ACKNOWLEDGMENTS

I had a ball doing the research for this guide, which is essentially an update and expansion of the Cape Region chapter from the second edition of *Baja Handbook*. For their inspiration, information, and hospitality, many thanks to Edelman Public Relations Worldwide, Ricardo Amador and Mar y Aventuras, Mauricio Moreno Beltrán, Guadalupe Céseña Chong, Jennifer Deaville, Lissa Fleming, Brian Westall González, Luis Klein, Hugh Kramer, Maribeth Mellin, Oscar and Elena Moreno, José Murrieta, Oscar Padilla, Jane Perkins, Karen (Kali) Rodríguez, Enrique Ojeda Santana, Jan Saucier and Westin Regina Los Cabos.

Thanks also to research assistant Chris Humphrey for braving a downpour on the slopes of the Sierra de La Laguna and for hiking the hotel circuit, and to Mike Persh for musical accompaniment.

IS THIS BOOK OUT OF DATE?

Between the time this book went to press and the time it reached the shelves, hotels have opened and closed, restaurants have changed hands, and roads have been repaired or fallen into disrepair. Also, prices have probably increased; therefore, all prices herein should be regarded as approximations and are not guaranteed by the publisher or author.

We want to keep this book as accurate and up to date as possible and would appreciate hearing about any errors or omissions you encounter while using *Cabo Handbook*.

If you have any noteworthy experiences (good or bad) with establishments listed in this book, please pass them along to us. If something is out of place on a map, tell us; if the best restaurant in town is not included, we'd like to know. Found a new route across the sierra? Share it with other Cape Region travelers. All contributions will be deeply appreciated and properly acknowledged. Address your letters to:

JOE CUMMINGS
CABO HANDBOOK
MOON PUBLICATIONS, INC.
P.O. BOX 3040
CHICO, CA 95927-3040, USA

BOB RACE

INTRODUCTION

With its crystalline shores embracing verdant mountains, the Cape Region of Baja California Sur is like a diamond-and-emerald pendant floating on azure seas. This once-remote corner of the Mexican republic offers striking tropical-desert scenery, uncommon wildlife, pristine beaches, friendly residents, and some of the best sportfishing in the world. Add a highly favorable year-round climate and you've got one of Mexico's most reliable yet relatively little-known travel experiences.

Los Cabos—the area extending from San José del Cabo to Cabo San Lucas—is currently the seventh most popular tourist destination in Mexico and the second fastest growing resort area in the country. Elsewhere in the Cape Region, historic mining and farming towns, the colorful waterfront state capital of La Paz, the interior sierras, and many miles of undeveloped beach on both sides of the peninsula receive but a trickle of visitors, many of them annual returnees for whom Cape explorations have become a pleasurable obsession.

THE LAND

BIRTH OF A PENINSULA

Baja California's Cape Region lies at the tip of the fourth-longest peninsula in the world (after the Kamchatka, Malay, and Antarctic), separated from mainland Mexico by roughly 250 km of ocean at the widest gap. This landmass wasn't always scissored from the rest of Mexico. At one time its entire length was attached to a broad tropical plain along Mexico's Pacific coast; about two-thirds of the area lay beneath the ocean. The 23-ton duck-billed hadrosaur roamed the region (its fossilized bones have been found near El Rosario) as did the mammoth, bison, hyracotherium (a fox-sized, primitive horse), and

camel. The peninsula's eventual divergence from the mainland came about as a result of the continual shifting of massive sections of the earth's surface called plates.

According to modern plate tectonics theory, Baja California and much of coastal California, U.S.A. to the north are part of the North Pacific Plate, while the rest of the North American continent belongs to the North American Plate. The boundary line between these two plates is the San Andreas Fault, which extends northward through the center of Mexico's Sea of Cortez and into the U.S., where it parallels the California coast on a southeast-northwest axis before veering off into the Pacific Ocean near San Francisco. The North Pacific and North American plates have shifted along this gap for millions of years, with the Pacific plate moving in a northwesterly direction at a current rate of about one to two inches a year.

This movement eventually tore basins in the earth's crust which allowed the Sea of Cortez to form, thus separating the land area west of the fault zone from land to the east. At one time the Sea of Cortez extended as far north as Palm Springs, California (U.S.A.); the sea would have continued moving northward at a gradual pace had it not met with the Colorado River. Silting in the Colorado River delta reversed the northward movement of the basins, holding the northern limit of the Sea of Cortez at a point well below what is now the U.S.-Mexican border. California's Salton Sea is a remnant of the northernmost extension of the Sea of Cortez, cut off by delta sedimentation.

As the peninsula moved slowly northwestward, the coastal plains tipped toward the west, creating a series of fault-block mountain ranges that include one of the Cape Region's most outstanding topographic features, the Sierra de La Laguna.

GEOGRAPHY

In many ways, Baja California's Cape Region has the most distinctive geography on the peninsula. The area receives substantially more rainfall than any other part of Baja California, save the Californian Region in the northeast. The Sierra de La Laguna—a topographic anomaly among Baja's mountain ranges (see "Mountains," below)—catches most of this rainfall, so the highlands here are more lushly vegetated than in the sierras to the north while the coastal lowlands remain fairly dry for beachgoing tourists. And unlike the rest of the peninsula, about a fourth of the Cape Region falls below the Tropic of Cancer. The combination of tropical latitude with moist uplands and dry coastal areas has created two unique biomes in the region—the Cape Oak-Piñon Woodlands and the Cape

Arid Tropical Forest—both of which are discussed below.

Mountains

Baja California's mountain ranges, or sierras, run down the center of the peninsula from northwest to southeast—a continuation of a mountain system that stretches southward from Alaska's Aleutian Islands to the spectacular rock formations at Cabo San Lucas. Like California's Sierra Nevada, Baja's high sierras typically feature granitic peaks topped by conifer forests. Because of the way in which the underground fault blocks tipped to create these sierras, the mountains tend to slope gradually down toward the west and fall off more dramatically toward the east. The Cape Region's Sierra de La Laguna, however, is an exception; it tips eastward so that its steepest slopes face west. It's also the only granitic fault-block range on the southern half of the peninsula—the others are volcanic.

The Sierra de La Laguna has been called an "island in the sky" because of its remarkable isolation from the Central Desert to the

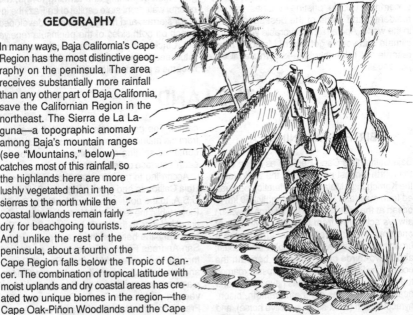

BOB RACE

north and the Gulf Coast Desert to the east. Up to 100 cm (40 inches) of rain falls annually on the peaks here, helping to support a unique ecosystem—the **Cape Oak-Piñon Woodlands.** These high-altitude woodlands harbor extensive stands of **Mexican piñon pine** and endemic oaks such as **madroño** and **palmita.** Lower down, abundant runoff sustains communities on either side of the range. Substantial underground springs supply water for orchards near the pueblos of Todos Santos, El Triunfo, and San Antonio. The western escarpment, facing the Pacific Ocean, is dissected by stream-eroded canyons and *arroyos* (streambeds) that are dry most of the year. But the arroyos on the eastern slopes are filled with water much of the year, enabling the areas around Miraflores, Santiago, and San Bartolo to support fruit and vegetable farming.

Deserts

About 25% of the Cape Region's total land area can be classified as desert, averaging less than 25 cm (10 inches) of rain per year. The Cape's desertlands belong to the Sonoran Desert, which extends across northwestern Mexico into parts of southeastern California and southern Arizona. But any visitor who has previously trav-

eled in other parts of the Sonoran Desert will note many subtle differences on the Cape. Because of the Cape's mountainous interior and the marine environment that surrounds it on three sides, the aridity of any given area can vary considerably. As a result, the Cape's desertlands belong to a subclassification of the Sonoran Desert known as the **Gulf Coast Desert.** This narrow subregion stretches along the Sea of Cortez from just below Bahía de los Angeles to the tip of the peninsula near San José del Cabo.

On average, the elevation is substantially higher here (with peaks up to 1,500 meters) than in the deserts to the north, and the terrain is marked by several broken sierras of granitic and volcanic rock. These sierras contain numerous arroyos and a few perennial streams that allow for sustainable farming.

The southern reaches of the Gulf Coast Desert receive a bit of extra precipitation from the occasional tropical storm that blows in from the south. As a result of the added moisture and elevation, many more trees and flowering cacti are found here than in other Baja deserts. Sea of Cortez islands to the east feature similar terrain, although the endemic vegetation varies from island to island.

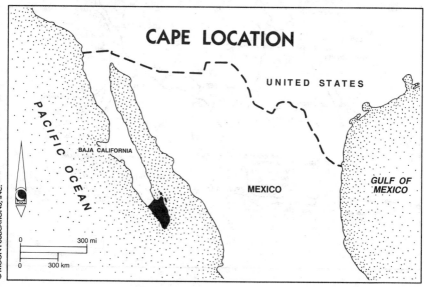

CAPE LOCATION

UNITED STATES

PACIFIC OCEAN

BAJA CALIFORNIA

MEXICO

GULF OF MEXICO

0   300 mi

0   300 km

© MOON PUBLICATIONS, INC.

PUNTA CONEJO

SAN JUAN DE
LA COSTA

ISLA ESPIRITU SANTO

PUNTA MARQUEZ

EL CHIVATO

*SEA OF
CORTEZ*

PLAYA TECOLOTE

**BAHIA
DE LA
PAZ**

PICHILINGUE

PUNTA COYOTE

EL CENTENARIO

11

LOS INOCENTES

LA PAZ
INTERNATIONAL
AIRPORT

LA PAZ

P A C I F I C   O C E A N

CAPE
REGION

19

286

*PICHILINGUE
PENINSULA*

CANAL DE CERRALVO

SAN PEDRO

MELITON
ALBANEZ

EL SARGENTO

*BAHIA DE
LA VENTANA*

LA VENTANA

*ISLA
CERRALVO*

EJIDO LA
MATANZA

EL CARRIZAL

EL TRIUNFO

SAN JUAN DE
LOS PLANES

*PUNTA ARENA
DE LA VENTANA*

PUNTA PERICO

LA PLAYITA

SAN ANTONIO

*BAHIA DE
LOS MUERTOS*

PUNTA LOBOS
TODOS SANTOS

1

EL PESCADERO

CARDONAL

PUNTA SAN PEDRO

PLAYA SAN PEDRITO

SAN BARTOLO

S I E R R A   D E   L A   L A G U N A

PUNTA PESCADERO

PLAYA LOS CERRITOS

LOS BARRILES

BAHIA DE PALMAS

PUNTA GASPAREÑO

COLONIA
ELIAS
CALLES

EL
AGUAJE

BUENA VISTA

19

AGUA
CALIENTE

SANTIAGO

MIRAFLORES

LA RIVERA

RIO CANDELARIA

CADUAÑO

PUNTA COLORADA

PLAYA MIGRIÑO

LA CANDELARIA

EL RINCON

SANTA ANITA
**LOS CABOS
INTERNATIONAL AIRPORT**
SAN JOSE VIEJO
SANTA ROSA
**SAN JOSE DEL
CABO**

RIO SAN JOSE

CABO PULMO   *CABO PULMO*

CABO FALSO

LOS FRAILES

CABO SAN LUCAS

1

PUEBLO LA PLAYA

BAHIA DE LOS FRAILES
PUNTA BOCA DEL TULE
RANCHO LA VINORAMA

BAHIA SAN LUCAS   *BAHIA CHILENO*   *PUNTA
PALMILLA*

LA FORTUNA

0   10 mi

0   10 km

© MOON PUBLICATIONS, INC.

Cape Arid Tropical Forest

The coastal areas of the Cape Region as well as the lower slopes of the Laguna and Giganta mountain ranges share characteristics typical of both tropical and arid biomes, hence the seemingly oxymoronic term "arid tropical forest." Like tropical forests worldwide, the lower Cape forests produce trees, shrubs, and undergrowth of varying heights that create a canopied effect. Mixed with this tangled growth are a profusion of succulents more associated with arid climes, including the **cardón-barbón,** a shorter cousin of the towering *cardón* found throughout Baja's deserts.

Much of the vegetation in the Cape Arid Tropical Forest is normally associated with the tropical thorn forests of coastal Colima and Guerrero on the Mexican mainland. Prominent marker plants unique to the Cape subregion include the **Tlaco palm, wild fig** *(zalate),* **wild plum** *(ciruelo),* **mauto,** and the alleged aphrodisiac herb **damiana.**

Coastal Wetlands

Wetland pockets lie in shallow areas along bays and lagoons in numerous spots along the Cape coast. They usually consist of **salt marshes,** which contain high concentrations of salt-tolerant plants such as cordgrass, eelgrass, saltwort, and salt cedar; or **mangrove forests,** containing one or more of the five species of mangrove

red mangrove

(mangle) common in Baja. Within any given wetland, the water level, salinity, and temperature can vary considerably; hence, an extensive variety of plants and animals can adapt to wetland areas. Because of this environmental variation, salt marshes and mangrove wetlands represent the most concentrated biomass areas on the planet. For most visitors, the main attraction of the wetlands is the abundance of waterfowl.

Areas with substantial wetlands in the Cape Region include Bahía de La Paz (mangrove forests), Todos Santos (mixed saltwater/freshwater estuarine marshes), and Estero San José (mixed saltwater/freshwater estuarine marshes).

Islands

The great preponderance of islands and islets surrounding the Baja California peninsula are found on the Sea of Cortez side; among the largest are Isla Espíritu Santo and Isla Cerralvo in the vicinity of La Paz. Many of these islands were created as the peninsula broke away from mainland Mexico and hence are "land-bridge" or "continental" islands rather than true oceanic islands. The islands are arid—their low elevation doesn't allow them to snag much of the rain that moves up from the south in summer. But because of their isolation, the Cortez islands feature a high number of endemic plant and animal species; at least half of the 120 cactus varieties found on the islands are endemic.

THE SEA OF CORTEZ

The Sea of Cortez was apparently named by Spanish sea captain Francisco de Ulloa after he sailed the entire perimeter of this body of water in 1539 and 1540 at the command of the most infamous of all Spanish conquistadors, Hernán Cortés. Four years previously Cortés had himself sailed the sea in an aborted attempt to colonize the peninsula. After de Ulloa's voyage, the name Mar de Cortés appeared intermittently on maps of the region, alternating with Mar Vermejo (Vermillion Sea, in reference to the color reflected from huge numbers of pelagic crabs) until the Mexican government officially renamed it the Gulf of California (Golfo de California) early in this century. Sailors, writers, and other assorted romantics, however, have continued to call it by its older name.

The sea is roughly 1,125 km (700 miles) long, with an average width of 150 km (93 miles). Oceanographers have divided it into four regions based on the prominent characteristics—depth, bottom contour, and marine productivity—of each zone. The northern quarter of the gulf, between the Colorado River delta and the Midriff Islands, is shallow in relation to the zones farther south because of silt deposited by the Colorado River, which has also rounded the bottom contours. The sea here is highly saline due to evaporation, and the tides vary in height by up to 10 meters (30 feet). Before the damming of the Colorado, the tidal bore created when the river met the incoming tide was powerful enough to sink ships.

The next region farther south encompasses the Midriff Islands, where basins reach depths of 820 meters (2,700 feet) and strong currents bring nutrients up from the bottom while aerating the water. This leads to an unusually high level of biological productivity, otherwise known as "good fishin'."

From the Midriff Islands to La Paz, basin depth doubles, silting is minimal, and water temperatures begin decreasing dramatically. The final sea zone below La Paz is oceanic, with trenches and submarine canyons over 3,650 meters (12,000 feet) deep. Around the tip of the cape, the Sea of Cortez meets the Pacific Ocean and their respective currents battle, producing some wicked riptides. This means that although the tip of the cape is the warmest area on the peninsula during the winter months, beach swimming can be treacherous.

The Sea of Cortez is biologically the richest body of water on the planet, with over 800 species of marine vertebrates and over 2,000 invertebrates at last count. The reported number rises with the publication of each new marine study.

CLIMATE

In satellite photographs of the North American continent snapped a hundred miles above the earth, Baja's Cape Region invariably jumps off the plate. The rest of the continent north and east may be obscured by whorls of clouds while the shores, plains, and mountains of the Cape are carved into the photographic image, remarkably clear. The chances of a day without rain in the winter are 95% in Baja, beating out Hawaii's 84% and Florida's 87%.

How does the Cape Region get so much sunshine? The simple answer is that it's positioned almost out of reach of the major weather systems that influence climate in western North America. Northwesterly storms from Eurasia and the Arctic bring rain and snow to the American Northwest and Midwest all winter long, while tropical storms roll across the South Pacific from Asia, dumping loads of rainfall along the lower Mexican coast and Central America in the summer.

The Cape is only slightly affected by the outer edges of these systems. Anchored between the warm, fish-filled waters of the Sea of Cortez and the heaving Pacific Ocean, bisected by plains and mountains, the Cape's isolated ecosystems range in climate from Mediterranean to desert to tropical. In some areas, overlapping microclimates defy classification, combining elements of semiarid, arid, subtropical, and tropical climes.

HOT AND COLD

Three variables influence temperatures at any given Cape location: elevation, latitude, and longitude. In plain talk, that means the higher you climb, the cooler it gets; the farther south you go, the warmer it gets; and it's always cooler on the Pacific side of the peninsula and warmer on the Sea of Cortez side. The Tropic of Cancer (approximate latitude 23.5° N) slices across the Cape Region from Todos Santos on the west coast, through Santiago in the interior, to the East Cape south of Bahía de Palmas. Tropical temperatures are thus the norm throughout the Cape except in the high sierra.

Pacific Coast

Because of prevailing ocean currents, the Pacific coast of the Cape shows the least overall variation in temperatures, staying relatively balmy year-round. From March to July, the California Current flows southward along the coast, bringing cooler temperatures from the north that moderate

*Playa Sirenita,
East Cape*

seasonal atmospheric warming, while in December and January the coast is warmed by the northward movement of the Davidson Current. These seasonal currents stabilize the air temperatures so that Cabo San Lucas, for example, averages 18° C (64° F) in January and 29° C (84° F) in August, a range of only 11° C (20° F).

Sea of Cortez
The Sea of Cortez has its own set of currents, sometimes lumped together as the Gulf Current, fed by tropical waters of the South Pacific traveling in a counterclockwise direction north along the mainland's upper Pacific coast and then south along the peninsular coast. As a result, the Sea of Cortez enjoys an average annual surface temperature of 24° C (75° F), significantly warmer than the Pacific's 18° C (64° F). The high rate of evaporation at the north end of the sea also contributes to warmer air temperatures; this combination of warm air and water temperatures means the Sea of Cortez can be classified as "tropical" over its entire length.

The weather along the East Cape is warm and sunny all winter long with average January temperatures around 23° C (74° F). In August, average temperatures are 31° C (88° F) in San José del Cabo, although daily high figures in the summer can easily reach 38° C (100° F) or more.

The Corridor
What's the weather like in between? Geographers officially place the boundary between the Pacific Ocean and the Sea of Cortez at Land's End, the rock formation near the entrance of Bahía San Lucas, Cabo San Lucas. But the area stretching along the tip of the Cape from Cabo San Lucas to San José del Cabo—known in the tourist industry as the "Corridor" (*Corredor Náutico* or "nautical corridor" in local Spanish)—mingles both Pacific and Cortez influences to create a microclimate that's warmer than Pacific locations yet cooler than Cortez areas. Overall, however, temperatures along the Corridor tend to be more in line with southern Sea of Cortez zones.

Chubascos, Coromuels, Cordonazos
Monthly average wind velocities for Baja California as a whole are moderate. From mid-May to mid-November, however, tropical storms from the south or east, known as *chubascos,* can bring high winds and rain to the coasts of the Cape Region. Although they usually blow over quickly, local mythology has it that if a *chubasco* lasts more than three hours, it will last a day; if it lasts more than a day, it will last three days; and if more than three days, it'll be a five-day blow.

Another Sea of Cortez weather pattern is the *cordonazo,* a small but fierce summer storm that originates locally and is usually spent within a few hours. A more welcome weather phenomenon is the *coromuel* of Bahía de La Paz, a stiff afternoon breeze that blows from offshore during the hot summer and early fall months. This wind was named for the English Lord Protector Cromwell, identified with English pirates who took advantage of the wind's regular occurrence for the plunder of ships trapped in the bay.

WET AND DRY

The "Land of Little Rain," as Baja has been called, isn't unique in its aridity since most of the earth's desert areas are found at latitudes between 15° and 30° either north or south of the equator; Baja is positioned roughly between 23° N and 31° N. Global convection currents in the atmosphere create a more or less permanent high-pressure shield over these zones, insulating them from the low-pressure fronts that bring rain clouds.

Rainfall in the Cape Region varies from under 25 cm (10 inches) per year in the driest areas east of the Sierra de La Laguna (from San José del Cabo north to La Paz) to upwards of 100 cm (40 inches) in the interior of the Sierra de La Laguna.

Variation in rainfall also occurs on a seasonal basis. In the Cape Region, rain usually arrives Aug.-Nov., peaking at an average of 5.8 cm in September for Cabo San Lucas and La Paz. Since mountain peaks trap rain clouds, the Cape's higher elevations invariably receive more rain than the low-lying coastal zones.

TRAVEL SEASONS

The flat end of the peninsula from San José del Cabo to Cabo San Lucas is warm year-round. Pacific influences generally moderate the heat July to September, while the tropic waters of the Gulf Current make this stretch the warmest coastal zone on the peninsula during winter months. Except for the occasional *chubasco* in late summer, the climate seems nearly perfect here, which is why "Los Cabos" has become such a popular vacation destination. Cabo San Lucas receives about 45% of its measurable annual rainfall—a total of 15-18 cm a year—in September, so if there's a month to avoid for weather reasons, that's the one.

The two months when you're least likely to have Los Cabos beaches to yourself are December and January, when large numbers of gringos come here seeking respite from rainstorms and blizzards.

FLORA

A thorough examination of all the plants and creatures of interest in the Cape Region might take volumes. The following sections cover some of either the most remarkable or most common forms of Cape plantlife. The complex interconnecting ecosystems of the peninsula and its islands hold a high number of unique species and remain relatively unexplored by biologists. Several botanists, marine biologists, zoologists, and paleontologists have undertaken solo research in the area, but only in the last three years has the first interdisciplinary team, sponsored by a Canadian university, begun studying the region.

CACTI

Cardón

One of the most common cacti throughout Baja, including the Cape Region, is the towering cardón (Pachycereus pringlei), the world's tallest species of cactus. Individuals can reach as high as 18 meters (60 feet) or more and weigh 12 tons, not counting the root system, which can spread up to 50 meters (150 feet) in diameter. More commonly they top out at seven to nine meters. The giant, pale green trunks feature 11-17 vertical ribs and may measure one meter thick. Some individuals live over 400 years.

The cardón is often confused with the smaller saguaro cactus of Sonora and Arizona; one major difference is that the branches of the cardón tend to be more vertical than those of the saguaro. The hardwood cores of cardón columns have been used by Bajacalifornios for centuries as building beams and fence posts. Among Mexicans, a cardón forest is called a cardonal.

Biznaga

Another extremely common and highly visible cactus is the biznaga or barrel cactus (genus Ferocactus). At least a dozen species grow in the Cape Region, most of them endemic. The cactus's English name refers to its shape, which is short and squat like a barrel. Most common varieties reach about waist-high. One variety, however, Ferocactus diguettii, growing only on

a few Sea of Cortez islands, easily reaches four meters (13 feet) in height and a meter (3.28 feet) in diameter. The spines of this cactus are often tinged red; from March to June the tops bloom with gorgeous yellow to red flowers. The Indians of Baja California Sur reportedly used hollowed-out biznagas as Dutch ovens, inserting food into the cavity along with heated stones, then sealing the cactus off till the food was cooked. The sturdy, curved spines also served as fishhooks in native fishing expeditions.

Pitahaya

Among Baja's original populations, another of the most important cacti was the **pitahaya dulce,** known among Anglos as organ pipe cactus. It has slender, vertical ribs that grow in clusters, and its spiny, orange-size fruit contains a sweet, juicy, pleasant-tasting pulp the color of red watermelon. According to accounts of Spanish missionaries, the Pericú Indians based their yearly calendar on the ripening of the fruit in late summer and early fall. During this season, the Indians engaged in a veritable fruit orgy, gorging themselves on the pulp until they fell asleep, then waking to begin eating again. The early Spanish explorers took the fruit with them on long sea journeys—its vitamin C content helped to prevent scurvy.

The pitahaya dulce is commonly found in Baja California south of the Sierra de San Borja, on several Sea of Cortez islands, and in Sonora and southern Arizona. A similar species, **pitahaya agria** (agria means sour in Spanish; dulce is sweet), branches more densely and lower to the ground, hence its English name **galloping cactus.** It grows throughout the peninsula and on most Sea of Cortez islands. The fruit of the pitahaya agria is similar in appearance to that of the pitahaya dulce but, as implied by the Spanish name, it's less sweet, more acidic. Both types of pitahaya fruit remain popular among Cape residents and travelers; the sweet ones ripen in July.

Opuntia

Another cactus variety well represented throughout Baja is the genus Opuntia, which includes all types known as **cholla** as well as the **nopal,** or **prickly pear.** Chollas are a bane to hikers because they're so prolific and densely covered with spines. A typical branch looks somewhat like braided or twisted rope. The cholla historically has had few domestic uses, although a tea made from the roots of the fuzzy-looking **teddy-bear cholla** (also called "jumping cholla" for its propensity to cling to the lower legs of hikers) is reportedly used by the Seri Indians as a diuretic.

In contrast, the much-loved prickly pear cactus has broad, flat stems and branches and a sparser distribution of spines. In northern Mexico and Baja its fleshy pads are a dietary staple. The most highly prized parts of the nopal are the young stem shoots, called *nopalitos,* and the ripe fruits, dubbed *tuna.* The flavor of the pads is a bit bland, like a cross between bell pepper and okra. The fruit, on the other hand, is juicy and sweet, and available in season in many Baja markets. If you want to taste it in the wild, remove the tunas carefully, cut them lengthwise with a sharp knife, and scoop out the insides with a spoon.

AGAVES

Yucca

One of the most common and striking desert plants is the yucca, which appears in several varieties throughout the Cape Region. Yuccas belong to the agave family, the largest member of which is the **tree yucca** *(Yucca valida),* called *datilillo* or "little date" for its resemblance to a date palm. Datilillos grow in clusters three to seven meters tall, their dagger-like blades supported by long woody trunks. This endemic is found throughout the plains and chaparral subregions on the Pacific side of the peninsula—just about anywhere except in the mountains.

Yuccas are extremely useful plants for rural Bajacalifornios. The fruit and flowers are edible (a candy called *colache* is made from the cooked flower buds), the roots can be boiled to make soap or leather softener, and the tough leaf fibers are used to make cordage, sandals, baskets, and mats.

Sotol

Very similar to yucca is another member of the agave family called *sotol* (genus *Nolina*). The

LOVE HERB

Probably the most well-known herb native to Baja's Cape Region is *damiana (Turnera diffusa),* a small shrub with bright, five-petaled yellow or golden flowers. The plant's aphrodisiac properties are its main claim to fame; these are often derided as nonsense by self-appointed Baja analysts. But according to botanist Norman C. Roberts, *damiana* "stimulates the genitourinary tract and is used in the treatment of sexual problems such as impotence, frigidity, sterility, and sexual exhaustion." Other benefits ascribed to the herb include use as a sedative and diuretic.

Damiana grows most commonly in rocky areas of the Cape Region but is also found as far away as Sonora, Texas, and in the West Indies. The two most common ways of ingesting the herb are in sweetened tea made from the leaves or in a liqueur containing *damiana* extract. In resort areas a "Baja margarita" substitutes *damiana liqueur* for triple sec.

leaves of a sotol are narrower and softer than those of a yucca; some sotols also produce long flower stalks similar to those of the century plant, though the flower buds occur along the entire length of the stalk instead of only at the top.

Perhaps the most spectacular variety of sotol in Baja is the native *Nolina beldingii,* sometimes called *palmita* because of its resemblance to a small palm tree. Palmitas, which can reach seven meters in height, grow clusters of thick leaves branching from their short, woody trunks.

The plant's native habitat is in the higher elevations of the Cape Region.

Maguey

More common are the many varieties of *maguey*, commonly called the century plant. Yet another member of the sizable Agave family, the *maguey* has broad, closely clustered leaves that grow at ground level without a visible trunk. In most species, the plant only flowers once in its lifetime, sending up a tall, slender stalk after maturation—typically at five to 20 years, depending on variety and locale. Early Anglo settlers in the southwestern U.S. spread the myth that agaves bloomed only once in a hundred years, hence the fanciful name "century plant."

The *maguey* was a very important food source to certain aboriginal populations, who harvested the plant just before it bloomed (when it's full of concentrated nutrients). Trimmed of its leaves, the heart of the plant was baked in an underground pit for one to three days, then eaten or stored. Some ranchers still prepare the agave in this manner today. As with datilillo, the leaf fibers are used as cordage for weaving various household goods.

BOB RACE

TREES

Palms

Seven varieties of palm grow wild in Baja California; four are native to the peninsula and islands while three are introduced species. Palms are very important to the local economy of the southern half of the peninsula, where they're most common. The long, straight trunks are used as roof beams, the leaves are used in basketry and for palapa roof and wall thatching, and the fruits provide a source of nutrition.

Among the most handsome Baja palm trees is the endemic **Tlaco palm** (also called *palma palmia* and *palma colorado*), common in the canyons and arroyos of the Cape Region mountains. The smooth, slender trunks, crowned by fan-shaped leaves, stand up to 20 meters (65.5 feet) tall. A closely related species, the Guadalupe Island palm, is native to Isla Guadalupe; its self-shedding

Tlaco palm

trunk (leaving little or no shag) has made it highly popular as a cultivated palm.

Baja's tallest palm variety is the endemic **Mexican fan palm** (also Baja California fan palm, skyduster, or *palma blanca*), which reaches heights of 27-30 meters (90-100 feet). As the name implies, its leaves are fan-shaped. Although it's not as durable as the Tlaco palm, the long trunk makes the tree highly useful for local construction. The fan palm's native habitats are north of the Cape Region in the Sierra de la Giganta and on Isla Angel de la Guarda, but it is used as an ornamental throughout Baja.

Two palm varieties were imported to Baja for their fruit value. The **date palm** was introduced to Baja by Jesuit missionaries and is now common near former mission sites, including San José del Cabo. The tree typically reaches 15-20 meters tall at maturity; the oblong fruit grows beneath feather-shaped leaves in large clusters, turning from pale yellow to dark brown as it ripens. Baja dates are eaten locally and shipped to mainland Mexico but are generally not considered of high enough quality for export. The 30-meter, feather-leafed **coconut palm** commonly grows along coastal areas of the Cape Region and is an important local food source.

Oaks and Pines

Tens of thousands of visitors drape themselves along Cape Region beaches every year without any inkling that in the Sierra de La Laguna mountains rising behind the coastal plains stands one of Mexico's most remarkable relic piñon–live oak woodlands. Two endemic species of oak (*encino*) found in the sierra include the **cape oak,** usually seen growing in higher canyons and arroyos, and the **black oak,** confined to the Cape Region's lower slopes.

The **Mexican piñon pine** (known as *pino piñonero* in Mexico) grows profusely at higher elevations in the Sierra de La Laguna, where the wood is a commonly used building material and the nuts are sometimes gathered for food.

Mimosas

This subfamily of the Leguminosae or pea family represents dozens of genera common to arid and semiarid zones all over the world. Characterized by linear seedpods and double rows of tiny leaves, common varieties in the Cape Region include the **mesquite** and various endemic kinds of **acacia.**

Indians have long used the trunk, roots, leaves, beans, and bark of the mesquite tree for a variety of purposes, from lumber to medicine. Ground mesquite leaves mixed with water form a balm for sore eyes, a remedy still used by *curanderos* (healers) in rural Mexico today. Chewing the leaves relieves toothache. Mesquite gum has also been used by various tribes as a balm for wounds, ceramic glue, dye, and digestive.

Mesquite beans are a good source of nutrition—a ripe bean pod, growing as long as nine inches, contains roughly 30% glucose and is high in protein. Many animals and birds savor the beans; horses will eat them until they're sick. Rural Mexicans grind the dried pods into a flour with which they make bread and a kind of beer. The Seri Indians, who live along the Sonoran coast of the Sea of Cortez, have separate names for eight different stages of the bean pod's development.

One of the prettiest endemic mimosas is the **palo blanco,** which has a tall, slender trunk with silver-white bark and a feathery crown that produces small, white, fragrant blossoms March-May. Bajacalifornios use the bark of the *palo blanco* to tan leather; at the end of the 19th century the main industry at Cabo San Lucas was the shipping of *palo blanco* bark to San Francisco tanneries.

Wild Figs

Three types of *Ficus* trees *(zalate),* one endemic, are common in the rocky areas of the Cape Region. In the village of Pueblo La Playa, east of San José del Cabo, stands a vintage collection of *zalates* of impressive stature.

Willows

Various cottonwoods *(alamo)* and willows *(sauz)* grow in higher elevations throughout the Cape Region. The endemic **huerivo** *(Populus brandegeei)* is a beautiful endemic cottonwood found in the canyons and arroyos of sierra. The tall, straight trunks reach heights of 30 meters and are highly valued as lumber for construction and furniture-making.

FAUNA

LAND MAMMALS

Had Charles Darwin happened to explore the peninsula and islands of Baja California instead of Ecuador's Galápagos Islands, he might well have arrived at the same conclusions about evolution. Baja's unique environment—an arid-to-tropical slice of mountains and plains isolated between two large bodies of water—has led to superlative endemism, or what one naturalist called "a nice degree of freakishness," among its plant and animal species.

One of the most widespread carnivores on the peninsula as well as on some Sea of Cortez islands is the **coyote,** which seems to be able to adapt itself equally well to mountain, desert, and coastal terrains. Anyone venturing into the interior of the peninsula is virtually guaranteed to spot at least one. In some areas they don't seem particularly afraid of humans although they always maintain a distance of at least 15 meters between themselves and larger mammals. A coyote will sometimes fish for crab, placing a furry tail in the water, waiting for a crab to grab on and then, with a flick of the tail, tossing the crab onto the beach. Before the crustacean can recover from the shock, the coyote is busy enjoying a fine crab feast.

Rarely sighted in the Sierra de La Laguna is the **mountain lion**—also called cougar, pan-

ther, or puma—which, like all cats, is mostly nocturnal. These beautiful creatures occasionally attack humans, so a degree of advance knowledge about their habits is necessary for those hiking in the sierras.

First, if you avoid hiking at night, you're much less likely to encounter a lion. If you do meet up with a lion, wildlife experts suggest you convince the beast you are not prey and may be dangerous yourself. Don't run from the animal, as this is an invitation to chase. Instead, shout, wave your hands, and, if the lion acts aggressively, throw stones at it. If you're carrying a backpack, raise it above your shoulders so that you appear larger to the lion. One or more of these actions is virtually guaranteed to frighten the lion away. If not, grab the biggest, heaviest stick you can find and fight it out to avoid becoming cat food.

Smaller, less intimidating carnivores commonly encountered in the Cape Region include the **gray fox, ringtail, bobcat, lynx, skunk, raccoon,** and **badger.**

One of the largest mammals still roaming wild in Baja is the **mule deer,** of which there is an endemic peninsular variety. Mule deer are most commonly seen on mountain slopes below 1,500 meters. Lesser numbers of **white-tailed deer** are usually found above this elevation. Deer are a popular source of meat for ranchers living in the sierras, who also use deerskin to make soft, homemade boots called *teguas.*

At least four varieties of rabbit hop around the Cape Region: the **brush rabbit, desert cottontail, black-tailed jackrabbit,** and the rare, endemic **black jackrabbit.** Each is especially adapted to its particular habitat. The long, upright ears of the black-tailed jackrabbit, for example, enable it to hear sounds from quite a distance, a necessity for an animal that is prey for practically every larger animal in the Cape Region. The more delicate ears of the desert cottontail act as radiators on hot desert days, allowing the rabbit to release excess body heat into the air.

The endemic black jackrabbit *(Lepus insularis)* is found only on Isla Espíritu Santo. Zoologists haven't yet been able to explain why the fur of this rabbit is mostly black, or why a cin-

ERIN DWYER

coyote

namon-red coloring appears along the ears and underparts.

The Cape supports a wide variety of common and not-so-common rodents—the **white-tailed antelope squirrel, marsh rice rat, Botta's pocket gopher,** and **piñon mouse,** to name a few. What may surprise some travelers is how many varieties manage to survive in the Gulf Desert. Among these are the **little desert pocket mouse, cactus mouse, desert wood rat,** and five endemic species of **kangaroo rat.**

MARINE MAMMALS

Sea Lions

Sixty-two percent of Baja's **California sea lions** or *lobos marinos (Zalophus californianus)* live in the Sea of Cortez—principally around the islands of San Esteban, San Jorge, Angel de la Guarda, San Pedro Mártir, and Espíritu Santo.

Cetaceans

The protected lagoons of Baja California's Pacific coast and the warm waters of the Sea of Cortez are practically made for whales and dolphins. Twenty-five species of cetaceans frequent Baja water, from the **blue whale,** the largest mammal on earth, to the **common dolphin** *(Delphinus delphis),* which is sometimes seen in the Sea of Cortez in pods as large as 10,000.

Whale species known to visit the Cape Region or make it their year-round habitat include **minke, fin, Sei, Bryde's, humpback, gray, goose-beaked, sperm, dwarf sperm, false killer, killer,** and **pilot.** Commonly seen dolphins are the **Pacific white-sided, bottlenosed, spotted, Risso's, spinner,** and **striped.**

The marine mammal usually of most interest to Cape whalewatchers is the **Pacific or California gray whale,** which migrates some 19,300 km (12,000 miles) a year between its feeding grounds above the Arctic Circle and its calving grounds in the Pacific lagoons of southern Baja California. The gray is the easiest of the whales to view since it frequents shallow coastal waters. Although the lagoons used by the grays for calving are found north of the Cape Region in south central Baja, the whales can sometimes be seen from shore as they make their way around the tip of the Cape to "exercise" the newly born calves.

Whalewatching: Like many two-legged mammals, gray whales prefer to spend their winters south of the border. During the Dec.-April calving season, whalewatching tours to the nearest calving lagoon (Bahía Magdalena, around 200 km/120 miles northwest of La Paz) can be arranged through hotels and travel agencies in La Paz, San José del Cabo, or Cabo San Lucas. **Sven-Olof Lindblad's Special Expeditions** (tel. 212-765-7740 or toll-free in the U.S./Canada 800-762-7740) arranges round-the-cape whalewatching trips between January and April, taking in the Pacific calving bays, several Sea of Cortez islands, La Paz, and Cabo San Lucas

close encounters of the barnacled kind

COURTESY OF SPECIAL EXPEDITIONS

aboard a comfortable 70-passenger, 152-foot ship. These programs receive high marks for both recreational and educational value.

FISH

The seas surrounding Baja California contain an amazing variety of marinelife. In the Sea of Cortez alone, around 800 varieties of fish have been identified. Marine biologists estimate a total of around 3,000 species, including invertebrates, between the Golfo de Santa Clara at the north end of the sea and the southern tip of Cabo San Lucas. This would make the area the richest sea, or gulf, in the world, a marine cornucopia that has inspired the nickname "God's Fishtank." The wide spectrum of aquatic environments along both coasts is largely responsible for this abundance and has led to Baja's reputation as a mecca for seafood aficionados as well as fishing and diving enthusiasts.

About 90% of all known Baja fish varieties are found close to the shores of the peninsula or its satellite islands. The Midriff Islands area in the center of the Sea of Cortez is especially rich in life—tidal surges aerate the water and stir up nutrients, supporting a thick food chain from plankton to fish to birds and sea lions. The Cortez, in fact, has acted as a giant fish trap, collecting an assortment of marine species over thousands of years from the nearby Pacific, the more distant equatorial zones of South America, and even the Caribbean, through a now-extinct water link that once existed between the two seas.

The information below represents only a brief overview of the many fish of common, everyday interest to Baja visitors and residents in contact with the aquatic world. Fish habitats are described below as being onshore, inshore, or offshore. Onshore fish frequent the edge of the tidal zone, and can be caught by casting from shore; inshore fish are in shallow waters accessible by small boat; and offshore fish lurk in the deep waters of the open Pacific or the southern Sea of Cortez. (See "Fishing," in the On the Road chapter.)

Billfish
The Cape Region is the undisputed world capital of sailfish and marlin fishing; just about every serious saltwater angler eventually considers a pilgrimage to La Paz or Cabo San Lucas. Six billfish species exist here in some numbers: **swordfish, sailfish,** and **striped, blue,** and **black marlin.** All are strong fighters, though the sailfish and striped marlin are generally the most acrobatic. Billfish inhabit a wide range of offshore waters in the Pacific and in the Sea of Cortez south of Bahía Magdalena and the Midriff Islands; the swordfish is found mostly on the Pacific side.

Corvinas and Croakers
About 30 species in Baja belong to this group of small- to medium-size fish that make croaking sounds. Varieties found inshore to onshore include **white seabass, Gulf corvina, orangemouth corvina, California corvina, yellowfin croaker,** and **spotfin croaker.**

Jack
Popular jacks include **yellowtail** (one of the most popular fish for use in *tacos de pescado*), **Pacific amberjack,** various **pompanos, jack crevalle,** and the strong-fighting **roosterfish,** named for its tall dorsal comb. These jacks are most preva-

yellowfin tuna

MARIO BAÑAGA JR. / PISCES FLEET

lent in inshore to onshore areas in the Sea of Cortez and in the Pacific south of Magdalena.

Dorado, Mackerel, and Tuna

Among the more sought-after food fish, found offshore to inshore throughout parts of both seas, are the **dorado**, sometimes called "dolphinfish" (though it isn't related to mammalian dolphins or porpoises) or mahimahi, its Hawaiian name; **sierra**, especially good in *ceviche* or marinated seafood salad; the knife-shaped **wahoo**, one of the fastest of all fish, reaching speeds of 50 knots; **Pacific bonito**; and three kinds of tuna—the **bluefin, albacore,** and highly prized **yellowfin.** Yellowfins can weigh up to 180 kilograms (400 pounds) and are among the best tasting of all tunas.

Bass

Sea bass are inshore fishes; different species dominate different Baja waters and all commonly find their way into Mexican seafood restaurants. The larger bass are called *garropas* (groupers), the smaller ones cabrillas.

Flatfish

These include flounder and halibut, usually called *lenguado* in Spanish. The most common variety found on the Pacific side is the **California halibut**; on the other side it's the **Cortez halibut.** Both make good eating and are often used in tourist areas for *tacos de pescado.*

Snapper

Generally found south of Magdalena and round the Cape as far north as the upper Sea of Cortez, locally popular snappers include **red snapper, yellow snapper, barred pargo,** and **dog snapper.** All snappers are called pargo in Spanish, except for the red snapper, which is *huachinango.* All are common food fish.

Sharks, Rays, and Squid

Of the more than 60 species of sharks found in Baja waters, some are rare and most stay clear of humans. The more common species are found offshore to inshore from Magdalena to the Midriff, and include the **smooth hammerhead, common thresher, bonito, sand, blue, blacktip,** and the world's largest fish, reaching up to 18 meters and 3,600 kilograms, the **whale shark.** Shark-fishing is an important activity in

Baja, supplying much of the seafood eaten locally. Hammerhead, thresher, bonito (mako), and leopard shark fillets are all very tasty.

KAREN McKINLEY

manta ray

Rays are common in warmer offshore-to-inshore waters throughout Baja. Many varieties feature barbed tailspines that can inflict a painful wound. Contrary to myth the barb is not actually venomous, although a ray "sting" can be extremely painful and easily becomes infected. Experienced beachgoers perform the "stingray shuffle" when walking on sandy bottoms. If you bump into a ray resting on the bottom, it will usually swim away; if you step on one, it's likely to give you a flick of the barb.

Common smaller rays found inshore include the **butterfly ray** and the aptly named **shovelnose guitarfish,** a ray with a thick tail and a flat head. Two species of rays are sometimes called "devilfish" because of their hornlike pectoral fins: the **mobula** and the huge **Pacific manta ray.** The Pacific manta possesses a "wingspan" of up to seven meters (23 feet) across and can weigh nearly two tons. Another fairly large ray, the **bat ray,** is sometimes confused with the manta, though it doesn't have the characteristic pectoral fins of the latter. A friendly manta will allow scuba divers to hitch rides by hanging on to the base of the pectorals.

CHALLENGES TO THE MARINE ENVIRONMENT

One of the major problems facing Baja fisheries is illegal fishing by unlicensed Japanese and Korean boats. Despite Mexico's ban on the netting of game-fish, many foreign vessels still use huge dredge nets and/or longlines to harvest marlin, swordfish, dorado, and other species legally reserved for sportfishing only—not to mention protected species such as porpoises and dolphins.

Novelist John Steinbeck, in his 1941 account of a scientific marine expedition into the Sea of Cortez accompanying marine biologist Ed Ricketts, described how he watched six Japanese shrimpers—weighing at least 600 tons each—purse-dredge the sea bottom, killing hundreds of tons of fish that were merely discarded after each dredging. One of his reactions: "Why the Mexican government should have permitted the complete destruction of a valuable food supply is one of those mysteries which have their ramifications possibly back in pockets it is not well to look into."

With government corruption apparently on the wane, Mexico is taking steps to curtail many of the commercial enterprises on the Sea of Cortez; in June 1993 the Mexican government declared the entire Sea of Cortez—coast, waters, and islands—a biosphere reserve. Expanding budgets mean it should become easier to enforce new regulations. One can only hope that intervention is soon enough and strong enough to preserve Mexico's great marine resources.

Squids of various species and sizes—most under 30 cm (one foot) in length—are found throughout the Pacific Ocean and Sea of Cortez. In deeper Pacific waters off the west coast glides the enormous **Humboldt squid,** which reaches lengths of 4.5 meters (15 feet) and may weigh as much as 150 kilograms (330 pounds). In the Cape Region squid (*calamar* in Spanish) is popularly eaten in *cocteles* or used as sportfishing bait.

Elongated Fish
These varieties share the characteristics of long, slender bodies and jaws like beaks. The sharp-toothed **California barracuda** swims in the Pacific from the border down to Cabo San Lucas while a smaller, more edible variety is found in the Sea of Cortez. In spite of their somewhat frightful appearance, barracudas rarely attack humans.

The silvery **flying fish** can be seen leaping above offshore waters throughout the Pacific and the lower Sea of Cortez. It is not generally considered a food fish. The most edible of the elongated fish is probably the acrobatic **Mexican needlefish,** or *agujón,* which reaches two meters in length and has green bones.

Shellfish
Baja's shores abound with deep-water and shallow-water shellfish species, including multiple varieties of **clams, oysters, mussels, scallops,** and **shrimp,** many of which have disappeared from coastal California, U.S.A. Baja's most famous shellfish is undoubtedly the **spiny lobster,** which appears on virtually every *mariscos* menu on the peninsula.

BIRDS

Hosting around 300 known species of birdlife, the peninsula and islands of Baja California are one of the most concentrated and undisturbed aviary habitats in North America. Ornithological research focusing on the Cape Region, however, is incomplete, and reference materials are difficult to come by; one of the most up-to-date works available is Peterson and Chalif's *A Field Guide to Mexican Birds,* last published in 1973.

Coastal and Pelagic Species
The vast majority of the Cape's native and migrating species are either coastal or open-sea (pelagic) birds. The Sea of Cortez islands are particularly rich in birdlife; the Mexican government has designated 49 of the islands as wildlife refuges to protect the many rare and endangered species there. Among the more notable island birds are the rare and clownish **blue-footed booby** and its more common cousins, the **brown booby** and the **masked booby.**

Common throughout the coastal areas of southern Baja is the **magnificent frigate,** called *tijera* (scissors) in Mexico because of its scissor-shaped tail. In spite of their seafood diet, frigates can't swim or even submerge their heads to catch fish—instead they glide high in the air on boomerang-

BOB RACE

magnificent frigate

shaped wings, swooping down to steal fish from other birds, especially slow-witted boobies.

Among the more commonly seen birds along the Sea of Cortez coast is the **brown pelican,** which in global terms is not so common. As a species, pelicans go back 30 million years; paleontologists use the modern pelican as a model for creating visual representations of the pteranodon, an extinct flying reptile with an eight-meter wingspan. Brown pelicans, the only truly marine species among the world's seven pelican species, dive 10-30 meters (30-100 feet) under water to catch fish. Other pelicans only dip their beaks beneath the surface, and tend to frequent inland waterways rather than marine habitats. Browns have almost entirely disappeared from the U.S. shores of the Gulf of Mexico, and are declining in the coastal islands of California—apparently due to the pesticide content of the Pacific Ocean. Baja's Cortez and Pacific coasts are among the last habitats where the brown pelican thrives.

Another noteworthy bird along the coast is the **fisher eagle,** which, as its name implies, catches and eats fish. The fisher eagle is also occasionally seen along freshwater rivers and around the Pacific lagoons.

Other coastal birds include two species of **cormorant,** the **long-billed curlew,** four species of **egret,** four species of **grebe,** 10 species of **gull,** three species of **heron,** the **belted kingbird,** two species of **ibis,** three species of **loon,** the **osprey,** the **American oystercatcher,** six species of **plover,** six species of **sandpiper,** the **tundra swan,** and seven species of **tern.**

Certain fish-eating birds are usually seen only by boaters since they tend to fly over open ocean. These pelagics include two species of **albatross,** the **black-legged kittiwake,** the **red phalarope,** three species of **shearwater,** the **surf scoter,** the **south polar skua,** five species of **storm petrel,** the **black tern,** and the **red-billed tropic bird.**

Estuarine and Inland Species

Another group of waterfowl in southern Baja frequents only freshwater ponds, *tinajas* (springs), lakes, streams, and marshes. These birds include two species of **bittern,** the **American coot,** two species of **duck,** the **snow goose,** the **northern harrier,** six species of **heron,** the **white-faced ibis,** the **common moorhen,** two species of **rail,** five species of **sandpiper,** the **lesser scaup,** the **shoveler,** the **common snipe,** the **sora,** the **roseate spoonbill,** the **wood stork,** three species of **teal,** the **northern waterthrush,** and the **American wigeon.** Some of these birds are native, others only winter over. One of the best, and most convenient, places to view such birdlife is the estuary in San José del Cabo.

In the sierras dwell the **golden eagle,** the **western flycatcher,** the **lesser goldfinch,** the **black-headed grosbeak,** the **red-tailed hawk,** two species of **hummingbird,** the **pheasant,** the **yellow-eyed junco,** the **white-breasted nuthatch,** the **mountain plover,** four species of **vireo,** eight species of **warbler,** the **acorn woodpecker,** and the **canyon wren.**

Common over desert and/or open country are three species of **falcon** (peregrine, prairie, and Cooper's), three species of **flycatcher,** six species of **hawk,** the **black-fronted hummingbird,** the **American kestrel,** the **merlin,** two species of **owl,** the **greater roadrunner,** eight species of **sparrow,** two species of **thrasher,** the **vernon,** the **turkey vulture,** the **ladder-backed woodpecker,** and the **cactus wren.**

REPTILES AND AMPHIBIANS

Among the slippery, slimy, scaly, crawly things that live in the Cape Region are around two dozen species of lizards, frogs, toads, turtles, and snakes.

Lizards

Four-legged reptilians of note include the **chuckwalla,** which is found on certain islands in the Sea of Cortez; it sometimes grows to nearly a meter in length. The chuckwalla drinks fresh water when available, storing it in sacs that gurgle when it walks; when a freshwater source is not available, the lizard imbibes saltwater, which it processes through a sort of in-

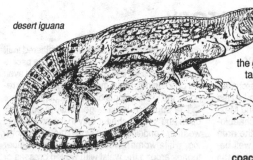

desert iguana

ERIN DWYER

Snakes

The rocky lowlands and chaparrals make perfect snake country. The bad news is that about half the known species are venomous; the good news is they rarely come into contact with humans. Scorpion stings far outnumber snakebites in Baja.

Harmless species include the **western blind snake, rosy boa, Baja California rat snake, spotted leaf-nosed snake, western patch-nosed snake, bullsnake, coachwhip, kingsnake, Baja sand snake,** and the **California lyre snake.**

The venomous kinds fall into two categories, one of which contains only a single snake species, the **yellow-bellied sea snake.** Sea snakes usually flee the vicinity when they sense human presence, but as a general precaution don't grab anything in the water that looks like a floating stick—that's how sea snakes deceive their prey.

The other category is the rattlesnakes, of which there are supposedly 18 species stretched out along Baja California. The most common species is the near-endemic **Baja California rattler** *(Crotalus enyo),* with a range that includes the lower three-fourths of the peninsula. Look for scaly mounds over the eyes if you care to make an identification. The most dangerous of Baja rattlers is the **Western diamondback**; it's the largest and therefore has the greatest potential to deliver fatal or near-fatal doses of venom. Fortunately the diamondback is mostly confined to the canyons of the northern sierras; I've never heard of a sighting in the Cape Region.

The general all-inclusive Spanish term for snake is *serpiente;* a nonvenomous snake is referred to as *culebra,* the venomous sort *víbora.* A rattlesnake is *un serpiente de cascabel* or simply *un cascabel.* An encouraging factoid: according to Spanish records, no missionary ever died of snakebite during the 300-year period of Spanish colonization of the New World.

ternal desalinator. Another good-sized lizard is the **desert iguana,** found throughout the Gulf Coast Desert and possibly farther north. Larger iguanas are sometimes eaten in ranchero stews and are said to taste better than chicken. The **coast horned lizard,** similar to the horny toad of the American Southwest, is another endemic.

Turtles

Of the six turtle varieties present, five are sea turtles: the **leatherback, green, hawksbill, western ridley,** and **loggerhead.** Because their eggs, meat, and shells are highly valued among coastal Mexican populations, all are on the endangered species list. The Mexican government has declared turtle hunting and turtle egg collecting illegal; the decimation of the turtles has slowed considerably but hasn't yet stopped. Bajacalifornios say they're upholding the laws while anglers along the mainland coast of the Sea of Cortez still take sea turtles.

The main culprit has apparently been Japan, which is the world's largest importer of sea turtles—including the endangered ridley and hawksbill, both of which the Japanese use for meat, turtle leather, and turtle-shell fashion accessories. In 1991 the Japanese government announced a ban on the importation of sea turtles, so perhaps the Sea of Cortez populations will soon make a comeback.

HISTORY

PRE-COLUMBIAN HISTORY

Because the Cape lacks spectacular archaeological remains, such as the Mayan and Aztec ruins in the southern reaches of mainland Mexico, it has largely been ignored by archaeologists. It is highly likely, however, that the area was inhabited by human populations well before the rest of Mexico. Baja California Sur was the logical termination for the coastal migration route followed by Asian groups who crossed the Bering Strait land bridge between Asia and North America beginning around 50,000 B.C.

The Cochimís and Guaycuras

Indian groups living in the central and southern reaches of the peninsula when the Spanish arrived were apparently much less advanced technologically than the Yumanos of northern Baja, not to mention Amerindian groups found in central and southern mainland Mexico. Because of the lack of archaeological research in these areas, the only record we have of these Indians is the one left us by Spanish accounts, which were undoubtedly biased in light of their mission to subordinate the peoples of the New World. Mission histories are full of lurid tales of Indian customs, many probably written to convince the Spanish crown of the desperate need to missionize the natives. Nevertheless, the Indians of central and southern Baja appeared to be among the more "primitive" of the tribes encountered by the Spanish in Mexico or Mesoamerica. In modern archaeological terms, they hadn't progressed beyond the Paleolithic epoch (the early Stone Age).

According to these accounts, the Guaycuras, divided into the Pericú, Huchiti, and Guaicura tribes, occupied the Cape Region. One fringe anthropological view has suggested a portion of the Guaycura tribes may have descended from Tahitian seafarers who were following the star Arcturus (overhead at latitude 22°) on their way to Hawaii when their boats were blown off course during bad weather. Whatever their place of origin, they spent most of their daylight hours searching for food; the men hunted small game or gathered shellfish while the women gathered fruit, seeds, and roots. If game was scarce, the people subsisted on a variety of insects and would even eat dried animal skins, including, according to reports, the leather boots of the conquistadors.

The southern Indians generally lived in the open and sought shelter only in the severest of weather conditions. Men wore little or no clothing, while women wore leather or yucca-fiber thongs around the waist with woven grasses or twigs suspended from the front and animal skins in the back. These garments were sometimes painted with bright colors. The tips of arrows and spears were generally of sharpened hardwood only, though chipped stone points were

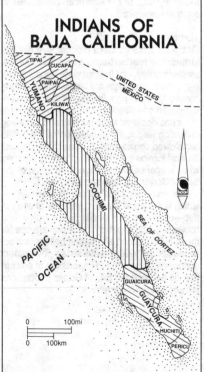

INDIANS OF
BAJA CALIFORNIA

occasionally used. The Guaycuras also used reed blowguns. The most important time of year among these Indians was when the fruit of the *pitahaya* cactus ripened; the fruit was then so abundant the Indians allegedly abandoned all activities save sleeping and eating.

None of the Guaycuras apparently left behind any artwork. This has been attributed to their harsh living environment; they may have had little time or energy for artistic pursuits. However, in the inland areas of the south central peninsula once inhabited by Cochimí and Guaycura tribes, numerous spectacular rock-art sites have been discovered. The Cochimís told the Spanish this rock art was created by a race of giants who'd preceded them. Almost nothing is known about this lost Indian culture, a people Baja rock-art expert Harry Crosby has dubbed "The Painters." Because rock-art sites in the Cape Region are less numerous than those found farther north in the Sierra de la Giganta and Sierra de San Francisco, modern researchers have almost totally neglected them.

THE SPANISH CONQUEST OF BAJA CALIFORNIA

Following 700 years of conflict with the Moors over control of the Iberian Peninsula, Spain in the 15th century emerged as the most powerful nation in Europe. Convinced that a Roman Catholic God was destined to rule the world with Spain as His emissary, the Spanish monarchy sent Christopher Columbus in search of a new route to the Far East. His mission was to establish contact with a mythical "Great Khan" in order to develop an alternate trade route with the Orient, since Arabs controlled the overland route through the Middle East. Along the way as many pagans as possible would be converted to Christianity. Once the Arab trade monopoly was broken, the Holy Land would be returned to Christian control.

Columbus's landing in the West Indies in 1492 was followed by Pope Alexander VI's historic 1493, decree which gave the Spanish rights to any new land discovered west of the Azores, as long as the Spanish made "God's name known there." Hence, the Spanish conquest of the New World started as a roundabout extension of the Holy Crusades.

A succession of Spanish expeditions into the Caribbean and Gulf of Mexico rapidly achieved the conquest of Mexico and Central America. Conquistador Hernán Cortés subdued the Valley of Mexico Aztecs in three years (1519-21), and the allegiance—or decimation—of other Aztecs and Mayans followed quickly.

Early California Explorations
When the Spanish conquistadors came to the western edge of mainland Mexico and looked beyond toward the landforms they could see above the sea, they concluded that Baja California was a huge island and the as-yet-unnamed Sea of Cortez led to the Atlantic. The idea of a "northwest passage" to the Atlantic persisted for years, even among seasoned explorers like Cabrillo, Drake, and Vizcaíno. Cortés himself directed four voyages from the mainland to the island of La California, although he actually accompanied only the third. The history of these early expeditions exposes the enmity and extreme sense of competition among those conquistadors supposedly working toward a common cause.

The first voyage, launched in 1532, never made it to the peninsula. The ships were captured in the Sea of Cortez by Nuño Guzmán, an archrival of Cortés operating farther north in Mexico. The next year a second expedition, under Captain Diego Becerra of the *Concepción*, suffered a mutiny in which the captain was killed. Basque pilot Fortún Jiménez took charge and the ship landed in Bahía de La Paz in early 1534. Thus the first European visitors to reach Baja California, a group of mutineers, arrived there just 42 years after Columbus touched down in the West Indies and nearly a century before the Pilgrims landed at Plymouth Rock.

Before they had much of a chance to explore, Jiménez and 22 of his crew were killed by Indians while filling their water casks at a spring. The survivors managed to sail the *Concepción* back to the mainland, where most were promptly captured by Guzmán. One of the escapees managed to reach Cortés with tales of rich caches of black pearls on a huge island with "cliffs and headlands and rocky coasts," as in the California of popular myth.

Cortés, inspired by these stories, organized and led a third expedition, partially financed by his own personal wealth. His party consisted of three ships and a group of 500 Spanish colonists that included women and children. They landed at the northeast end of Bahía de La Paz—which Cortés named Santa Cruz—in May of 1535, the same year New Spain was officially established. Although Cortés apparently found pearls in abundance, his attempt to colonize the peninsula lasted only two years, by which time disease, hostile Indians, and *chubascos* had driven the colonists back to the mainland.

The fourth attempt by Cortés to establish a Spanish foothold on California soil was led by the highly competent Captain Francisco de Ulloa, who'd accompanied Cortés on the failed Santa Cruz expedition. Cortés stayed behind on this one, hoping Ulloa's expedition would be able to find a more hospitable California beachhead. Ulloa set sail from Acapulco with two ships in July 1539, and over the next eight months he managed to explore the entire perimeter of the Sea of Cortez, reaching the mouth of the Río Colorado and rounding the Cape along the Pacific coast as far north as Isla Cedros.

Upon reaching Isla Cedros, Ulloa reportedly sent one ship back to Acapulco for supplies; it isn't known for certain what happened to the other vessel. According to some historical accounts, Ulloa found his way back to the mainland and was murdered by one of his own crew near Guadalajara; other accounts say he disappeared north of Isla Cedros. At any rate, his written report of the voyage—which indicated Baja was not an island but a peninsula—didn't surface until a hundred years later. His biggest contribution to the geography of the times was the naming of the Mar de Cortés, now the Sea of Cortez, or Gulf of California.

After squandering most of his wealth in futile attempts to explore Baja California, Cortés was recalled to Spain in 1541, never to return to Mexican shores. In his place, Spain dispatched experienced Portuguese navigator Juan Rodríguez Cabrillo in 1542 with orders to explore the Pacific coast. Starting from the southern tip of the peninsula, his expedition made it as far north as the Oregon coast and mapped several major bays along the way, including those of San Diego and Monterey. Cabrillo himself never made it past California's Santa Barbara Islands; he died there following a mysterious fall.

Manila galleon

Manila Galleons and Privateers

Meanwhile on the other side of the globe, events were unfolding that would influence Baja California's history for the next 250 years. Although Portuguese navigator Ferdinand Magellan reached the Philippines in 1521, it wasn't until 1565 that López de Legaspi defeated the archipelago's native defenders. Immediately thereafter, Estéban Rodríguez and Padre Andrés de Urdaneta pioneered a ship route from Manila to the New World that took advantage of the 14,500-km (9,000-mile) Japanese Current across the northern Pacific, thus establishing a trade connection between the Orient and New Spain.

The ships making the annual roundtrip voyages between Manila and Acapulco beginning in 1566 came to be called "Manila galleons." The lengthy sea journey was very difficult, however, because of the lack of fresh water during the final weeks of the five- to seven-month eastward crossing. This provided further impetus for establishing some sort of settlement in lower California where ships could put in for water and supplies.

A California landfall became even more desirable when in 1572 the Manila galleons started carrying shipments of gold, silks, and spices to New Spain. The ships were so heavy they became easy prey for faster pirate vessels. By

1580, England's Sir Francis Drake had entered the Pacific via the Straits of Magellan and circumnavigated the globe, thus ending Spanish dominion over the seas. Drake plundered Spanish ships with regularity, and as news of the treasure-laden ships spread, other English as well as Dutch privateers were lured into the Pacific.

Their raids on Spanish ships became an embarrassment to the crown and a drain on Spanish wealth, so the Spaniards were forced to seek out harbors along Baja's Cape Region where they could hide. Since the first land sighting on the east Pacific leg of the Manila-Acapulco voyage was below the peninsula's midpoint, the Cape Region was the logical choice for a landing. Following much experimentation, Bahía San Lucas and Bahía de La Paz became the two harbors most frequently used.

Eventually, however, the keen privateers figured out how to trap Spanish ships in the very bays their crews sought for protection. Thomas Cavendish plundered the Manila galleon *Santa Ana* at Cabo San Lucas in 1587, and so many ships were captured in Bahía de La Paz that the landfall there, originally called Santa Cruz by Cortés, eventually earned the name Pichilingue, a Spanish mispronunciation of Vlissingen, the provenance of most of the Dutch pirates.

Pirating continued off the Baja coast throughout the entire 250-year history of the Manila-Acapulco voyages. One of the more celebrated English privateers in later years was Woodes Rogers, who arrived in the Pacific in 1709 and captured the Manila galleon *Encarnación* off Cabo San Lucas. On his way to Baja California that same year Rogers rescued Alexander Selkirk, a sailor marooned on an island off the coast of Chile for four years. Selkirk served as shipmaster on Rogers's vessel and later became the inspiration for Daniel Defoe's 1719 novel *Robinson Crusoe.*

Further Exploration and Colonization Attempts

As the Spaniards' need for a permanent settlement in California grew more dire, coastal explorations were resumed after a hiatus of over 50 years. Cabrillo was succeeded by merchant-turned-admiral Sebastián Vizcaíno, who in 1596 landed at the same bay on the southeast coast chosen by his predecessors, Jiménez and Cortés. This time, however, the natives were

friendly—perhaps because it was *pitahaya* fruit season when they arrived—and Vizcaíno named the site La Paz ("Peace"). Loading up on *pitahaya* fruit—effective for preventing scurvy— and pearls, Vizcaíno continued northward along the Sea of Cortez coast, stopping to gather more pearls before returning to the mainland.

In 1602 Vizcaíno commanded a second, more ambitious expedition that sailed along the Pacific coast to near present-day Mendocino in California. His names for various points and bays along the coasts of both Californias superseded most of those bestowed by Cabrillo and Cortés.

Upon his return Vizcaíno told his superiors that the Monterey Bay area of California was well suited to colonization. However, because he was no longer in favor with New Spain's fickle viceroys, no one paid much attention to his findings and he was reassigned to an obscure Sinaloa port. The cartographer for the voyage, Gerónimo Martínez, was beheaded for forgery, although his maps of the Californias remained the best available for over 200 years.

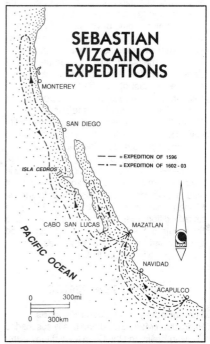

SEBASTIAN VIZCAINO EXPEDITIONS

MONTEREY

SAN DIEGO

— — = EXPEDITION OF 1596
— · — = EXPEDITION OF 1602 - 03

ISLA CEDROS

CABO SAN LUCAS   MAZATLAN

PACIFIC OCEAN

NAVIDAD

ACAPULCO

0   300mi

0   300km

© MOON PUBLICATIONS, INC.

This neglect of California's potential enabled an Englishman to put first claim to the territory. Sir Francis Drake, who landed at what is now Drake's Bay in northern California during his 1578-80 voyage, christened the land New Albion on behalf of the English crown. Like the Spanish maps of the time, his maps depicted California as an island.

For a time Spain left both Californias unexplored. In 1615 Captain Juan de Iturbi obtained the first official concession for peninsular pearl diving but no land settlement was established. After two of his ships were captured by Dutch privateers off Cabo San Lucas, de Iturbi's remaining vessel sailed northward in the Sea of Cortez as far as the 28th parallel, harvesting pearls along the way. Because of dwindling provisions, they were forced to turn back to the mainland after only a few months.

The peninsula remained unconquered by the Spanish for another 80 years. In 1683 Spain's Royal Council for the Indies authorized an expedition under Admiral Isidor Atondo y Antillón and Padre Eusebio Francisco Kino that managed to occupy an area of La Paz for 3.5 months before being driven back to the mainland by dwindling provisions and hostile natives. After two months of rest and provisioning on the mainland, they crossed the Sea of Cortez again, this time establishing a mission and presidio just above the 26th parallel at a place they named San Bruno. Supported by a friendly Indian population, the mission lasted 19 months. Lack of water and food—they had to rely on supply ships from the mainland—forced Kino and Atondo back to the mainland.

Kino never returned to Baja California but later became famous for his missionary efforts in northwestern Mexico and Arizona, where he is said to have converted thousands of Indians to Roman Catholicism. In 1701 he accompanied an expedition from the northwest of Sonora to the mouth of the Río Colorado that confirmed Ulloa's claim that Baja California was a peninsula. He died in Sonora in 1711.

THE MISSION PERIOD

The Founding of the Jesuit Missions

Padre Juan María Salvatierra finally succeeded in giving Spain and the Church what they want-

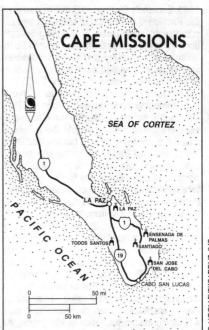

ed—a permanent Spanish settlement on the Baja California peninsula. Backed by the mainland missionary system, a 30,000-peso annual subsidy from the Royal Council of the Indies, and a contingent of Spanish soldiers, Salvatierra landed in San Bruno in October 1697, located a better water source 24 km south of the original presidio, and proceeded to establish the mother of all California missions, Nuestra Señora de Loreto.

The founding of the Loreto mission initiated what Baja historians usually call "the Jesuit missionary period," lasting from 1697 to 1767. During this interval, the Jesuits established 20 missions, stretching from the southern tip of the peninsula to near present-day Cataviña in central Baja. That wasn't a spectacular accomplishment compared with the progress of mainland colonization, but lower California was a much more difficult area to colonize. It had taken 167 years from the time the first Spaniard had set foot on her shores until the first successful settlement was established on Baja California soil.

The Spanish mission system basically worked like this: the padres, always in the company of armed escorts, approached groups of natives and offered them the protection of the Church and the Spanish crown in return for a willingness to undergo religious instruction. Those natives who agreed were congregated at a suitable spot and directed to build a mission. The mission in turn became a refuge for the Indians and a place for them to learn European farming techniques and other trades, as well as Catholic ways. Once pacification was complete, the mission became a secularized church community (pueblo) and the missionaries moved on to new areas.

The system worked well with the docile Indians of Central Mexico but was often unsuccessful among the nomadic, fiercely independent Indians of northern Mexico and Baja. Elsewhere in Mexico and Latin America, the norm was to secularize after 10 years; in Baja, the Spanish Church never voluntarily secularized its missions.

Amateur historians like to say the Californias were missionized by the cross, not the sword. This was actually no more true in Baja than it was for the mainland, although the military presence was indeed less—but only because the Jesuits were given greater administrative power in Baja and had to finance themselves, and their militia, through Church funds. The conversion techniques were the same: natives who obeyed the padres were rewarded with land and protection, those who rebelled were punished, those who organized rebellions were executed. Apologists claim the padres never endorsed violence, but if this were true, they wouldn't have brought along the militia in the first place.

A contemporary report of the founding of Misión San Juan Bautista describes how Padres Salvatierra and Pedro de Ugarte approached the natives of Liguí in 1703:

The two Padres, the soldier who accompanied them and two Christian Indians were given a real fright by a large band of Indians who fired a shower of arrows toward them, but after the soldier . . . discharged his musket into the air the Indians threw down their weapons and prostrated themselves on the earth, presently sitting up to await the coming of the Padres. Through an interpreter, Padre Salvatierra explained to them the purpose of their visit, and distributed among them some small gifts, expressing the hope that Padre Pedro de Ugarte might return later and be welcomed by them. Before leaving they brought 48 Indian children for baptism.

Indian Revolts, Disease, and the Decline of the Jesuits

Several times during the Jesuit period, groups of Indians revolted against missionization. The most significant rebellion occurred in 1734-36 among the Pericú Indians of the southern peninsula. Apparently the revolt was triggered by Padre Nicolás Tamaral's injunction against polygamy—long a practice among the Pericús and Guaicuras, tribes in which women outnumbered men. The punishment of a Pericú shaman under the injunction doubled the perceived assault on native culture and a group of disaffected Indians organized themselves against the entire mission structure.

In October 1734, the Pericús attacked and burned the missions at Santiago and San José del Cabo, killing Padre Tamaral and his counterpart at Santiago. They also set fire to the mission in Loreto, although the padre there escaped unharmed and was able to send to the mainland for assistance. The provincial governor of Sinaloa, after receiving letters from Loreto describing the uprising, dispatched a ship from the mainland with 60 Yaqui warriors and a number of Spanish soldiers. The troops marched from mission to mission, meeting little resistance from the poorly equipped Pericús.

Unrest among the Pericús continued for another two years, a situation that led to the founding of a large presidio at San José del Cabo. As a further precaution, the garrisons at every mission in the south were expanded by 10 soldiers each. Besides reinforcing the missions, this increased military presence encouraged Manila galleons to make Cabo San Lucas a regular stop on their return voyages from the Orient.

In the years to follow, epidemics of smallpox, syphilis, and measles—diseases borne by Europeans for which Indians had no natural immunity—decimated the Indian population. In 1538 Padre Jacobo Baegert of Misión San Luis Gonzaga estimated the Baja Indian population at about 50,000. In three outbreaks of smallpox in 1742, 1744, and 1748, an estimated 42,000, or five-sixths of the Indian population, perished. Gathering the natives into mission settlements only hastened their demise, intensifying the spread of contagions. A significant number of Indians also lost their lives in continued rebellions against the padres. The La Paz mission was abandoned in 1748; by 1767 only one member of the entire Huchiti branch of the Guaycura nation survived.

As the southern Indians died out, the missionaries moved quickly northward, seeking new sheep for their flocks. The last four missions established by the Jesuits, Santa Gertrudis (1752), San Borja (1762), Calamajué (1766), and Santa María (1767), were scattered widely in northern Baja in an obvious push toward California.

In 1767 King Charles III ordered the expulsion of the Jesuit Order from all Spanish dominions, including Baja California. Accounts of the expulsion disagree as to the reasons behind his action. According to crown representatives, the Jesuits were too power-hungry and would no longer be held accountable for their actions. The Jesuits themselves claimed persecution because they'd dared criticize corruption among the nobility and royalty of Europe. Whatever the reason, in 1768 the 16 Jesuit padres of Baja found themselves herded onto a ship bound for the mainland port of San Blas, where the same ship received a contingent of Franciscan padres sent to replace them.

Franciscan and Dominican padres succeeded the Jesuits, but by the end of the 18th century it was clear that Spain and the Church could no longer afford to support the Baja missions. The peninsula's Indian population had dwindled to less than 5,000 by 1800, and, without an abundance of free native labor, maintaining a colony wasn't an easy task. The California missions to the north seemed much more promising—water was more readily available and the Indian labor force was more docile and plentiful. The growing unrest in Mexico placed the peninsula even lower on Spain's list of priorities.

INDEPENDENCE FROM SPAIN

The Catholic Church in Mexico had amassed huge amounts of wealth by the beginning of the 19th century and had become lenders to the colony's growing entrepreneurial class. At the other end of the economic spectrum, the increasing numbers of mestizos—Mexican-born residents of mixed Spanish and Indian ancestry—were denied land ownership and other rights, and were generally treated as second-class citizens.

Fearing the Church was becoming too powerful, King Charles III of Spain decreed in 1804 that all church funds be turned over to the royal coffers. As padres all over Mexico were forced to comply with the decree, calling back large sums of money lent out to entrepreneurs, economic chaos ensued. Mexicans blamed their economic and social problems on Spain's remote rule; when Napoleon invaded Spain in 1808, limiting authority to Spanish loyalists in Mexico City, the disaffected clergy began planning a revolt.

Mexico's struggle for independence from Spain began on 16 September 1810, a date celebrated annually as Diez y Seis or Mexican Independence Day. Padre Miguel Hidalgo y Costilla issued a call for independence entitled the Grito de Dolores ("Dolores Cry") in the mainland province of Guanajuato. Although the rebels who gathered around Hidalgo soon captured Zacatecas, Valladolid, and San Luis Potosí, Mexico wasn't completely free of Spanish rule for another 11 years. When Hidalgo was captured and executed by loyalists, another padre took his place and the fighting continued until Mexico City acceded to the demands of the rebels in 1821.

The 1821 Plan de Iguala treaty between Spain and Mexico guaranteed three political underpinnings of the new regime: the religious dominance of the Catholic Church, a constitutional monarchy, and equal rights for mestizos as well as Mexican-born Spaniards. Former Viceroy Agustín de Iturbide was appointed emperor of the new republic, but his reign only lasted two years before he was overthrown by another junta that established a short-lived federal republic called Los Estados Unidos de México—the United States of Mexico—in 1824.

Over the next six years the Mexican republic endured two more coups; it wasn't until 1829 that all Spanish troops were expelled from Mexico. In 1832 all non-Dominican missions in Baja were secularized and converted to parish churches. The Dominican missions of the northern peninsula were allowed to remain because they were considered the only outposts of civilization north of La Paz and Loreto, and as such were important links with prospering Alta California. Another change in policy involved the encouragement of Anglo-American immigration to the northeastern Mexican state of Coahuila y Texas—a policy that would have profound implications later on.

The Mexican-American War

In 1833 Antonio López de Santa Anna, a megalomaniac general in charge of enforcing the expulsion of Spanish troops, seized power and revoked the Constitution of 1824, thus initiating a series of events that eventually led to a war with the U.S. and the resultant loss of huge amounts of territory. During the first 30 years of Mexican independence, Mexico changed governments 50 times; Santa Anna—who called himself the "Napoleon of the West"—headed 11 of these regimes.

Mexican citizens everywhere were angry at the revocation of their republican constitution by a self-appointed dictator. But none were more frustrated than the Anglo-American immigrants who had voluntarily abandoned their U.S. citizenship in order to take Mexican citizenship under the Constitution of 1824 and live in the northern half of Coahuila y Texas. In 1836 the "Texicans" declared an independent Republic of Texas, fought and lost San Antonio's infamous Battle of the Alamo, and then routed Santa Anna's troops at San Jacinto, Texas.

Defeated and captured, Santa Anna signed the Velasco Agreement, which guaranteed Texas independence and recognized the Rio Grande as the border between Mexico and the new Texan republic. There matters lay until the U.S. granted statehood to the near-bankrupt republic in 1845. Santa Anna's government refused to recognize the Velasco Agreement, claiming Texas only extended as far south as the Nueces River, about 160 km north of the Rio Grande at the widest gap. When the U.S. Army moved into the area south of the Nueces, Santa Anna retaliated by sending troops across the Rio Grande, thus initiating the Mexican-American War.

After a series of skirmishes along the Rio Grande, U.S. President James Polk ordered the army to invade Mexico. In Baja California,

Mexican and American forces engaged at Santo Tomás, Mulegé, La Paz, and San José del Cabo. Mexico City finally fell to U.S. troops in March 1847, and Santa Anna signed the Treaty of Guadalupe Hidalgo in 1848. In the treaty, Mexico conceded not only the Rio Grande area of Texas but part of New Mexico and all of California for a payment of US$25 million and the cancellation of all Mexican debt.

In retrospect, it is likely the annexation of Texas was part of a U.S. plan to provoke Mexico into declaring war so the U.S. could gain more of the Southwest. The war so damaged Mexico's already weakened economy that in 1853 Santa Anna sold Arizona and southern New Mexico to the U.S. for another US$10 million. During that same year, American freebooter William Walker sailed to La Paz and declared himself "President of Lower California." He and his mercenary troops fled upon hearing that Mexican forces were on the way. He was later tried—and acquitted—in the U.S. for violation of neutrality laws. Walker was executed after a similar escapade in Nicaragua two years later.

For the Mexican population, already strongly dissatisfied with Santa Anna, these losses of territory became the final straw; in 1855 Santa Anna was overthrown by populist Benito Juárez.

Depopulation of the Peninsula, Civil War, and Reform

The second half of the 19th century was even more turbulent for Mexico than the first. At the end of the Mexican-American War, the California Gold Rush of 1849 lured many Mexicans and Indians away from the peninsula to seek their fortunes in California, reducing Baja's already scant population even further and transforming it into a haven for bandits, pirates, and an assortment of other outlaws and misfits. Only six Dominican padres remained on the peninsula by the 1880s.

Meanwhile back on the mainland, a civil war (called the "War of Reform" in Mexico) erupted in 1858, following the removal of Santa Anna, in which self-appointed governments in Mexico City and Veracruz vied for national authority. Once again, Church wealth was the principal issue. The liberals, under Zapotec Indian lawyer Benito Juárez, had promulgated a new constitution in 1857 and passed a law further

KAREN MCKINLEY

Benito Juárez

Foreign Investment in Baja California

In Baja, Díaz and the "Porfiriato" encouraged foreign investment on a large scale, and in the 1880s vast land tracts were sold to American or European mining, farming, manufacturing, and railway concessions. All but the mining concessions met failure within a few years, mainly because the investors weren't prepared to deal with the peninsula's demanding climate and lack of transportation.

Mineral excavation in turn-of-the-century Baja enjoyed a boom—gold, silver, copper, and gypsum were the main finds, along with graphite, mercury, nickel, and sulfur. One of the most successful mining endeavors was that of Compañía del Boleo, a French mining syndicate in Santa Rosalía that for many years was the largest copper-mining and smelting operation in Mexico.

INTO THE TWENTIETH CENTURY

The Mexican Revolution

By the early 1900s, it was obvious that the gap between rich and poor was increasing, caused by the extreme pro-capitalist policies of the Díaz regime and the lack of a political voice for workers and peasants. In response to the situation, a liberal opposition group, using Texas as a base, formed in exile, organizing strikes throughout the country. This forced Díaz to announce an election in 1910; his opponent was Francisco Madero, a liberal from Coahuila. As it became clear that Madero was garnering mass support, Díaz imprisoned him on trumped-up charges.

Upon his release, Madero fled to Texas and began organizing the overthrow of the Díaz government. The rebels, with the assistance of the colorful bandit-turned-revolutionary Pancho Villa and peasant-hero Emiliano Zapata, managed to gain control of the northern Mexican states of Sonora and Chihuahua. Unable to contain the revolution, Díaz resigned in May of 1910 and Madero was elected president. His one-time allies, however, broke into several factions—the Zapatistas, Reyistas, Vasquistas, and Felicistas, named for the leaders of each movement—and Madero was executed in 1913. Baja California had its own faction, the Magonistas, who briefly held Tijuana in 1911.

For the next six years the various factions played musical chairs with national leadership,

restricting the financial powers of the Church; all Church property save for the church buildings themselves had to be sold or otherwise relinquished. A reactionary opposition group took control of Mexico City and fighting continued until 1861, when the liberals won and Juárez was elected president.

Juárez immediately had to deal with the 1862 French invasion of Mexico, which came in response to Mexico's nonpayment of debts to France. Napoleon's first invading force was defeated at Puebla on the Gulf of Mexico coast, but the following year the French captured the port and continued onward to take Mexico City, where they installed Austrian Ferdinand Maximilian as emperor of Mexico. Under U.S. pressure, the French gradually withdrew from Mexico and Juárez was back in power by 1867.

Over the next four years Juárez initiated many economic and educational reforms. Upon his death in 1872, political opponent Porfirio Díaz took over and continued reforms begun by Juárez, albeit in a more authoritarian manner. Díaz and/or his cronies ruled for the next 28 years, suspending political freedoms but modernizing the country's education and transportation systems.

and Mexico remained extremely unstable until revolutionary leader Venustiano Carranza emerged as president. Carranza held a historic convention that resulted in the Constitution of 1917, the current Mexican constitution. This document established the *ejido* program to return lands traditionally cultivated by the Indian peasantry, but taken away by rich ranch and plantation owners under Díaz, to local communities throughout Mexico. Three years later opponent Álvaro Obregón and his supporters overthrew Carranza.

Obregón managed to hang onto the office for four years, establishing important educational reforms; he was followed in 1924 by Plutarco Elías Calles. Calles instituted wide-reaching agrarian reforms, including the redistribution of three million hectares of land. He also participated in the establishment of the National Revolutionary Party (PNR), the forerunner of the Institutional Revolutionary Party (PRI), Mexico's dominant party today.

U.S. Prohibition
In the same year that Obregón took power in Mexico City, the U.S. government amended its own constitution to make the consumption, manufacture, and sale of alcoholic beverages a federal offense. This proved to be a disastrous experiment for the U.S., ushering in an era of organized crime, but was a boon to Baja California development. Americans began rushing across the border to buy booze from the restaurants, cantinas, and liquor stores of northern Mexico.

Border towns added casinos and brothels to the assortment of liquor venues and became so prosperous that the municipal leadership was able to lobby successfully for the division of Baja California into northern and southern territories. On the negative side, the border towns became renowned as world sleaze capitals. Their reputations persisted long after Prohibition ended in 1933 and the Mexican government outlawed gambling—prostitution remained legal—in 1938.

Nationalist Reforms and World War II
The year 1938 proved a turning point in modern Mexican history as PNR candidate Lázaro Cárdenas ascended to the presidency. Cárdenas, a mestizo with Tarascan Indian heritage, instituted the most sweeping social reforms of any national leader to date, effecting significant changes in education, labor, agriculture, and commerce.

His land reforms included the redistribution of 18.6 million hectares (46 million acres) among newly created *ejidos*—a legacy that is as hot a topic for debate today as it was then. Foreign-owned oil interests were expropriated and a national oil company, Petróleos Mexicanos (PEMEX), was established. These reforms frightened off foreign investors for many years and it has been only very recently that Mexico has reattracted foreign capital. Cárdenas also reorganized the PNR as the Mexican Revolution Party (PRM—Partido de la Revolución Mexicana), which soon changed its name to the Institutional Revolutionary Party (PRI—Partido Revolucionario Institucional).

Baja Statehood and the Transpeninsular Highway
After the war Mexico continued to industrialize and the economy remained relatively stable under one PRI president after another. In 1952 the Territory of (Northern) Baja California was declared Mexico's 29th state as its population moved past the 80,000 required for statehood. Northern Baja was, in fact, better off economically than most of the rest of the country. The boomtowns of Tijuana and Mexicali were servicing a fast-growing border economy and Valle de Mexicali farming competed well with California's Imperial Valley. In 1958 it was determined that Baja was second only to Mexico City in the number of automobiles per capita.

Meanwhile wealthy Americans had been flying to La Paz and Cabo San Lucas since the late 1940s to fish the teeming waters of the Sea of Cortez, and in 1948 several Hollywood celebrities (including Bing Crosby, John Wayne, and Desi Arnaz), built a resort known as Las Cruces on the Cortez coast east of La Paz. In 1958 a lone American investor constructed the Hotel Palmilla at Punta Palmilla on the Corridor, and others quickly followed with the Hotel Cabo San Lucas, Hotel Hacienda, and Hotel Finisterra in Cabo San Lucas, along with Rancho Buena Vista on Bahía de Palmas.

Throughout the 1960s most of Baja south of Ensenada remained benevolently neglected, which led travel writers of the time to employ the famous catchphrase, "the forgotten peninsula." The Cape Region was a little-known beach and sportfishing destination limited to pilots, diehard anglers, and celebrities. The overall population of the Territory of Southern Baja California was stagnating, perhaps even decreasing; except for La Paz, it was limited to tiny collections of hardy souls here and there who scratched for cash as rancheros or *pescadores* (fishermen). Even La Paz was just a step above a sleepy backwater port, although its status as a duty-free port was beginning to attract a steady trickle of mainland Mexicans.

By the 1970s it was obvious that southern Baja wasn't going to catch up with northern Baja unless transportation between the south, north, and mainland improved. Travel between Tijuana and La Paz took up to 10 days via rough dirt tracks. Construction of the Transpeninsular Highway (Mexico 1) was finally completed in 1973, connecting Tijuana with Cabo San Lucas for the first time. In less than a year, the population of Baja California Sur passed the 80,000 mark and the territory became Mexico's 30th state.

The 1,700-km-long Transpeninsular Highway has greatly contributed to the modernization of one of Mexico's last frontiers. Fishing and agricultural cooperatives can now transport their products to the border or to the ports of Santa Rosalía, Guerrero Negro, and La Paz. The highway has brought Americans, Canadians, and Europeans deep into the peninsula in greater numbers than ever before, and the revenue from their visits provides another means of livelihood for the people of Baja.

Like the border visitors of the Prohibition years, those foreigners who come to the Cape Region in the 1990s are seeking something that's scarce in their own countries. For some it may be the unfenced desert solitude, for others the pristine beaches or historic mission towns. The challenge of the future for the Cape's burgeoning tourist industry is how to develop and maintain an adequate infrastructure without sacrificing those qualities that make Baja California Sur unique.

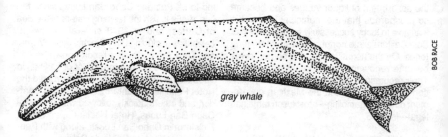

gray whale

BOB RACE

THE PEOPLE

The people of Baja California Sur are in many ways a breed apart from their compatriots on the mainland, which they call *la otra banda,* "the other edge." As Mexico's last frontier, El Sur continues to attract residents seeking something they haven't been able to find on the mainland, whether it's the rugged, independent life of the interior deserts and sierras or the tropical ambience of La Paz or Los Cabos.

For the rest of Mexico, Baja California Sur occupies a place in the national psyche somewhat analagous to that of Hawaii for many Americans. It's seen as a place that's part of the nation yet almost out of reach, an exotic destination most of the population will never have an opportunity to see. Hence, mainlanders typically regard people native to Baja California Sur as somehow "different" from themselves.

The enticements of a highly favorable climate, bounteous sea, and wide-open spaces has drawn a mix of native Bajacalifornios, transplanted Mexicans, and gringos to the Cape Region. The region as a whole—from La Paz to Cabo San Lucas and everywhere in between—receives less than 350,000 tourists a year (roughly one-tenth the number that visits the city of San Francisco in a year). About 40% of these visitors hail from elsewhere in Mexico while the other 60% come from the U.S., Canada, Europe, Asia, and Latin America.

Approximately 370,500 people live in Baja California Sur, most of them in La Paz, San José del Cabo, or Cabo San Lucas. Obviously, most of the Cape Region is very sparsely populated—the average density, even if these and all other Baja cities are included in the estimate, is only 1.5 persons per square km (about four persons per square mile). Outside the three most populated cities it's less than one person per 26 square km (one body per 10 square miles).

Mexico's population growth rate is currently estimated at 1.9% per annum, relatively low for a developing country. The average for the Cape Region is probably higher than the national average because of immigration. Yet Baja California Sur remains the country's least populated state.

ORIGINS

Bajacalifornios are an unusually varied lot. Elsewhere in Mexico, the average citizen is a mix of two heritages, Spanish and Indian. In the Cape Region the mix is typically more complicated, mainly because southern Baja remained a frontier much longer than most of the mainland and northern Baja, attracting people who arrived in the New World long after the Spanish colonized the Mexican mainland. It was 167 years after

enjoying the bounteous sea

WHAT'S A GRINGO?

The Latin-American Spanish word *gringo,* reportedly a corruption of the Spanish word *greigo* or "Greek," has different meanings in different parts of Latin America. In Argentina or Uruguay, for example, it is used to refer to anyone of Italian descent. In Mexico and Central America, it is almost always reserved for persons of northern European descent, especially those from the U.S. and Canada. In Cabo Pulmo, I once heard a naive, newly arrived white Canadian archaeologist comment that it would be easy for him to carry out his research in Baja because he wasn't a gringo. (Sorry pal, but you're a gringo, too.) In spite of everyday linguistic evidence to the contrary, many non-Spanish speakers insist that only Americans are gringos. The Mexicans, however, have a more precise epithet for Americans: *yanquis* or "Yankees."

Is gringo a derogatory term? It can certainly be used that way. Most of the time, however, it's simply an unconscious racial identification of neutral value. Educated Mexicans tend not to use it; instead they would typically say *norteamericano* or *americano* for Americans—some Mexicans insist on the former even though the term is a slight to Canadians who, after all, are North Americans, too—*canadiense* for Canadians, *alemán* for Germans, and so forth. Expatriate North Americans and Europeans living in Baja frequently refer to themselves and their expat friends as gringos.

aren't even citizens; many of them are North Americans or Europeans who've retired to Baja. A lesser number are gringos who've simply dropped out of the rat race. With the recent relaxation of investment and trade laws, a growing number of nonnationals are also setting up businesses on the Cape.

LANGUAGE

As in the rest of Mexico, Spanish is the most widely spoken language in Baja California Sur. English is widely spoken by merchants, hotel staff, and travel agents in La Paz, San José del Cabo, and Cabo San Lucas. Even in these cities, however, you can count on finding English-speaking Mexicans only within each city's tourist districts. Outside of tourist areas, and especially in smaller towns in the sierra, it's somewhat rare to encounter anyone who speaks more than a few words of English.

If you plan to restrict your daily schedule to hotel, beach, restaurant, and nightclub visits, you'll get by fine using English. But if you don't speak Spanish and you hope to do the Cape circuit or to explore the interior a bit, you'd be wise to learn at least enough of the language to cope with everyday transactions. Knowing a little Spanish will not only mitigate communication problems, it will also bring you more respect among the local Mexicans, who quite naturally resent foreign visitors who expect Mexicans to abandon their mother tongue whenever a gringo approaches. A popular sign seen in tourist restaurants reads "We promise not to laugh at your broken Spanish if you won't laugh at our broken English."

Dictionaries and Phrasebooks

The Glossary and Spanish Phrasebook at the back of this book will get you started on a basic vocabulary in *español.* For further study, you'll want a dictionary and a larger phrasebook. One of the best portable dictionaries for the Spanish

the conquest of Mexico before the Spanish were able to maintain a permanent settlement on the peninsula; by this time, tales of the Californias were on the tongues of adventurers throughout the world. The first paved highway between the Cape Region and the U.S. border was completed only 21 years ago.

By the end of the 19th century the Cape had become a favorite spot for sea-weary sailors to jump ship. The eastern shores of the peninsula were placid, and there was little chance deserters would be rounded up and incarcerated by local militia, who were scarce then and remain so today. Most of the ex-sailors who retired in this manner were English, but during WW I a few Germans and other Europeans came ashore. Their ship captains might have considered them cowardly deserters, but survival in southern Baja in the 19th and early 20th centuries was possible only for the brave, hardy, and resourceful.

Since in a very real sense much of Baja is still a frontier area—with more immigrants wandering in year by year—Baja's demographics have yet to solidify into recognizable pie-graph proportions. About two percent of the population student is the paperback *University of Chicago Spanish-English, English-Spanish Dictionary,* which emphasizes New World usages and contains useful sections on grammar and pronunciation. If even this small volume is too large for your backpack, the *Collins Gem Dictionary: Spanish-English, English-Spanish* comes in a tiny 4-by-3.5-by-1-inch edition with a sturdy plastic cover and over 40,000 entries.

Berlitz's *Latin-American Spanish For Travellers* is a small phrasebook divided by topics and situations (e.g., grammar, hotel, eating out, post office). Not all the phrases and terms it contains are used in Baja, but it's better than nothing.

One of the best references for off-the-road adventurers is Burleson's and Riskind's *Backcountry Mexico: A Traveler's Guide and Phrase Book* (University of Texas Press). Although it's rather bulky for carrying in a backpack and is oriented toward travel in northern mainland Mexico, it contains many words and phrases of value to sierra hikers and campers.

Pacific bonito

BOB RACE

BOB RACE

ON THE ROAD

TRAVEL HIGHLIGHTS

Time, money, and personal inclinations will compel most visitors to make advance decisions as to which parts of the Cape Region they'll see and which they'll have to leave out. The following list, organized by theme rather than geographic area, contains what I consider the "best" of what the Cape Region has to offer.

Beaches: Playa del Amor, Cabo San Lucas; Playa Balandra, La Paz; Playa San Pedrito, West Cape; Playa Santa María, The Corridor

Islands: Isla Cerralvo; Isla Espíritu Santo

Desert Environments: La Candelaria; Todos Santos to Rancho Los Inocentes

Sierra Towns: San Bartolo; Santiago

Nightlife: Cabo San Lucas; San José del Cabo

Hiking and Backpacking: Cañón San Dionísio; La Laguna

Surfing: La Pastora, West Cape; Playa Costa Azul, San José del Cabo; Playa San Pedro, West Cape

Windsurfing: Bahía de La Ventana, near La Paz; Bahía de Palmas, East Cape

Kayaking: Bahía de La Paz; Isla Espíritu Santo

Snorkeling and Diving: Cabo Pulmo, East Cape; El Bajo, near La Paz; Los Islotes, near La Paz

Fishing: Bahía de Palmas, East Cape; Bancos Gorda, near San José del Cabo; Banco San Jaime, near Cabo San Lucas; Punta Pescadero to Punta Perico, East Cape

The Cape Loop
Those with enough time and money to rent a car in La Paz, San José del Cabo, or Cabo San Lucas can make a rewarding circular route around the Cape Region via paved highways Mexico 1 and Mexico 19. Extending a total distance of approximately 564 km (350 miles), this route will take visitors along the lower slopes of the Sierra de La Laguna, through the sierra's former mining towns, across the Plains of La Paz, and along the coastlines of the East and West Capes as well as the "Corredor Naútico" between San José del Cabo and Cabo San Lucas.

This loop can be comfortably driven in two or three days (see the Cape Distances chart for distances and driving times of various segments), but visitors with additional time will be able to stop more frequently and see more of the region. The more adventurous can widen the loop by taking the sandy Camino Rural Costero ("Rural Coastal Road")—see "La Ribera to San José del Cabo" in the Central and East Cape chapter for details.

SPORTS AND RECREATION

The Cape Region's major attractions largely fall under this heading—from trekking in the Sierra de La Laguna to scuba diving off Cabo Pulmo. An added bonus is that, for the most part, you can enjoy outdoor recreation at little or no cost. User demand is low, and when fees are involved they're usually quite reasonable.

HIKING AND BACKPACKING

Trails
Hiking trails, from wide, 150-year-old paths created by Indians or shepherds to smaller, more recent trails worn by hikers, crisscross the Sierra de La Laguna. Signposts, however, are scarce—it's a good idea to scout an area first and ask questions locally about the best way to get from point A to point B. Although it's sometimes tempting to venture off established trails, that's a good way to get lost; you might also contribute to the destruction of delicate ecosystems. Light trails that don't seem to go anywhere may be cattle or coyote trails, which connect surface water sources. See the "Sierra de La Laguna" section in the Central and East Cape chapter for information on specific trails.

Maps
Topographic maps, which chart trails and elevation differentials, are helpful for extended hiking and backpacking in the sierra. **Map Centre** (2611 University Ave., San Diego, CA 92104-2894, tel. 619-291-3630, fax 291-3840) and **Map Link** (25 E. Mason, Santa Barbara, CA 93101, tel. 805-965-4402, fax 805-962-0884) carry a complete line of Baja topo maps in three scales (1:1,000,000, 1:250,000, and 1:50,000) that are sold separately according to region. The maps cost around US$6 each. Both stores will mail out a map listing on request.

What to Bring
Day Hikes: For a hike of a day or less, all you need is sturdy footwear (light, high-topped hiking boots are preferable to sneakers in rocky terrains) and whatever food or water you plan to consume for the day (count on at least two liters of water per person for chaparral or lower sierra hiking, more if the weather is hot).

Overnight Hiking/Backpacking: Longer hikes obviously require more preparation and equipment. Bring enough clothing to remain comfortable at both ends of the temperature spectrum; on the Pacific side of the sierra, days tend to be warm, nights chilly. A three-season backpacking tent and a light sleeping bag, for temperatures down to 2° C/35° F in the sierra, usually suffice for shelter.

Good hiking boots are essential. Thick lug soles with steel shanks are preferable, as they provide protection from sharp rocks and spiny plants. Bring along a first-aid kit that includes an elastic bandage for sprains and snakebite treatment, and a pair of tweezers for removing thorns and cactus spines. Also pack flashlight, compass, waterproof matches, knife, extra batteries, foul-weather gear, and signal device (mirror or whistle).

Water and Food: Always carry plenty of water; a minimum of four liters per person per full day of walking, five in hot weather. Although springs and *tinajas* exist in the sierra, the water level varies considerably and you shouldn't count on finding water sources along the way. If you need drinking water from one of these sources, always boil it first for at least 10 minutes or treat it with iodine or a water filter designed to remove impurities. Bring enough food for the duration of your hike (count on about 1.5 pounds of dry food per person per day), plus one or two days extra. One to three nestable pans will suffice for up to six hikers, along with a spoon, small plastic bowl, and cup for each person.

Camping Tips

Campsites: In addition to all the usual rules for choosing campsites, don't camp beneath coconut palms (a falling coconut could knock down your tent or fracture your skull) or in arroyos (danger of flash floods).

Fires and Waste Disposal: Open fires are permitted just about anywhere in the Cape Region except within city limits. Dead or fallen hardwood is plentiful in the upper sierra; lower down, cactus skeletons—especially *pitahaya* and cholla—make excellent fuel. Scrap lumber suitable for firewood can sometimes be salvaged from town dumps. Imitate the locals and keep your fires small. Never leave hot coals or ashes behind; smother with sand—or water, if you can spare it—till cool to the touch.

Pack out all trash that won't burn, including cigarette butts; they take 10-12 years to decompose. Bury human waste six inches down, and don't use soap in streams or springs.

Island Camping: If you happen to have the blessed opportunity to camp on any of the Sea of Cortez islands like Espíritu Santo, Cerralvo, or

Partida, check your bags thoroughly before landing on the island to make sure you haven't inadvertently brought along any animal species (including insects or insect eggs) that aren't native to the island. Such introduced species can wreak havoc on fragile island ecologies. Pack out all human waste as well as trash; carrying along a port-a-potty and deep-sixing its contents at sea after you leave the island is the most convenient way to deal with the former.

FISHING

The Cape Region's reputation as one of the best sportfishing regions in the world is well deserved. Nowhere else will you find as many varieties of fish in an area as compact and accessible as the waters surrounding the Cape. Although it's most famous for its acrobatic billfish—marlin, sailfish, and swordfish—and other deep-sea fishing, the Cape also offers opportunities for surf casters, small-boaters, and sport divers, as well as folks who don't yet know a rod from a reel.

Onshore Fishing

Most accessible to travelers, since it doesn't require a boat, is onshore or surf fishing, which you can enjoy anywhere along the coast you can get a line into the water.

Surf fishing is best on the Pacific coast between Playa El Migriño and El Carrizal (north of Todos Santos), at beaches along the Corridor, and almost anywhere on the Sea of Cortez between San José del Cabo and La Paz. Common onshore fish include surfperch, cabezón, sand bass, ladyfish, halibut, corvinas, opaleye, leopard shark, and triggerfish. Surf fishing the submarine canyons along the shore of the East Cape can actually yield roosterfish, California yellowtail, and yellowfin tuna for anglers using the right tackle, and onshore catches of dorado and even marlin are not unknown. All of these except the marlin are considered excellent food fish, and even the marlin is edible when smoked.

Inshore Fishing

Anyone with access to a small boat, either a skiff trailered in or a rented panga (an open fiberglass skiff that's usually five to six meters long and powered by a 40-60 hp outboard motor), can enjoy inshore fishing at depths of up to around 50-100 meters. Common inshore catches include many of the surf fishes mentioned above, plus various kinds of groupers, seabass, bonito shark, sculpin (scorpionfish), barracuda, sierra, pompano, amberjack, red and yellow snapper, pargo, and cabrilla. Cabrilla, however, must be released when caught.

Larger gamefish occasionally taken inshore are the bluefin and yellowfin tuna, yellowtail, dorado, jack crevalle, and roosterfish. Again, all fish mentioned make good eating.

Offshore Fishing

The bigger gamefish are found in deeper waters—over 200 meters (100 fathoms)—and require bigger tackle and more technique, including specialized trolling methods prescribed for each type of fish. Larger boats—fishing cruisers—are usually necessary simply because of the distance from shore to the fishing area. In the Cape Region, however, you can reach depths of over 200 meters in less than 1.5 km. These areas are accessible by skiff or panga, though strong seasonal currents are sometimes a problem, requiring a larger outboard motor. Contrary to the popular image of Cabo San Lucas sportfishing, it isn't necessary to use a boat equipped with fighting chairs to catch the big ones, although it's undoubtedly more comfortable.

Because of the special tackle and techniques involved in offshore fishing, many Cape visitors hire local fishing guides—who usually provide boats and tackle—to transport them to offshore fishing grounds. A sometimes less expensive alternative involves signing up for fishing cruises that take groups of tourist anglers out on big powerboats.

Most offshore anglers go after striped, blue, or black marlin, sailfish, swordfish, wahoo, dorado, roosterfish, yellowtail, and tuna. These fish are large, powerful fighters, requiring a certain skill in handling rod and line. The billfish are the most acrobatic, performing high leaps and pirouettes when hooked; wahoo and roosterfish will also "greyhound," performing a series of long, low jumps while swimming rapidly in one direction.

Of the billfish, only the swordfish is considered good eating. The rest are traditionally re-

garded as trophy fish, meant to be stuffed and mounted in the den or living room. To their credit, an increasing number of anglers these days release billfish after catch; many outfitters discourage or even forbid the taking of these beautiful creatures unless the fish has been badly injured in the fight.

The wahoo, dorado, roosterfish, yellowtail, and various tunas all make excellent eating.

Fishing Seasons

Fish are biting somewhere in Cape waters all year round. But water temperature, ocean currents, weather patterns, fish migrations, and other variables mean you usually won't find the same type of fish in the same spot in, say, December as in July. The Cape Region presents a complex set of fishing conditions that vary from month to month and year to year. An unusually dry year in the American Southwest, for example, lessens the outflow of nutrients from the Colorado River into the Sea of Cortez, diminishing the store of plankton and other small marine creatures at the bottom of the Cortez food chain. This in turn affects populations of larger fish, from sea bass to whale sharks. All the various "fishing calendars," obviously, can serve only as general guidelines.

A few generalizations are possible. The greatest variety and number of gamefish swim the widest range of Cape waters from April through October, when the water temperatures are very warm. During the winter, many species migrate south.

Fortunately for winter anglers, exceptions abound. The widely distributed California yellowtail, for example, is present year-round, migrating up and down the Sea of Cortez—La Paz and the East Cape in the winter, central to northern Cortez in the summer—as well as the lower Pacific coast. Sierra peak season is winter, when they're found in abundance along the Pacific coast. Wahoo generally spend December through April at the Cape, moving up toward Bahía Magdalena and the southern Cortez in the warmer months.

If your trip occurs between December and April, head for Cabo San Lucas or San José del Cabo; from May to November you can angle anywhere along a horseshoe-shaped loop extending from Bahía Magdalena on the Pacific side to above La Paz on the Cortez.

FISH TRANSLATOR

Mexican guides who lead sportfishing trips often use the local terms for gamefish; when they don't, the English terms they use aren't always correct. This works the other way, too—many gringos use incorrect Spanish names for Baja fish, which can cause confusion when asking about local fishing conditions. Here is a key to some of the more common translations:

albacore tuna—*albacora*
barracuda—*picuda*
black seabass—*mero prieto*
bluefin tuna—*atún de aleta azul*
blue marlin—*marlín azul*
dolphinfish (mahimahi)—*dorado*
grouper (generic)—*garropa*
halibut—*lenguado*
hammerhead shark—*cornuda*
jack crevalle—*toro*
ladyfish—*sabalo*
mackerel—*sierra, makerela*
manta ray—*manta*
octopus—*pulpo*
Pacific amberjack—*pez fuerte*

perch (generic)—*mojarra*
pompano—*palometa*
puffer (generic)—*bolete*
red snapper—*huachinango*
roosterfish—*papagallo, pez gallo*
sailfish—*pez vela*
sea bass (cabrilla)—*cabrilla*
shark (generic)—*tiburón*
small shark—*cazón*
squid—*calamar*
stingray (generic)—*raya*
striped marlin—*marlín rayado*
swordfish—*pez espada*
triggerfish—*cochi*
wahoo—*sierra wahoo, peto*
whale shark—*pez sapo*
white seabass—*corvina blanca*
yellowfin tuna—*atún de aleta; amarilla*
yellowtail—*jurel*

Pez is the generic word for fish. Once fish has been caught and is ready for cooking (or has been cooked), it's called *pescado*.

As a final caveat, remember that an unusually warm winter means better fishing all over Baja; likewise a particularly cold winter forces many fish far south, making even Cabo San Lucas, the "fisherman's paradise," less productive.

Equipment

Although bait and tackle are available at shops in La Paz and Cabo San Lucas, you can't count on finding exactly what you want; supplies are variable. The more expensive fishing fleets supply or rent good fishing gear, while the budget-oriented outfits provide very spotty equipment. If you're inclined toward using one of the no-frills outfitters in order to economize, you ought to have your gear assembled before arrival.

A full fishing kit containing tackle for every conceivable Cape Region sportfishing possibility would probably weigh in excess of 70 kilograms. Seasoned anglers claim you can get by in just about any situation with four basic rigs: two trolling rods with appropriate reels and 50- to 80-pound test monofilament line for offshore fishing, one medium-duty eight- or nine-foot rod

and spinner with 30-pound mono for surf casting and onshore fishing, and a six-foot light spinning rig loaded with four- to eight-pound line for bait fishing, freshwater fishing, or light surf casting. Two trolling rigs are recommended because these are the rods used against fish most likely to yank your outfit into the sea; it's always best to have a spare.

No matter how many rods you bring into Mexico, you're legally permitted to fish with only one at a time. Electric reels are permitted for use by handicapped persons only.

Bait: What a fish will take at any given moment is highly variable, hence the properly equipped angler comes prepared with an array of natural and artificial bait. Live or frozen bait—including everything from squid to mackerel to clams—is available near the more frequented fishing areas; you can also easily catch your own bait with a light rig. A cooler is necessary for keeping bait fresh; hired boats will usually supply them. Among the vast selection of artificial lures available, the most reliable seem to be those perennials that imitate live bait, such as spoons, lead-heads, candybars, swimmers, and, for offshore fishing, trolling heads. Bring along a few of each in different colors and sizes. You can purchase a few highly specialized lures, such as marlin heads and wahoo specials, in Cabo San Lucas.

Tide Tables: Serious onshore-inshore anglers should bring along a set of current tide tables so they can decide what time to wake up in the morning.

Legal Requirements

The red tape surrounding fishing in Mexico is minimal. The basic requirement is that anyone over 16 who intends to fish must possess a Mexican fishing license; technically, this includes all persons aboard boats equipped with fishing tackle, whether they plan to fish or not. This is important to remember for anyone going along on fishing trips as a spectator.

A single license is valid for all types of fishing, anywhere in Mexico, and is issued for periods of one day, one week, one month, or one year. A license is usually included in the price of sportfishing cruises, but not necessarily on panga trips—if you don't have a license, be sure to ask if one is provided before embarking on a guided trip. The cost of a Mexican license has risen steadily over the last few years but remains less expensive than most fishing licenses in the U.S. or Canada.

Fishing licenses are available from a number of sources, including tackle shops and Mexican insurance companies near the U.S.-Mexico border. They can be obtained by mail from the **Mexico Department of Fisheries (PESCA)** (2559 Fifth Ave., Suite 101, San Diego, CA 92103-6622, tel. 619-233-6956, fax 233-0344) or from California branches of the **American Automobile Association (AAA), Club Mex** (P.O. Box 1646, Bonita, CA 92002-1646, tel. 619-585-3033), and **Discover Baja Travel Club** (3065 Clairemont Drive, San Diego, CA 92117, tel. 619-275-4225, toll-free 800-727-BAJA).

Mexican Regulations: The general daily bag limit is 10 fish per person, including no more than five of any one species. Certain fish varieties are further protected as follows (per-day limits): one full-grown marlin, sailfish, or swordfish; two dorado, roosterfish, shad, tarpon, or shark. Extended sportfishing by boat is limited to three consecutive days if the daily bag limit is reached each of the three days.

Bag limits are the same for free divers as for rod-and-reelers. Only handheld spears and band-powered spearguns—no gas guns or power-heads—are permitted and no tanks or compressors may be used. A further weight limitation permits no more than 25 kilograms (55 lbs) of fish in a day's catch of five specimens, or one specimen of unlimited weight. Gill nets, purse nets, and every other kind of net except for handling nets are prohibited for use by nonresident aliens, as are traps, explosives, and poisons.

The taking of shellfish—clams, oysters, abalone, shrimp, and lobster—by nonresident aliens is officially prohibited. However, taking a reasonable amount—no more than can be eaten in a meal or two—is customarily permitted. This regulation is in place to protect Mexican fishing unions; even buying shellfish from local sources is prohibited unless you purchase from a public market or *cooperativa*. Obtain a receipt in case of inspection.

Totuavas, sea turtles, and cabrilla are protected species that cannot be taken by anyone. Nor can any fish be caught for "ornamental purposes" (e.g., for aquarium use). Mexican fishing regulations are subject to change; check with the Mexico Department of Fisheries for the latest version before embarking on a fishing expedition.

Two areas off limits to all fishing are Bahía Cabo San Lucas harbor and Pulmo Reef, the only official fish sanctuaries along the peninsular coast. Many other areas probably ought to be protected for educational and recreational purposes, since the government-regulated bag limits help to preserve fish species but not fish habitats. Fishing, boating, diving, and other aquatic activities can wreak havoc on lagoons and delicate reef systems—use special care when traversing these areas. Never drop an anchor or a fishing line on a coral reef; such contact can cause irreversible damage to reef systems.

U.S. Customs and California State Regulations: Once you've obeyed Mexican fishing regulations and bagged a load of fish, you still have to conform to U.S. Customs regulations if you wish to re-enter the U.S. with your catch. Fortunately, U.S. regulations conform with Mexican bag limits, so that whatever you've legally caught south of the border can be transported north. The U.S. state of California further requires anyone transporting fish into the state to present a completed California Declaration of

Entry form, available at the border or at any international airport. To facilitate the identification of the transported fish, some part of each fish—head, tail, or skin—must be left intact. In other words, you can't just show up at the customs station with a cooler full of anonymous fish fillets.

BOATING

Recreational boating along Baja's peninsular and island coastlines has been popular since the 1950s. In the days before the Transpeninsular Highway, it was one of the safest, if slowest, ways of traveling from California to the southern peninsula. Despite recent improvements in highway travel, interest in navigating Baja waters has only increased. The main difference now is that smaller vessels can be trailered or cartopped down the peninsula, saving days and weeks that might otherwise be spent just reaching your cruising destination.

An extremely wide range of pleasure boats plies Baja waters, from sea kayaks to huge motor

yachts. The most heavily navigated areas lie along the northwest coast between San Diego and Ensenada and in the Cabo San Lucas to La Paz corridor, but even these waters are relatively uncrowded compared to the marinas and bays of California. Cabo San Lucas, the most popular southern Baja harbor, checks in only around 1,200 foreign-owned vessels or so per year, an average of less than 3.3 arrivals per day.

Cartopping
The most popular boats for short-range cruising, fishing, and diving are those that can be transported on top of a car, RV, or truck—aluminum skiffs in the 12- to 15-foot range. This type of boat can be launched just about anywhere; larger, trailered boats are restricted to boat launches with trailer access. The most appropriate outboard motor size for a boat this size is 15- to 20-horsepower; larger motors are generally too heavy to carry separately from the boat, a necessity for cartopping.

If you decide to transport a skiff or sea kayak on top of your vehicle, be sure to use a sturdy, reliable rack or loader with a bowline to the front bumper and plenty of tie-downs. The rough road surfaces typical of even Baja's best highways can make it difficult to keep a boat in place; crosswinds are also a problem in many areas. Frequent load checks are necessary.

Inflatables
Rugged inflatable boats, such as those manufactured by Achilles or Zodiac, are well-suited to coastal navigation from Cabo San Lucas around to the East Cape. You can carry them on top or even in the cargo area of a large car or truck and inflate them with a foot pump or compressor as needed. A small 24-hp outboard motor is the best source of power. Inquire at **Pacific Marine Supply** (2084 Canon St., San Diego, CA 92106, tel. 619-223-7194, fax 223-9054) for the latest gear.

Trailering
Larger boats that require trailering because of their weight are much less versatile than cartop boats. A trailered boat must be floated off its trailer at a launch site, and on the entire peninsula fewer than 20 launches—five or six on the Pacific side, the remainder on the Sea of Cortez—offer trailer access. Another disadvantage to boat trailering is that Baja road conditions

make towing a slow, unpleasant task. On the other hand, if one of these spots happens to be your destination and you plan to stay awhile, the added cruising range of a larger vessel might be worthwhile.

Ocean Cruising

The typical ocean cruiser on the Pacific side is a 12- to 24-meter (40- to 80-foot) powerboat; on the Cortez side, 10- to 18-meter (35- to 60-foot) sailboats are popular. Properly equipped and crewed, these boats can navigate long distances and serve as homes away from home. Smaller motor-powered vessels are usually prevented from ocean cruising simply because of the lack of available fueling stations—their smaller fuel capacities greatly diminish cruising range. Sailboats smaller than nine meters (30 feet) have a similar problem because of the lack of storage space for food and water.

If you want to try your hand at ocean cruising, contact **Cortez Yacht Charters** (7888 Ostrow St., San Diego, CA 92111, tel. 619-469-4255).

Charts and Tide Tables

The best nautical charts for Baja waters are those compiled by the U.S. government. They come in two series: the Coastal Series, which covers the entire Pacific and Cortez coastlines in three large charts (numbers 21008, 21014, and 21017) with a scale of around 1:650,000 each; and the Golfo de California Series, which offers much larger-scale maps—from 1:30,000 for La Paz to 1:290,610 for the entire Cape Region—of selected areas along the Cortez coast and around the Cape. The nautical surveys that resulted in both series occurred between 1873 and 1901, so many of the place-names are out of date.

You can purchase these charts individually from the **Defense Mapping Agency** (Washington, D.C. 20315-0010, tel. 800-826-0342 or 301-227-2495). Two of the Coastal Series are out of print, however, and others may eventually drop from sight as well. A much better, and less expensive source of these charts is *Charlie's Charts: The Western Coast of Mexico (Including Baja)*, a compilation of all U.S. nautical charts from San Diego to Guatemala, including those currently unavailable from the DMA. The charts have been extensively updated from the DMA originals, with more recent markings for anchorages, boat ramps, hazards, and fishing and

diving spots. The spiral-bound volume costs around US$5 and is available from **Charles E. Wood,** Box 1244, Station A, Surrey, B.C., Canada V3W 1G0. It's also available in many Alta California marine supply stores. Some outlets may carry an earlier version called *ChartGuide*.

Tide tables are published annually; to cover the entire Baja coastline you'll need two sets, one that pertains to the Pacific tides and one for the Sea of Cortez tides. Either or both are available from **Map Link** (25 E. Mason, Santa Barbara, CA, 93101, tel. 805-965-4402, fax 962-0884) or marine supply stores. You can also order Sea of Cortez tide tables from the **University of Arizona** Printing and Publishing Dept. (Room 102, West Stadium, Tucson, AZ 85721, tel. 602-621-2572, fax 621-6458).

Legal Requirements

Boat Permits: Any nonresident foreigner operating a boat in Mexican waters who intends to fish from that boat is required to carry a Mexican boat permit as well as a fishing permit. Even if you transport a boat to Baja with no fishing tackle and no plans to fish, it's a good idea to obtain a boat permit; first, because you might change your mind when you see all the fish everyone else is pulling in, and second, because you never know when you might end up carrying a passenger with fishing tackle. *All* boats used for fishing require a permit, whether cartopped, trailered, carried inside a motor vehicle, or sailed on the open seas.

Permits are available by mail from the Mexico Department of Fisheries or from the Discover Baja Travel Club. A boat permit is valid for 12 months; fees vary according to the length of the craft.

Port Check-ins: If you launch a boat at a Mexican port, specifically within the jurisdiction of a Captain of the Port (COTP), you must comply with official check-in procedures. This simply involves reporting to the COTP office and completing some forms. The only time it's a hassle is when the Captain isn't present; you may have to wait around a few hours. Some ports charge filing fees of up to US$15.

Anytime you enter another COTP's jurisdiction, you're required to check in. In everyday practice, boaters only go through this formality when spending the night at a port with a COTP office.

Checking out is not required until you leave the port of origin—i.e., the port at which you first launched. If you're on a cruise from a foreign country, you should check out at the last port with a COTP on your return itinerary. Current COTPs in Baja are located at Ensenada, Guerrero Negro, Bahía Magdalena (San Carlos), Cabo San Lucas, San José del Cabo, La Paz, Puerto Escondido, Loreto, Mulegé, Santa Rosalía, Bahía de los Angeles, and San Felipe.

Fuel, Supplies, and Repairs

At present only permanent marinas in Cabo San Lucas and La Paz (or farther north in Ensenada, Puerto Escondido, and Santa Rosalía) offer fuel year-round. Elsewhere you must count on your own reserves or try your luck at canneries, boatyards, and fish camps, where prices will probably exceed official PEMEX rates. Often at places other than marinas you'll have to go ashore and haul your own fuel back to the boat; come prepared with as many extra fuel containers as you can manage.

La Paz is the Cape Region's best source of marine supplies and repairs. As with all other motorized conveyances in Mexico, it's best to bring along plenty of spare parts, especially props, filters, water pumps, shear pins, hoses, and belts. Don't forget to bring along at least one life jacket per person—statistics show that in 80% of all boating fatalities, the victims weren't wearing them.

Ocean cruisers might consider equipping their boats with **desalinators. Recovery Engineering** (tel. 800-548-0406 in the U.S. and Canada) has developed a new line of reverse-osmosis desalinators that run off 12-volt power sources and produce as much as 12.5 liters of drinking water per hour from seawater. The company also manufactures a hand-pumped survival version for life rafts that weighs just over one kilogram.

SEA KAYAKING

Kayaking is one of the best ways to experience the Cape Region coasts, yet few North American kayakers seem to make it this far south. Coves, inlets, water caves, and beaches inaccessible to skiffs or 4WD vehicles are easily approached in a kayak, especially on the Sea of Cortez. The Cortez is truly a world-class kayaking environment, as more and more kayakers discover each year. La Paz in particular is an excellent place to learn sea-kayaking skills because of the abundance of bays, coves, and islands nearby.

Kayaking on the Pacific side is for the experienced paddler only. High surf and strong currents require equal quantities of strength and expertise. Finding a beach campsite isn't too difficult, but reaching it through the surf might be.

Equipment

Sea kayaks can be rented from sports outfitters in La Paz and Cabo San Lucas. Outfitters in La Paz favor traditional closed-cockpit models

Kayaking is a great way to explore coastal waters.

Costa Azul

designed for coldwater zones, even though nearby waters are quite warm most of the year. Cabo San Lucas outfitters often carry both closed- and open-cockpit styles. For extended winter touring, the closed-top boats are preferable—cool winds can make even warm spray feel cold on the skin. For shorter winter trips or summer excursions, the open-top has certain advantages. Since the paddler sits on top of the deck rather than underneath it, the open-top is much easier to exit and thus somewhat safer overall. Open-cockpit kayaks are also easier to paddle and more stable than traditional kayaks—just about anyone can paddle one with little or no practice. But they do maneuver a bit more slowly due to a wider beam and higher center of gravity.

If you're on your way to Baja by vehicle and need kayaking equipment or supplies, two convenient stops are **Southwest Sea Kayaks** (1310 Rosecrans St., San Diego, CA 92106, tel. 619-222-3616) or **Southwind Kayak Center** (17855 Sky Park Circle A, Irvine, CA 92714, tel. 714-261-0200 or 800-SOUTHWIND). Both stores offer rentals as well as sales.

Maps and Tide Tables: Nautical charts are of little use for kayak navigation. A better choice is 1:50,000-scale topo maps, available from Map Link or Map Centre. Tide tables are also valuable.

Organized Kayak Trips

A great way to learn sea kayaking is to join an organized trip led by experienced kayakers. The Cape Region's best companies, **Baja Expeditions** and **Mar y Aventuras,** lead kayak trips out of La Paz year round; see the La Paz section for details.

WINDSURFING

From November through March, the Sea of Cortez is a windsurfer's paradise, particularly along the East Cape. La Paz is also a very good area, even in summer, when a strong breeze called El Coromuel comes in just about every afternoon. The best spots here lie along the mostly deserted beaches of the peninsula northeast of town—Punta Balandra to Punta Coyote. When nothing's blowing in the Bahía de La Paz vicinity, dedicated windsurfers can shuttle west across the peninsula to check out the action at Punta Marquéz on the Pacific side, only 72 km (45 miles) away.

Los Barriles on Bahía de Palmas, along the East Cape, is one of the more accessible windsurfing areas in southern Baja. The wind blows a steady 18-30 knots all winter long and wave-sailing is possible in some spots. During the season, uphauling is usually out of the question due to chop and high winds, so ability to waterstart is a prerequisite for windsurfing in this area.

Los Barriles is also home to the **Baja Vela Highwind Center** (tel. 415-322-0613 or 800-223-5443 in the U.S. and Canada), which offers highly rated instruction and package deals from mid-November through mid-March. Even if you're not a participant in one of its windsurfing vacations, you may be able to arrange for service and parts.

The Pacific side of Baja generally demands more experience from the sailboarder. Those who can handle high surf and strong winds will love it. None of the Cape Region's Pacific shores, however, are protected from major swells, so the novice should attempt only fair-weather sailing.

SURFING

Cape Region surfers are blessed; they can enjoy both winter and summer wave action within a rough hundred-km radius. The winter swell from the northwest creates point breaks along the Pacific shore from Punta Marquéz all the way to Migriño. Some breaks, such as those at San Pedrito and Cerritos, are well known; others are found at "secret" spots that only locals are supposed to know about. Soul surfers will find these without much trouble.

During summer's southern swell, the place to be is the Corridor between Cabo San Lucas and San José del Cabo, where beach breaks predominate at dependable spots like Costa Azul ("Zipper's"). When the southern swell is really happening, surfable waves wrap right around San José del Cabo as far north up the Sea of Cortez as Los Barriles. More information on Pacific and Cortez breaks can be found in the appropriate destination sections.

Equipment
Surfing is a low-tech sport, so the scarcity of surf shops in Baja is not a major problem. For any extended trip down the coast, carry both a short and a long board—or a gun for the northwest shores of Isla Natividad or Islas de Todos Santos in winter; longboards aren't used much in the Cape Region, however. Besides wax and a cooler, about the only other items you need to bring are a fiberglass-patching kit for bad dings and a first-aid kit for routine surf injuries. Most surf spots are far from medical assistance—don't forget butterfly bandages. Boards can be repaired at just about any boatyard on the coast, since most Mexican pangas are made of fiberglass and require a lot of patching.

Small surf shops in San José del Cabo and Cabo San Lucas sell boards, surfwear, and ac-cessories. The best is San José's **Killer Hook.** You can buy Mexican-made boards—San Miguel and Cactus brands—for about US$50-75 less than what they cost north of the border, about US$100 less than retail for a comparable American or Japanese board.

Tide charts come in handy for predicting low and high tides; a pocket-sized tide calendar available from **Tidelines** (P.O. Box 431, Encinitas, CA 92024, tel. 619-753-1747) charts daily tide changes from Crescent City, California, to Manzanillo, Mexico, with +/- corrections for a Los Angeles baseline.

SNORKELING AND SCUBA DIVING

The semitropical Sea of Cortez coral reefs at the southern tip of the Cape Region are among the least known dive locations in Mexico, yet because they're so close to shore they're also among the most accessible. Cape marinelife is concentrated in two types of environments: natural reefs, of either rock or hard coral; and shipwrecks, which develop into artificial reefs over time.

Heavy swells and surging along the Pacific coast mean that Pacific diving should only be tackled by experienced scuba divers or with an experienced underwater guide.

Cape Diving
Because it lies at the intersection of the Pacific and the Cortez, the Cape Region makes a particularly varied dive location. The Sea of Cortez alone offers one of the richest marine ecosystems in the world; sea lions, numerous whale and dolphin varieties, manta rays, amberjacks, and schooling hammerhead sharks are all part of a thick food chain stimulated by cold-water upwellings amid the over 100 islands and islets that dot the Cortez. Larger species native to temperate northern waters mix with colorful, smaller species of tropical origins that have found their way north from Central and South American waters, thus providing underwater scenery that is especially vivid and varied.

Rock reefs are abundant throughout the lower Cortez islands near La Paz, where tidal conditions are generally calm and the water is relatively warm all year round. Marinelife is plentiful and varied at such rock reef sites, and spearfishing is excellent in many areas. From La Paz south, onshore water temperatures usually hover between 21° C (70° F) and 29° C (85° F) year-round, making the southern Cortez the most popular diving destination on this side of Baja. Water visibility is best from July through October, when it exceeds 30 meters (100 feet); this is also when the air temperature is warmest, often reaching well over 32° C (90° F).

La Paz has several dive shops; popular local dive sites are numerous and include Playa Balandra (mostly snorkeling), Roca Suwanee, Isla Espíritu Santo, Isla Partida, the *Salvatierra* shipwreck, El Bajito Reef, Los Islotes, and El Bajo Seamount. El Bajo is famous for its summer population of giant manta rays, who seem unusually disposed toward allowing divers to hitch rides on their *alas* (pectoral fins). Schooling hammerhead sharks are also common during the summer months—they're very rarely aggressive toward divers when swimming in schools, so El Bajo makes an excellent observation area.

The Cabo Pulmo and Los Cabos areas are served by several small dive operations. The East Cape is known for Pulmo Reef, the only hard coral reef in the Sea of Cortez. This reef consists of a series of eight volcanic ridges inhabited by profuse coral life. The coral attracts a wide variety of fish of all sizes and colors; other, smaller reefs, as well as shipwrecks, lie in the general vicinity. Because most underwater attractions are close to shore, this area is perfect for diving from small boats or open-cockpit kayaks. Some of the reef fingers can even be reached from shore.

Several coves along the coast toward Cabo San Lucas make good snorkeling sites. Bahía Cabo San Lucas itself is a protected marine park; the rocks and points along the bayshore are suitable for snorkelers and novice scuba divers while the deep submarine canyon just 45 meters offshore attracts experienced thrillseekers. This canyon is known for its intriguing "sandfalls," streams of falling sand channeled between rocks along the canyon walls. Nearby Playa Santa María and Playa Chileno, on the way east toward San José del Cabo, are popular snorkeling areas with soft corals at either end of a large cove.

Equipment

Dive shops throughout the Cape Region are well-stocked with standard diving and snorkeling equipment. Novice divers won't need to bring anything; experienced divers who are picky about their equipment may want to bring along any specialized gear they're accustomed to. Since most equipment sold or rented in Cape dive shops is imported from the U.S., stocks vary from season to season. Purchase prices are also generally a little higher in Mexico than north of the border.

At Cabo San Lucas and around the Cape as far north as La Paz, a light suit may be necessary from late November through March; shorties or ordinary swimsuits will suffice the rest of the year. In summer, many Sea of Cortez divers wear Lycra skins to protect against jellyfish stings.

Because divers and anglers occasionally frequent the same areas, a good diving knife is essential for dealing with wayward fishing line. Bring two knives so you'll have a spare. Include extra O-rings, CO_2 cartridges for flotation vests, and rubber slings for spearguns, and bring a wetsuit patching kit if you plan to dive away from resort areas.

Air: Dependable air for scuba tanks is available in La Paz, Cabo Pulmo, and Cabo San Lucas. Always check the compressor first, however, to make sure it's well maintained and running clean. Divers with extensive Baja experience usually carry a portable compressor not only to avoid contaminated air, but to use in areas where tank refills aren't available.

Recompression Chambers: In late 1994 a hyperbaric decompression chamber, equipped with two compressors, an oxygen analyzer, closed-circuit TV, and a hotline to Divers Alert Network (DAN), was installed at Plaza Marina (next to Plaza Las Glorias) in Cabo San Lucas for use by local and visiting divers. The next nearest full-time, dependable recompression facility is the Hyperbaric Medicine Center (tel. 619-543-5222) at the University of California Medical Center in San Diego. The HMC is open Mon.-Fri. 0730-1630, and for emergencies.

Organized Dive Trips and Instruction

The greatest number of dive shops leading dive excursions operate out of Cabo San Lucas. Many of the dive shops in Cabo San Lucas also offer instruction and PADI scuba certification.

In Cabo Pulmo on the East Cape, two small operations guide dive trips; one, **Pepe's Dive Center** (P.O. Box 532, Cabo San Lucas, BCS, tel./fax in La Ribera 114-5-39-00, ext. 193), also offers instruction and PADI certification at very reasonable rates. If you're planning on doing a Pulmo dive, it's considerably less expensive to arrange it here than in Cabo San Lucas on the other end of the Cape—assuming you can arrange your own transport.

La Paz has two or three reliable outfitters who offer guided dives and instruction/certification, relatively few considering the numerous offshore dive sites in the vicinity. The oldest, **Baja Expeditions** (2625 Garnet Ave., San Diego, CA 92109, tel. 619-581-3311 or 800-943-6967), offers well-organized, extended dive trips on live-aboard boats to El Bajo and other offshore sites from June to November.

chilipepper fish

BOB RACE

ACCOMMODATIONS

Places to stay in the Cape Region run the gamut from free beach camping to plush resort hotels. Visitors who plan on doing the Cape circuit will have a greater range of options at any given location if they bring along camping gear.

HOTELS AND MOTELS

Unlike the closely spaced, vertical high-rises of Cancún, Acapulco, and other major Mexican resorts, Cape Region hotels tend more toward the organic than the geometric. Even in the Los Cabos area, they're more likely to hide behind a rocky cliff or occupy a secluded cove, spreading out along a sandy swath rather than towering over it. Often their shapes and colors mimic the surrounding environment, as at the Westin Regina Resort near San José del Cabo or the Hotel Solmar Suites next to Cabo San Lucas.

At many hotels and motels, midweek rates are lower than weekend rates, and high-season rates top low-season rates. For most Cape hotels, the high season runs November to March. Some places charge a higher peak-season rate Jan.-March; in purely statistical terms, March usually scores the highest annual hotel occupancy.

Obviously one way to save money on accommodations is to visit the Cape in the off-season, i.e., April-October. The Cape Region's climate is livable year-round; summer temperatures of 37° C/100° F on the Cortez coast are usually mitigated by sea breezes and relatively low humidity (see "Climate" in this book's Introduction for further specifics).

Whatever the rack rate, you can usually get the price down by bargaining (except during peak periods, e.g., Christmas, spring break, and Easter). When making a reservation and/or when checking in, be sure to clarify whether the room rate includes meals—occasionally it does. Asking for a room without meals is an easy way to bring the rate down, or simply ask if there's anything cheaper.

Most hotels add a 10% national hotel tax to quoted rates. Some also add a 10% service charge. When quoted a room rate, be sure to ask whether it includes tax and service—to avoid a 20% surprise over posted rates when you check out.

Budget

Many hotels and motels in the Cape Region are considerably less expensive than their counterparts in the U.S., Canada, or Europe. Even Los Cabos rates tend to line up slightly lower than rates at most other beach resorts in Mexico (the San José–Cabo San Lucas Corridor is an exception). In the budget range, you'll find a simple but clean room with private bath and double bed for around US$20-35 in Cabo San Lucas, Todos Santos, and San José. Soap, towels, toilet paper, and purified drinking water are usually provided; in some places you may have to ask. Rooms in this price range usually don't offer air conditioners but fans may be available.

Lodging under US$15 per night is rare unless you stay at a youth hostel, *casa de huéspedes,* or *pensión,* where bathrooms are usually shared. The term *baño collectivo* indicates shared bathroom facilities.

Medium-Priced

The largest number of hotels and motels in the Cape Region fall into the US$40-70 range. Some are older Mexican-style hotels just a bit larger than those in the budget range while others are American-style motels; most everything in this price range comes with air-conditioning.

Luxury and Resort Hotels

Higher-end places are found all along the coast from La Paz around to Cabo San Lucas. Prices for international-class accommodations average around US$80-120. A few Cape resorts charge US$250 and higher for particular rooms or suites. Some of these places are good values, while others are definitely overpriced. When in doubt, stick to the less-expensive hotels. Or ask about "specials"; places that normally cost US$150 a night are sometimes available at 50% discounts.

Hotel Reservation Services

Most of the hotels and motels mentioned in this guidebook will take advance reservations directly by phone or mail. Some North American visitors may find it more convenient to use reservation services offered in the United States. **Baja Hotel Reservations** (18552 MacArthur Blvd., Suite 205, Irvine, CA 92715, tel. 714-476-5555, toll-free 800-347-2252 in the U.S./Canada), for example, specializes in luxury hotels, including the Hotel Los Arcos in La Paz and the Hotel Finisterra in Cabo San Lucas.

Baja Reservations (tel. 800-368-4334 in the U.S./Canada) handles bookings for the Playa del Sol, Punta Colorada, and Palmas de Cortez in the Buena Vista/Los Barriles area.

Delfin Hotels and Resorts (330 High St., Santa Cruz, CA 95060, tel. 408-459-9494 or toll-free 800-524-5104) handles reservations for several condominiums and hotels in San José del Cabo (La Jolla, Misiones del Cabo) and Cabo San Lucas (Terrasol Cabo, Marina Cabo Plaza, Casa Rafael).

GUESTHOUSES AND HOSTELS

Casas de Huéspedes; Pensiones

Aside from free or very basic campgrounds, *casas de huéspedes* (guesthouses) and *pensiones* (boardinghouses) are the cheapest places to stay in the Cape Region. Unfortunately for budgeters they aren't very plentiful except in La Paz. The typical *casa de huéspedes* offers rooms with shared bath *(baño colectivo)* for US$3.60-5.40; US$5.40-7.20 with private bath. A pensión costs about the same

but may include meals. At either, most lodgers are staying for a week or more but the proprietors are usually happy to accept guests by the night.

The main difference between these and budget hotels/motels—besides rates—is that they're usually located in old houses or other buildings (e.g., convents) that have been converted for guesthouse use. Soap, towels, toilet paper, and drinking water are usually provided, but as with budget hotels and motels you may have to ask.

Youth Hostels

Baja has one youth hostel (*villa deportivas juvenile,* or youth sports villa) each in La Paz and Cabo San Lucas. They feature shared dormitory-style rooms where each guest is assigned a bed and a locker. Bathing facilities are always communal and guests must supply their own soap and towels. Rates are US$3 per night (US$3.60 for non-Hostelling International members); temporary memberships can be purchased for US$1.20. Food is available at hostel cafeterias for US$1.20-1.80 per meal.

Staying at youth hostels is a great way to meet young Mexicans and improve your Spanish; English is rarely spoken. About the only drawback is that the hostels tend to be inconveniently located some distance from the center of town, so transport can be a problem. For the fitness-oriented, they're ideal; sports facilities usually include gym, swimming pool, and courts for basketball, volleyball, and tennis.

*Westin Regina Resort
Los Cabos*

The isolated, idyllic beaches of the Cape Region offer numerous camping opportunities.

CAMPING

The Cape Region has more campgrounds, RV parks, and other camping areas for its size than anywhere else in Mexico. Because the population density of the Cape is so dramatically low, it's easy to find beach campsites offering idyllic settings and precious solitude, often for free. For travelers who like the outdoors, it's also an excellent way to slash accommodation costs. A recent tourist study found that over 50% of Baja's foreign overnight visitors typically camp rather than stay in hotels.

Campgrounds and RV Parks

The Cape Region offers roughly 20 private campgrounds that charge fees ranging from around US$3 for a place with virtually zero facilities to as high as US$15 for a developed RV park with full water, electrical, and sewage hookups, plus recreation facilities. Most campgrounds charge around US$3-5 for tent camping, US$6-12 for full hookups.

If you can forego permanent toilet and bathing facilities you won't have to pay anything to camp, since there's a virtually limitless selection of free camping spots, from beaches to deserts to mountain slopes. You won't necessarily need 4WD to reach these potential campsites, as plenty of turnouts and graded dirt *ramales* (branch roads) off the main highways can be negotiated by just about any type of vehicle.

FOOD AND DRINK

Much of what Bajacalifornios eat can be considered northern Mexican cuisine. Because northern Mexico is generally better suited to ranching than farming, ranch-style cooking tends to prevail in rural areas, which means that ranch products—meat and dairy foods—are highly favored.

Unlike the northern mainland, however, just about any point in the Cape Region is less than a couple of hours' drive from the seashore, so seafood predominates here more than elsewhere in northern Mexico—or probably anywhere else in Mexico for that matter. In fact, in most places on the Cape, seafood is more common than meat or poultry. If there's anything unique about Cape cuisine, it's the blending of ranch cooking with coastal culture, which has resulted in such distinctive food creations as the *taco de pescado* (fish taco).

WHERE TO EAT

The Cape's larger towns—La Paz, San José del Cabo, and Cabo San Lucas—offer everything from humble sidewalk taco stands to four-star hotel restaurants. Elsewhere the choices are fewer and more basic. In small towns there may be only two or three restaurants serving standard Mexican

dishes or, if near the coast, *mariscos* (seafood). Sometimes the best meals on the road come from what you improvise yourself after a visit to a local *tienda de abarrotes* (grocery store).

Most hotels on the Cape have restaurants and in small towns and remote areas these may be among the best (and only) choices. A few hotel restaurants, such as the Arrecife Restaurant in the Westin Regina Resort near San José, are worthwhile culinary destinations in and of themselves. In Cabo San Lucas, the Cape's vacation capital, restaurants with humorous names like The Giggling Marlin and Squid Roe cater to tourist tastes by serving a hybrid menu of common Mexican dishes, seafood, and burgers.

Local Color

Taquerías, small, inexpensive diners where tacos are assembled before your eyes (sort of the Mexican equivalent to the old-fashioned American hamburger stand), tend to be found in areas where there's a lot of foot traffic—near bus terminals, for example. The good ones are packed with taco-eaters in the early evening. In La Paz and San José del Cabo, other economical alternatives include *loncherías*—small, cafe-style places that usually serve *almuerzo* (late breakfast/early lunch) and *comida* (the main, midday meal). *Loncherías* typically stay

Streetside grills provide aromatic ambience and great food.

ANTOJITOS

burrito—a flour tortilla rolled around meat, beans, or seafood fillings

chalupa—a crisp, whole tortilla topped with beans, meat, etc. (also known as a *tostada*)

chiles rellenos—mild poblano chiles stuffed with cheese, deep-fried in an egg batter, and served with a *ranchero* sauce (tomatoes, onions, and chiles)

enchilada—a corn tortilla dipped in chile sauce, then folded or rolled around a filling of meat, chicken, seafood, or cheese and baked in an oven

flauta—a small corn tortilla roll, usually stuffed with beef or chicken and fried

picadillo—a spicy salad of chopped or ground meat with chiles and onions (also known as *salpicón*)

quesadilla—a flour tortilla folded over sliced cheese and grilled; ask the cook to add *chiles rajas* (pepper strips) for extra flavor

taco—a corn tortilla folded or rolled around anything and eaten with the hands; *tacos de pescado,* or "fish tacos," are the closest thing Baja has to a regional specialty

tamal—cornmeal *(masa)* dough wrapped in a corn husk and steamed; sometimes stuffed with corn, olives, pork, or turkey

torta—a sandwich made with a Mexican-style roll (*bolillo/birote* or the larger *pan telera*); one of the most popular is the *torta de milanesa,* made with breaded, deep-fried veal or pork

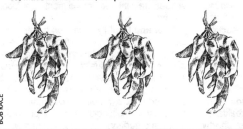

BOB RACE

open 1100-1700. Municipal markets in La Paz and San José feature rows of *loncherías* serving inexpensive basic meals and *antojitos* (snacks or one-plate dishes). Some *loncherías* offer *comida corrida,* a daily fixed-price meal that includes a beverage, an entree or two, side dishes, and possibly dessert.

Cafes are similar to loncherías except that they may open earlier and serve *desayuno* (breakfast) in addition to other meals.

Ordering and Paying

You really don't need much Spanish to get by in a restaurant (in most hotel restaurants, you won't need any at all). Stating what you want, plus *por favor* (please), will usually do the trick (e.g., *dos cervezas, por favor,* "two beers, please"). Don't forget to say *gracias* (thank you). The menu is called *el menú* or, much less commonly in Baja, *la carta.* As a last resort, you can always point to what you want on the menu.

La cuenta is the bill. A tip *(la propina)* of about 15% is expected at any restaurant with table service; look to see if it's already been added to the bill before placing a tip on the table.

WHAT TO EAT

Tortillas

A Mexican meal is not a meal without tortillas, the round, flat, pancake-like disks eaten with nearly any nondessert dish, including salads, meats, seafood, beans, and vegetables. Both wheat-flour and cornmeal tortillas are commonly consumed in the Cape Region. Among northern Mexicans, it is said that meat and poultry dishes taste best with flour tortillas while vegetable dishes go best with corn. Most restaurants offer a choice of the two. If you order tortillas without specifying, you may get *¿de harina o de maíz?* as a response.

Although prepackaged tortillas are available in *supermercados* (supermarkets), most Mexicans buy them fresh from neighborhood *tortillerías* or make them at home. Many restaurants and cafes in the Cape region, and virtually all *loncherías* and *taquerías,* serve only fresh tortillas—tortillas made the same day, or the night before. If you're used to prepackaged tortillas—which is what most Mexican eateries in the U.S. or Canada serve—you're in for a pleasurable surprise when you raise a fresh, hot, homemade tortilla to your nose for the first time.

RESTAURANT RATING KEY

$	Less than US$4 per meal
$$	US$4-8 per meal
$$$	US$9-16 per meal
$$$$	Over US$16 per meal

Ratings are based on
the average price of an entree.

Incidentally, a tortilla has two sides, an inside and an outside, that dictate which direction the tortilla is best folded when wrapping it around food. The side with the thinner layer—sometimes called the *pancita,* or belly—should face the inside when folding the tortilla. If you notice the outside of your tortilla cracking, with pieces peeling off onto the table, you've probably folded it with the *pancita* outside instead of inside.

Antojitos

This word literally means "little whims," thus implying snacks to many people. However, the word also refers to any food that can be ordered, served, and eaten quickly—in other words, Mexican fast food. Typical *antojitos* include tamales, enchiladas, burritos, *flautas,* chiles rellenos, chalupas, *picadillo,* quesadillas, *tortas,* and tacos.

Breakfasts

Menus at tourist restaurants are often confusing because some of the same "breakfast" dishes may end up on more than one section of the menu. Mexicans have two kinds of breakfasts, an early one called *desayuno,* eaten shortly after rising, and a second called *almuerzo* that's usually taken around 1100. To further confuse the issue, Spanish-English dictionaries usually translate *almuerzo* as "lunch," while bilingual menus often read "breakfast."

The most common Mexican *desayuno* is simply *pan dulce* (sweet pastry) and/or *bolillos* (torpedo-shaped, European-style rolls) with coffee and/or milk. Cereal is also sometimes eaten for *desayuno;* e.g., *avena* (oatmeal), *crema de trigo* (cream of wheat), or *hojuelas de maíz* (corn flakes).

The heavier eggs-and-frijoles dishes known widely as "Mexican breakfasts" in the U.S. and Canada are usually taken as *almuerzo,* the late breakfast, which is most typically reserved for

weekends and holidays. Eggs come in a variety of ways, including *huevos revueltos* (scrambled eggs), *huevos duros* (hard-boiled eggs), *huevos escafaldos* (soft-boiled eggs), *huevos estrellados* (eggs fried sunny side up), *huevos a la mexicana* (also *huevos mexicanos,* eggs scrambled with chopped tomato, onion, and chiles), *huevos rancheros* (fried eggs served on a tortilla), and *huevos con chorizo* (eggs scrambled with ground sausage), *con tocino* (with bacon), or *con jamón* (with ham). All egg dishes usually come with frijoles and tortillas.

One of the cheapest and tastiest *almuerzos* is *chilaquiles,* tortilla chips in a chile gravy with crumbled cheese on top. Eggs and/or chicken can be added to *chilaquiles* as options. Another economic choice is *molletes,* a split *bolillo* spread with mashed beans and melted cheese, served with salsa on the side.

Entrees

The main dish or *el plato fuerte* of any meal can be a grander version of an *antojito,* a regional specialty from another part of Mexico (*mole poblano,* for example), or something the *cocineros* (cooks) dream up themselves. Typical entrees are centered around meats, seafood, or poultry.

Meat and Poultry: Common meats include *carne de res* (beef), *puerco* (pork), and *borrego* (lamb). *Jamón* (ham), *chorizo* (sausage), and *tocino* (bacon) are usually reserved for *almuerzo.* Steak may appear on menus as *bistec, bistek, biftec,* or steak. *Venado* (deer meat or venison) and *conejo* (rabbit) are commonly served on ranchos. Poultry dishes include *pollo* (chicken), *pavo* (turkey), and, less frequently, *pato* (duck) and *codorniz* (quail).

Seafood: *Mariscos* entrees on the menu are often seasonal or dependent on the "catch of the day." Often just the word *pescado,* along with the method of cooking (e.g., *pescado al mojo de ajo*), will appear. If you need to know exactly what kind of fish, just ask *"¿Hay cuál tipo de pescado?"*—although in some cases the only response you'll get is something generic like *pescado blanco* ("white fish"). For specific fish names, see the Special Topic "Fish Translator."

Baja's number-one seafood specialty is the *taco de pescado* (fish taco). If you haven't ever tried one, you're most likely wondering "What's the big deal—a fish taco?" Eat one, though, and

COOKING METHODS

Entree items, whether meat, poultry, or seafood, are most commonly prepared in one of the following styles:

adobo, adobada—marinated or stewed in a sauce of vinegar, chiles, and spices

a la birria—roasted on a spit (usually goat)

a la parilla—broiled

albóndigas—meatballs

al carbón—charcoal-grilled

a la veracruzana—seafood (often *huachinanga*, red snapper) cooked with tomatoes, onions, and olives

al mojo de ajo—in a garlic sauce

al pastor—slowly roasted on a vertical spit

al vapor—steamed

asada—grilled

barbacoa—pit-roasted

con arroz—steamed with rice

encebollado—cooked with onions

entomado—cooked with tomatoes

empanizada—breaded

frito—fried

guisado—in a spicy stew

machaca—dried and shredded

you're hooked for life. Short, tender, fresh fish filets are battered and fried quickly, then folded into a steaming corn tortilla with a variety of condiments including *salsa fresca* (chopped tomatoes, onions, chiles, and lime juice), marinated cabbage (similar to coleslaw in the States), *guacamole* (a savory avocado paste), and sometimes a squirt of mayonnaise. ¡La última! Any kind of white-fleshed fish can be used—the best fish tacos are those made from yellowtail *(jurel)*, halibut *(lenguado)*, or dorado *(dorado)*.

Shellfish are also quite popular on Baja menus: *ostiones* (oysters), *almejas* (clams), *callos* (scallops), *jaiba* (small crab), *cangrejo* (large crab), *camarones* (shrimp), *langosta* (lobster), *langostina* (crayfish, also called *cucarachas*), and *abulón* (abalone). They can be ordered as *cocteles* (cocktails—steamed or boiled and served with lime and salsa), *en sus conchas* (in the shell), or in many other ways.

Other Dishes

Beans: The beans most preferred in the Cape Region, as on the northern mainland, are pinto beans, usually dried beans boiled until soft, then mashed and fried with lard or vegetable oil (usually the former) to make *frijoles*. Often this preparation is called *frijoles refritos*, or "refried beans," although they're not really refried except when reheated. Sometimes the beans are served whole, in their own broth, as *frijoles de olla* (boiled beans) or with bits of roast pork as *frijoles a la charra* (ranch-style beans). Frijoles can be served with any meal of the day, including breakfast.

Cheese: Even the most remote rancho will usually have some cheese around, so if your appetite isn't stimulated by the *iguana guisada* simmering on the hearth, you can usually ask for chiles rellenos (mild poblano chiles stuffed with cheese and fried in an egg batter) or quesadillas (cheese melted in folded flour tortillas). A meal of beans, tortillas, and cheese provides a complete source of protein for travelers who choose to avoid meat, poultry, or seafood for health, economic, or moral reasons.

Many ranchos produce their own *queso fresco*, "fresh cheese" made from raw cow's, goat's, or sheep's milk. To make *queso fresco*, the rancheros first cure the milk with homemade rennet (from a calf's fourth stomach) until the milk separates, then press the curds with weights (sometimes under flat rocks lined with cloth) to remove excess moisture. In more elaborate operations, the initial pressing is then ground up and repressed into small round cakes. If you want to buy some queso fresco, look for *Hay queso* signs as you pass ranchos. If you're very fortunate, you might even come across *queso de apoyo*, an extra-rich cheese made from heavy cream.

Soup: The general menu term for soup is *sopa*, although a thick soup with lots of ingredients is usually a *caldo*.

Vegetables: Although vegetables are sometimes served as side dishes with *comidas corridas*, with restaurant entrees, or in salads *(ensaladas)*, they're seldom listed separately on the menu. Many types of vegetables are grown in the Cape Region, particularly in the lower elevations on the east side of the Sierra de La Laguna and in the vicinity of Todos Santos and Pescadero. Several small farms in the Todos Santos area specialize in organic produce.

paletería y nevería

Salsas and Condiments

Any restaurant, cafe, *lonchería,* or *taquería* will offer a variety of salsas. Sometimes only certain salsas are served with certain dishes, while at other times one, two, or even three salsas are stationed on every table. Often each place has its own unique salsa recipes—canned or bottled salsas are rarely used.

There are as many types of salsas as there are Mexican dishes—red, green, yellow, brown, hot, mild, salty, sweet, thick, thin, blended, and chunky. The most typical is the *salsa casera* (house salsa), a simple, fresh concoction of chopped chiles, onions, and tomatoes mixed with salt, lime juice, and cilantro. This is what you usually get with the complimentary basket of *totopos* (tortilla chips) served at the beginning of every Mexican meal. Another common offering is *salsa verde* (green sauce), made with a base of tomatillos, a small, tart, green tomato-like vegetable. Some salsas are *picante,* or spicy hot (also *picosa*), so it's always a good idea to test a bit before pouring the stuff over everything on your plate.

Whole pickled chiles are sometimes served on the side as a condiment, especially with tacos. Salt *(sal)* is usually on the table, although it's rarely needed since Mexican dishes tend to be prepared with plenty of salt. Black pepper is *pimiento negro,* and if it's not on the table it's normally available for the asking. Butter is *mantequilla,* sometimes served with flour tortillas.

In *taquerías,* guacamole (mashed avocado blended with onions, chiles, salt, and some-times other ingredients) is always served as a condiment. In restaurants it may be served as a salad or with tortilla chips.

Desserts and Sweets

The most popular of Mexican desserts, or *postres,* is a delicious egg custard called *flan.* It's listed on virtually every tourist restaurant menu, along with *helado* (ice cream). Other sweet alternatives include pastries found in *panaderías* (bakeries) and the frosty offerings at the ubiquitous *paleterías.* Strictly speaking, a *paletería* serves only *paletas,* flavored ice on sticks (like American popsicles but with a much wider range of flavors), but many also serve *nieve,* literally "snow," flavored ice served in bowls or cones like ice cream.

Dulcerías are candy shops that sell a huge variety of sticky Mexican sweets, usually wrapped individually. Often brightly decorated, *dulcerías* are oriented toward children and sometimes carry inexpensive toys as well as sweets. The larger ones sell piñatas, colorful papier-mâché figures filled with candy and small gifts and hung at parties; on special occasions, children are allowed to break them with sticks, releasing all the goodies inside. Traditionally piñatas are crafted to resemble common animals, but these days you'll see all kinds of shapes, including "Teenage Mutant Tortugas de Ninja."

In Todos Santos, once an important sugar-cane-growing area, a local specialty is *panocha,* a candy made from raw sugar.

(top) looking west from Sierra de La Laguna;
(bottom) Playa San Pedrito (Chris Humphrey)

(top) La Candelaria, West Cape; (bottom) Estero San José

BUYING GROCERIES

The cheapest way to feed yourself while traveling around the Cape Region is the same way you save money at home, by buying groceries at the store and preparing meals on your own. While it may not have any dining spots to speak of, even the smallest town will have a little grocery store or corner market. A ripe avocado, a chunk of *queso fresco*, and a couple of *bolillos* can make a fine, easy-to-fix meal.

The humblest type of store is the small family-owned *tienda de abarrotes*, usually recognizable by the single word *abarrotes*—"groceries"—printed somewhere on the outside (*tienda* means "store"). These stock the basics—tortillas, dried beans, flour, herbs and spices, bottled water, a few vegetables, possibly *bolillos* and *queso fresco*—as well as limited household goods like soap and laundry detergent. Like the 7-Eleven back home, the food at the average *tienda de abarrotes* is not particularly inexpensive.

A better deal, when you can find one, is the government-sponsored CONASUPO (an acronym for Compañía Nacional de Subsistencias Populares). CONASUPOs carry many of the same items as *tiendas de abarrotes*, but at government-subsidized prices. Not every item is cheaper, however, so it pays to shop around. A large, supermarket-style CONASUPO is called CONASUPER. Even less expensive are markets operated by ISSSTE (Instituto de Seguridad y Servicios Sociales para Trabajadores del Estado).

Privately run, American-style supermarkets, found in La Paz, San José, and Cabo San Lucas, are called *supers* or *supermercados*. Like their North American counterparts, they're usually well stocked with a wide variety of meats, baked goods, vegetables, household goods, and beer and liquor, including many common U.S. brands. The supermarket at Plaza Aramburo in Cabo San Lucas has a better variety of foodstuffs than many American supermarkets! As in the rest of North America, supermarket prices are often cheaper than those in smaller grocery stores.

La Paz and San José support *mercados municipales* (municipal markets), large warehouse-type structures where meat, fruit, and vegetable producers sell their goods directly to the public. Prices are often very good at these markets but it helps if you know how to bargain.

Panaderías: You can often purchase a few bakery items at all of the above-named stores, but the best place to buy them, naturally, is at their source—a *panadería* (literally, "breadery," i.e., bakery). The typical *panadería* produces tasty *bolillos* (Mexican rolls), *pastels* (cakes), and *pan dulce* (cookies and sweet pastries). To select bakery items from the shelves of a *panadería*, simply imitate the other customers—pick up a pair of tongs and a tray from the counter near the cash register and help yourself, cafeteria-style.

Tortillerías: Unless you make them yourself, the best place to buy tortillas is where they make them fresh every day. Restaurants, *tiendas*, and home cooks will purchase from the local *tortillería* to avoid spending hours at a *metate* (grinder) and *comal* (griddle). The automated process at a *tortillería* uses giant electric grinders and conveyor belts to transform whole corn into fresh tortillas, which you purchase by weight, not number. A kilo yields about 40 average, 12-cm tortillas; you can order by the *cuarto* or *medio* (quarter or half kilo). The government-subsidized prices are quite low.

DRINKING

Nonalcoholic Beverages
Cold Drinks: The water and ice served in restaurants in the Cape Region is always purified—it's not necessary to order *agua mineral* (mineral water) unless you need the minerals. Likewise, the water used as an ingredient in "handmade" drinks, e.g., *licuados* or *aguas frescas,* also comes from purified sources. Actually most Cape residents—Mexicans and foreigners alike—drink right out of the tap because the source, Sierra de La Laguna spring water, is perfectly safe.

Licuados are similar to American "smoothies"—fruit blended with water, ice, honey or sugar, and sometimes milk or raw eggs, to produce something like a fruit shake. Any place that makes *licuados* will also make orange juice, *jugo de naranja.*

Aguas frescas are the colorful beverages sold from huge glass jars on the streets of larger cities, or at carnivals, usually during hot weather. They're made by boiling the pulp of various fruits, grains, or seeds with water, then straining it and adding large chunks of ice. *Arroz* (rice) and *horchata* (melon-seed) are two of the tastiest *aguas*.

American soft drinks *(refrescos)* like 7UP, Coke, and Pepsi are common; their Mexican equivalents are just as good. An apple-flavored soft drink called Manzanita is quite popular.

Hot Drinks: Coffee is served in a variety of ways. The best, when you can find it—ranchos sometimes serve it—is traditional Mexican-style coffee, which is made by filtering near-boiling water through fine-ground coffee in a slender cloth sack. Instant coffee *(nescafé)* is often served at small restaurants and cafes; a jar of instant coffee may be sitting on the table for you to add to hot water. When there's a choice, a request for *café de olla* (pot coffee) should bring you real brewed coffee. When you order coffee in a Mexican restaurant, some servers will ask *de grano o de agua?* (literally "grain or water?"), meaning "brewed or instant?" One of the better Mexican brands found in supermarkets is Café Combate.

Café con leche is the Mexican version of café au lait, i.e., coffee and hot milk mixed in near-equal proportions. *Café con crema* (coffee with cream) is not as available; when it is, it usually means a cup of coffee with a packet of nondairy creamer on the side. Espresso machines are popping up everywhere in the resort areas of Cabo San Lucas and San José del Cabo; most of the time the so-called "espressos" and "capuccinos" produced bear only a passing resemblance to the real stuff. (A major exception is Caffé Todos Santos in Todos Santos, where the espresso drinks are consistently good.)

Hot chocolate *(chocolate)* is fairly common on Mexican menus. It's usually served very sweet and may contain cinnamon, ground almonds, and other flavorings. A thicker version that is made with cornmeal—almost a chocolate pudding—is called *champurrado* or *atole*.

Black tea *(té negro)* is not popular among Bajacalifornios although you may see it on tourist menus. Ask for *té helado* or *té frío* if you want iced tea. At home many Mexicans drink *té de manzanilla* (chamomile tea) or *té de yerba buena* (mint tea) in the evenings.

BAR LINGO

cantinero—bartender
cerveza—beer
una fría—a cold one
envase, botella—bottle
casco—empty bottle
una copita, un tragito—a drink
vaso, copa—glass
la cruda—hangover
sin hielo—without ice
con hielo—with ice
botanas—snacks

Alcoholic Beverages

Drinking laws in Mexico are quite minimal. The legal drinking age in Mexico is 18 years, and it's illegal to carry open containers of alcoholic beverages in a vehicle. Booze of every kind is widely available in bars, restaurants, grocery stores, and *licorerías* (liquor stores). *Borracho* means both "drunk" (as an adjective) and "drunkard."

Cerveza: The most popular and available beer brand in southern Baja and the Cape Region is Pacífico, from Mazatlán, just across the Sea of Cortez from La Paz. Tecate, brewed in the town of the same name in northern Baja, is the second most popular label. Both brands are good-tasting, light- to medium-weight brews, with Tecate holding a slight edge (more hops) over Pacífico. You can't compare either of these with their export equivalents in the U.S., since Mexican breweries produce a separate brew for American consumption that's lighter in taste and lighter on the alcohol content. It's always better in Mexico.

Other major Mexican brands such as Corona, Dos Equis (ordered by Mexicans as "Lager"), Superior, Carta Blanca, Bohemia, and Negra Modelo are available in tourist restaurants, but you'll notice the locals stick pretty much to Tecate and Pacífico, perhaps out of regional loyalty.

The cheapest sources for beer are the brewery's agents or distributors. Look for signs saying *agencia, subagencia, cervezería,* or *deposito*. There you can return deposit bottles for cash or credit. You can buy beer by the bottle *(envase)*,

TEQUILA

Mexico's national drink has been in production since at least the time of the Aztecs; the Spaniards levied a tax on tequila as early as 1608. The liquor's name was taken from the Ticuila Indians of Jalisco, who mastered the process of distilling an extract from the *Agave tequiliana*, or **blue agave,** a process still employed by tequila distilleries today. Native to Jalisco, this succulent is the only agave that produces true tequila as certified by the Mexican government. Look for the initials DGN—for *Dirección General de Normas*—on the label.

Much of the tequila-making process is still carried out *a mano* (by hand). In the traditional method, the mature heart of the tequila agave, which looks like a huge pineapple and weighs 20-60 kilograms, is roasted in a pit for 24 hours, then shredded and ground by mule- or horse-powered mills. After the juice is extracted from the pulp and fermented in ceramic pots, it's distilled in copper stills to produce the basic tequila, which is always clear and colorless with an alcohol content of around 40%.

"Gold" tequilas are produced by aging in imported oak barrels. After six months the liquor can be bottled as *reposado* or "rested" tequila; after three years it's truly *añejo* or "aged."

José Cuervo, Sauza, and Herradura are well-established tequila labels with international reputations. Of the three, Herradura is said to employ the most traditional methods, and tequila connoisseurs generally prefer it over the other two. But don't take their word for it, try a few *probaditos* (little proofs) for yourself. One of the best places to experiment is Cabo San Lucas' Caballo Blanco Restaurant, where the bar stocks over 35 varieties of tequila. Don't try tasting them all in one night or you'll probably never drink tequila again.

Mezcal And The Worm

The distillate of other agave plants—also known as *magueys* or century plants—is called mezcal. The same roasting and distilling process is used for mezcal as for tequila. Actually, tequila, too, is a mezcal, but no drinker calls it that, just as no one in a U.S. bar orders "whiskey" when they mean to specify scotch or bourbon.

The caterpillar-like grub floating at the bottom of a bottle of mezcal is the *gusano de maguey* (maguey worm), which lives on the maguey plant itself. They're safe to eat—just about anything pickled in mezcal would be—but not particularly appetizing. By the time you hit the bottom of the bottle, though, who cares?

Tequila Drinks

The usual way to drink tequila is straight up, followed by a water or beer chaser. Licking a few grains of salt before taking a shot and sucking a lime wedge afterward makes it go down smoother. The salt raises a protective coating of saliva on the tongue while the lime juice scours the tongue of salt and tequila residues.

Tequila con sangrita, in which a shot of tequila is chased with a shot of *sangrita*, is a slightly more elegant method of consumption. Sangrita is a bright red mix of orange juice, lime juice, grenadine, red chile powder, and salt.

An old tequila standby is the much-abused margarita, a tart Tex-Mex cocktail made with tequila, lime juice, and Cointreau (usually "Controy" or triplesec in Mexico) served in a salt-rimmed glass. A true margarita is shaken and served on the rocks (crushed or blended ice tends to kill the flavor), but just about every gringo in Baja seems to drink "frozen" margaritas, in which the ice is mixed in a blender with the other ingredients. A "Baja margarita" substitutes Baja's own damiana liqueur for the triplesec. The damiana herb is said to be an aphrodisiac.

can *(bote)*, six-pack *(canastilla)*, or case *(cartón)*. Large, liter-size bottles are called *ballenas* ("whales") or *caguamas* ("sea turtles") and are quite popular. When buying beer at an *agencia* or *deposito,* specify *fría* if you want cold beer, otherwise you'll get beer *al tiempo* (at room temperature).

Wine: Baja is one of Mexico's major wine-production areas and Baja wines are commonly served in restaurants. Two of the more reliable labels are Domecq and Santo Tomás, both produced in northern Baja. A broad selection of varietals is available, including cabernet sauvignon, chardonnay, chenin blanc, pinot noir, barbera, and zinfandel. These and other grapes are also blended to produce cheaper *vino tinto* (red wine) and *vino blanco* (white wine). When ordering wine in Spanish at a bar, you may want to specify *vino de uva* ("grape wine"), as *vino* alone can refer to distilled liquors as well as wine. *Vino blanco,* in fact, can be interpreted as cheap tequila.

Liquor: Tequila is Mexico's national drink and also the most popular distilled liquor in Baja. If you're keen on sampling Mexico's best, head for Pancho's Restaurant in Cabo San Lucas, said to have the largest selection of tequilas in the entire country.

The second most popular liquor is brandy, followed closely by *ron* (rum), both produced in Mexico for export as well as domestic consumption. A favorite rum drink is the *cuba libre* (Free Cuba), called *cuba* for short—a mix of rum, Coke, and lime juice over ice. Similar is the *cuba de uva,* which substitutes brandy for rum. Other hard liquors—gin, vodka, scotch—may be available only at hotel bars and tourist restaurants.

Cantinas and Bars: Traditionally, a cantina is a Mexican-style drinking venue for males only, but in modern Mexico the distinction between "bar" and "cantina" is becoming increasingly blurred. True cantinas are rare in the Cape Region except in the smaller towns of the interior, where you may occasionally stumble upon a palapa-roofed, palm- or *carrizo*-walled structure festooned with blinking Christmas lights. Inside are a few tables and chairs and a handful of *borrachos;* if any women are present, they're either serving the booze or serving as hired "dates." The only drink choices will be beer, Mexican brandy, and cheap tequila or *aguardiente*—moonshine. Often when you order tequila in a place like this, you'll be served a large glass of *aguardiente,* considered an acceptable substitute.

Bars, on the other hand, are found in most hotels and in the downtown districts of La Paz, San José, and Cabo San Lucas. They've developed largely as social venues for tourists or for a younger generation of Mexicans for whom the cantina is passé. A bar, in contrast to a cantina, will offer a variety of beer, wine, and distilled liquor. By Mexican standards, bars are considered very upscale places to hang out, so they aren't extremely popular—many young Mexicans would rather drink at a disco where they can dance, too.

HEALTH AND SAFETY

By and large, Baja California's Cape Region is a very healthy place. Sanitation standards are high compared to many other parts of Mexico and the tap water quality in many areas is superior to that in most of California. The visitor's main health concerns are not food or water sources but avoiding mishaps while driving, boating, diving, surfing, or otherwise enjoying the Cape's great outdoor life. Health issues directly concerned with these activities are covered under the relevant sections in this book.

FOOD AND WATER

Visitors who use common sense will probably never come down with food- or water-related illnesses while traveling in Cabo. The first rule is not to overdo it during the first few days of your trip—eat and drink in moderation. Shoveling down huge amounts of tasty, often heavy Mexican foods along with pitchers of margaritas or strong Mexican beer is liable to make anyone sick from pure overindulgence. If you're not used to the spices and different ways of cooking, it's best to ingest small amounts at first.

Second, take it easy with foods offered by street vendors, since this is where you're most likely to suffer from unsanitary conditions. Eat only foods that have been thoroughly cooked and are served either stove-hot or refrigerator-cold. Many gringos eat street food without any problems whatsoever, but it pays to be cautious, especially if it's your first time in Mexico. Concerned with the risk of cholera, the Baja California Sur state government in July 1992 banned the sale of ice cream or *ceviche* by street vendors.

Doctors usually advise against eating peeled, raw fruit and vegetables in Baja. Once the peel is removed, it is virtually impossible to disinfect produce. Unpeeled fruits and vegetables washed in purified water and dried with a clean cloth are usually okay. After all, plenty of Mexican fruit is consumed daily in Canada and the United States.

Hotels and restaurants serve only purified drinking water and ice, so there's no need to ask for mineral water or refuse ice. Most residents, both foreign and Mexican, drink the tap water, which comes from uncontaminated underground springs. To be safe, however, first-time visitors are advised not to consume tap water except in hotels where the water system is purified—if so, you'll be informed by a notice over the washbasin in your room. Most grocery stores sell bottled purified water. Water purification tablets, iodine crystals, water filters, and the like aren't necessary for Cape travel unless you plan on extensive backpacking (see "Sports and Recreation," above).

Turista

People who've never traveled to a foreign country may undergo a period of adjustment to the new gastrointestinal flora that comes with new territory. There's really no way to avoid the differences wrought by sheer distance. Unfortunately, the adjustment is sometimes unpleasant for some people.

Mexican doctors call gastrointestinal upset of this sort *turista* since it affects tourists but not the local population. The usual symptoms of *turista*—also known by the gringo tags "Montezuma's Revenge" and "the Aztec Two-Step"—are nausea and diarrhea, sometimes with stomach cramps and a low fever. Again, eating and drinking in moderation will help prevent the worst of the symptoms, whch rarely persist more than a day or two. And if it's any consolation, Mexicans often get sick the first time they go to the U.S. or Canada.

Prevention and Treatment: Many Mexico travelers swear by a preventive regimen of Pepto-Bismol begun the day before arrival in country. Opinions vary as to how much of the pink stuff is necessary to ward off or tame the foreign flora, but a person probably shoudn't exceed the recommended daily dose. Taper off after four days or so until you stop using it altogether.

If you come down with a case of *turista*, the best thing to do is drink plenty of fluids. Adults should drink at least three liters a day, a child under 37 kilos (80 pounds) at least a liter a day. Lay off tea, coffee, milk, fruit juices, and booze. Eat only bland foods, nothing spicy, fatty, or fried, and take it easy. Pepto-Bismol or similar pectin-based remedies usually help. Some people like to mask the symptoms with a strong over-the-counter medication like Immodium AD (loperamide is the active ingredient), but though this can be very effective, it isn't a cure. Only time will cure traveler's diarrhea.

If the symptoms are unusually severe (especially if there's blood in the stools) or persist more than one or two days, see a doctor. Most hotels can arrange a doctor's visit or you can contact a Mexican tourist office or U.S. Consulate for recommendations.

SUNBURN AND DEHYDRATION

Sunburn probably afflicts more Cabo visitors than all other illnesses and injuries combined. The sunlight in Baja can be exceptionally strong, especially along the coast. For outdoor forays, sun protection is a must, whatever the activity. The longer you're in the sun, the more protection you'll need.

A hat, sunglasses, and plenty of sunscreen or sunblock make a good start. Bring along a sunscreen with a sun protection factor (SPF) of at least 25, even if you don't plan on using it all the time. Apply it to *all* exposed parts of your body—don't forget the hands, top of the feet, and neck. Men should remember to cover thinned-out or bald areas on the scalp. Sunscreen must be reapplied after swimming or after periods of heavy perspiration.

If you're going boating, don't leave shore with just a bathing suit. Bring along an opaque shirt—preferably with long sleeves—and a pair of long pants. Since you can never know for certain whether your boat might get stranded or lost at sea for a period of time (if, for example, the motor conks out and you get caught in an offshore current), you shouldn't be without extra clothing for emergencies.

It's also important to drink plenty of water and/or nonalcoholic, non-caffeinated fluids to avoid dehydration. Alcohol and caffeine—including the caffeine in iced tea and Coke—will increase your potential for dehydration. Symptoms of dehydration include darker-than-usual urine or inability to urinate, flushed face, profuse sweating or an unusual lack thereof, and sometimes headache, dizziness, and general feeling of malaise. Extreme cases of dehydra-

tion can lead to heat exhaustion or even heatstroke, in which the victim may become delirious and/or convulse. If either condition is suspected, get the victim out of the sun immediately, cover with a wet sheet or towel, and administer a rehydration fluid that replaces lost water and salts. If you can get the victim to a doctor, all the better—heatstroke can be very serious.

Rehydration Formula: If Gatorade or a similar rehydration fluid isn't available you can mix your own by combining the following ingredients: 1 liter (4 cups or 1 quart) purified water or diluted fruit juice; 2 tablespoons sugar or honey; one quarter teaspoon salt; and one quarter teaspoon bicarbonate of soda. If soda isn't available, use another quarter teaspoon salt. The victim should drink this mixture at regular intervals until symptoms subside substantially. Four or more liters may be necessary in moderate cases, more in severe cases.

MOTION SICKNESS

Visitors with little or no boating experience who join offshore fishing cruises sometimes experience motion sickness caused by the movement of a boat over ocean swells. The repeated pitching and rolling affects a person's sense of equilibrium to the point of nausea. Known as "seasickness" *(mareado),* it can be a very unpleasant experience not only for those green at the gills but for fellow passengers anxious lest the victim spew on them.

The best way to prevent motion sickness is to take one of the preventives commonly available from a pharmacist: promethazine (sold as Phenergan in the U.S.), dimenhydrinate (Dramamine), or scopolamine (Transderm Scop). The latter is available as an adhesive patch worn behind the ear—the time-release action is allegedly more effective than tablets. These medications should be consumed *before* boarding the vessel, not after the onset of symptoms. It's also not a good idea to eat a large meal before getting on a boat.

If you start to feel seasick while out on the bounding main, certain actions can lessen the likelihood that it will get worse. First, do not lie down. Often the first symptom of motion sickness is drowsiness, and if you give in to the impulse you'll almost certainly guarantee a worsening of the condition. Second, stay in the open air rather than below decks—fresh air usually helps. Finally, fix your gaze on the horizon; this will help steady your disturbed inner ear, the proximate cause of motion sickness.

BITES AND STINGS

Mosquitoes and *Jejenes*

Mosquitoes breed in standing water. Since standing water isn't that common in arid Baja, neither are mosquitoes. Exceptions include palm oases, estuaries, and marshes when there isn't a strong breeze around to keep them at bay. The easiest way to avoid mosquito bites is to apply insect repellent to exposed areas of the skin and clothing whenever the mossies are out and biting. For most species, this means between dusk and dawn.

The most effective repellents are those containing a high concentration of DEET (N,N-diethyl-metatoluamide). People with an aversion to applying synthetics to the skin can try citronella (lemongrass oil), which is also effective but requires more frequent application.

More common than mosquitoes in estuarial areas are *jejenes*, tiny flying insects known as "no-see-ums" among North Americans—you almost never see them while they're biting. The same repellents effective for mosquitoes will usually do the trick with *jejenes*.

For relief from the itchiness of mosquito bites, try rubbing a bit of hand soap on the affected areas. Jejene bites will usually stop itching in less than 10 minutes if you refrain from scratching them. Excessive scratching of either type of bite can lead to infection, so be mindful of what your fingers are up to.

In spite of the presence of the occasional mosquito, the U.S. Centers for Disease Control has declared all of Baja California Sur malaria-free.

Wasps, Bees, and Hornets

Although stings from these flying insects can be very painful, they aren't of mortal danger to most people. If you're allergic to such stings and plan to travel in remote areas of Baja, consider obtaining anti-allergy medication from your doctor before leaving home. At the very least, carry a supply of Benadryl or similar over-the-counter antihistamine. Dramamine (dimenhydrinate) also usually helps mitigate allergic reactions.

For relief from a wasp/bee/hornet sting you can apply a paste of baking soda and water to the affected area. Liquids containing ammonia, including urine, also help relieve pain. If a stinger is visible, remove it—by scraping if possible, or with tweezers—before applying any remedies. If a stung limb becomes unusually swollen or if the victim exhibits symptoms of a severe allergic reaction—difficulty in breathing, agitation, hives—seek medical assistance.

Ticks

If you find a tick embedded in your skin, don't try to pull it out—this may leave the head and pincers under your skin and lead to infection. Covering the tick with petroleum jelly, mineral oil, gasoline, kerosene, or alcohol will usually cause the tick to release its hold in order to avoid suffocation.

Burning the tick with a cigarette butt or hot match usually succeeds only in killing it—when you pull it out, the head and pincers may not come with it. Stick with the suffocation method and if the beast still doesn't come out, use tweezers.

Scorpions

The venom of scorpions *(alacranes)* varies in strength from individual to individual and species to species, but the sting is rarely dangerous to adults. It can be very painful, however, resulting in partial numbness and swelling that lasts several days. In Baja, the small yellow scorpions inflict more painful stings than the larger, dark-colored ones.

The best treatment begins with persuading the victim to lie down and relax to slow the

BOB RACE

spread of the venom. Keep the affected area below the level of the heart. Ice packs on the sting may relieve pain and mitigate swelling; aspirin also helps.

Children who weigh less than about 13 kilos (30 pounds) should receive medical attention when stung by a scorpion. Doctors in La Paz, San José, and Cabo San Lucas usually have ready access to scorpion antivenin *(anti-alacrán)*, but it should only be administered under qualified medical supervision. Mexicans often keep on hand a bottle of alcohol containing dead scorpions; applied to a scorpion sting, this alcohol solution reportedly acts as an effective antivenin.

Avoiding Scorpions: Scorpions prefer damp, dark, warm places—dead brush, rock piles, fallen logs—so exercise particular caution when placing your hands in or near such areas. Hands are the scorpion's most common target on the human body; campers should wear gloves when handling firewood in Baja.

Other favorite spots for scorpions are crumpled clothing and bedding. In Gulf Desert areas of the Cape, always check your bedsheets or sleeping bag for scorpions before climbing in. In the same environments, shake out your shoes and clothing before putting them on.

POISONOUS SEA CREATURES

Various marine animals carry poisons in parts of their bodies that can inflict painful stings on humans. In Baja, such creatures include jellyfish, Portuguese men-of-war, cone shells, stingrays, sea urchins, and various fishes with poisonous spines.

The best way to avoid jellyfish and Portuguese men-of-war is to scope out the water before going in—if you see any nasties floating around, try another beach. You can avoid stingrays by shuffling your feet in the sand as you walk in shallow surf—this will usually cause rays resting in the sand to swim away.

To avoid cone shell and sea urchin stings, wear shoes in the water; several sport shoe manufacturers now produce specialized water shoes. You can also often spot cones and urchins in clear water, especially when wearing a diving mask.

Anglers should take care when handling landed fish to avoid poisonous spine wounds. If you

don't know how to avoid the spines while handling a fish, let someone more experienced show you how.

The treatment for stings from all of the above is the same: remove all tentacles, barbs, or spines from the affected area; wash with rubbing alcohol or diluted ammonia (urine will do in a pinch) to remove as much venom as possible; and wrap the area in cloth to reduce the flow of oxygen to the wound until pain subsides. If an acute allergic reaction occurs, get the victim to a doctor or clinic as quickly as possible.

MEDICAL ASSISTANCE

The quality of basic medical treatment, including dentistry, is relatively high in Cape cities and larger towns; ask at a tourist office or at your consulate for recommendations. Public IMSS hospitals can be found in La Paz, San José, and Cabo San Lucas; Cabo's hospital is quite modern. There are public clinics or Red Cross (Cruz Roja) stations in nearly every other town.

Emergency Evacuation
San Diego's **Air-Evac International** provides emergency 24-hour airlift service (or, in the border areas, ground ambulance) from Baja to U.S. hospitals in the San Diego area. The emergency number is (619) 278-3822; for inquiries call (800) 254-2569 in the U.S., 95-800-10-09-96 in Mexico. Air-Evac accepts collect calls; payment can be made with a credit card or through your health insurance company. Providing the same service is **Critical Air Medicine** (tel. 619-571-0482 or 800-247-8325 in California, 800-633-8326 elsewhere in the U.S., 95-800-10-02-68 in Mexico).

SAFETY

Statistics clearly show that violent crime is much less common in Mexico than anywhere in the United States. In Baja California Sur crime statistics are over 90% lower than the U.S. national average. Yet Americans seem to be the most paranoid of all visitors to Mexico.

Historical reasons, to a large degree, account for this paranoia. Chief among them is the general border lawlessness that was the norm very early in this century. The turn of the century and early 1900s was an era of border disputes and common banditry on both sides of the border, all the way from the Texas Gulf coast to California's Pacific coast. Americans living in these areas came to fear *bandidos* who stole livestock and occasionally robbed the Anglo ranchers themselves, while the Mexicans in turn feared American cattle rustlers, horse thieves, gunslingers, and the infamous Texas Rangers, a private militia whose conduct at the time fell somewhere between that of the Hell's Angels motorcycle gang and the Los Angeles Police Department.

Soon after this era had begun to wane, as politics on both sides of the border stabilized, the U.S. Prohibition experiment sent millions of Americans scrambling into Mexican border towns for booze. In the illicit atmosphere, boozers were soon rubbing elbows with gamblers and whoremongers, and it wasn't long before Mexican border towns gained an even more unsavory reputation.

Once Prohibition was lifted, Americans had no reason to come to Mexico solely for drinking purposes and the border towns began cleaning up their acts. Among the uninformed and inexperienced, however, the border-town image remains, sadly mixing with the equally outdated bandido tales to prevent many Americans from enjoying the pleasures of life south of the border.

Historically the Cape Region has never had any banditry to speak of; neither the author nor anyone in the author's acquaintance has ever been robbed in the Cape (or, for that matter, anywhere in Mexico). Compared to Hawaii or Florida, the Cape is many, many times safer in terms of crimes committed against tourists.

Precautions: In general, visitors to Cabo should take the same precautions they would when traveling anywhere in their own countries or abroad. Keep money and valuables secured, either in a hotel safe or safety deposit box, or in a money belt or other hard-to-reach place on your person. Keep an eye on cameras, purses, etc., to make sure you don't leave them behind in restaurants, hotels, or campgrounds. At night, lock the doors to your hotel room and vehicle.

Private campgrounds usually have some kind of security, if only a night watchman, to keep out intruders. Secluded beach campsites seem to be safe due to their seclusion—around the Cape Region it's rare for crime to occur in such areas. Nonetheless, don't leave items of value lying around outside your tent, camper, or RV at night.

IMMIGRATION AND CUSTOMS

ENTRY REGULATIONS

U.S. and Canadian Citizens
A U.S. or Canadian citizen visiting Mexico solely for tourism, transit, or study purposes is not required to obtain a visa. All U.S. or Canadian visitors crossing the Mexican border for more than 72 hours or going farther south than Ensenada must carry validated "tourist cards" (Form FMT), which aren't actually cards but slips of paper. These are available free of charge at any Mexican consulate or Mexican tourist office, from many travel agencies, on flights to Mexico, or at the border.

The tourist card is valid for stays of up to 180 days and must be used within 90 days of issuance. Your card becomes invalid once you exit the country—you're supposed to surrender it at the border—even if your 180 days hasn't expired. If you'll be entering and leaving Mexico more than once during your trip, you should request a multiple-entry tourist card, available from Mexican consulates.

Validation: Once you cross the border or land at an airport on an international flight, your tourist card must be validated by a Mexican immigration officer. If you're flying into La Paz or Los Cabos, you will automatically be channeled through brief immigration procedures. If you're driving down, you can arrange this at any *migración* office in Baja (all *municipio* seats have them), but it's accomplished most conveniently at the border crossing itself or at the immigration office in Ensenada (right around the corner from the tourist information booth on Blvd. Costero).

Minors: Before 1991, Mexican regulations required children under the age of 18 crossing the border without one or both parents to carry a notarized letter granting permission from the absent parent, or both parents if both were absent. This regulation is no longer in effect, but we've heard that some Mexican border officers, as well as airline check-in crews, are still asking for the letter, apparently unaware that the regulation has been rescinded. Hence unaccompanied minors or minors traveling with only one parent should be prepared for all situations with notarized letters. In cases of divorce, separation, or death, the minor should carry notarized papers documenting the situation.

In reality, minors with tourist cards are rarely asked for these documents. Children under 15 may be included on their parents' tourist card but this means neither the child nor the parents can legally exit Mexico without the other.

Citizens from Other Countries

Tourists from countries other than the U.S. or Canada may need visas in advance of arrival in Mexico. Citizens of Australia, New Zealand, and most western European countries can usually obtain free, no-photo visas at the border or international airport of entry; be sure to check with a Mexican embassy or consulate first, as visa regulations change from year to year.

If you apply in person at a Mexican embassy or consulate, a tourist visa can generally be obtained on the day of application.

Pets

Dogs and cats may be brought into Mexico if each is accompanied by a **vaccination certificate** that proves the animal has been vaccinated or treated for rabies, hepatitis, pip, and leptospirosis. You'll also need a **health certificate** issued no more than 72 hours before entry and signed by a registered veterinarian. Upon recrossing the border into the U.S., the U.S. Customs Service will ask to see the vaccination certificate.

Since 1992 the requirement that the health certificate be stamped with a visa at the border or at a Mexican consulate has been repealed. The certificate is still necessary; the visa isn't.

Long-Term Visas

Special *inmigrante rentista* visas (FM-2 status) are issued to foreigners who choose to reside in Mexico on a "permanent income" basis. This most often applies to foreigners who retire in Mexico, though it's also used by artists, writers, and other self-employed foreign residents. With this visa you're allowed to import one motor vehicle as well as your household belongings into Mexico tax-free.

The basic requirements for this visa are that applicants forego any kind of employment in Mexico while residing in the country and show proof in the form of bank statements of a regular source of foreign-earned income amounting to at least US$1,500 per month, plus US$500 for each dependent over the age of 15, e.g., US$2,000 for a couple. A pile of paperwork, including a "letter of good conduct" from the applicant's local police department, must accompany the initial application, along with an immigration tax payment (currently US$121) and various application fees totaling around US$75. The visa must be renewed annually but the renewal can be accomplished at any immigration office in Mexico—there's one in every *municipio*. After five years in Mexico, an *inmigrante rentista* is eligible to apply for *inmigrado* status, which confers all the rights of citizenship, including employment in Mexico, save the right to vote.

Similar to the FM-2 but easier to obtain is the FM-3, or *no inmigrante visitante,* visa, which requires an income of US$1,200 a month plus US$500 for each dependent. The FM-3 is annually renewable for five years, at which point you must start the application process over again.

Many foreigners who have retired in Baja manage do so on the regular 180-day tourist visa; every six months they dash across the border and return with a new tourist card, issued at the border, on the same day. This method bypasses all the red tape and income requirements of the retirement visa.

CUSTOMS

Entering Mexico

Officially, tourists are supposed to bring only those items into Mexico that will be of use during their trip. This means you can bring in practically anything as long as it doesn't appear in large enough quantities to qualify for resale. Boats require special permits. (See "Legal Requirements" under "Boating" in the "Sports and Recreation" section).

Foreign-registered motor vehicles—cars, trucks, RVs, motorcycles, etc.—do not require permits for travel anywhere on the Baja California peninsula. However, if you plan to take a vehicle registered outside Mexico onto one of the vehicle ferries that sail from Baja to the mainland, or if you plan to drive farther east than San Luis Río Colorado in Sonora, you must obtain an auto permit. These are available from any Mexican consulate abroad, at the border, or from the ferry office in La Paz. For further information on vehicle permits, see "Getting There," following.

Into the U.S.
Visitors returning to the U.S. from Mexico may have their luggage inspected by U.S. Customs officials. The hassle can be minimized by giving brief, straight answers to their questions and cooperating with any requests to open your luggage, vehicle storage compartments, or anything else. Occasionally the officers use dogs to sniff luggage or vehicles for contraband or illegal aliens.

Customs Duties: Nearly 3,000 items—including all handicrafts—made in Mexico are exempt from any U.S. customs duties. Adults over 21 are allowed one quart of alcoholic beverages and 200 cigarettes (or 100 cigars) per person. All other purchases or gifts up to a total value of US$400 within any 31-day period can be brought into the U.S. duty-free. Under the new North American Free Trade Agreement (NAFTA), import duties on most Mexican goods are gradually being phased out.

Plant and Animal Prohibitions
The following fruits and vegetables cannot be brought into the U.S. from Mexico: oranges, grapefruits, mangoes, avocados (unless the pits are removed), and potatoes (including yams and sweet potatoes). All other fruits are permitted.

Other prohibited plant materials are straw (including packing materials and items stuffed with straw), hay, unprocessed cotton, sugarcane, and any plants in soil, including houseplants.

Animals and animal products that cannot be imported include wild and domesticated birds, pork or pork products, and eggs. Beef, mutton, venison, and other meats are permitted up to 50 pounds total per person.

Customs regulations can change at any time, so if you want to verify the regulations on a purchase before risking duties or confiscation at the border, check with a U.S. consulate in Baja before crossing. Now that NAFTA is a fact, expect sweeping changes in customs regulations—toward more leniency—in both directions.

LEGAL MATTERS

All foreign visitors in Mexico are subject to Mexican legal codes, which are based on Roman and Napoleonic law. The most distinctive features of the Mexican judiciary system, compared to Anglo-American systems, are that the system doesn't provide for trials by jury (the judge decides) nor writs of habeas corpus (though you must be charged within 72 hours of incarceration). Furthermore, bail is rarely granted to an arrested foreigner—for many offenses, not even Mexican nationals are allowed bail. Hence, once arrested and jailed for a serious offense, it can be very difficult to arrange release. The lesson here is: Don't get involved in matters that might result in your arrest. This primarily means anything having to do with drugs or guns.

The oft-repeated saw that in Mexico an arrested person is considered guilty until proven innocent is no more true south of the border than north. As in Canada or the U.S., an arrested person is considered a criminal *suspect* until the courts confirm or deny guilt. You have the right to notify your consulate if detained.

Mexican federal police *(federales)*, mostly under pressure from the U.S., occasionally set up roadblocks to conduct searches for drugs. Such roadblocks are now rare in Baja, however, due to past complaints from tourists who drove regularly on the peninsula. If your vehicle is stopped by a roadblock, be as cooperative as possible. If there are any irregularities or if you object to the way in which the procedure is carried out, make note of the incident—including whatever badge numbers, names, or license numbers you can obtain discreetly—and later file a report with the Mexican Attorney General for Tourist Protection. A conviction of possession of any illegal drug carries with it a minimum prison sentence of seven years.

La Mordida
In the past, Mexican police had a reputation for hassling foreigners, especially those who drove their own vehicles in Mexico. Tales of the legendary *mordida* (literally, "bite"), or minor bribe, supposedly a necessary part of navigating one's

way around Mexico, swelled way out of proportion to reality but were nonetheless based on real incidents.

For several years now, the Mexican police have for the most part ceased singling out foreigners for arrest, partly as a result of anticorruption efforts by the federal government but more importantly because of a conscious effort to attract more tourists. Most foreign visitors who drive in Mexico these days complete their trips without any police hassles. Over the last five years, I haven't heard of a single incident involving *mordida* for traffic violations anywhere in the Cape Region. (See "Getting Around," following, for tips on traffic laws and dealing with traffic police.)

In Case of Arrest

If you get into trouble with Mexican law, for whatever reason, you should try to contact your nearest consulate in Baja. Embassies and consulates for each town are listed under the respective destination chapters. You can also contact the local offices of the Secretary of Tourism—see the sections on each town for phone numbers and addresses. In Baja California Sur, the Secretary of Tourism office in La Paz is the best place to look for help. These agencies routinely handle emergency legal matters involving visiting foreigners; you stand a much better chance of resolving legal difficulties with their assistance.

MONEY, MEASUREMENTS, AND COMMUNICATIONS

MONEY

Currency

The unit of exchange in Mexico is the peso, which under the "old peso" system appeared in coins of 50, 100, 500, and 1,000 pesos, or in bills of 1,000, 5,000, 10,000, 20,000, 50,000, and 100,000.

In January 1993 the government introduced the *nuevo peso* or "new peso," a currency that simply knocks three zeros off the old peso. Ten new pesos, for example, equals 10,000 old pesos. The first new peso notes were exact copies of old peso notes without the three zeros. A 10,000-peso note read 10 pesos but otherwise looked exactly the same. The new pesos come in denominations of N$10, N$20, N$50, N$100, N$200, and N$500. In late 1994 a new set of bills for the N$10, N$20, and N$50 denominations was issued; the new currency is 17% smaller than the old peso and earlier new peso bills. To further clarify the distinction between old and new peso bills, the historic personages pictured on each of these "new" new peso notes (as opposed to "old" new peso notes) was changed from Lázaro Cárdenas to Emiliano Zapata on the N$10 bill, from Andrés Quintana Roo to Benito Juárez on the N$20 bill, and from Cuauhtémoc to José María Morelos on the N$50 bill.

Old peso denominations of 50,000 and 100,000, along with their new peso equivalents, N$50 and N$100, can be difficult to break, so try to get them changed as soon as possible to secure a good supply of smaller notes. New peso N$200 and N$500 bills are almost impossible to break except when used for large purchases.

In addition to the new bills, new peso and *centavo* coins have been issued in denominations of 5¢, 10¢, 20¢, 50¢, N$1, N$2, N$5, and N$10.

Until the older currency passes from circulation, both kinds of pesos, in any combination, are legal tender throughout Mexico. In remote villages where the new peso isn't yet common, there may be some initial reluctance to accept new pesos. Usually there's someone around who will vouch for the validity of the new currency. In larger towns and tourist areas, old pesos are steadily becoming less common than new pesos, especially in the Cape Region.

The $ symbol is often used for indicating old peso as well as dollar prices. New peso prices are indicated by the symbol N$. While it's highly unlikely you'll ever confuse the two—since the exchange ratio is so high for old pesos—you should ask when in doubt. New peso prices are much closer to what a dollar price might be, hence there's more potential for confusion between dollars and new pesos; but since new peso prices are clearly marked with the symbol N$, this usually isn't a problem. Sometimes the abbreviation m.n. will appear next to a price—this means *moneda nacional* ("national money") and usually refers to old pesos.

When quoting prices verbally, Mexican vendors ordinarily refer to new peso prices. Even under the old peso system, they often abbreviated a verbal price quote by omitting the word *mil* (thousand) since few things cost less than 1,000 pesos. Thus *doce cinco* meant *doce mil quiniento* (12,500 old pesos) and under the new system means 12 new pesos plus fifty *centavo* or N$12.50. More correctly this would be spoken as *doce cincuenta* or "twelve fifty."

Since the smallest new peso coin is 5¢, all payments are rounded off to the nearest multiple of five *centavo*. For a marked price of N$8.52 (8,520 old pesos), for example, you actually only pay N$8.50; for a N$8.53 price you pay N$8.55.

Most places on the Cape will take U.S. dollars as well as pesos. Paying with pesos, however, usually means a better deal when the price is fixed in pesos; if you pay in dollars, the vendor can determine the exchange rate. If a T-shirt, for example, is marked at N$30, and the bank rate is N$6.5 per dollar, you'll pay only US$4.60 for the T-shirt with pesos changed at the bank. However, if you ask to pay in dollars, the vendor may charge US$5.45, figuring an exchange of

N$5.5 per US$1 since vendors have the right—by custom rather than law—to charge whatever exchange rate they wish. If you're bargaining for price, it really doesn't matter what currency you use as long as you stick to one currency from start to finish.

Some stores in smaller towns prefer not to take dollars since this means keeping track of two currencies and makes banking more complicated. PEMEX stations sometimes refuse dollars—attendants are usually too busy to stop and calculate rates.

Devaluation
The value of the Mexican peso has been in a downward spiral since 1976 when the government decided to allow the national currency to "float" on the international money market. From 1976 to 1987 the exchange rate slid from eight pesos to the dollar to over 2,000. In 1988 the Bank of Mexico instituted measures to slow the decline to less than a *centavo* per day by the end of 1992. Since the switch to the new peso in '93, the peso actually gained in value against the U.S. dollar for a while, then slipped again. At press time, it was around N$6.25 per US$1.

Changing Money
Banks: Banks offer the best exchange rate for buying pesos and they all offer the same rate, set by the Bank of Mexico. This rate is usually posted behind the counter where foreign exchange is handled. Banks also accept a wide range of foreign currencies, including Swiss francs, German marks, British pounds, Japanese yen, and Canadian dollars. Either cash or traveler's checks are accepted. The main drawbacks with banks are the long lines and short hours (Mon.-Fri. 0900-1330); the foreign-exchange service usually closes at noon or 1230.

Moneychangers: The second best rate is at the *casa de cambio* or private moneychanging office. The *casa de cambio* either knocks a few pesos off the going bank rate or charges a percentage commission. It pays to shop around for the best *casa de cambio* rates since some places charge considerably more than others. Rates are usually posted; *compra* refers to the buying rate for US$ (how many pesos you'll receive per dollar), while *venda* is the selling rate (how many pesos you must pay to receive a

dollar). As with banks, the difference between the buying and selling rates is the moneychangers' profit, unless they charge commissions on top of it.

Moneychangers are usually open much later than banks; some even work evening hours, which makes them immeasurably more convenient than banks. United States dollar currency is generally preferred, though many *casas* will also accept Canadian dollars. However, Canadians should always keep a reserve supply of U.S. dollars for instances when Canadian currency isn't accepted. Moneychangers usually accept traveler's checks; some border-town casas, however, accept only cash.

Only the larger towns and tourist centers offer moneychanging offices. In smaller towns you'll have to resort to a bank or local merchant. Many storekeepers will be happy to buy dollars at a highly variable and sometimes negotiable rate. Few will take traveler's checks, however, unless you make a purchase.

Moneychangers at Mexican airports offer notoriously low rates. Try to buy pesos in advance if arriving by air, or pay with dollars until you can get to a bank or *casa de cambio*.

Hotels: Hotels, motels, *pensiones,* and other lodgings generally offer the lowest exchange rates. If you're trying to save money, avoid changing currency where you stay. Pay for your room in pesos if possible, since the same low rate often applies to room charges paid in dollars.

Credit Cards
Plastic money (primarily Visa and MasterCard) is widely accepted in the Cape Region at large hotels, at restaurants catering to tourists or businesspeople, at car rental agencies (you can't rent a car without a credit card), and at shops in tourist centers or large cities. Usually card displays at the cash register or on the door will announce that *tarjetas de crédito* (credit cards) are accepted. If in doubt, flash one and ask *"¿Se acepta tarjetas de crédito?"* or simply *"¿Está bien?"* A reference to *efectivo* means "cash."

Credit cards are not accepted at PEMEX stations. In 1991 the Mexican government announced plans to introduce a special "tourist credit card" that would be valid at PEMEX outlets; so far, *nada.* If and when the plan is finally realized, travel agencies abroad should know the details.

Paying for goods and services in Baja with credit cards that are paid through U.S. or Canadian banks can save you money since the exchange rate will usually dip farther in the dollar's favor by the time the transaction is posted at your bank. Many shops and some hotels, however, add a 3-6% surcharge to bills paid with a card, which more than offsets the exchange rate differential.

Cash advances on credit card accounts—a very useful service for emergencies—are available at Mexican banks. Banamex will accept MasterCard debit cards ("cash" or "check" cards), a more convenient way to carry travel funds than either cash or traveler's checks. Bancomer ATMs will accept Visa cards; at Banca Serfín you can arrange cash advances or withdrawals using either Visa or MasterCard, but only at the exchange counters, not from Banca Serfín ATMs.

Estimating Costs

Inflation in Mexico currently runs around 22% per annum, in large part due to the continued weakening of the peso on international markets, but also because of a slight relaxation of wage and price controls. This means that when estimating travel costs based on prices quoted in this book, some allowance must be made for inflation. Although peso prices will increase in direct proportion to the inflation rate, this isn't necessarily so for prices figured in dollars, since the dollar continues to gain in value against the peso.

Because of fluctuations in the peso-dollar ratio, and in an effort to keep prices up to date, all prices in this book are quoted in dollars. This doesn't mean, however, that there won't be any increase in prices by the time you arrive. A couple of phone calls to hotels for price quotes should give you an idea how much rates have increased, if at all; this difference can be applied as a percentage to all other prices for a rough estimate of costs.

Tipping

A tip of 10-15% is customary at restaurants with table service unless a service charge is added to the bill. Luggage handling at hotels or airports warrants a tip of US$.50, or the equivalent in pesos, per bag. A few hotels maintain a no-tipping policy; details will be posted in your room. The tipping of chambermaids is optional.

You don't need to tip PEMEX station attendants unless they wash your windows, check the oil, or perform other extra services beyond pumping gas. The equivalent of US$.30 to US$.60 in pesos is sufficient. When the change due on a gasoline purchase is less than N$1 it's customary to let the attendant keep the change.

The Mexican government collects an *impuesta al valor agregado* (IVA) or "value added tax" on all goods and services, including hotel and restaurant bills and international phone calls Before 1992 the IVA was 15%, but in an effort to boost consumption the tax has been reduced to 10%. Hotels and restaurants were supposed to pass the five percent tax savings on to the consumer by dropping prices accordingly; as a result you may see menus that read "five percent solidarity discount included."

MEASUREMENTS

Mexico uses the metric system as the official system of weights and measures. This means the distance between La Paz and San José del Cabo is measured in kilometers, cheese is weighed in grams or kilograms, a hot day in San Felipe is 32° C, gasoline is sold by the liter, and a big fish is two meters long. A chart at the end of this book converts pounds, gallons, and miles to kilos, liters, and kilometers, and vice versa.

Bajacalifornios used to dealing with American tourists often use the Anglo-American and metric systems interchangeably. Even rancheros in remote areas occasionally use *millas* (miles) as a measure.

In this book, distances are rendered in kilometers, often followed by miles in parentheses for the benefit of American readers and for checking against American odometers. All road markers in Mexico employ the metric system. Dimensions and weights are usually quoted using the metric system, except when feet or pounds are culturally more appropriate, as in prescribing monofilament fishing line.

COMMUNICATIONS

Time

Baja California Sur lies in the mountain time zone but does not observe daylight savings time. Hence from November to April, BCS time runs the same as in the mountain time zone (as followed in the U.S. and Canada), while the remainder of the year BCS is an hour behind mountain time.

Time in Mexico is commonly expressed according to the 24-hour clock, from 0001 to 2400 (one minute past midnight to midnight). A restaurant posting hours of 1100-2200, for example, is open from 11 a.m. to 10 p.m. To conform to the Mexican system, all times in this guidebook follow the 24-hour clock.

Electricity

Mexico's electrical system is the same as those in the U.S. and Canada: 110 volts, 60 cycles, alternating current (AC). Electrical outlets are of the North American type, designed to work with appliances with standard double-bladed plugs. Small towns in some rural areas may experience brief interruptions of electrical service or periods of brownout (voltage decrease). In a few villages, gasoline-powered generators are the only sources of electricity and they may be turned off during the day.

Postal Service

The Mexican postal service, though quite reliable, is relatively slow. Most towns in Baja have a post office (oficina de correos) where you can receive poste restante mail. Have correspondents address mail in your name, last name capitalized, followed by a/c Lista de Correos, the town name, and the state; e.g., Joe CUMMINGS, a/c Lista de Correos, Todos Santos, Baja California Sur, Mexico.

In small towns and villages, residents often don't use street addresses, simply scrawling the addressee's name followed by domicilio conocido ("known residence") and the name of the town or village. Even in large towns and cities, addresses may bear the name of the street without a building number (sin número, abbreviated as "s/n"), or will mention the nearest cross streets (e.g., ent. Abasolo y Revolución, or "between Abasolo and Revolución").

Many foreigners who are seasonal Cape residents have their mail sent in care of a hotel or RV park. You can rent boxes at many Mexican post offices but the initial application process often takes several weeks. Todos Santos, Cabo San Lucas, and La Paz have private mail companies (similar to Mail Boxes, Etc.) that also rent boxes with minimal red tape.

For mail to the U.S., many residents save their letters and parcels until a friend or relative makes a trip across the border. A letter mailed to Los Angeles from Cabo San Lucas will take as much as two weeks, while one mailed from Chula Vista, California (opposite Tijuana) will take only two days.

Telephone Services

Telmex, the national telephone company, has improved its services considerably over the last few years. Local phone calls are relatively cheap—pay phones take a 10-peso coin—as are long distance calls within Mexico. Connections are usually good, though you may have to wait a long time to get through to the operator during such busy periods as Sundays and holidays.

If you don't want to use a phone booth or a hotel/RV-park phone (hotels and RV parks usually add surcharges to both local and long-distance calls), you can make a call during business hours from a TelMex office. Only large towns offer TelMex offices with public telecommunications facilities; a small town may offer a private telephone office (usually called caseta de teléfono), often set up in the corner of a local shop, where you can make calls. Like hotels, private telephone offices add surcharges to calls.

Making International Calls: To direct dial an international call to the U.S. or Canada, dial 95 plus the area code and number for a station-to-station call or 96 plus area code and number for a person-to-person call. For countries besides Canada and the U.S., dial 98 and 99 respectively. Long-distance international calls are heavily taxed and cost more than equivalent international calls from the U.S. or Canada.

To reach toll-free (800) numbers in Mexico from the U.S. or Canada, dial 91 first. From Mexico, you can reach AT&T by dialing 95-800-462-4240, a toll-free call that connects you with a USADirect system. For MCI the number is 95-800-674-7000, for Sprint 95-800-977-8000. The appropriate long-distance operator can then place a collect call on your behalf or, if you have an AT&T, MCI, or Sprint phone card, charge the call to your account. If you try these numbers from a hotel phone, be sure the hotel operator realizes the call is toll free; some hotel operators

TELEPHONE CODES

To call a number in Mexico from outside the country, dial 011 + 52 + area code + number. Example: To call the number 2-47-61 in La Paz from the U.S., dial 011 (international dialing code) + 52 (Mexico country code) + 112 (La Paz area code) + 2-47-61 (the phone number in La Paz). You must dial the country code and local area code before the local number.

IN MEXICO

Information (national): 01
Long-distance operator (national): 02
Time: 03
Information (local): 04
Mexico City area code: 05
Police: 06
Spanish-English emergency information: 07
International operator: 09

LONG-DISTANCE DIRECT DIALING FROM MEXICO

station to station (in Mexico): 91 + area code + number
person to person (in Mexico): 92 + area code + number
station to station (to U.S. and Canada): 95 + area code + number
person to person (to U.S. and Canada): 96 + area code + number
station to station (to other countries): 98 + area code + number
person to person (to other countries): 99 + area code + number

BAJA CALIFORNIA SUR AREA CODES

La Paz: 112
San José del Cabo/Cabo San Lucas: 114
Todos Santos: 114

use their own timers to assess phone charges. Another way to reach AT&T is to dial **01 on the tan-colored LADATEL phones (the ones that accept LADATEL phone cards) or on blue pay phones.

Warning: TelMex international rates now run about the same as AT&T's, sometimes cheaper (depending on time of day and call destination). Since the deregulation of telephone service in Mexico, several private, U.S.-based long-distance phone companies have set up shop in Mexico to take advantage of undiscerning tourists. Often the same company operates under several different corporate names in the same area, charging at least 40% more per international call then TelMex, AT&T, MCI, or Sprint—as much as US$14 for the first minute,

plus US$4 each additional minute! A percentage of these charges usually goes to the hotel or private phone office offering the service. At most private phone offices it's cheaper to use TelMex than these fly-by-night U.S. companies, even if you have to pay a service charge on top of TelMex rates. Unless you're independently wealthy, always ask which company is being used before you arrange an international call through a hotel or private phone office.

Collect: For international service, calling collect saves money and hassles. On some pay phones and all private phones, you can make collect calls to the U.S. and Canada directly by dialing the prefix 92 before the area code and number. This is the easiest way to make a collect call. If you end up with a local operator instead, in Spanish the magic words are *por cobrar* (collect), prefaced by the name of the place you're calling (e.g., *"a los Estados Unidos, por favor— por cobrar"*). This will connect you to an English-speaking international operator. You're supposed to be able to obtain an international operator directly by dialing 09, but this number doesn't always work. For best results, speak slowly and clearly.

Local Numbers: Most telephone numbers in the Cape Region consist of five digits. There's no standard way of hyphenating the numbers; a five-digit number may appear as 211-13, 2-1113, or 2-11-13. For the sake of consistency the latter form, which seems to be the most common in Mexico, is used in this book.

Business Hours

The typical small business is open Mon.-Fri. 0900-1400, closed until 1600 or 1700, then reopened until 1900 or 2000. Retail businesses are usually open on Saturday as well. Official government offices typically maintain an 0830-1530 schedule, although Secretary of Tourism offices usually open again from 1700 to 1900.

Banks are open Mon.-Fri. 0830-1330, but the foreign currency exchange service usually closes around noon—probably to lock in the exchange rate before afternoon adjustments.

SERVICES AND INFORMATION

TRAVEL SERVICES

Tourist Information

Mexico's federal tourist bureau, the Secretaría de Turismo (SECTUR), has one state office in La Paz where you'll find a variety of free brochures, maps, hotel and restaurant lists, and information on local activities. It's between Km 6 and 5 on Mexico 1 (Av. Abasolo); tel. 2-11-99, fax 2-77-22.

Outside Mexico the government staffs 12 Mexican Government Tourism Offices (MGTO) to handle requests for tourist information. Seven are located in the United States. The information they provide on the Cape Region, however, is rather minimal.

Travel Clubs

Baja's popularity as a boating and RV destination has spawned three California-based travel clubs that specialize in recreational travel on the peninsula and along the Pacific coast of mainland Mexico. Membership benefits include discounts (usually 10-20%) at various hotels, restaurants, and other tourist-oriented establishments in Mexico; discounted group auto and boat insurance; the opportunity to participate in such club events as tours and fiestas; and subscriptions to newsletters containing tips from other club members, short travel features, and the latest information on road conditions and Mexican tourism policy. The clubs can also arrange tourist cards, boat permits, and fishing licenses by mail.

ClubMex and Discover Baja specialize in road (especially RV) travel and publish monthly newsletters, while Vagabundos del Mar is oriented toward boaters and publishes its newsletter every two months. Both ClubMex and Discover Baja invite members or potential members to visit their San Diego area offices on the way to Baja for up-to-date road and weather information. **Discover Baja** can be contacted at

3065 Clairemont Drive, San Diego, CA 92117 (tel. 619-275-4225 or toll-free 800-727-BAJA). Contact **ClubMex** at 3450 Bonita Rd., Suite 107, Chula Vista, CA (tel. 619-585-3033, fax 420-8133); the company's mailing address is P.O. Box 1646, Bonita, CA 91902-1646. Write or call **Vagabundos del Mar** at P.O. Box 824, Isleton, CA 95641 (tel. 707-374-5511, fax 374-6843).

MAPS

For general road travel in the Cape Region, the maps in this guidebook should suffice. If you're planning to drive farther north than La Paz, you can pick up one of the many Baja California maps available to visitors. Two maps are particularly well-suited to general-purpose Baja road travel. One is published by the Automobile Club of Southern California and is available from most AAA offices; maps are free to AAA members. This map is easy to read, accurate, and detailed enough for any border-to-cape auto trip. Its excellent graphics include topographic shading.

International Travel Map Productions (ITM) publishes a well-researched map that's a bit harder to find, especially in the United States. Map and travel stores may carry it, or it can be ordered from ITM, P.O. Box 2290, Vancouver, B.C. V6B 3W5, Canada. In spite of its smaller scale (one inch: 15.78 miles or 25.4 km), the ITM map is far more detailed than the AAA map and all distances are entered in kilometers as well as miles. Many dirt roads, trails, and destinations unmarked on the AAA map appear on the ITM map. In addition, the map features contour lines in 200-meter intervals and is annotated with useful historical and sightseeing information. The main drawback of this map is that it's so detailed it's difficult to read. In addition, the map's graphics scheme uses far too much red, a color particularly difficult to read in low light.

Topographical Maps

Since differences in elevation often determine backcountry route selection, hikers, kayakers, mountain bikers, and off-road drivers should consider obtaining topographical maps in advance of their arrival in the Cape Region. For information on what's available and where to get it, see "Hiking and Backpacking" under "Sports and Recreation," above. Topo maps are difficult to come by in the Cape Region; in La Paz, the Instituto Nacional de Estadística Geografía e Informática (INEGI), on Calle Rosales between calles V.G. Farias and Altamirano, sells topo maps for Baja California Sur for around US\$4 a sheet.

BUYING OR LEASING PROPERTY IN BAJA

The Mexican government allows both resident and nonresident foreigners to own Mexican real estate—both land and buildings—with certain restrictions. Under the Constitution of 1857, foreign ownership of land by direct title is permitted only in areas more than 100 km (62 miles) from any international border and 50 km (31 miles) from any sea coast. In Baja California, this limits prospective buyers to areas in the interior of the peninsula where services—water, electricity, sewage, telephone—are often nonexistent.

However, since 1973 the Mexican government has offered a way for foreigners to acquire lots that fall outside the geographic lim-

its, including coastal property. For transactions of this nature, the Ministry of Foreign Affairs issues permits to foreigners allowing them to create limited real estate trusts, administered by Mexican banks, with themselves as beneficiaries. Originally, these trusts were valid for 30-year nonrenewable terms only. In 1989 the government further liberalized real estate regulations so that the trusts (called *fideicomisos*) could be renewed at the end of each 30-year term for an additional 30-year term, with no limit on the number of renewals. In December 1993 the basic term for bank trusts was lengthened to 50 years, a period that may be long enough to attract U.S. housing lenders. Until now U.S. lenders have remained aloof from the *fideicomiso* market. *Fideicomisos* can be bought and sold among foreigners, at market rates, just like fee-simple property.

Needless to say, Baja real estate prices have increased substantially as a result of this change in policy. An estimated 40,000 foreigners now reside in Baja California Norte alone, some of them Americans who commute to San Diego for work. The priciest coastal properties are those near the U.S.-Mexico border and on the Cape, but prices are still substantially below what's available in coastal California. The outlook for Cape Region real estate at the moment is bright; purchases made at the right time, in the right place, can be very good investments, but just like at home it pays to shop around carefully.

Beach lots large enough for a two- or three-bedroom home in the La Paz area are avail-

home under construction in The Corridor

able for US$15,000 and up. In Cabo San Lucas or San José, house lots cost at least three times this, though condos are available for not much more. Elsewhere on the Cape—on the East Cape or north of Todos Santos—survivalist types can find beach hideaways with no services for even less; in remote areas, total annual lease payments run as low as US$500-1000. With a desalinator, generator or solar cells, propane stove and refrigerator, and perhaps an airplane to get in and out, you can live in considerable style. Historic Cape pueblos such as Todos Santos, San Antonio, and Santiago offer lots of promise because they're developing so gradually and, for the most part, with taste and sensitivity for the land and culture. In terms of creature comforts, these towns lie somewhere between the convenience of Los Cabos and the remoteness of beach camps.

Precautions: Before you rush off to grab Cape land, you should be aware that a lot of people get burned in Mexican real estate deals. It's best to deal through an established, reputable real estate agent. The American company Century 21 has opened a franchise in Baja, and although it generally represents only the more expensive properties, Century 21 people can be very helpful with information on real estate trusts. Mexican tourist offices in Baja also often carry information on residential property. It also helps to talk to current owner-residents about which real estate companies have the best and worst reputations.

Many sellers ask that the full purchase price be paid up front. Because a large number of gringos buy land in Mexico with cash, some Mexicans assume this is customary for all North Americans. Paying up front is not the automatic procedure for Mexicans themselves, who often make down payments and then send in monthly time payments; mortgage terms similar to those found in Canada and the U.S. are available in Mexico, though they are difficult for non-residents to obtain. Even if you have the cash, don't hand over more than half the full amount until you have the *fideicomiso* papers in hand.

Once again, investigate the realtor thoroughly before signing on the dotted line. Mexico doesn't require salespersons or brokers to obtain any sort of real estate license, hence many North Americans who couldn't make the grade in the U.S. or Canada now work in Mexico.

Time Shares

Time-share salespeople are the scourge of Cape resort areas, especially Cabo San Lucas, where they hang out on street corners and in hotel lobbies, hounding every tourist that passes by. These hustlers, who are sometimes gringos, will try almost anything to convince you to sign on the dotted line, on the spot—including denying that what they're selling is a time-share. In the last couple of years the situation has improved and the time-share touts seem a bit more low-key than three or four years ago.

It pays to hold off on any decision until you've made inquiries among current time-share residents at the development and checked with your consulate to see if there have been any complaints. Time-share developments typically begin selling when construction has just begun—sometimes they don't get finished, or when they do they don't shape up as promised. Also, because time-share owners aren't year-round residents, they usually lack both a sense of community and a sense of responsibility toward the local environment. For the developer, time-shares mean huge profits, as the same space is sold repeatedly in one-week segments. Since land in Baja is relatively inexpensive, considering the charming scenery and climate, it seems to attract get-rich-quick developers who show a decided lack of respect for the fragile Baja environment. Finally, keep in mind that from an investment perspective, time-shares don't appreciate in value as much as single-owner properties, if they appreciate at all (not very likely).

This is not to say there aren't any good time-share opportunities on the Cape. But, in general, as with any real estate deal, it pays to proceed very cautiously. Don't be cajoled into buying without considering all the options.

GETTING THERE

BY AIR

International Flights

The Cape Region boasts two international airports, **Los Cabos International Airport** (airport code: SJD) near San José del Cabo, and **Marquéz de León International Airport** (LAP) near La Paz. Both field flights from the U.S.—the only country with direct international flights to the Cape—as well as from mainland Mexico.

Los Cabos, a modern airport about 15 km (nine miles) north of San José, receives daily direct flights from Houston, Los Angeles, San Diego, San Francisco, Oakland, and Phoenix, with connections to many other U.S. cities. Only

one Mexican airline, Mexicana, flies to Los Cabos from mainland Mexico.

The La Paz airport primarily serves Mexican carriers, with direct flights from Los Angeles and various cities on the Mexican mainland.

For a general overview of what's available, see the "Airlines in the Cape Region" chart and "Air Routes (Direct Service)" map in this chapter. For specific information on regularly scheduled flights to the previously mentioned airports, see the La Paz and San José del Cabo "Getting There" sections.

Private Planes

The Cape Region, particularly the East Cape, is a popular destination among North American

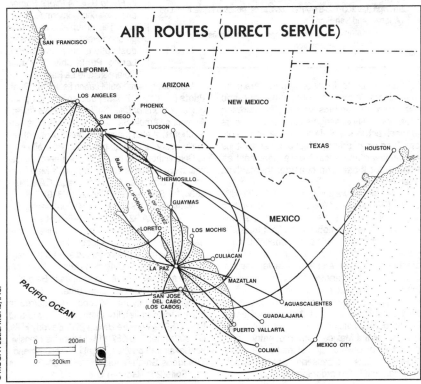

AIR ROUTES (DIRECT SERVICE)

© MOON PUBLICATIONS, INC.

AIRLINES IN THE CAPE REGION

Aero California (tel. 800-237-6225); to La Paz; nonstop flights from Culiacán, Guadalajara, Hermosillo, Loreto, Los Angeles, Los Mochis, Mazatlán, Mexico City, and Tijuana.

Aero California (tel. 800-237-6225); to Los Cabos; nonstop flights from Los Angeles and Phoenix.

Aeroméxico (tel. 800-237-6639); to La Paz; nonstop flights from Culiacán, Mexico City; connecting flights from Acapulco, Chihuahua, Ciudad Juárez, Guadalajara, León, Los Angeles, Monterrey, New York, Puerto Vallarta, Tijuana, and Tucson.

Alaska Airlines (tel. 800-426-0333); to Los Cabos; nonstop flights from Los Angeles and San Diego; connecting flights from Anchorage, Palm Springs, Phoenix, Portland, San Francisco, and Seattle.

Continental Airlines (tel. 800-525-0280); to Los Cabos; nonstop flights from Houston.

Mexicana Airlines (tel. 800-531-7921); to Los Cabos; nonstop flights from Los Angeles.

SunTrips (tel. 800-786-8747); to Los Cabos; nonstop flights from Los Angeles and San Francisco.

All routings subject to change; call the airlines for the latest information.

At the moment aviation fuel is more expensive in Mexico than in the U.S., so most pilots stop at Brown Field (San Diego County) or Calexico (Imperial County) to top off before crossing the border. Another reason to take on fuel at the border is because it's only available at or near a fraction of the bush strips; careful planning is required.

A reliable source of information for anyone considering a private flight to Baja is **Flight Log** (P.O. Box 2465, Fullerton, CA 91623, tel. 310-391-4464 or 714-521-2531). Flight Log's US$25 membership fee covers a newsletter subscription, a copy of *Flying Baja: A Pilot's Primer,* and a telephone information service. This group also organizes group "adventure" flights to Baja destinations such as Mulegé, Loreto, Punta Chivato, Punta Colorada, and La Paz.

light-aircraft pilots. Entry procedures are minimal, air traffic over the peninsula light, and nearly a dozen airstrips are available, allowing pilots and their passengers in a matter of hours to reach corners of Baja otherwise accessible only by days of driving. Most of these airstrips are unpaved and unstaffed—a significant attraction for those who consider themselves bush pilots.

Private aircraft weighing less than 12,500 kilograms (27,500 pounds) and carrying fewer than 14 passengers are subject to the same customs procedures as automobiles and light trucks. In cases where the plane's owner doesn't accompany the aircraft, flights are further restricted to single-engine craft with five or fewer passengers. Cargo is restricted to the personal belongings of pilot and passengers.

Flight plans must be filed in advance with the Mexican airport nearest the point of entry. Southbound, pilots must clear immigration and customs at the Mexican airport of entry; northbound, stops on each side of the border are required for pilots and passengers to satisfy both Mexican and U.S. border formalities.

A San Diego–area outfit calling itself **Baja Bush Pilots** (tel. 619-297-5587) publishes a 384-page guide, *Airports of Baja California and Northwest Mexico,* by Arnold Senterfitt, which contains aerial photos, sketch maps, and descriptions of virtually every landing strip in Baja. Few pilots fly to Baja without this book. Mexican aeronautical charts are available from San Diego's Map Centre (2611 University Ave., San Diego, CA 92104-2894, tel. 619-291-3630, fax 291-3840).

Nelly's Pilot Supply (1424 Continental St., San Diego, CA 92173, tel. 619-661-6099, 800-677-8046, fax 661-2597) at Brown Field near San Ysidro offers Baja guidebooks, pilot manuals, and flight supplies oriented toward the Baja pilot. Nelly's also has its own *Baja Nelly's Flight Guide to Mexico,* covering airports in Baja plus Brown Field, Calexico, and Yuma.

Planes that fly into Mexico are required to carry Mexican liability insurance. Lewis and Lewis (8929 Wilshire Blvd. #200, Beverly Hills, CA 90211, tel. 310-657-1112) offers inexpensive annual aircraft policies. Flight Log recommends Thaddeus Smith & Associates (12443 Lewis St., Suite 201, Garden Grove, CA 92640, tel.

714-938-9469). Every pilot must show a valid insurance policy at the border to clear customs. In addition, U.S. Customs requires an annual inspection for planes flying into the U.S., whether American- or foreign-owned; the inspection costs US$25 but is good for an unlimited number of entries per year.

For further information on flying regulations in Baja, contact a Mexican consulate or the Departmento de Transport Aéreo Internacional (Edificio Torre, Aeropuerto Internacional de la Ciudad de México, México, D.F.) or Flight Log.

BY LAND

Most Cape visitors arrive by air, but a significant number—many of them repeat visitors—drive all the way down the peninsula from the U.S.-Mexico border. Public transport by Mexican bus is also possible from the border.

Full details on the transpeninsular road trip—by private vehicle and by bus—are available in *Baja Handbook* (Moon Publications, 1994).

Bus to Tijuana
Greyhound Bus Lines (tel. 619-239-9171 in San Diego, 213-620-1200 in L.A.) operates 18 buses a day between 0040 and 2340 from Los Angeles to Tijuana via San Diego. The fare is US$14.50 one way (or US$29 roundtrip) from L.A., US$4 (or US$7 roundtrip) from San Diego. Buses leave from the downtown Greyhound Trailways terminals in each city and terminate at Tijuana's downtown terminal at Calle Comercio and Avenida Madero. The trip from San Diego is about 35 minutes when traffic is light; in the reverse direction it usually takes around 55 minutes. Mexican Customs doesn't make everyone get off the bus at the border; U.S. Customs does. From Los Angeles, the bus journey is about three hours. Boxed bicycles may accompany paying passengers at no extra charge.

The cheapest bus transport to the border from San Diego is the Metropolitan Transit System's city bus no. 932, which travels from the downtown area (Centre City) to San Ysidro every 30 minutes from 0540 to 2135 (0612 to 2105 weekends and holidays) for just US$1.50. Because it makes several stops along the way, the city bus takes an hour and 20 minutes to reach San Ysidro. For schedule information, call (619) 233-3004.

Buses to La Paz
See "Intercity Bus Service" in the Getting Around chapter for details on bus routes between the border and the Cape Region.

From Mainland Mexico
Transportes Norte de Sonora and **Autotransportes del Pacífico** operate long-distance express buses to Mexicali and Tijuana from various towns in Guanajuato, Nayarit, Sonora, Chihuahua, Michoacán, Jalisco, Sinaloa, Zacatecas, Querétaro, and México City.

Green Tortoise
To those who have never traveled by Green Tortoise, it's difficult to describe the experience. Imagine a sort of youth hostel on wheels, with a bit of a '60s spirit, and you'll begin to get the idea. The buses are refurbished Greyhounds with convertible beds and tables, comfortable but a bit of a tight squeeze at night when everyone's lying down. That's also when the bus travels. Great way to meet people.

Green Tortoise operates nine-day (US$249-269) and 14-day (US$349-399) trips to Baja Nov.-April that begin in San Francisco (pickups in L.A. are possible) and range as far south as La Paz. Prices are very reasonable—less than the full roundtrip airfare alone between San Francisco and La Paz—and include roundtrip transport and lodging on the bus, along with guided hikes and side trips to remote Baja beaches. The food fund adds another US$5 per day to the trip; communal meals cover about 70% of the meals—some meals are left to the participants. The trips include an optional windsurfing and sailing program available for an additional fee. All things considered, it's a travel bargain and a novel introduction to Baja.

For further information, contact Green Tortoise Adventure Travel (P.O. Box 24459, San Francisco, CA 94124, tel. 800-227-4766).

Driving
If you're contemplating the drive and have limited time, figure on making it from Tijuana to Cabo in three eight-hour days (Cataviña first night, Santa Rosalía or Mulegé second night) or 2.5 dawn-to-dusk days (Guerrero Negro first night, La Paz second night). If you stretch your itinerary to include a week's driving time each way, you'll have a safer trip and more of an op-

portunity to enjoy the sights along the way.

The red tape for driving into Baja is extremely minimal. In fact, no vehicle permits of any kind are required, no matter how long you stay in Baja, unless you plan to cross to the mainland by road (via San Luis Río Colorado) or ferry (Santa Rosalía or La Paz).

Insurance: Before driving into Baja, drivers should arrange for Mexican vehicle insurance. No matter what your own insurance company may tell you, Mexican authorities don't recognize foreign insurance policies for private vehicles in Mexico.

Vehicle insurance isn't required by law in Mexico but it's a good idea to carry a Mexican liability policy anyway; without it, a minor traffic accident can turn into a nightmare. Short-term insurance—as little as one day's worth—can be arranged at any of several agencies found in nearly every border town between the Pacific Ocean and the Gulf of Mexico. One of the most popular and least expensive is **Oscar Padilla Mexican Insurance,** which has insured North American motorists since 1951. Padilla premiums for a multiple-entry, one-year, comprehensive policy for Baja/Northwest Mexico start at around US$90 for under US$5000 in coverage and rise to US$489 for US$150,000 worth of coverage; liability only costs US$53 per year. The main office is located at 1660 Hotel Circle N., Suite 735, San Diego, CA 92108 (tel. 619-688-1776 or 800-258-8600).

Another good source of Mexican insurance is **International Gateway Insurance Brokers** (tel. 800-423-2646), with rates just a few dollars higher than Padilla's. Its "Tour Aid" service includes US$3,000 accident coverage, emergency towing to US$100 for autos or US$200 for motorhomes, emergency road service to US$100, hospital guarantee to US$500, parts service (they ship parts from the U.S. to Mexico for the cost of parts only), and legal service. Tour Aid is available for US$20 a year or is included with the insurance.

Those in a hurry might prefer **Instant Mexico Insurance Services.** IMIS sits at the last exit before the San Ysidro/Tijuana border crossing at 223 Via de San Ysidro (tel. 619-428-4714 or 800-638-0999). It's open 24 hours and in addition to insurance offers tourist cards, fishing and boating permits, maps, guidebooks, and other Baja requisites.

Several agencies in Tijuana and Ensenada offer annual policies that charge you only for those days you're actually in Mexico. Of course, this requires a trip south of the border to obtain such a policy, so you'll need a day's worth of border insurance beforehand. One agency north of the border that can arrange Mexican liability insurance on a per-use basis is **Anserv Insurance Services** (tel. 619-233-5444 or 800-262-1994 in Alta California, tel. 800-654-7504 elsewhere in the U.S. and Canada). Rates are as low as US$1 a day based on 60 days' minimum use per policy year. The ClubMex, Discover Baja, and Vagabundos del Mar travel clubs (see "Services and Information," above, for addresses and phone numbers) offer low group-insurance rates for members, ranging from US$53 a year for liability-only to US$90 a year for US$5000 worth of collision, fire, theft, and glass insurance. Add another US$15-20 for each additional US$5000 in coverage. These group policies are offered on a yearly basis only; they can't be purchased by the day, week, or month.

Some insurance companies try to justify higher premiums by claiming their policies cover repairs performed in the U.S. or Canada, pointing out that less expensive insurance is valid only for repairs in Mexico. In most cases, such an argument is irrelevant; the primary reason you need Mexican insurance is to protect yourself against liability in the event of an accident. In cases where your vehicle is disabled, repairs will have to be performed in Mexico anyway. Even if you obtain a policy that covers U.S./Canada repairs, chances are it won't cover transport of a disabled vehicle to the border. However, North American visitors driving vehicles with difficult-to-obtain parts might want to consider a policy valid for U.S./Canada repairs.

Whichever policy you choose, always make photocopies of it and keep originals and copies in separate, safe places. It's also a good idea to carry a photocopy of the first page—the "declaration" or "renewal of declaration" sheet—of your home country policy as Mexican law requires you cross the border with at least six months' worth of home-country insurance.

Temporary Vehicle Import Permits

If you're only driving in the states of Baja California and Baja California Sur, you won't need one of these. However, if you plan to take a vehicle aboard a ferry bound for the mainland from Santa Rosalía or La Paz, you will need a temporary vehicle import permit before you'll be allowed to book a ferry ticket. To receive this permit, you simply drive your vehicle to a Mexican customs office (this can be done at any official border crossing or in La Paz) and present the following: a valid state registration for the vehicle (or similar document certifying legal ownership), a driver's license, and a credit card (Visa, MasterCard, American Express, or Diner's Club) issued outside Mexico.

If you are leasing or renting the vehicle, you'll also have to present a leasing or rental contract made out to the person bringing the vehicle into Mexico. If the vehicle belongs to someone else (e.g., a friend or relative), you must present a notarized letter from the owner giving you permission to take the vehicle to Mexico. Contrary to rumor, you aren't required to present the "pink slip" or ownership certificate unless the state registration certificate is for some reason unavailable.

Once the Mexican customs officials have approved your documents, you'll proceed to a Banjército (Banco del Ejército or Military Bank) office attached to the customs facilities and your credit card account will be charged US$12 for the permit fee. This fee must be paid by credit card; cash is not accepted. If you don't have a credit card, you'll have to post a bond (1% to 2% of the vehicle's blue-book value) issued by an authorized Mexican bond company, a very time-consuming and expensive procedure. Banjército is the bank used for all Mexican customs charges; the operating hours for each module are the same as for the border crossing at which it's located.

Once the US$12 fee has been charged to your credit card, the permit is issued, with a validity period equal to that shown on your tourist card or visa. You may drive back and forth across the border—at any crossing—as many times as you wish during the permit's validity. You are supposed to surrender the permit at the border when your trip is over, however.

In the U.S., further information on temporary vehicle importation can be obtained by calling (800) 446-8277. Under a new agreement between the American Automobile Association (AAA) and the Mexican government, U.S. motorists with credit cards are able to obtain both tourist cards and auto permits from AAA offices in Texas, New Mexico, Arizona, and California.

If you're renting a car with Mexican license tags, none of the above is necessary, of course.

BY SEA

Ferry

Two passenger-vehicle ferry services currently connect La Paz with the Mexican mainland—one runs to Topolobampo, the other to Mazatlán. The passenger-vehicle service that used to operate between Cabo San Lucas and Puerto Vallarta was terminated in 1989, and a jetfoil called *Baja Express* that ran between La Paz and Topolobampo in 1992 ceased operations after less than a year due to financial difficulties.

With passenger-vehicle ferries anyone driving on the mainland can reach the Cape Region without a time-consuming trip all the way around the Sea of Cortez. Many drivers from the North American west coast use Baja ferry services as an alternative way of reaching the mainland, since it allows them to avoid Mexico 15 (or its expensive toll equivalent, Mexico 15-D) on the way to Mazatlán and points farther south.

A third ferry service is available between Santa Rosalía in central Baja and Guaymas, Sonora, on the mainland. Moon's *Baja Handbook* and *Northern Mexico Handbook* contain complete information on this route.

Fares and Classes: A few years ago the vehicle ferry system was privatized under the directorship of Grupo SEMATUR (Servicios Marítimos y Turísticos) de California, S.A., and fares are now market-priced rather than subsidized. The fares listed here were valid as of late 1994; allow for average inflation, roughly 15% per year, when making ferry plans.

Passenger fares are based on class: *salón* (bus-style reclining seats in various general seating areas), *turista* (shared bunk rooms with washbasins), and *cabina* (small, private cabins with two single berths and toilet facilities). Some ferryboats also feature an additional *especial* class with large, deluxe cabins. Vehicle fares are based on the length of the vehicle—the longer the rig, the higher the fare. All fares must be paid in pesos.

Note: Signs at all vehicle ferry ticket offices warn that passenger tickets will not be issued to pregnant women.

Reservations: Whether it was the fare increases or the reorganization of management under private auspices, ferry reservations are now much easier to make than they were several years ago. Generally speaking, if you show up at the ferry terminal one day in advance of your desired voyage, you should be able to get passenger tickets. To book vehicle passage, you must hold a valid temporary vehicle import permit (see above).

Salón seats are sold on a first-come, first-served basis; *turista* can be reserved three days or more in advance; a *cabina* can be reserved a month or more in advance. During holiday periods—especially Semana Santa (the weeks before Easter Sunday) and Christmas week, when you might want to avoid ferry service altogether—you should try to pick up your tickets at least a week or two in advance. Reservations must be confirmed 15 days before departure date for the La Paz–Mazatlán and La Paz–Topolobampo routes.

SEMATUR operates ticket offices at each of its ferry piers for advance as well as day-of-departure sales. SEMATUR also operates a city office (tel. 112-5-38-33 or 5-46-66) at Calle Guillermo Prieto and 5 de Mayo in La Paz. This office accepts pesos, U.S. dollars, Visa, and MasterCard as payment for ferry tickets; it's open for ticket sales and reservations daily 0800-1300.

A number of Mexican travel agencies are authorized to handle ticket reservations and sales in La Paz (Viajes Transpeninsulares, tel. 112-2-03-99; Viajes Perla, tel. 2-86-66; Viajes Cabo Falso, tel. 5-23-93 or 2-41-31), Los Mochis (Viajes Paotam, tel. 681-5-19-14), and Mazatlán (Turismo Coral, tel. 69-81-32-90; Marza Tours, tel. 86-08-96; Viajes Attiq, tel. 84-24-00). SEMATUR's toll-free information and reservation telephone number in Mexico is 91-800-6-96-96; this number can be dialed from the U.S. and Canada.

Topolobampo–La Paz: Topolobampo is a small port town that serves the Los Mochis area.

An interesting way to reach Baja's Cape Region from, say, Texas is to take the Chihuahua al Pacífico train via Creel and the Barrancas del Cobre ("Copper Canyon," Mexico's equivalent of the Grand Canyon) to Los Mochis, then the Topolobampo ferry to La Paz. Ferries on this route are mostly devoted to cargo, with a smaller *salón* section. During holiday periods, more passenger space is usually available.

The ferry leaves Topolobampo daily (except Sunday) at 0900 and arrives in La Paz about 1800. Eastbound, the ferry departs La Paz daily (except Tuesday) at 2000, arriving at Topolobampo around 0600. On westbound Thursday and Friday departures, all four classes are available; on Monday, Tuesday, Wednesday, and Saturday only *salón* class tickets are sold. Eastbound all four classes are available on Wednesday and Thursday; other days offer *salón* only. Passenger tickets cost US$13 *salón*, US$26.50 *turista*, US$40 *cabina*, and US$53 *especial*. Auto, truck, or van fares are US$83; with trailers to nine meters US$150 or to 17 meters US$282; buses and motorhomes US$142; motorcycles US$11.

Mazatlán–La Paz: At the moment this is the most full-service passenger-vehicle ferry available between Baja and the mainland. Each of the three craft that regularly ply this route offers *salón, turista, cabina,* and *especial* classes plus a restaurant-bar, disco, video lounge, and *cafetería*.

Ferries depart each port daily at 1500, arriving on the other side at around 0900. Westbound, all four classes are available Fri.-Wed., *salón* class only on Thursday; for eastbound departures it's *salón* only on Wednesday, all four classes the rest of the week. Passenger fares are US$20 *salón*, US$40 *turista*, US$60 *cabina*, and US$80 *especial*. For vehicles, fares are: auto, truck, or van to five meters US$136; with trailers to nine meters US$246; with trailers 15-19 meters (49-62 feet) US$465; buses and motorhomes US$231; motorcycles US$18.

GETTING AROUND

If you've driven your own vehicle down to the Cape Region, you'll have a ready set of wheels for exploring all the Cape offers. If not, cars are easily rented in La Paz, San José del Cabo, and Cabo San Lucas. You can also visit almost every town by public intercity bus.

BY BUS OR TAXI

Intercity Bus Service

Baja's reliable intercity bus transportation covers the peninsula from Tijuana to Cabo San Lucas. The longest direct ride available is the Tijuana–La Paz route (about 25-28 hours), operated by **Autotransportes Aguila** and **Tres Estrellas de Oro.** For a bus trip all the way to Cabo, you have to disembark in La Paz and change to one of the many La Paz–Cabo San Lucas buses. Central and southern Baja feature two other intercity bus companies, **ABC** (Autobuses Baja California) and **Autotransportes de La Paz.**

Special express buses with air-conditioning, onboard toilets, and reclining seats are used on long-distance trips. Buses used on shorter trips may or may not have air conditioning, but are always tolerably comfortable. The infamous "chicken buses" of southern Mexico and Central America don't exist in Baja.

Fares are moderate. A Tijuana–La Paz ticket on a *primera* or first-class bus costs about US$45; second class is half that. The La Paz–Cabo San Lucas run is around US$6.50. Reservations aren't accepted for bus travel. Buses usually depart several times daily, so you simply show up at the bus terminal around the time you want to leave. Buses ply the 35 km (22 miles) stretch between San José del Cabo and Cabo San Lucas frequently all day long for US$1.50 each way.

All the Spanish you need for riding a bus is *boleto* (ticket), the name of your destination (have a map handy just in case), and a reasonable command of spoken Spanish numbers for quoted fares (although the fare is always posted somewhere on the ticket office wall).

City Buses

La Paz has a comprehensive city bus system with fares averaging US$.10 to US$.30, payable in *pesos only*. City buses come in a variety of sizes and shapes, from 12-passenger vans *(colectivos)* to painted school buses and huge modern vessels with automatic doors. The destination or general route—typically a street name—is usually painted somewhere on the front of the bus or displayed on a marquee over the front windshield.

Intercity bus service in Baja is extensive and reliable.

Printed bus schedules are either hard to come by or nonexistent. If you can't figure out which bus to take by comparing the destination sign with a map, just ask other waiting bus passengers or, if your Spanish isn't up to that, make inquiries at the tourist office.

Route Taxis

La Paz also features *taxis de ruta,* specially licensed cars that follow set routes similar to and often paralleling the bus routes. These vehicles are usually large American station wagons that hold up to 12 passengers. Unlike city buses, you can flag them down anywhere along the route. The destination is usually painted in whitewash on the windshield but locals often distinguish the route by the taxis' two-tone color scheme. A *roja y crema* may run from the central bus station to a market on the outskirts of town while a *negro y azul* may travel from the plaza to the main shopping district. Other than the terminating points of the route at either end, there are no predetermined taxi stops; passengers must let the driver know where they want off. As on city buses, route taxi fares are the same no matter where you disembark. Usually they're only a bit higher than bus fares, around US$.25-.40.

Hire Taxis

Regular hire taxis congregate at hotels and designated taxi stands in La Paz, San José del Cabo, and Cabo San Lucas. Sometimes fares are posted at the hotel or taxi stand, but often you must ask for a fare quote. If possible, try to find out the fare from hotel staff or a friendly resident before approaching a taxi driver—you'll feel more secure about not getting ripped off. If the quoted fare doesn't match what you've been told in advance, you can negotiate or try another driver. Fortunately, most Cape taxi drivers will quote the correct fare immediately.

In smaller towns with no buses or route taxis you may sometimes find a few regular hire taxis hanging out by the town plaza. They're generally used for reaching out-of-town destinations, since anyplace without a city bus system is small enough to wander around on foot. Although the locals pay a set fare based on distance, gringos are sometimes quoted a much higher fare. Dig in and negotiate until it's reasonable. Even if you can afford the higher fare, you owe it to other foreign visitors not to encourage price-gouging.

CYCLING

Among North American cyclists, Baja California Sur is the most popular area in all of Mexico. Traffic is relatively light, the scenery is striking, and cyclists can pull over and camp just about anywhere.

Touring or mountain bike? If you plan to stay on paved highways, a touring bike would be the best choice, as it's lighter and faster than a mountain bike. On the other hand, the Cape offers so many great off-highway rides—like the the lower sierra and the Camino Rural Costero along the East Cape—that anyone who has the time and equipment should consider a mountain bike. Off-road riding requires a stronger frame, higher clearance, and wider tires.

Many interesting trail rides lie within the 386-km (240-mile) loop that circles the Cape from La Paz to Cabo San Lucas via the Sierra de La Laguna and back via Todos Santos and the west coastal plains. The lower eastern escarpment of the sierra in particular—west of Santiago and Miraflores—is fat-tire heaven, offering rides through tropical-arid thorn forests and, if you can handle steep grades and bike portage, subalpine meadows. The unpaved road network along the coast between San José and La Paz will astound even the most jaded dirt bikers as it takes them past deserted white-sand coves with coral reefs, over jagged desert peaks, and then down into lush San Juan de los Planes.

Because the Cape sun can be particularly strong when you're on paved surfaces, which both reflect and radiate heat, you may find an 1100-1500 siesta necessary no matter what time of year you ride. Don't forget to bring sunglasses and plenty of high-SPF sunscreen.

Equipment and Repairs

Whether you're riding a mountain or touring bike, you'll need the same basic essentials to handle long-distance Baja riding. If you plan to camp along the way, you'll need the usual camping and first-aid gear, selected to fit your panniers. Camping is often your only choice on transpeninsular trips, since cyclists simply can't make the mileage from hotel to hotel in central Baja. On the other hand, if you're only doing the Cape loop you can easily bike from hotel to hotel.

Helmets are particularly important; a head injury is even more serious when you're in the middle of nowhere. A helmet will also keep direct sun off the top of your skull. A rearview mirror is a must for keeping an eye on motorists coming from behind on narrow roads. A locking cable is preferable to a clunky U-lock for long-distance trips since it weighs less, although bicycle theft isn't much of a problem in Baja. The only other security you might need is a removable handlebar bag for carrying camera and valuables; you can take the bag with you when stopping at restaurants or tiendas and fill it with snacks for eating on the fly.

Water is an uppermost consideration on overnight trips. No matter what the time of year, cyclists should carry four one-liter bottles of water per day. The one-liter bottles used for cycling are more puncture-resistant than water containers designed for camping. Punctures are always a concern in Baja because of all the trees and plants bearing spines.

Tires: The puncture threat means you should outfit your bike with heavy-duty tires and tubes. Bring along two or three spare tubes, one spare tire, a tire gauge, and a complete tire repair kit. You should also carry duct tape and moleskin—or commercial plastic booting—to use as booting material against sidewall cuts caused by sharp rocks or cactus.

Rack: Check nuts and bolts daily and retighten as necessary. Applying Locktite should lessen the need for retightening—carry a small supply along with extra nuts and bolts. Baling wire can be used for improvised repairs; carry two or three meters along with wirecutters.

Other Repairs: Bike shops can be found in La Paz and Cabo San Lucas. Although the Mexicans who run these shops can sometimes perform miraculous repairs using nothing resembling a bike's original parts, it's safer to come prepared with spares, especially for parts that aren't easily jury-rigged. At a minimum, carry a spare freewheel, a rear derailleur, and all the wrenches and screwdrivers necessary to work on your bike. If in addition you bring along several extra spokes, cables, and a spare chain, you'll be ready for just about any repair scenario.

Bicycle Transport
All airlines that fly to the Cape Region will allow you to check bikes as luggage as long as they're boxed. Bus lines will transport bikes of paying passengers in bus luggage compartments for no additional cost, but again bikes should be boxed. For return trips from Baja, you should be able to pick up a box from bicycle shops in La Paz or Cabo San Lucas, or build your own from discarded cardboard boxes.

Guided Bicycle Trips
If you're unsure of your off-road cycling skills, you might want to tackle the Cape with an experienced cycle guide. **Backroads** (1616 Fifth St., Berkeley, CA 94710-1740, tel. 510-527-1555, fax 527-1444) organizes fully outfitted, six- and seven-day mountain-biking trips in the Cape Region for US$798-1095.

DRIVING IN THE CAPE REGION

Before the 1973 completion of the Transpeninsular Highway (Mexico 1), only hardened off-road vehicles with equally sturdy drivers ever made it to the Cape. Nowadays, with paved Mexico 1 and paved Mexico 19 forming a loop around the Cape, the region is perfectly safe for ordinary folks driving ordinary passenger cars, as long as they employ a little ordinary common sense. For the adventurer, there remain miles of unpaved roads that will take you as far from civilization as anyone would care to go. Such off-highway digressions are perfect for those who might agree with one of naturalist Joseph Krutch's famous Baja fiats:

Baja California is a wonderful example of how much bad roads can do for a country. Bad roads act as filters. They separate those who are sufficiently appreciative of what lies beyond the blacktop to be willing to undergo mild inconvenience from that much larger number of travelers which is not willing. The rougher the road, the finer the filter.

Cape Roads
Two paved national highways grace the Cape Region: Mexico 1 (the Transpeninsular, from Tijuana to Cabo San Lucas) and Mexico 19 (between Cabo San Lucas and San Pedro, via Todos Santos). The only paved state highway is

CAPE DISTANCES

SECTION	DISTANCE	TIME
La Paz to San Pedro via Mexico 1	24 km (15 miles)	30 minutes
San Pedro to Todos Santos via Mexico 19	51 km (32 miles)	45 minutes
Todos Santos to Cabo San Lucas via Mexico 19	72 km (45 miles)	1 hour, 30 minutes
La Paz to Cabo San Lucas via Mexico 1 and Mexico 19	147 km (92 miles)	2 hours
La Paz to Los Barriles via Mexico 1	105 km (65 miles)	1 hour, 45 minutes
Los Barriles to San José del Cabo via Mexico 1	81 km (50 miles)	1 hour, 30 minutes
San José del Cabo to Cabo San Lucas via Mexico 1	34 km (21 miles)	30 minutes
La Paz to Cabo San Lucas via Mexico 1	221 km (137 miles)	2 hours, 30 minutes

BCS 286, the relatively short blacktop running between La Paz and San Juan de los Planes. These three highways enable drivers to visit all of the Cape's major towns and resort areas, including La Paz, Los Barriles, Santiago, San José del Cabo, the Corridor (the 28-km/18-mile stretch between San José and Cabo San Lucas), Cabo San Lucas, and Todos Santos.

An as yet unnamed paved road leads east of Mexico 1 at Las Cuevas to a point about six miles south of the East Cape community of La Ribera. Eventually, according to local authorities, this paved road will extend all the way down the East Cape to San José. Meanwhile a decent, unpaved, fair-weather road parallels this coastline.

The lower eastern escarpment of the Sierra de La Laguna is bisected by Mexico 1, which offers the only paved-road access to the mountains.

Off-Highway Travel

The Cape's unpaved roads vary considerably, from rutted jeep tracks to elevated, graded, gravel boulevards. The trouble with the graded unpaved roads is that they tend to degenerate quickly between gradings into washboard surfaces impossible to drive at anything but very low speeds (8-16 kph/5-10 mph)—unless you want to risk crushed vertebrae and a dropped transmission.

The effect of these unpaved roads on you and your vehicle depends a lot on what you're driving. Some off-highway Baja navigators drive pickups with customized shocks and suspension that enable a driver to float over the worst washboard surfaces. Other drivers—like many of the local residents who can't afford heavy-duty, customized rigs—learn to drive slowly and appreciate the scenery.

The best unpaved roads are probably those that have evolved more or less naturally, with little or no grading. When the weather's dry, some of these roads ride better than the Transpeninsular. Of course, unpaved roads may sometimes start out quite nicely but get increasingly worse with each passing mile, to the point where even the most intrepid explorers are forced to turn around. At other times, a road will suddenly improve after a long stretch of cavernous potholes and caved-in sides. Weather is a big determining factor; even the best ungraded, unpaved roads are often impassable during or following a hard rain.

How do you know when to turn around? There's always an element of risk when driving down a dirt road for the first—or even the hundredth—time, but it helps to ask around before embarking on a road that doesn't see much traffic. A good road map can also assist with such decisions. The AAA map (see "Services and Information," above) classifies unpaved roads into four categories: gravel, graded, dirt, and poor. The annotated ITM map uses a similar but more specific fourfold system: gravel, graded, unimproved dirt, and vehicular track. Although neither of these maps is entirely up to date or 100% accurate, using one or both in conjunction with local input will greatly improve your decision-making. A topographical map could be of considerable value to a 4WD navigator as well, since sometimes it's the steep canyon grades that call up defeat.

Even with the best planning there's always the possibility of getting stuck in muddy or sandy areas. Anyone engaging in serious off-highway driving should carry along a sturdy shovel for digging out mired wheels. Another handy trick for negotiating soft ground is to let the air out of your tires to a pressure of around 12-15 psi. This really works, but you should also carry along a 12-volt air compressor, one that will plug into the cigarette lighter, for pumping the tires back up after you're on firm ground again.

Driving Precautions

The first rule of Baja driving, no matter what kind of road you're on, is *never* take the road for granted. Any highway in Baja, including the Transpeninsular, can serve up 100 meters of smooth, seamless blacktop followed immediately by 100 meters of contiguous potholes or large patches of missing asphalt. A cow, horse, or burro could be right around the next curve, or

road to Candelaria

a large dog can leap out in front of your vehicle just as you fasten your eyes on a turkey vulture drying its wings on top of a tall *cardón*.

The speed limits set by the Mexican government—80 km per hour (48 mph) on most highways—are very reasonable for Baja's highway conditions. Obey them and you'll be much safer than if you try to keep the speedometer needle in the spot you're accustomed to. Wandering livestock, relatively narrow highway widths (6-8 meters/19-25 feet max), and inconsistent highway maintenance mean you simply can't drive at U.S.-Canada speeds.

Many Cape roadways suffer from a conspicuous lack of shoulders. This doesn't mean you won't find any places to pull off—gravel turnouts appear fairly regularly, and in many areas you can drive directly onto the roadside from the highway. It just means you can't count on a safe margin in an emergency situation. At the very least, an emergency turnout will raise a lot of rocks and dirt—small dangers in themselves—and in some spots, like in the sierras around San Antonio, leaving the highway can launch you and your vehicle into a thousand-foot freefall. Guardrails are often flimsy or nonexistent.

Yet another reason not to take the road for granted is the number of sometimes unmarked blind curves and blind hilltops frequently encountered. Never assume a clear path around a curve or over a hilltop—potential obstructions include an oblivious 18-wheeler or bus passing in the opposite direction, wandering livestock, rockslides, or road washouts. To be on the safe side, keep toward the outside edge of your own lane. Commercial truck drivers in Mexico roar down the road as if they're exempt from all speed limits, almost always flying at least 40 kph over the posted limit.

Rule number two is never drive the highways at night. Except along the Corridor portion of Mexico 1 between San José and Cabo San Lucas, highways have no lighting. In addition, reflectors and even painted lines are absent from many highway sections; even if no other vehicles besides your own were on the road at night, you could easily overshoot an unexpected curve. Add to this the fact that many poorly maintained local vehicles have nonfunctioning headlights, taillights, or brakelights, and it should be obvious that trying to make highway miles after sundown is crazy. Some locals do it, but they're used to local conditions and know the roads relatively well. Still, a high proportion of car accidents in Baja—around 80% according to insurance companies—occur at night.

Specific Hazards: When you see road signs marked Vado or Zona De Vados, slow down. The word *vado* is most often translated as "dip," but in Baja it usually means more than a slight depression in the road—it's any place where the road intersects an *arroyo,* or dry stream wash. The danger lies not only in the sudden grade drop but in the potential for running into a recently accumulated body of water. Some *vados* feature measuring sticks marked in meters; when water is present, you'll know roughly how deep it is. If you come to a *vado* full of water with no measuring stick, get out of your vehicle and measure the depth yourself using a mesquite branch or other suitable object. *Vados* aren't always signposted, so stay alert—they appear even on relatively flat terrain.

In towns, pueblos, *ejidos,* or anywhere else people live in Mexico, you'll encounter *topes* (speed bumps). Often unpainted and unsignposted, they can really sneak up on you. Some *topes* are real industrial-strength tire-poppers, so always take it very slow when traversing them. You'll notice that Mexican drivers seem to have more respect for speed bumps than for stop signs or traffic lights.

Highway Signs

One of the pleasures of driving in the Cape Region is the relative absence of signs cluttering the roadside. Billboards, in fact, are virtually nonexistent. The Mexican government does have a system of highway signs, however, based on common international sign conventions followed throughout most of the world; these can be very helpful as long as you know what they mean. Most display self-explanatory symbols (e.g., a silhouette of a man holding a shovel means "men working").

Cautionary sign captions are especially helpful, including Curva Peligrosa (Dangerous Curve), Despacio (Slow), and Zona de Vados (Dip Zone). Other common highway signs include: Desviación (Detour), No Tire Basura (Don't Throw Trash), Conserve Su Derecha (Keep to the Right), Concida Cambio de Luces (Dim Your Lights), No Rebase (No Passing), and No Hay Paso (Road Closed).

Along the highways as well as on many secondary roads, you can measure driving progress with the assistance of regularly spaced kilometer markers, usually black lettering on a reflective white background.

ROADSIDE RELIGION

Along Baja's roadways you'll occasionally see small roadside crosses—sometimes in clusters—or shrines. Often placed at fatal accident sites, each cross marks a soul's point of departure from this world. Larger shrines containing Christ or Virgin figures are erected to confer blessings or protection on passing motorists. These vary from simple enclosures made of vegetable oil cans to elaborate sculptural designs.

In the brush beside the track there was a little heap of light, and as we came closer to it we saw a rough wooden cross lighted indirectly. The cross-arm was bound to the staff with a thong, and the whole cross seemed to glow, alone in the darkness. When we came close we saw that a kerosene can stood on the ground and that in it was a candle which threw its feeble light upward on the cross. And our companion told us how a man had come from a fishing boat, sick and weak and tired. He tried to get home, but at this spot he fell down and died. And his family put the little cross and the candle there to mark the place. And eventually they would put up a stronger cross. It seems good to mark and to remember for a little while the place where a man died. This is his one whole lonely act in all his life. In every other thing, even in his birth, he is bound close to others, but the moment of his dying is his own.

—JOHN STEINBECK,
THE LOG FROM THE SEA OF CORTEZ

(previous page) Los Islotes;
(this page, top) Caleta El Candelero, Isla Espíritu Santo; (this page, bottom) Bahía Chileno

HIGHWAY SIGNS

STOP

RAILROAD CROSSING

CEDA EL PASO
YIELD RIGHT OF WAY

TOPES
SPEED BUMPS

CIRCULACION
ONE WAY

DOBLE CIRCULACION
TWO WAY

E
PARKING

NO
NO PARKING

DIP (across arroyo)

DIP (across arroyo)

PARADA
BUS STOP

CONSERVE SU DERECHA
KEEP TO THE RIGHT

© MOON PUBLICATIONS, INC.

If you're having tire trouble, look for home-made signs reading "Llantera," which indicate tire repair shops.

Traffic Offenses

Although Mexican traffic police don't go out of their way to persecute foreign drivers, it may seem that way when you're the foreigner who's stopped. The more cautiously you drive, the less likely you'll inadvertently transgress local traffic codes. This would seem like obvious advice, but for some reason many visiting motorists in Baja drive as if they thought there were no traffic laws in Mexico. Most of these people seem to have California plates.

If you're stopped by a *tránsito* (traffic cop), the first rule is to behave in a patient, civil manner. The officer might then let you off with just a warning. If the officer decides to make a case of it, you'll be asked to proceed to the nearest police post or station, where a fine will be assessed and collected. This is a perfectly legal request. But if the cop suggests or even hints at being paid on the spot, you're being hit up for *la mordida,* the minor bribe.

In Baja, requests for *mordida* from foreigners—for traffic offenses, at least—have become increasingly rare, and the government is making admirable progress toward stamping the practice out altogether. If confronted with such a situation, you have two choices. Mexico's Attorney General for the Protection of Tourists recommends you insist on going to the nearest station to pay the fine, and that as you pay you request a receipt. Such a request may result in all charges being dropped. If you don't feel like taking the time for a trip to the station, you can choose to negotiate the "fine" on the spot. Doing so, however, won't contribute to the shrinking of the *mordida* phenomenon.

Speeding citations are rare, but when they are issued the fine is usally equivalent to one day's Mexican minimum wage (US$5) per each kilometer per hour above the speed limit you were estimated to be driving. Aside from speeding on Mexico 1-D, driving the wrong direction on one-way streets and running stop signs are the two most common traffic violations among foreign drivers in Baja. Some intersections may display no vertical stop ("Alto") signs at all, only broad stripes painted on the pavement indicating where vehicles are supposed to stop. The best practice is to assume you're supposed to stop at every single intersection in the city, which is pretty close to the truth. A sign reading "Cuatro Altos" means the intersection is a four-way stop.

Insurance

It's very important to carry a Mexican liability-insurance policy on your vehicle while driving in Baja. In case of an accident, such a policy could keep you from going to jail. For details on Mexican insurance, see "Driving" under "Getting There," above.

Fuel

The only automotive fuel commercially available in Mexico is sold at government-owned PEMEX stations. Unlike many parts of Mexico, PEMEX stations are fairly plentiful in the Cape Region, though it's always best to top off your tank whenever it reaches the half-empty mark and there's a PEMEX station at hand.

Three kinds of fuel are available: leaded ("Nova"), a higher-octane unleaded ("Magna Sin"), and diesel. All three are priced by PEMEX according to standard rates and shouldn't vary from station to station. All three fuels are somewhat more expensive in Mexico than their equivalents in the U.S. or Canada; the price is usually marked in pesos on the pump. The pump readout often accommodates only three or four digits, so a N$25 (25,000-peso) sale may appear as 2500, 25.00, 250, or 25.0. Although this may sound like it could be a problem when paying up, it's not once you're used to seeing it.

It helps to get out of your vehicle to keep an eye on the pumping procedures. If you're confused by the pump readout, currency conversion, or price per liter, carry a handheld calculator to make sure it all adds up; a calculator held in clear view will deter most potential grifters. As new pumps are added they will be calibrated to read in nuevo pesos to conform to the new currency system instituted in January 1992. This should make calculations considerably easier.

As of 1995, official government fuel prices per liter were US$.20 for Magna Sin (about US$.76 per gallon), US$.19 for Nova (US$.72/gallon), and US$.14 for diesel (US$.53/gallon). Since PEMEX is government-owned, you don't see the week-to-week price fluctuations common in countries where oil companies are privately owned and rates influenced by small changes in international oil prices. But fuel prices calculated in dollars may fluctuate as the peso continues its roller-coaster ride.

Rumors about the quality of PEMEX fuels sometimes suggest an extra fuel filter or additive are necessary. This may have been the case 10 or more years ago, but nowadays PEMEX fuel seems to perform well with all types of vehicles.

The main problem with PEMEX fuel remains the availability of Magna Sin; not all stations carry unleaded gasoline. In a pinch, you can use leaded gas in vehicles intended for unleaded without an appreciative difference in performance. Adding a can of octane booster to each tankful seems to help. You shouldn't be forced to burn more than a tankful of leaded here and there, if at all, since most PEMEX stations in the Cape Region dispense unleaded; in fact, Magna Sin is now more widely available in Baja than in mainland Mexico. All gas stations mentioned in this guidebook generally stock Magna Sin unless otherwise noted.

Other availability-related problems include long lines at small-town stations and the occasional selling out of one or all types of fuel at a particular station. To notify customers, the hose will usually be draped over the top of a pump when it's empty.

Liquefied Petroleum Gas (LPG): LPG fuel is available in most towns. The price per liter is about the same as for Magna Sin when bought for vehicular purposes. LPG sold for heating and cooking is subsidized and costs less than in the U.S. or Canada. The difficulty is finding it. Look for signs reading *butano*.

Oil: Motor oil is widely available at *tiendas* and PEMEX stations throughout the Cape. If your vehicle takes anything lower (thinner) than 30-weight, however, you'd better bring along your own; most places stock only 30- or 40-weight oil.

Parts and Repairs
Good auto shops and mechanics are available in La Paz, San José, and Cabo San Lucas. Elsewhere, if you have a breakdown, it's either do it yourself or rely on the mercy of passing drivers. In areas where you can find a mechanic, the following makes can usually be serviced: Chevrolet, Dodge, Ford, Nissan, Toyota, and Volkswagen. For anything else, you should carry spare filters, plugs, points, hoses, belts, and gaskets—even for the shortest of trips.

Green Angels
The Secretaría de Turismo operates a fleet of green trucks called Angeles Verdes ("Green Angels") that patrol Baja's highways and offer professional assistance to anyone with automotive problems. Each truck carries a first-aid kit, a shortwave radio, gasoline, and a variety of common auto parts. They're usually staffed by two uniformed employees, one of whom may speak some English. The drivers will perform minor repairs for the cost of the parts and can provide towing for distances up to 24 km (15 miles). If they can't remedy the problem or tow your vehicle to a nearby mechanic, they'll give you a lift and/or arrange for other assistance.

The trucks supposedly patrol assigned highway sections at least twice a day; the author's experience is that the Green Angels are much more commonly seen in south central Baja, where they're most needed due to the longer distances between towns.

Trailers, Motorhomes, Campers, and Vans
The Cape is a popular destination for RVers. Not only are there plenty of campgrounds with services, but you can pull off the road and camp just about anywhere outside the cities, with few restrictions. Those restrictions that do exist are largely physical; numerous places simply can't accommodate a wide trailer or motorhome because of narrow roadways, steep grades, or sharp curves. Even the Transpeninsular is tight in some places. In fact, you shouldn't even attempt a Baja trip in any rig wider than three meters (nine feet).

Probably the rig most suited to Baja travel is a well-equipped camper or van. With a bed, two five-gallon water containers, a small propane stove and refrigerator, and a portable toilet, you can travel just as independently as someone driving a 40-foot motorhome. Add a deep-cycle RV battery under the hood and you can run a variety of electrical appliances for at least a week without turning over your engine. For extra power, mount a solar panel on top of the cab or camper.

More complete information on managing the entire transpeninsular journey by RV is available in Moon's *Baja Handbook*.

automotive angels

Car Rental

You can rent cars in La Paz, San José del Cabo, and Cabo San Lucas. At many agencies, various Volkswagen models are all that's available; most rental places charge daily rates of around US$25-29 for a VW bug, US$46 for a Golf, and US$55-63 for a van (called "Combi" in Mexico). Nissan Tsuru II (equivalent to the Sentra) models cost around US$55 a day, a Jeep Wrangler around US$65. In general, rental rates are lowest from the airport agencies at Los Cabos International Airport, highest in downtown Cabo San Lucas or anywhere in La Paz; at the latter locations, fees ranging from US$.18 to US$.30 per kilometer are often added to the above rates. All rates include Mexican liability insurance, but not collision damage. For added collision coverage, figure an extra US$6-10 a day.

If you're planning on driving long distances, you can save money by arranging a flat rate with no kilometer costs. If you can rent by the week, the savings increase considerably. The best deal in Baja on an advance reservation is from Avis International: a new, made-in-Mexico VW bug (no air-conditioning or radio) for US$174 per week, with unlimited free kilometers. You might be able to negotiate an equally low rate on a walk-up basis from any of the agencies at Los Cabos International.

The VW bug, incidentally, is one of the best non-4WD passenger cars for Baja travel since its engine is air-cooled (no radiator boil-overs) and over the drive wheels (good traction), and its road clearance is a bit above average.

Motorcycles

The entire Cape Region is excellent motorcycle country. The winding sierra roads are especially challenging and since traffic is generally light you can really let it rip. Another advantage of motorcycle travel is that if your bike gets mired in soft ground, you can almost always extricate it without assistance.

As with automotive travel in Baja, pre-departure planning is important. You should be able to carry enough gear in two panniers and a backpack (tied down on the rear) for a trip all the way down the peninsula.

Good motorcycle mechanics are hard to find in the Cape Region—you should be entirely self-reliant to make this trip safely and successfully. Besides the usual camping and first-aid gear, bikers should carry all tools needed for routine maintenance, spare brake shoes, a tire repair kit, spare levers, an extra battery, a clutch cable, spare light bulbs, a four-liter reserve gas can, and a spare helmet visor.

The same driving precautions that apply to four-wheel driving should be followed by bikers as well. Special care should be taken when negotiating blind curves since buses and trucks in Mexico aren't used to seeing motorcycles on the highway. As with bicycle touring, motorcyclists may find that an 1100-1500 siesta is necessary to avoid the sun's worst rays.

BOB RACE

LA PAZ

Ensconced along the largest bay on Baja's Sea of Cortez coast, La Paz is a city of 180,000 noted for its attractive *malecón* (waterfront) backed by swaying palms and pastel-colored buildings, its splendid sunsets, easygoing pace, and near-perfect climate, and its proximity to uncrowded beaches and pristine islands. Many Baja travelers—Mexicans and gringos alike—cite La Paz ("Peace") as their favorite city on the Baja California peninsula; a few even go as far as to pronounce it their favorite in all of Mexico. Nowadays Cabo San Lucas, 221 km (137 miles) farther south, receives more attention than La Paz in the North American press, which suits La Paz fans fine since it means fewer tourists.

Of all the cities in Baja, La Paz is steeped most profoundly in mainland Mexico's traditions; it was the first major European settlement on the peninsula, and has long been a haven for Mexicans dissatisfied with life on the mainland. Many *paceños* (La Paz natives) are descendants of mainlanders who sailed to La Paz to avoid the political turmoil of 19th and early 20th century mainland Mexico. And it's not uncommon to meet more recent Mexican emigrés who have resettled in La Paz after becoming fed up with modern-day political machinations in Mexico City, Guadalajara, or Monterrey. *Paceños* are proud of the many ways in which their city lives up to its name.

The city offers a wide variety of accommodations and dining venues, well-stocked supermarkets, marine supplies, and a ferry terminal with daily departures for Mazatlán and Topolobampo across the Sea of Cortez. Minor traffic snarls are common in *el centro,* the downtown area, but can be avoided by using Blvd. Forjadores, a wide avenue skirting the southern section of the city. Along the bay, La Paz remains much as John Steinbeck described it in 1941:

> *La Paz grew in fascination as we approached. The square, iron-shuttered colonial houses stood up right in back of the beach with rows of beautiful trees in front of them. It is a lovely place. There is a broad promenade along the water lined with benches, named for dead residents of the city, where one may rest oneself. . . . [A] cloud of delight hangs over the distant city from the time when it was the great pearl center of the world. . . . Guaymas is busier, they say, and Mazatlán gayer, but La Paz is antigua.*

CLIMATE AND TRAVEL SEASONS

The most pleasant time of year to visit La Paz is mid-October through May, when days are balmy, evenings cool. In January, maximum temperatures average 22° C (72° F), minimum temperatures 14° C (57° F). Temperatures for July average 35° C (96° F) maximum, 24° C (75° F) minimum. Hot summer afternoons are moderated somewhat by the daily arrival of the *coromuel,* a strong onshore breeze that bedevils yachties trying to escape the harbor but cools down the rest of the population.

La Paz and vicinity average only around 15 cm (six inches) of rainfall per year, over half generally falling during the Aug.-Sept. *chubasco* (tropical storm) season. Full-fledged *chubascos* with gale-force winds actually reach La Paz only every couple of years. Most of the time the area receives only the remote influences of storms centered along mainland Mexico's lower west coast.

Over the last few years, February has been La Paz's peak tourist month. Even then you should be able to find a hotel room easily since the average hotel occupancy rate runs 45-50% all year round.

HISTORY

Early Spanish Contact

When the Spanish first landed on the shores of Bahía de La Paz in the early 16th century, the area was inhabited by migrating bands of Guaicura and Pericú Indians, who allegedly called their homeland "Airapi." Hunters and gatherers, these Indian groups lived mostly on shellfish, small game, and wild plants. As artifacts on display at La Paz's Museum of Anthropology demonstrate, they were also skilled weavers and potters.

Into this peaceful scene entered the first European, a Basque mutineer named Fortún Jiménez who commandeered the Spanish ship *Concepción* on the Sea of Cortez in 1533. Originally under the command of Capt. Diego Becerra, the *Concepción* had been sent to explore the sea on behalf of Spain's most infamous conquistador, Hernán Cortés. After executing the captain, Jiménez landed at Bahía de La Paz in early 1534, where he and 22 of his crew were killed by Indians while filling their water casks at a spring. The survivors sailed the *Concepción* back to the mainland, where the ship was immediately captured by Cortés's New Spain rival, Nuño Guzmán. At least one crew member man-

Hernán Cortés

aged to escape and returned to Cortés with descriptions of a huge, beautiful bay filled with pearl-oyster beds.

Cortés himself landed at the northeast end of the bay, probably at Pichilingue near the present ferry terminal, in May 1535, naming it Puerto de Santa Cruz. Cortés was able to effect a truce with local Indians, but his attempt at establishing a permanent Spanish colony lasted only through 1538, when the colonists were forced to abandon the peninsula due to supply problems.

The next Spaniard to visit the bay was famed explorer Sebastián Vizcaíno, who landed here in 1596 during his long voyage around the peninsula's perimeter and north to California. Because he and his crew were treated so well by the Pericús, Vizcaíno named the bay Bahía de La Paz ("Bay of Peace").

Pirates and Colonization

Baja California remained free of Spaniards another 100 years before the successful establishment of a mission colony at Loreto to the north. By this time, English and Dutch pirates were plundering New Spain's Manila galleons as they returned from the Orient weighted down with gold, silks, and spices. One of the free-

ENGLISH PIRATES ON THE SEA OF CORTEZ

Sir Francis Drake, Thomas Cavendish, William Dampier, Woodes Rogers, Thomas Dover, and other English privateers left behind a colorful Baja legacy. In spite of Spain's repeated attempts to colonize the peninsula, throughout the Spanish colonial period the pirates probably gained more wealth in the Californias than the Spanish themselves. For 250 years they plagued the Manila galleons off the coast of the Californias, finding the bays and lagoons of Baja's Cape Region perfect hiding places from which to launch attacks on treasure-laden ships.

In La Paz, using their knowledge of the strong breeze that blows into the harbor every summer afternoon, the pirates attacked Spanish galleons while the vessels were effectively trapped in the bay. Four centuries after the first Manila-Acapulco voyages, this afternoon wind is still known as *El Coromuel*, named for the Puritan Cromwells—father and son—who ruled successively as Lord Protectors of England.

The Disappearance of the *Desire*

The most notorious of the Pacific privateers was Sir Thomas Cavendish, whose greatest feat of plunder occurred at Cabo San Lucas in 1587. There his two English vessels, *Desire* and *Content*, commandeered the Spanish galleon *Santa Ana* following a protracted sea battle. After looting the *Santa Ana's* cargo holds and setting its crew and passengers ashore, Cavendish set fire to the ship. The Spanish crew later retrieved the burned hulk, and restored the galleon for a return to Acapulco.

The plundered treasure, meanwhile, was divided between the *Desire* and *Content*. The ships set sail for England immediately, but during the first night of their triumphant voyage, the *Desire* disappeared. Cavendish reported in England that the captain and crew of the *Desire* must have scuttled the ship on a nearby island and disappeared with the loot. Neither the wreckage of the vessel nor the treasure was ever discovered; some historians speculate that at least part of the missing wealth remains buried near the Cape.

A Visit by Robinson Crusoe

In 1709, famed corsair Woodes Rogers landed in La Paz after rescuing a seaman who'd been marooned five years on a deserted island off Chile's coast. The rescued man was Alexander Selkirk, whose island sojourn became the inspiration for Daniel Defoe's *Robinson Crusoe,* published in 1719. Selkirk was aboard Rogers's *Dover* when the crew captured the Spanish galleon *Nuestra Señora de la Encarnación y el Desengaño* off Cabo San Lucas in 1709; he served as sailing master on the ship's return voyage to England the following year.

---

booters' favorite staging areas was Bahía de La Paz, which contained numerous *ensenadas* (coves) and inlets perfect for concealing their swift corsairs. When Spanish crews put in for water, the pirates raided the galleons, often using their knowledge of strong afternoon winds to attack the ships when they were effectively pinned down.

Increased pirate activity in the late 17th and early 18th centuries created the need for a Spanish presence in the Cape Region. In 1719 Padre Juan de Ugarte, then President of the Missions, contracted a master shipbuilder to construct a ship for the specific purpose of exploring the Sea of Cortez coast and improving supply lines with the mainland. The barque *El Triunfo de la Cruz,* assembled of native Baja hardwood at the Mulegé estuary, made its first sailing to Bahía de La Paz in 1720 with Ugarte and Padre Jaime Bravo as passengers.

Ugarte and Bravo founded the mission community of Nuestra Señora del Pilar de La Paz at the current city site. The padres didn't find the Pericús to be as friendly this time around; Scottish padre William (Guillermo) Gordon replaced Bravo in 1728 as chief missionary but the mission lasted only until 1749, when it was abandoned following a series of Indian rebellions. By this time, another mission, along with a presidio, had been founded farther south at San José del Cabo—a better location for monitoring pirate activity.

La Paz Reborn

Left with European diseases and without the support of the mission system, the local Pericú population dwindled quickly. By 1811, Mexican ranchers and *pescadores* who had settled along the Bahía de La Paz started their own town, which they named La Paz after the bay. After

THE PEARLS OF LA PAZ

Pearls develop from sand grains or other small particles that manage to get between an oyster's mantle and its shell. The oyster secretes a substance that cushions it from the irritation of the particle—if the grain moves freely during the secretion buildup, the pearl is more or less spherical; if it stays in one place or is embedded in the shell, it becomes a "baroque" pearl. Even when an oyster doesn't contain a pearl, the interior of the shell is valued for its rainbow luster, known as mother-of-pearl. Only particular mollusk varieties within the family Pteridae, found only in certain coastal areas off East Asia, Panama, and Baja California, can form pearls.

Pearl gathering in the New World goes back at least 7,000 years. When the Spanish found Indians along the Sea of Cortez coast wearing pearls and pearl shells as hair ornaments in the early 16th century, they quickly added pearls to the list of exploitable resources in Mexico. Finding the source of the luminescent, milky-white spheres—oysterbeds—became a priority of marine expeditions off Mexico's west coast.

After a Spanish mutineer reported the presence of pearls in Bahía de la Paz in 1533, harvesting them became one of Cortés's primary interests in exploring Baja's lower Sea of Cortez coast. Between 1535, when Cortés finally managed to establish a temporary settlement at Bahía de la Paz, and 1697, when Jesuit padres began missionizing the Baja peninsula, untold thousands of pearls were harvested. The Jesuits, however, strongly objected to any secular exploitation of the peninsula, preferring to keep Baja within the domain of the Church. Hence during the mission period (1697-1768), pearling was restricted to sporadic illegal harvests; still, many pearls found their way to Europe, where they encrusted the robes of bishops and Spanish royalty.

In the mid-19th century, following the secularization of Baja missions, the Baja pearl industry was revived by armadores (entrepreneurs) who hired Yaqui divers from Sonora to scour the shallow bays, coves,

and island shores between Mulegé and La Paz. The invention of diving suits in 1874 revolutionized pearling by allowing divers access to deeper waters. By 1889 the world pearling industry was dominated by Compañía Perlífera de Baja California, based in La Paz.

Intensive harvesting rapidly depleted the oysterbeds, and between 1936 and 1941 most of the remaining pearl oysters were wiped out by an unknown disease. Many La Paz residents today believe the disease was somehow introduced by the Japanese to eliminate Mexican competition in the pearl industry, but it's more likely the disease simply took advantage of an already weakened population.

The mystique of La Paz pearls continued long after the industry's demise. John Steinbeck based his novella *The Pearl* on a famous pearl story he heard while visiting La Paz in 1941. According to one version of the original legend, hundreds of *paceño* pearlers used to gather at Punta El Mechudo (north of La Paz near Isla San José) each year to celebrate the final dive of the pearling season. The last pearl taken at this event was traditionally dedicated to the Virgin of Guadalupe, Mexico's national patron saint. During one such gathering, so the story goes, the final dive had already been concluded when a pearler entered the sea. When reminded that the pearl "para la Virgen" had already been harvested, he answered "I'm not going for the Virgin's pearl, this one's going to be for the devil!" and promptly dove.

The diver never surfaced nor was his body ever found. Thinking that Satan had taken him at his word, other pearl divers declared the area off the point taboo and never harvested pearls there again. Today they still say that if you dive to the bottom you'll find the blasphemous pearler's ghost sitting in the sand, his hair and beard grown very long, holding a huge pearl in his green hands. The nearby headland is named El Mechudo, "The Hair-Disheveled," for the ghost.

Loreto was severely damaged during a hurricane in 1829, the capital of Baja California Sur was moved to burgeoning La Paz, where it's remained ever since.

During the Mexican-American War (1846-48), the city was occupied by U.S. troops; the soldiers left when the Californias were split by the 1848 Treaty of Hidalgo. But American General

William Walker, dissatisfied with the treaty and hoping to add another slaveholder state to counter the growing U.S. abolitionist movement, formed his own army of "New York Volunteers" and retook La Paz in November 1853. Proclaiming himself "President of the Republic of Sonora," Walker lasted only six months before he and his mercenaries fled upon hearing that the U.S. wouldn't back their claims, and that the Mexican Army was on its way to La Paz from the mainland. Walker was tried in the U.S. for violation of neutrality laws, fined, and two years later was executed by the Nicaraguan army for attempting a similar takeover of Nicaragua.

La Paz remained a sleepy tropic seaport, known only for pearl harvesting, until it was declared a duty-free port following WW II. After an epizootic disease killed off the entire pearl-oyster population, the city's economic focus turned to farming and trade with the mainland. During Mexico's postwar economic boom, mainland Mexicans crossed the Sea of Cortez in

droves to buy imported merchandise; enchanted by La Paz itself, many stayed on.

In the '50s, La Paz became well-known as a fishing resort and was visited by a succession of North American literati and Hollywood celebrities, thus initiating the city's reputation as an international vacation spot. But until the Transpeninsular Highway was completed in 1973, the city remained for the most part a tourist destination for mainland Mexicans.

Statehood was bestowed on the Territory of Baja California Sur in 1974, with La Paz as its capital. Linked by air, ferry, and highway to mainland Mexico and the U.S., the city has

grown considerably yet managed to maintain its tropic port ambience. As a tourist destination, it remains more Mexican than foreign—of the 129,000 leisure visitors who came to La Paz in 1993, Mexican nationals outnumbered foreigners three to one.

SIGHTS

Museo de Antropología

Baja California history buffs shouldn't miss this well-designed museum (tel. 2-01-62) at calles 5 de Mayo and Altamirano. Three floors of exhibits cover Cape Region anthropology from prehistoric to colonial and modern times. On display are fossils, minerals, Indian artifacts, dioramas of Indian and colonial life, and maps of rock-painting sites throughout central and southern Baja. Labels are in Spanish only.

A small gift section offers Spanish-language books in the fields of anthropology, archaeology, and art history, including such hard-to-find volumes as the *Catalogo Nacional de los Monumentos Históricos Inmuebles de Baja California Sur,* an inventory of historical buildings in the *municipios* of San Antonio, San José del Cabo, Santiago, and Todos Santos.

Next to the museum is an older building that has served La Paz as a hospital, prison, and, more recently, the **Biblioteca Justo Sierra,** a children's library. Behind the library is an ethnobotanical garden dedicated to the exhibition of medicinal herbs and sculpture from the region.

Admission to the museum is free; daily hours are 0900-1800.

Plaza Constitución (Jardín Velazco)

La Paz's tidy downtown *zócalo* is enclosed by calles 5 de Mayo, Revolución de 1910, Madero, and Av. Independencia. At the southwest side of the plaza is the post-missionary-style **Catedral de Nuestra Señora de La Paz,** which replaced La Paz's original mission church in 1861. Although the twin-towered brick edifice looms over the plaza, it lacks the charm of earlier Jesuit missions.

At the northwest side of Plaza Constitución, opposite the cathedral, is the **Biblioteca de História de las Californias** (Library of Californias' History). Housed in the 1880s-era former Casa de Gobierno ("Government House"), the library is filled with Spanish- and English-language volumes on Alta and Baja California history. The general public is welcome to use the library for research purposes; it's open Mon.-Fri. 0900-1800, Saturday 0900-1500. For library information, call 2-01-62.

La Unidad Cultural Profesor Jesus Castro Agundez

This cultural center at calles Farías and Legaspy, in the area of the city known as Cuatro Molinos ("Four Windmills"), includes an art gallery, community art school, and city archives. Also part of the complex is the **Teatro de la Ciudad** (City Theater, tel. 5-02-07), a 1,500-seat performing-arts facility that hosts musical,

Catedral de Nuestra Señora de La Paz

theatrical, and dance performances throughout the year.

The four windmills next to the theater pay tribute to a time when La Paz relied on windmills to pump water and generate electricity. Another symbolic display in the complex is **La Rotunda de los Sudcalifornianos Illustres,** a circle of sculpted figures representing Baja California Sur's most illustrious heroes. Most of the historical personages honored at the Rotunda are former teachers or soldiers.

Malecón

One of the city's major attractions is the pleasant five-km *malecón,* a seawall promenade along the northwest side of Paseo Alvaro Obregón extending from Calle 5 de Febrero (Mexico 1 south) to the northeastern city limits. Palm-shaded benches are conveniently situated at intervals along the walkway for watching sailboats and yachts coming in and out of the bay. The best time of day for people-watching is around sunset, when the city begins cooling off, the sun dyes the waterfront orange, and *paceños* take to the *malecón* for an evening stroll. Snacks and cold beverages are available at several palapa bars along the way.

Universities

As Baja California Sur's educational center, La Paz supports a large number of schools at the primary, secondary, and tertiary levels. Most prominent among the latter is the **Universidad Autonomía de Baja California Sur** ("University of South Baja California") on Blvd. Forjadores, with an enrollment of around 2,000 and reputable programs in agriculture, engineering, and business. The **Instituto Tecnológico de La Paz** ("Technological Institute of La Paz"), also on Blvd. Forjadores, enrolls approximately 3,000 students and is primarily known for its commercial-fishing department.

ACCOMMODATIONS

La Paz offers the most varied—and least expensive—selection of places to stay of any place in the Cape Region. Room rates in La Paz are quite reasonable for a seaside area, with most rooms falling in the US$25-65 range.

Bahía de La Paz

Downtown Hotels and Motels

In 1941 Max Miller, author of *Land Where Time Stands Still,* wrote:

> *The Hotel Perla is the place to stay. For an American there's no other choice unless he wishes to rent a room with a Mexican family or live in a Mexican board-and-rooming house. . . . [T]he Mexicans themselves expect an American to stay at the Hotel Perla. If he doesn't stay there when he first arrives, then he's in La Paz for no good reason. He's under suspicion.*

Time hasn't stood still in La Paz, but the *malecón's* **Hotel Perla** (tel. 112-2-07-77, fax 5-53-63) is still one of the most popular hotels in the city. The Perla's location at Paseo Obregón 1570, right at the center of the *malecón* and just a few steps away from the main shopping district, cannot be beat. La Terraza, the hotel's downstairs, open-air restaurant, remains a favorite gathering place for La Paz residents and visitors alike, while the upstairs nightclub draws a mostly local crowd. Clean rooms with high ceilings, a/c, TV, and telephones cost US$42 s, US$48 d, US$52 t. Indoor parking is available on the ground floor.

Another *malecón* standby around since the dawn of La Paz's tourist industry is **Cabañas de los Arcos** (tel. 2-27-44; in U.S./Canada, tel. 714-476-5555 or 800-347-2252) at Paseo Obregón 498. Built in 1954, during La Paz's heyday as an exotic playground for Hollywood celebrities, Los Arcos became the city's first center for sportfishing trips. *Paceño*-owned Los Arcos has a newer hotel section which, like the *cabañas,* faces the *malecón* and bay. Rooms in the *cabaña* section cost US$75 s, US$77 d, US$81 t; each comes with a/c and a fireplace; a newer wing behind the *cabaña* section and swimming pool contains junior suites, which rent at the same daily rates but don't have fireplaces.

In the much larger Hotel Los Arcos section less than a 100 meters down the street from the original *cabañas,* a/c rooms go for US$75 s, US$77 d, US$85 t (add US$3 for bay-view rooms, US$10 for suites). In addition to a pool,

this section offers a coffeeshop, restaurant, bar, gift shop, sauna rooms, massage service, and sportfishing tours.

Around the corner at Calle Allende 36-B, just a half block from the *malecón,* the **Hotel Mediterrané** (tel./fax 5-11-95) features large, airy rooms in a small, two-story white stucco building for US$35-40.

Budget Hotels: Around the corner from Hotel Los Arcos at Calle Bravo 110, the friendly **Hotel Lorimar** (tel. 5-38-22) is a long-time budget favorite with European, Canadian, and American visitors. Clean, well-maintained rooms with a/c cost US$19-21. The proprietors speak English but are happy to let you practice your Spanish.

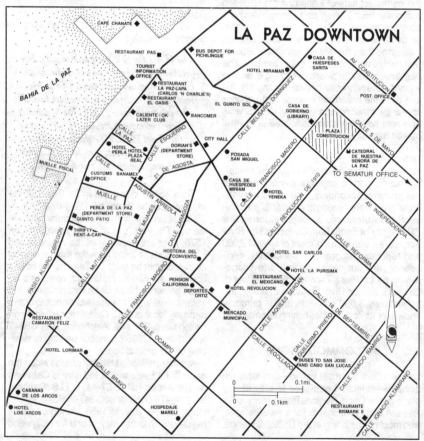

They can also arrange kayaking and diving trips through local outfitters. The Lorimar is just a block off the *malecón;* guests often meet in the cozy upstairs dining area to exchange travel tips.

The **Hotel Plaza Real** (Callejón La Paz and Calle Esquerro, tel. 2-93-33), a block off the *malecón* and right around the corner from the Hotel Perla, is a three-story, modern hotel popular with middle-class Mexican businesspeople. Rooms with a/c and TV cost just US$23.30 s, US$26.66 d; the downstairs coffeeshop is a popular local spot for breakfast and Mexican food.

Also a block off Paseo Obregón at calles 5 de Mayo and Domínguez, the three-story, apartment-style **Hotel Miramar** (tel. 2-06-72, fax 2-06-82) features clean, modern rooms with a/c, minibar, and TV w/VCR for US$29 s, US$33 d. Some rooms come with balconies and bay views at no extra charge, so be sure to ask what's available.

Hotel Pekin (Paseo Obregón at Calle Guadalupe Victoria, tel. 5-09-95), facing the *malecón* and attached to the Chinese restaurant of similar name (Nuevo Pekin), offers clean rooms with a/c and TV (some with bay views) for US$21 s, US$23 d, US$24 t in a two-story building with vaguely Asian architecture.

Farther downtown, a good budget choice is the well-kept and efficient **Hotel La Purísima** (calles 16 de Septiembre and Serdán, tel. 2-34-44), a three-story business hotel near the municipal market featuring rooms with a/c, fan, and TV for US$18 s, US$21 d, or US$27 t. The service is excellent, and gringos are rarely seen in this hotel so it's a good choice for visitors looking to immerse themselves in urban Mexican culture. **Hotel San Carlos** (calles Revolución and 16 de Septiembre, tel. 2-04-44), on the second floor of a large corner building on the same block, has dingy but cheap rooms with balcony and fan for US$11-15 s/d.

Around the corner from the San Carlos on calles Revolución and Degollado, the **Hotel Revolución** (formerly Hotel María Cristina, tel. 5-80-22) occupies two stories of a three-story orange structure. Sixteen adequate rooms (but not as good as the Purísima's) cost US$17 s plus US$3 for each additional guest.

Although in name it's a hotel, **Hotel Yeneka** (tel. 5-46-88), at Calle Madero 1520 between Calle 16 de Septiembre and Av. Independencia, looks and operates much like a guesthouse.

Long known on the backpacker circuit, the Yeneka is built around a courtyard filled with tropical vegetation, a rusting Model T, and an amazing collection of other items giving the appearance of an ongoing garage sale. Almost everything is painted green; a pet monkey swings from tree to tree. Basic, scruffy rooms cost US$15 s, US$18 d, US$22 t.

North of Downtown: Club El Moro (tel. 2-40-84), a whitewashed, Moorish-style place on landscaped grounds at Km 2, La Paz–Pichilingue Rd., offers one-bedroom suites for US$60, two-bedroom suites for US$80. Weekly and monthly rates are available on request; many repeat visitors opt for the long-term rates. On the grounds are a pool, restaurant, and bar. Buses heading downtown pass the hotel frequently during daylight hours; otherwise it's a two-km (1.2-mile) walk to the town center.

Just a bit farther north at Km 2.5 on the La Paz–Pichilingue Rd., the palm-encircled **Hotel Palmira** (tel. 2-40-00, fax 5-39-59; tel. 800-336-5454 in the U.S./Canada) caters to conventioneers as well as vacationers with its large meeting rooms, banquet halls, and quiet garden rooms for US$66 s/d. Other facilities include a pool, tennis court, restaurant, bar, and disco.

In a residential neighborhood in the northwest part of the city, the friendly **Hotel Gardenias** (Calle Serdán Norte 520, tel. 2-30-88) is a large, modern, two-story hotel built around a pleasant courtyard and pool. Clean rooms with a/c and TV cost a reasonable US$26 s, US$30 d; it's popular among Mexicans. Although the hotel's street address reads Calle Serdán, the entrance is actually on Guerrero between Serdán and Gmo. Prieto.

Bayfront Hotels: You'll pay a bit more to stay next to the water rather than along the *malecón.* None of the bayfront hotels are within easy walking distance of the *malecón* or downtown La Paz although taxis are always available.

Opposite the Hotel Palmira adjacent to the plush Marina Palmira at Km 2.5, La Paz–Pichilingue Rd., stands the new **Suites Marinas** (tel. 2-62-54, fax 2-62-77), where US$75 s/d buys a night in a well-designed studio suite with kitchenette. For US$120 you can have a more spacious master suite with attached kitchenette, and for US$150 the kitchenette is separated by a wall. Facilities include new tennis courts, a large pool, and an outdoor bar; boat slips are available nearby for visiting yachties.

La Concha Beach Resort (tel. 2-65-44, fax 2-62-18; tel. 213-943-1369 or 800-999-2252 in the U.S./Canada) sits on Playa Caimancito (near Km 5, La Paz–Pichilingue Rd.), the city's closest swimming beach. Well-kept rooms, all with bay views, cost US$77 s/d, US$128 suite. The hotel, once a training center for the now-defunct El Presidente chain, features a pool, restaurant, bar, gift shop, and aquatic sports center.

South of the *malecón* and Marina de La Paz, **Hotel La Posada de Engelbert** (A.P. 152, La Paz, BCS or P.O. Box 397, Bonita, CA 91908, tel. 2-04-11, fax 2-06-63; tel. 619-421-2062 in the U.S./Canada) at calles Nuevo Reforma and Playa Sur offers 25 Mediterranean-style suites and cottages for US$55 and US$75 respectively; the cottages come with fireplaces. A pool, tennis court, restaurant, and bar fill out the compound. In recent years the Posada has been more or less taken over by visiting American college students participating in short-term marine biology programs. The facilities have suffered accordingly; the programs, so say rumors, will be discontinued after 1995. With a little renovation, the Posada, originally built by pop crooner Engelbert Humperdinck for the Hollywood set, could regain its faded glamour.

Farther south, at Km 5.5 on the highway that eventually curves north toward Ciudad Constitución, construction on the new **Villas del Mar** is nearing completion; this bayside hotel should be open by the time you read this. The Mediterranean-style suites stand opposite the state tourism office next to the site where the long-awaited FIDEPAZ marina has yet to appear. Rates will probably run in the US$80-140 range.

The **Vista Coral** condos at Marina de La Paz, past the southwest end of the *malecón*, are open now and some units may be available for rent by the night. Inquire at the friendly Marina de La Paz office (tel. 2-16-46, fax 5-59-00).

Highway Hotels: If you're blazing through town on your way south to Los Cabos, two hotels along the highway here make convenient stops. **Motel Villa del Sol** (tel. 5-78-20, fax 2-19-20) offers a newish motel-style complex with rooms encircling a parking area near Km 5 on Mexico 1. Rooms with a/c, bath, and TV cost US$25-28.

Farther in toward the city at Km 3.5, well-kept

Motel Calafia (tel. 2-58-22) has similarly arranged rooms but slightly higher rates.

Pensiones, Casas de Huéspedes, Hosterías

La Paz offers more budget accommodations—*pensiones, hosterías,* and *casas de huéspedes*—than any other city in Baja. Doubles with a private shower are readily available for under US$7.20—a steal by modern Baja standards. Long-term visitors can often get a room for around US$3.60 a night. On the downside, accommodations in this price range come without air-conditioning, a significant inconvenience July-Oct., and since most of them are located in the downtown commercial zone they can be a bit noisy, with open windows and vented doors contributing to the influx of noise. But if you can do without air-conditioned silence, these are fairly clean, friendly, safe, and economical choices.

As old as the city itself is **Pensión California** (tel. 2-28-96), housed in a former 18th-century convent at Calle Degollado 209 between Revolución de 1910 and Madero. The interior courtyard of this rambling Moorish-style building contains a tropical garden of sorts and a display of old and new paintings. Some by local artists, some from the mainland—including an 18th-century Silva in a 17th-century baroque frame—they lend a distinctly Bohemian feel to the atmosphere. Rooms are very basic—little more than a few worn sticks of furniture, fan, and hot shower—but reasonably comfortable. Rates are US$5.10 s or d, US$6 for up to four people, or US$7.80 for a room sleeping six. Discounts are possible for long-term stays. Practically every backpacker on the Baja circuit turns up at the Pensión California at one time or another.

Just around the corner at Calle Madero 85 is another former convent, operated by the same family that owns Pensión California. At the **Hostería del Convento** (tel. 2-35-08) room rates are roughly the same as at Pensión California, although the place is more funky and faded. Even less expensive is **Casa de Huéspedes Miriam** (tel. 2-11-04), Calle 16 de Septiembre 202 between calles Domínguez and Madero, where a cell-like but clean room costs US$4 s, US$4.80 d. The water supply can be iffy.

One of the better values in this category is the **Posada San Miguel** (tel. 2-18-02), Calle Domínguez 1510, a colorful colonial-style inn built around a tiled courtyard. The basic, almost bare rooms have fairly hard beds and cost US$6 s, US$7.20 d, but the courtyard entrance is a major plus. You may want to borrow a broom to sweep your room before settling in.

Seemingly undiscovered by gringo budget travelers (a surprise since it's such good value), the family-run **Casa de Huéspedes Sarita** (tel. 2-42-74) at Calle Domínguez 254 offers a cozy front balcony sitting area and clean rooms with attached bath for just US$4.55 s, US$5.40 d, N$8.15 t.

At **Hospedaje Mareli** (tel. 2-15-17), Calle Serdán Sur 283, you can rent adequate a/c rooms by the month for US$99.60-108. When there's a vacant room you can sometimes get a daily rate of US$9.

La Paz has an official youth hostel at the **Instituto de la Juventud y el Deporte** (tel. 2-46-15), a sports complex on Blvd. Forjadores (Km 3) near Calle 5 de Febrero. A bed in a gender-segregated, four-person dorm costs US$3.60 a night, US$3 with a Hostelling International card; all ages welcome. Facilities include pool, gym, cafeteria, and volleyball and basketball courts. The hostel is distant from the town center and more expensive for two people than a budget hotel, considering the cost per bed. But it's closer to the main bus terminal than the downtown lodgings.

Camping and RV Parks

Free beach camping is available north of the Pichilingue ferry terminal at Playa Pichilingue, Playa Balandra (Puerto Balandra), Playa El Tecolote, and Playa El Coyote. Except for El Tecolote, none of these beaches have sources of fresh water; all supplies must be brought from La Paz. Two restaurants at El Tecolote supply food and beverages.

In and around La Paz are seven trailer parks—six at the western edge of the city off Mexico 1 and one to the south off BCS 286. Starting from the west (Mexico 1 south), the first is **City View RV Park** (tel. 5-77-99, ext. 188) in the settlement of El Centenario, about 15 km northwest of La Paz on the edge of Ensenada de La Paz. Here you'll find 35 well-kept pull-through sites with full hookups for US$9 a night, plus 20 tent/camper sites with sewer only for US$6. Flush toilets and hot showers are available, and attached to the park is a family-

run *fábrica* where souvenir figurines are made. A bit farther south off the same highway is **Los Aripez (Oasis de Aripez) RV Park** (tel. 5-10-25), just before Km 15 in El Centenario. Popular among Transpeninsular voyagers making short La Paz stopovers, full-hookup slots here cost US$10 for two, plus US$2 per each additional person; facilities include showers, flush toilets, laundry, restaurant, bar, and access to the shallow Ensenada de La Paz (also known as Ensenada de Aripez), where you can launch boats. No tentsites are available.

Next along Mexico 1, five km (three miles) west of the city near the state tourism office, is the well-maintained **Casa Blanca RV Park** (tel. 2-00-09, fax 5-11-42), where over 40 full-hookup sites are US$10 a night for two persons plus US$2 for each additional guest. The facility includes showers, flush toilets, a pool, tennis courts, spa, laundry, restaurant, and a small market.

A kilometer closer to the city center and surrounded by a high wall, **El Cardón Trailer Park** (mailing address: A.P. 104, La Paz, BCS; tel. 2-00-78, fax 2-12-61), at Km 4 features 80 shaded well-tended palapa sites with full hookups for US$8-10 for two, plus US$1 each additional person; tents permitted. El Cardón offers a pool, groceries, flush toilets, hot showers, dump station, and laundry.

Just before the defunct Hotel Gran Baja, off Av. Abasolo (Mexico 1) near the VW dealer, is the upscale, 95-slot **La Paz Trailer Park** (A.P. 482, La Paz, BCS; tel. 5-06-02 or 2-87-87, fax 2-99-38). Full hookups or tentsites cost US$13-15 for two plus US$3 per additional guest; facilities include showers, flush toilets, potable tap water, pool, jacuzzi, tennis court, laundry, restaurant, and bar.

A bit farther east toward the city center, off Calle Nayarit on the bay, is the smallish, palm-planted **Aquamarina RV Park** (mailing address: A.P. 133, La Paz, BCS; tel. 2-37-61). A favorite among boaters and divers, Aquamarina features its own marina, complete with boat ramp, storage facilities, and air for scuba tanks, plus showers, flush toilets, potable tap water, pool, and laundry facilities. Full-hookup sites are US$14 for two, plus US$2 per additional guest.

The little-frequented **El Carrizal RV Park** (tel. 2-33-24) boasts 168 RV spaces about two km south of La Paz off BCS 286, the state highway to San Juan de los Planes. Full hookups at El Carrizal cost US$9; facilities include a large pool, showers, flush toilets, and laundry.

FOOD

La Paz offers dining venues for all tastes and budgets, and as might be expected in a coastal city, the seafood selection is particularly good. In the afternoons, the downtown area centered around the *malecón* and Calle 16 de Septiembre features a number of street vendors serving fish tacos and *cocteles*. One of the best stands for fish, shrimp, and clam tacos is **Super Tacos de Baja California Hmnos. González,** at the corner of Arreola and Esquerro opposite the Banamex.

During the daytime, the cluster of *loncherías* in the **Mercado Municipal Francisco E. Madero,** Revolución and Degollado, serves as a very inexpensive grazing spot for *antojitos* and *comidas corridas.*

Seafood

$$-$$$ **Restaurant Bermejo,** Los Arcos Hotel, Paseo Obregón: One of the better hotel restaurants, enhanced by its location overlooking the *malecón*—ask for a window table—and presided over by an Italian chef. The menu features mostly seafood, steak, and pasta; open daily noon-midnight.

$$ **Bismark II** (tel. 2-48-54), Degollado and Altamirano: A casual, family-run restaurant specializing in lobster, abalone, and *carne asada.* All meals start with the restaurant's unique *totopos*—instead of chips, they're fried whole tortillas—served with a smooth guacamole. The *ceviche* is also very good. Open daily 0800-2200.

$$ **Restaurant Camarón Feliz** ("Happy Shrimp") (tel. 2-90-11), Obregón and Bravo: A small, cutesy seafood place on a traffic island near Hotel Los Arcos; very good *cocteles de camarones* (shrimp cocktails). Open daily noon to midnight.

$$ **Restaurant La Mar y Peña** (tel. 2-99-49), Calle 16 de Septiembre between Isabel la Católica and Albañez: Operated by local seafood wholesalers Mar y Peña, this small airconditioned restaurant has a terrific menu that features practically everything that swims, including several *machaca* (dried and shredded) versions. Credit cards accepted. Open daily for lunch and dinner.

$$-$$ **Palapa Adriana** (tel. 2-83-29), on the beach at Paseo Obregón, between 5 de Mayo and Constitución: One of the *malecón*'s original palapa restaurant-bars, with fresh seafood, *carnes rajas* (grilled steak), and Mexican standards. Funky and very reasonable. Open weekdays 1000-2300, weekends till 0200 (with occasional live music).

Mexican

$ **Café San Francisco** (tel. 2-74-79), next to the Hotel Mediterrané on Calle Allende: Very inexpensive but tasty Mexican meals served in a clean, bright, airy cafe. Open 0730-2100 daily; comida corrida available 1300-1600.

$$ **El Oasis Restaurant and Bar** (tel. 5-76-66), Paseo Obregón between 16 de Septiembre and La Paz, next to Carlos'n Charlie's: A sidewalk patio restaurant with a large menu of seafood, steaks, and Mexican dishes. It has taken a year or so for this place to gain a clientele, but it seems to be working out. Open daily 1100-0100; live music in the evening.

$$-$$$ **La Paz-Lapa de Carlos'n Charlie's** (tel. 2-92-90), Obregón and 16 de Septiembre: One of the latest installments in the Grupo Anderson chain that includes Squid Roe and Señor Frog's. The atmosphere is much more low-key than the usual Anderson enterprise, with the interior decor featuring old Mexican movie posters. The menu emphasizes good Mexican fare, seafood (try the *ceviche paceño*), and steak dishes; much of the clientele is Mexican. The terrace tables usually catch a breeze. Open daily noon-midnight.

Restaurant El Mexicano (tel. 2-89-65), Calle Serdán at 16 de Septiembre: Menudo, seafood, and Mexican standards; nothing special but it's cheap. Open daily 0730-2200.

$$ **PAS,** Paseo Obregón and Av. Independencia, on the *malecón:* This relatively new, upmarket spot on the waterfront features a wide selection of well-prepared Mexican standards for breakfast, lunch, and dinner.

$$-$$ **Restaurant Plaza Real** (tel. 2-93-33), Hotel Plaza Real, Calle Esquerro and Callejón La Paz: A very popular coffee-shop-style place with moderate prices, efficient service, and good Mexican food. Open Sun.-Fri. 0700-2300, Saturday 0700-1300.

$ **Super Pollo,** three locations: Calle 5 de

Febrero at Gómez Farías; 5 de Mayo at Gómez Farías; and Blvd. Forjadores at Loreto. A good, economic choice for *pollo asado al carbón estilo Sinaloa* (Sinaloa-style grilled chicken), sold with tortillas and salsa. Eat in or take out; open daily 1100-2200.

American

$-$$ The Dock Café, Marina de La Paz, at the bay end of Calle Legaspy: Visiting and resident yachties crowd this small, casual diner for fried chicken, hamburgers, fish and chips, bagels, salads, steaks, American breakfasts, and homemade apple pie. A blues trio occasionally performs in the evening. Open Sun.-Tues. and Thursday 0800-2200, Fri.-Sat. 0800-midnight; closed Wednesday.

$$ El Molino Steak House (tel. 2-61-91), Legaspy and Topete, near Marina de La Paz: Although the house specialty is American-style steaks, this large palapa restaurant is very popular with local residents. It's open Mon.-Sat. 1100-2300; most nights there are mariachis.

$$ Restaurant Grill Campestre (tel. 5-63-34), opposite the FIDE-PAZ building on Mexico 1 North, near Km 5.5: Popular with gringos and Mexicans alike for barbecued ribs, Cobb salad, and other American specialties. Open daily for lunch and dinner.

International

$-$$ Comidalandia, Av. Ortega near Juárez: This peculiar two-vendor complex mates **La Vaca Loca Texas BBQ** with **Ichiban Comida Japonesa,** both good. Open Mon.-Thurs. 1100-1600, Fri.-Sat. 11-1800.

$$-$$$ El Taste (tel. 2-81-21), Paseo Obregón at Juárez: An old-timer featuring steaks, Mexican, and seafood, patronized by a mostly tourist and expat clientele. Open daily for breakfast, lunch, and dinner.

$-$$ Restaurant Dragón (tel. 2-13-72), 16 de Septiembre and Esquerro: La Paz's tiny Chinatown harbors five or six Chinese restaurants,

of which this is generally considered the best. Basically Cantonese, with Mexican influences; open daily 1300-2130.

$-$$ Romeo, Calle Madero near Legaspy: Many La Paz expats claim this place makes the best pizza in the city. Open Tues.-Sun. 1100-2200.

$$ La Fabula Pizza, four locations: Paseo Obregón at Av. Independencia; 5 de Mayo 310 (opposite the cathedral); La Católica at Allende; Blvd. Kino 2530. American-style pizza and Italian specialties; open daily for lunch and dinner.

$$ La Terraza (tel. 2-07-77), Paseo Obregón 1570: This outdoor cafe beneath the Hotel Perla has an extensive menu of seafood, Mexican, steak, and Italian dishes that attracts a steady crowd of both tourists and locals. It's the best place in town for people-watching, and the food is reasonably priced and reasonably tasty.

$ Los Arcos Cafetería, Hotel Los Arcos, Paseo Obregón: A self-service coffeeshop with inexpensive Mexican and international dishes; open daily 0600-2200.

$$ Trattoria La Pazta (tel. 5-11-95), Hotel Mediterrané, Calle Allende, a half block off the *malecón:* A Swiss-run restaurant specializing in pasta and other Italian specialties. Open Wed.-Mon. 1300-2200.

Vegetarian

$ El Quinto Sol (tel. 2-16-92), Domínguez and Av. Independencia: This natural food/vegetarian store includes a cafe section serving *tortas, comida corrida,* pastries, salads, granola, fruit and vegetable juices, and yogurt.

$ Tonantzin, 5 de Mayo and Serdán (one block east of the plaza): Whole wheat bread, yogurt, *licuados,* juices, and herbs. Open Mon.-Sat. 0800-2000, Sunday 0800-1500.

Ice Cream

Downtown La Paz is packed with tiendas selling *nieves* (Mexican-style ice cream) and *paletas* (popsicles). **Mr. Yeti** is a big one, with branches on Paseo Obregón and Calle Madero. A personal favorite is tiny **La Fuente** on Paseo Obregón between Degollado and Muelle; though small, this place offers an amazing variety of flavors (including *capirotada,* a Mexican bread pudding), as well as *licuados, aguas frescas,* and all-fruit *paletas.*

For American-style ice cream, head for the reliable **Helados Bing** at Esquerro and La Paz (opposite Hotel Plaza Real).

Cafes
$-$$ **Café Chanate:** Although it's only open in late afternoon and evening (Mon.-Thurs. 1600-2200, Fri.-Sat. 1800-midnight), this cozy cafe on the waterfront opposite Calle 16 de Septiembre serves the best coffee and espresso drinks in the city. Pastries, cakes, and Mexican snacks such as *molletes* (beans and melted cheese on an open *bolillo*) are available. See "Entertainment and Events," following, for details on evening events.

Groceries
The **Mercado Municipal Francisco E. Madero,** at Revolución and Degollado, houses a collection of vendor stalls purveying fresh fish, meats, fruit, vegetables, and baked goods at nonsubsidized free-market prices. Since prices are usually posted, no bargaining is necessary. Opposite the market on Degollado, **Panaficadora Lilia** sells fresh *bolillos* and *pan dulce* daily. Nearby at the corner of Revolución and Bravo is a *tortillería.* Other traditional markets include **Mercado Bravo** (at Bravo and G. Prieto) and **Mercado Abastos** (Blvd. Las Garzas).

La Paz features several supermarkets, including the large **CCC** (Centro Comercial California) outlets at Av. Abasolo and Colima and at La Católica and Bravo. Another good supermarket chain is **Supermercados Aramburo,** with branches at Madero and Hidalgo, 16 de Septiembre and Altamirano, and Durango 130 Sur (between Ocampo and Degollado). These carry American-brand packaged foods as well as Mexican products, but prices are about twice what you'd usually pay elsewhere in town. The government-subsidized **ISSSTE Tienda** at calles Altamirano and Bravo has the best grocery prices in the city, although the selection varies according to what ISSSTE purchased cheaply that week. The **Tienda Militar** ("Mili-

tary Store") on Calle 5 de Mayo at Padre Kino offers a larger selection than ISSSTE Tienda and is almost as inexpensive.

Two stores in La Paz specialize in natural foods. **El Quinto Sol** (Domínguez at Av. Independencia) offers natural juices, wheat gluten, soybean meat substitutes that include soybean chorizo, whole wheat flour, herbs, yogurt, and ice cream, as well as a few ready-to-eat items like tortas and salads. **Los Girasoles** (Calle Revolución between Hidalgo and Morelos, tel. 2-55-90) operates a bakery and sells veggie sandwiches, yogurt, granola, vitamins, and various whole grains. **Tonantzin,** at 5 de Mayo and Serdán, is similar.

At the other end of the nutritional spectrum are two *dulcerías* (sweet shops) on the corner of calles Ocampo and Serdán. **Dulcería Perla** has a complete selection of traditional and modern Mexican sweets, while **Dulcería Aladino** on the opposite corner specializes in candy-filled piñatas, including a few in the shape of Teenage Mutant Ninja Turtles.

Fresh-roasted coffee beans can be purchased at the outlets of **Cafe Combate** (Calle 5 de Mayo 1056) or **Cafe El Marino** (Gmo. Prieto at 16 de Septiembre).

ENTERTAINMENT AND EVENTS

Bars and Cafes
The **Bar Pelicanos,** overlooking the *malecón* in Hotel Los Arcos, is a large, sedate watering hole popular among tourists and Old Hands. It's worth at least one visit to peruse the old photos along the back wall; subjects include a motley array of unnamed vaqueros and revolutionaries, as well as Pancho Villa, General Blackjack Pershing, President Dwight Eisenhower, Emiliano Zapata, and Clark Gable posing with a marlin. The bar is open daily 1000-0100.

On the beach side of Paseo Obregón, three blocks west of Hotel Los Arcos, is the casual and sometimes lively palapa bar **La Caleta,** where the clientele is predominantly local. Yachties from the nearby Marina de La Paz occasionally arrive via Zodiac rafts, which they park on the adjacent beach. Drinks are reasonably priced, with a 1600-2000 happy hour, and there's usually live guitar music after 2100 or so.

At the laid-back **Club Intimo,** in a historic building at Calle Esquerro 60 near the Hotel Perla, patrons listen to recorded jazz or play chess over quiet drinks (cocktails, beer, wine, coffee, and juices) and complimentary peanuts. On weekends the patio behind the bar hosts live bands. Club Intimo is open nightly 1900-0300. Just up the street on the same block, the slightly seedy **Peña Folklórico Misión** features live *norteña* bands nightly.

Café Chanate, opposite Calle 16 de Septiembre on the *malecón,* is a comfortable, European-style coffeehouse with espresso drinks, light meals, and recorded music—mostly jazz, blues, and Latin from the 1920s-'40s. On Wednesday evenings the cafe's "Cine Club" screens art films on video, while the second and fourth Thursdays of each month are reserved for opera videos; on Friday nights there's usually live music. A few books on Baja are available for sale. The Chanate is open Mon.-Thurs. 1600-2200, Fri.-Sat. 1800-midnight.

Billiards

Casino Club Billiares, opposite the southwest corner of the plaza (Calle Revolución de 1910 at Av. Independencia), has some of the nicest playing tables and cues I've seen in Mexico. To play costs US$4 per hour—rather upscale by Mexican standards. Local shooters are happy to demonstrate the two most popular games: *billiares,* a three-ball game played on a table with no pockets; and "pool," wherein ball numbers 3-15 are lined up along the edge of the table and sunk in order (the person who sinks the 15 wins). Some players are also familiar with eight-ball as played in the United States.

Discos and Nightclubs

Living up to its laid-back reputation, La Paz isn't big on discos. The most popular dance spot among young *paceños* is the two-story **5to Patio** (Quinto Patio) on Paseo Obregón between Muelle and Degollado; often the music is live. A slightly older crowd frequents **Varitas** on Av. Independencia downtown, near El Quinto Sol natural foods store and Plaza Constitución, for dancing to recorded and live music. A mixed tourist/local crowd patronizes the Hotel Palmira's disco, **El Rollo,** which features international and Latin recordings and occasional live music. The **Cabaña Club,** at the Hotel Perla, usually offers live *norteña* and *tecnobanda* music and attracts a more local crowd.

Bullfights and *Charreadas*

The municipal stadium at Constitución and Verdad occasionally hosts *corridas de toros* in the late winter months, usually Feb.-March.

Paceños are more active in *charrería* than in bullfighting, and you can attend *charreadas* (Mexican-style rodeos) at **Lienzo Charro Guadalupano,** located just south of the city on the west side of Mexico 1 on the way to San Pedro. For information on the latest schedules for *charreadas* and *corridas de toro,* contact the state tourism office between Km 6 and 5 on Mexico 1 (Av. Abasolo) opposite the FIDEPAZ Marina; tel. 2-11-99, fax 2-77-22. A *gran charreada* is usually held to celebrate Cinco de Mayo (5 May).

Events

La Paz's biggest annual celebration is **Carnaval,** held for six days before Ash Wednesday in mid-February. Carnaval is also held in the Mexican cities of Mazatlán, Ensenada, and Veracruz, but

Carnaval connoisseurs claim La Paz's is the best—perhaps because the city's *malecón* makes a perfect parade route.

As at all Mexican Carnavals, the festival begins with the Quema de Mal Humor, or "Burning of Bad Humor," in which an effigy representing an unpopular public figure is burned. Other events include the crowning of La Reina del Carnaval ("Carnaval Queen") and El Rey Feo ("Ugly King"), colorful costumed parades, music, dancing, feasting, cockfights, and fireworks. The festival culminates in El Día del Marido Oprimido, the "Day of the Oppressed Husband"—23.5 hours of symbolic freedom for married men to do whatever they wish—followed by a masquerade ball on the Tuesday evening before Ash Wednesday.

Also prominent on the city's yearly events calendar is the **Fiesta de La Paz** (officially known as "Fiesta de la Fundación de la Ciudad de La Paz"), held 3 May, the anniversary of the founding of the city. The state tourist office can provide up-to-date details on festival scheduling and venues.

SHOPPING

Until recently, imported merchandise could be purchased in La Paz free of import duties and sales tax. The city's duty-free status was recalled in 1989, however, and sales tax is now commensurate with the rest of Mexico's. But the city still offers some of Baja's best shopping in terms of value and variety, starting with the downtown department stores of **Dorian's** (calles 16 de Septiembre and Esquerro) and **La Perla de La Paz** (calles Arreola and Mutualismo). Dorian's resembles a typical middle-class, American-style department store; La Perla is more of a discount department store, featuring a good supply of coolers (ice chests), toiletries, housewares, and liquors at low prices.

Along Paseo Obregón in the vicinity of the Hotel Perla and Hotel Los Arcos are a number of souvenir and handicraft shops of varying quality. One of the better ones is **Artesanías La Antigua California,** at Paseo Obregón 220, which sells quality folk arts and crafts from the mainland. Away from the downtown area, the **Centro de Arte Regional** (calles Chiapas and Encinas) produces and sells pottery, while **Arte-** sanía **Cuauhtémoc** (Av. Abasolo between Jalisco and Nayarit) weaves rugs, blankets, wall-hangings, tablecloths, and other cotton or wool items. Custom orders are available, and customers are welcome to watch the weavers at their looms in back of the shop. Opposite Artesanía Cuauhtémoc on Av. Abasalo, **Casa María** carries a good selection of *artesanías,* furniture, and decorating accessories.

For tourist-variety souvenirs, especially T-shirts, **Bye-Bye** (four blocks east of Hotel Perla on Paseo Obregón) is a good choice. **Soko's Curios** (Paseo Obregón and 16 de Septiembre) is strictly for collectors of Mexican kitsch.

For bottom-dollar bargains on clothing and housewares, browse the **Mercado Municipal Francisco E. Madero** at Revolución and Degollado. Inexpensive electronics, watches, and jewelry are available at a string of shops along calles Domínguez and Madero between Av. Independencia and Calle 16 de Septiembre, and along a pedestrian alley off Calle 16 de Septiembre near Dorian's department store.

Deportes Ortíz (tel. 2-12-09), on Calle Degollado almost opposite Pensión California, carries a modest selection of camping, diving, and other sports equipment.

SPORTS AND RECREATION

Beaches
Bahía de La Paz is scalloped with 10 signed, public beaches. Most inviting are the seven beaches strung out northeast of La Paz along Península de Pichilingue—they get better the farther you get from the city. **Playa Palmira,** around four km (2.5 miles) east of downtown La Paz via the La Paz–Pichilingue Rd., is now monopolized by the Hotel Palmira and Marina de Palmira. A kilometer farther, the small but pleasant **Playa El Coromuel** offers restaurant-bar service, a waterslide, *palapas,* and toilets. In front of La Concha Beach Resort near Km 5, **Playa Caimancito** (named for an offshore rock formation that resembles a small gator) features a rock reef within swimming distance of the grayish beach. Although it's close to the city and resort developments, you can see a surprising number of tropical fish here; incoming tide is the best time for swimming or snorkeling.

Playa del Tesoro, 14 km (8.5 miles) from the city, is another casual, semi-urban beach with palapas and a restaurant. The beach was purportedly named for a cache of silver coins unearthed by crews building a road to the Pichilingue ferry terminal near the beach. Just southwest of El Tesoro, a dirt road leads to hidden **Playa Punta Colorada,** a small, quiet cove surrounded by red-hued hills that protect it from the sights and sounds of the La Paz–Pichilingue Road.

At Km 17, just beyond the SEMATUR ferry terminal, is **Playa Pichilingue,** the only public beach in the La Paz vicinity with restrooms available 24 hours for campers. The beach also has a modest palapa restaurant.

After Pichilingue the once-sandy track has been replaced by pavement as far as Playa Tecolote. The turnoff for **Playa Balandra** appears five km (three miles) beyond Pichilingue, then it's another 800 meters (half-mile) to the parking area and beach. Several palapas, brick barbecue pits, and trash barrels have been installed by the city. Depending on the tide, the large, shallow bay of Puerto Balandra actually forms several beaches, some of them long sandbars. Ringed by cliffs and steep hills, the bay is a beautiful and usually secluded spot, perfect for wading in the clear, warm waters. Clams are fairly abundant; a coral reef at the south end of the bay offers decent snorkeling. Climb the rock cliffs—carefully—for sweeping bay views. Camping is permitted at Balandra, but oftentimes a lack of breeze brings out the *jejenes* (no-see-ums), especially in the late summer and early fall. The beaches sometimes draw crowds on weekends.

About three km (1.5 miles) beyond the Playa Balandra turnoff is **Playa El Tecolote,** a wide, long, pretty beach backed by vegetated dunes. Because Tecolote is open to the stiff breezes of Canal de San Lorenzo, the camping here is usually insect-free. Two palapa-style restaurants, **El Tecolote** and **Palapa Azul,** sell seafood and cold beverages, and rent pangas, beach chairs and umbrellas, fishing gear, and plastic canoes. Free municipal palapas and barbecue grills have been added along the beach north and south of the restaurants. If you visit during the week the place is almost deserted.

Isla Espíritu Santo, 6.5 km (four miles) away, is clearly visible in the distance; you can hire a

BEACHES AND ISLANDS NEAR LA PAZ

panga from Palapa Azul to cross the channel for around US$40-50. See the section immediately following for more details on this island and others nearby.

From Tecolote the road returns to sand as it winds across the peninsula for about 13 km (eight miles) before ending at remote **Playa Coyote.** Along the way shorter roads branch off to rocky coves suitable for camping. Don't tackle this road expecting to find the perfect white-sand beach; the farther northeast from Tecolote you go, the stonier and browner the beaches become. South of Playa Coyote a network of sand roads lead to Puerto Mejia and **Las Cruces.** Named for three crosses topping a bluff near the cove where Cortés supposedly landed, the latter served as a supply port for Isla Cerralvo pearl beds during the pearl era. Abandoned in the 1930s after the pearl-bearing oysters died out, Las Cruces became a fly-in getaway for Hollywood celebrities in the 1940s and '50s. Rumors say some of the fabulous beach villas are still occupied on occasion, but the road's final approach is so difficult (intentionally so, according to the stories) that few people have been able to confirm or refute the rumors.

West of La Paz: At the northwest end of Ensenada de la Paz, the bay cul-de-sac created by Peninsula El Mogote, are **Playa El Comitán** and **Playa Las Hamacas,** both shallow beaches tending toward mudflats in low tide. Because the waters of the *ensenada* are enclosed by city development, and the channel outlet to open sea is relatively narrow, swimming is not a prime attraction at these two beaches.

Of more natural interest on this side of the bay is **Peninsula El Mogote** itself, an 11-km (seven-mile) thumb of land jutting across the top of Ensenada de La Paz directly opposite the city. The southern shore of the peninsula is rimmed by mangrove, while the north side facing the open bay offers clean water and a long beach sullied only by everyday flotsam left by the sea. It's not uncommon to see dolphins swimming by. Local myth says that if you eat the wild plums of the *ciruelo (Cryptocarpa edulis)* growing on El Mogote's sand dunes, you'll never want to leave La Paz. As there is no ready road access to El Mogote, the easiest way to reach the peninsula is by kayak from the Marina de La Paz area (see "Kayak Trips," below, for more information). Most kayakers land on the mangrove side facing Ensenada de La Paz, then walk across the peninsula's narrow isthmus to reach the bay/ocean side.

Isla Espíritu Santo,
Isla Partida, and Los Islotes
The large and small islands clustered just north of Península de Pichilingue offer an amazing variety of recreational possibilities both in and out of the water. The 22.5-km-long (14-mile-

Isla Espíritu Santo

long) **Isla Espíritu Santo** and its smaller immediate neighbor to the north, **Isla Partida,** are excellent destinations for all manner of watercraft from sea kayaks to yachts. Sandy beaches and large coves along the western shores of both islands provide numerous opportunities for small-craft landings and camping. In full sun, the sand-bottom reflections of these bays create such a bright, translucent color that white seagulls flying over them are transformed into glowing blue-green UFOs.

Rock reefs provide good snorkeling at **Punta Prieta** at the north end of Bahía San Gabriel toward Espíritu Santo's southwestern tip; at the west end of **Isla Ballena,** an islet off the northwest coast of the Espíritu Santo; at three islets in **Caleta El Candelero** toward the island's northern end; and off **Punta Bonanza** on Espíritu Santo's southeast side.

Even if you don't snorkel, picturesque, sand-bottomed **Bahía San Gabriel** is worth a visit to see the ruined walls of a pearlery dating to the early 1900s. The low walls form an inner lagoon

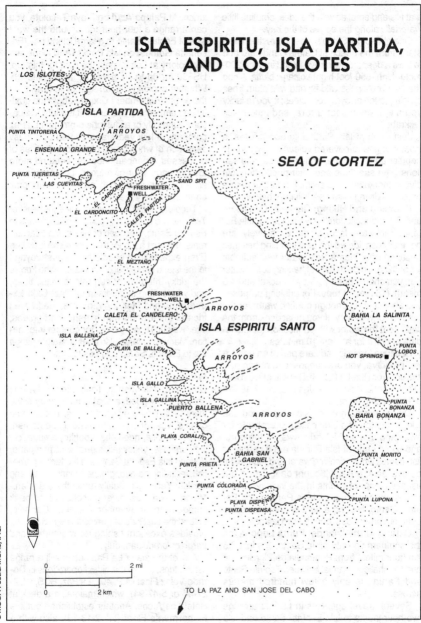

ISLA ESPIRITU, ISLA PARTIDA, AND LOS ISLOTES

LOS ISLOTES

ISLA PARTIDA

PUNTA TINTORERA *ARROYOS*

ENSENADA GRANDE

SEA OF CORTEZ

PUNTA TIJERETAS
LAS CUEVITAS *SAND SPIT*

EL CARDONAL
FRESHWATER WELL

EL CARDONCITO
CALETA PARTIDA

EL MEZTAÑO

FRESHWATER WELL

CALETA EL CANDELERO *ARROYOS*

BAHIA LA SALINITA

ISLA ESPIRITU SANTO

ISLA BALLENA

PLAYA DE BALLENA

PUNTA LOBOS

HOT SPRINGS

ISLA GALLO

ISLA GALLINA
PUERTO BALLENA *ARROYOS*

PUNTA BONANZA
BAHIA BONANZA

PLAYA CORALITO

BAHIA SAN GABRIEL

PUNTA PRIETA

PUNTA MORITO

PUNTA COLORADA

PLAYA DISPENSA
PUNTA DISPENSA

PUNTA LUPONA

© MOON PUBLICATIONS, INC.

0   2 mi
0   2 km

TO LA PAZ AND SAN JOSE DEL CABO

that fills and empties with the tides, creating little waterfalls along the edges of the bay.

One of Espíritu Santo's most interesting hikes starts from the beach at Caleta Candelero and follows a deep, rocky arroyo inland into the 200-meter-high (650-foot-high) volcanic bluffs. Along the way you'll pass wild fig and wild plum trees clinging to the arroyo's rock sides; if you're lucky you might even spot a rare, endemic black jackrabbit.

Just north of Isla Partida lie **Los Islotes,** a cluster of guano-covered volcanic rock islands popular among divers, anglers, birds, and sea lions. The sea lions and their pups often join divers/snorkelers for a swim. For further details on scuba diving sites see "Diving," below.

Camping and Hiking: Caleta El Candelero and El Cardoncito, on the west sides of Isla Espíritu Santo and Isla Partida respectively, are generally considered the best camping beaches because each has a freshwater well suitable for bathing. To be certain of hauling some water out, you should bring your own bucket and 4.5 meters (15 feet) of rope. For drinking purposes you should bring enough purified water for the duration of your stay. If you must drink from the well, treat the water with purification tablets/iodine or boil it for at least 10 minutes.

Because these islands are part of an ecological preserve, you are supposed to obtain permission from the La Paz SEDESOL office (Blvd. Olachea and Palacio de Justicia, tel. 2-16-99) before setting up camp.

On the northern tip of Isla Partida you can hike to the top of a bluff called **El Embudo** for sweeping sea and island views. At the north and south ends of Isla Partida are a couple of fish camps where drinking water and food might be available, but don't count on it. There are usually plenty of yachts in the vicinity. A narrow sandbar almost bridges Partida and Espíritu Santo, leaving a tight channel for small boat movement between the two islands.

Getting to the Islands: Punta Lupona, on the southern tip of Espíritu Santo, lies just 6.5 km (four miles) from Península de Pichilingue, and the shallow channel between Espíritu Santo and Partida is only a few hundred meters across.

Several travel agencies in La Paz arrange two-hour jaunts to Isla Espíritu Santo and Isla Partida for around US$40 per person including lunch. At **Palapa Azul** on Playa Tecolote, you can arrange a four-hour trip around the west side of Espíritu Santo to a large island bay (Ensenada Grande) on Isla Partida and to the sea lion colony at Los Islotes; the cost for this trip, US$90 for up to six persons, includes lunch. Whether booking with an agency in town or at the beach, remember to inquire about the quality and contents of the lunch. If the lunch situation sounds iffy or awful (one prominent La Paz company a few years ago served one lousy sandwich of white bread glued to two slices of processed American cheese), demand more food or carry your own lunch. Life preservers are another variable worth inquiring about; some boats don't carry them.

Tecolote or the smaller beaches just east of Tecolote are good put-in points for kayak trips to Espíritu Santo. Because of winds and tidal currents, this isn't a trip for the novice sea kayaker. Even experienced paddlers on a first voyage to the island should follow someone who knows the tricky interplay of currents, shoals, tides, and winds. Two outfitters in La Paz, **Baja Expeditions** and **Mar y Aventuras,** lead kayak trips to the islands with experienced guides; see "Kayak Trips," below, for contact information. Mar y Aventuras also does a straight panga trip to Espíritu Santo and Los Islotes.

Fishing

Outer bay and offshore fishing in the La Paz area are very good; a boat is mandatory since there's little onshore or surf fishing. The bay and canals west of the islands hold roosterfish, pargo, cabrilla, needlefish, bonito, amberjack, jack crevalle, yellowtail, sierra, and pompano. Beyond Isla Espíritu Santo are the larger gamefish, including dorado, grouper, marlin, tuna, and sailfish. Yellowtail usually run in the area Jan.-March, while most other gamefish reach peak numbers April-November. Canal de Cerralvo, around the east side of Península de Pichilingue, provides excellent fishing for roosterfish and *pargo colorado* Jan.-July.

Any of the major La Paz hotels will arrange fishing trips; one of the oldest operations is **Dorado Velez Fleet** (A.P. 402, La Paz, BCS, tel. 2-27-44 or 5-47-94), which maintains a desk at Hotel Los Arcos. Another established outfit is **Fisherman's Fleet** (tel. 2-13-13), also with a desk at Los Arcos. You can arrange guides and boats at the pier just east of the Pichilingue ferry terminal. Panga fishing trips in the bay generally cost US$80-90 a day for two people, beyond Isla Espíritu Santo or to Canal de Cerralvo figure around US$160. Long-range fishing cruises run US$200-300 a day and usually accommodate up to four anglers.

Anglers with a sturdy set of wheels and their own tackle can drive the desolate road north from El Centenario (west of La Paz on the way to Ciudad Constitución) to **Punta El Mechudo** and **San Evaristo** at the northernmost end of Bahía de La Paz, where the onshore and inshore fishing—for grouper, snapper, pargo, cabrilla, sierra, dorado, and yellowfin—is almost as good as in the Canal de Cerralvo. Most visiting anglers camp on either side of Punta El Mechudo. The road is paved for the first 40 km (25 miles) as far as the phosphate-mining town of San Juan de la Costa, then graded gravel for the final 53 km (33 miles) to San Evaristo.

Fishing tackle is available at **Deportiva La Paz** (tel. 2-73-33), Paseo Obregón 1680.

Boating

With a huge, protected bay, one private and four public marinas, and several boatyards and marine supply stores, La Paz is Baja California's largest and best-equipped boating center. Northeast of town, on the Canal de La Paz at Km 2.5, the well-planned **Marina Palmira** (mailing address: A.P. 34, La Paz, BCS; tel. 2- 42-77, fax 5-39-59) currently offers 146 slips with electricity for yachts up to 42.5 meters (140 feet), as well as dry-storage facilities, a market, laundry, marine supplies, fuel, and boat launch. This marina also offers crewed and bareboat yacht charters. Daily slip rates range US$15-60 depending on the size of the boat, with discounts for long-term moorings; boats up to 90 feet are charged US$5.10 per foot per month, larger craft cost US$6-7.20 per foot per month. Condos adjacent to the marina are also available for rent by the day, week, or month.

At the west end of the *malecón* (calles Topete and Legaspy) is the **Marina de La Paz** (tel. 2-16-46, fax 5-59-00; mailing address: A.P. 290, La Paz, BCS), owned by original panga designer Malcolm "Mac" Shroyer. Facilities include a launch ramp, fuel dock, market with groceries and marine supplies, water and electricity outlets, laundry, showers, restrooms, a chandlery,

boat and vehicle storage, and 68 slips. Daily rates range from US$8.40 for a six- to nine-meter (20- to 30-foot) craft to US$30 for anything over 20 meters (63 feet), up to a maximum of 22.8 meters (75 feet). The daily rate is discounted June-Oct.; monthly rates start at US$142. Showers cost US$.60. Marina de La Paz is by far the most popular marina in the bay and is often full Nov.-May; call or write in advance to check for vacancies before sailing in.

The well-established **Abaroa Boat Yard,** at the end of Calle Navarro near the Marina de La Paz, offers mooring facilities for up to 25 boats but is usually full; the rates are the lowest in La Paz. Still under construction is La Paz's fourth docking facility, the government-financed **FIDEPAZ Marina** on the waterfront near the state tourist office at the west end of Canal de La Paz. According to FIDEPAZ officials, the facility—if ever actually completed—will offer over 400 slips. Yet another pipe dream is a marina called **Costa Baja** north of the Marina Palmira.

You can launch trailered and cartopped boats at Marina de La Paz, Marina Palmira, Abaroa Boat Yard, Aquamarina RV Park, and Pichilingue. Smaller boats and kayaks can put in at any of the public beaches.

Pangas: If you're in the market for a new panga, La Paz is the panga capital of Mexico. Until 1968, when American Mac Shroyer designed and built the first molded fiberglass pangas, many Sea of Cortez fishermen still used dugout canoes of Indian design; glass pangas made in La Paz are now sold all over Mexico.

Embarcaciones Arca (tel. 2-08-74, fax 2-08-23) makes and sells pangas at a factory at Juárez and Gmo. Prieto. The standard panga is sold in 18-, 20-, or 22-foot lengths, but the factory can accommodate special orders as long as 36 feet. The standard panga outboard motor is a "cinco-cinco caballos," 55 horsepower. Prices run US$3200-4200 each, depending on whether canopy, stowage compartment, or other options are included.

Kayak Trips: Two area outfits operate guided kayak trips in the region, **Baja Expeditions** (see "Dive Shops," below) and **Mar y Aventuras.** Baja Expeditions offers five- to eight-day sea kayaking tours around Isla Espíritu Santo (March-May and Oct.-Jan. only) or nine-day coastal paddles between Bahía Agua Verde (south of Loreto) and La Paz. A more adventurous nine-day, open-water kayak trip hops among the islands of Espíritu Santo, Los Islotes, San José, Santa Cruz, Santa Catalina, and Santa Marta. Both nine-day trips are available Oct.-April only. Rates range from US$695 for the five-day Espíritu Santo trip to US$1195 for the Loreto–La Paz paddle.

Mar y Aventuras (tel. 2-70-39, fax 3-05-59), at Calle Tepete 564 between 5 de Febrero and Navarro (near Abaroa Boat Yard and Marina de La Paz) is geared toward kayak renters and day-trippers as well as persons interested in multiday guided tours. Five-day expeditions around Isla Espíritu Santo (Oct.-April only) cost US$700-800 depending on the number of participants. In addition to the longer trips, they offer six-hour bay kayak tours to visit Peninsula El Mogote's mangrove and beach areas for just US$35 per person including lunch, as well as an all-day paddling and snorkeling trip to Playa Balandra for US$40 per person. Custom-designed kayak trips of any length can be arranged.

Experienced kayakers can also rent kayaks from Mar y Aventuras for paddling to El Mogote or to the islands on their own. The company rents open-top kayaks for US$12 a day, closed-top touring kayaks for US$18 including PFD, paddle, and spray deck. Also available for rent are snorkeling gear, wetsuits, tents, and sleeping bags. Mar y Aventuras can be reached May-Sept. at 181 Jardine Rte., Gardiner, MT 59030 U.S.A., tel. (406) 848-7550.

Parts and Repairs: Marina de La Paz is the best local source of information about boating needs; a marine supply store on the premises stocks many everyday nautical items. A booklet by Janet Calvert entitled *La Paz Boater's Guide to Goods and Services,* available at the marina, contains a thorough list of all boatyards, outboard-motor shops, and marine supply stores in La Paz. Boaters at the marina can also offer recommendations for the best places to obtain boat parts and repairs.

Diving

Some of Baja's best dive sites lie in the La Paz vicinity, but most are accessible only by boat. As elsewhere in the Sea of Cortez, the optimum diving months are May-Aug., when visibility reaches 30 meters (100 feet) or more and water temperatures run around 27° C (80° F). In Sep-

tember tropical storms are an obstacle and during the late fall and winter months high winds and changing currents reduce visibility to 10-15 meters (35-50 feet). A light wetsuit is necessary any time except June-August.

One of the most popular diving spots is the wreck of the *Salvatierra,* a 91-meter (300-foot) La Paz–Topolobampo ferry that went down in the Canal de San Lorenzo in 1976. The hull lies about 2.5 km (1.5 miles) southeast of the southern tip of Isla Espíritu Santo at a depth of approximately 10 fathoms (18 meters/60 feet). Encrusted with sponges, sea fans, mollusks, and gorgonians, the wreck attracts numerous varieties of tropical fish, including groupers, barracuda, angelfish, goatfish, parrotfish, moray eels, and rays.

Along the western shores of **Isla Espíritu Santo** and **Isla Partida** are several good diving reefs. Bahía San Gabriel, a large cove along Espíritu Santo's southwest shore, features a shallow boulder reef (San Rafaelito) at its northern end suitable for both scuba diving and snorkeling. Similar rock reefs—along with submarine caves—can be found farther north off Espíritu Santo's western shore near Caleta El Candelero, extending from the west side of **Isla Ballena.**

One of the most colorful dive sites in the vicinity is **Los Islotes,** the tiny islet group off the north end of Isla Partida. Boulder reefs and underwater pinnacles off the north and northeast shores draw large marine species, including schools of hammerhead sharks, manta rays, and other pelagic (open-ocean) fish. A nearby cove is home to around 300 sea lions who seem to enjoy swimming alongside divers and performing tricks for the camera. Late in the breeding season (Jan.-May) is the best time to visit the colony, since this is when the adolescent pups are most playful.

To the southwest of Los Islotes lies **El Bajito,** a large rock reef that extends to within six meters (20 feet) of the sea's surface; the base of the reef meets a sandy bottom at about 24-28 meters (80-90 feet). The diverse marinelife frequenting the reef includes grouper, cabrilla, and an unusually large number of morays; attached to the rocks are gorgonians, sea fans, and a variety of other invertebrate creatures.

A group of three sea pinnacles called **El Bajo** (also known as Marisla Seamount), about 13 km (8.2 miles) northeast of Los Islotes, is renowned for the presence of large pelagics such as marlin, sharks (hammerhead, blacktip, tiger, and silvertip), dorado, corvina, and manta rays. Mantas frequent El Bajo from July to mid-October, and for unknown reasons often allow divers in this area to "hitch" rides by holding onto their backs near the pectoral fins. Whale sharks, the largest fish in the world, are occasionally seen near El Bajo during the same months, as are pilot whales.

Due to strong tidal currents, El Bajito and El Bajo are best left to experienced open-ocean divers.

Southeast of Península de Pichilingue, the somewhat more remote **Isla Cerralvo** offers several additional diving opportunities. Even more remote—generally reached by live-aboard trips—are **Isla Santa Cruz** and **Islas Las Animas** to the north. The former is known for rock reefs at depths of around 17 meters (35 feet) with a profusion of sea horses, while the latter reportedly offers the greatest variety of diving experiences—caves, hammerheads, whale sharks, sea lions—of any site in the Sea of Cortez. Only Baja Expeditions leads Santa Cruz and Animas dives at the moment.

Dive Shops: The granddaddy of all dive outfits in La Paz is Fernando Aguilar's **Baja Buceo y Servicio** ("Baja Diving Service") (tel. 2-18-26, fax 2-86-44) at Av. Independencia 107-B. Besides offering equipment sales and rental, Aguilar organizes dive trips to the *Salvatierra,* Los Islotes, or other nearby sites for US$70 a day including guide, transport, lunch, unlimited sodas and beer, weight belt, and two tanks. Dive trips to El Bajo and Isla Cerralvo cost US$80. For all trips, add US$10 for full gear. Basic scuba certification costs US$90; a complete open-water diving certification course is available for US$280. In addition, BBS offers snorkeling trips for US$40 to Playa Encantada and the sea lion colony, as well as windsurfing equipment and instruction. Available rental equipment includes regulators, BCDs, wetsuits, masks, snorkels, fins, tanks, weight belts, booties, and portable air compressors.

Baja Expeditions (tel. 5-38-28), at Calle Sonora 586 just off Av. Abasolo, offers a variety of daylong and live-aboard dive programs in the La Paz vicinity. Most of these—particularly the live-aboard trips on the 86-foot *Don José*—are booked out of the U.S. office (2625 Garnet Ave., San Diego, CA 92109, tel. 619-581-3311 or 800-843-6967), but it's occasionally possible to sign up in La Paz when space is available. An eight-day live-aboard excursion costs US$1395.

Day excursions aboard Baja Expeditions' 50-foot *Río Rita* dive boat can be booked in La Paz at a rate of US$135 per person per day, which covers weights and tanks, up to three separate dives, breakfast, lunch, and afternoon snacks. US$325 per person buys a three-day package that includes three nights of hotel accommodations, usually at Los Arcos, and two days of diving.

Diving equipment and air fills are available at **Deportiva La Paz** (tel./fax 2-73-33), Paseo Obregón 1680. The shop doesn't organize dive trips.

LA PAZ INFORMATION AND SERVICES

Tourist Offices

Baja California Sur's SECTUR office (tel. 2-11-99, fax 2-77-22) lies between Km 6 and 5 on Mexico 1 (Av. Abasolo) opposite the FIDEPAZ Marina. The friendly staff speaks English and can assist with most tourist inquiries; the Attorney for the Protection of Tourists is also stationed here. The office maintains an information booth for the distribution of maps and brochures on the *malecón* near Calle 16 de Septiembre. Office and booth are open Mon.-Sat. 0800-1900.

Newspapers

Two Spanish-language dailies are published in La Paz: *Diario Peninsular* and *El Sudcaliforniano.*

Librería Contiempo, a bookstore on Calle Arreola at Paseo Obregón, carries *The News* from Mexico City.

Changing Money

Several banks and moneychangers are located in the area around Calle 16 de Septiembre. As elsewhere in Baja, the foreign-exchange service at banks is only open Mon.-Fri. before noon. Both Bancomer and Banamex have ATMs.

Moneychangers *(casas de cambio)* stay open till early evening and on Saturday, but are closed on Sunday, when your only alternative is to change money at a hotel at lower rates. Pesos

USEFUL LA PAZ
TELEPHONE NUMBERS
(La Paz area code: 112)

Police: 2-07-81
Red Cross: 2-11-11 or 2-12-22
Green Angels: 5-96-77 or 2-77-62
Highway Patrol: 2-03-69 or 2-87-98
IMSS Hospital: 2-73-77
Tourist Attorney: 2-59-39
State Tourism Office: 2-11-99
Immigration: 2-04-29
Ferry Office: 5-38-33 or 5-51-17

are a must for everyday purchases in La Paz; city merchants are not as receptive to U.S.-dollar transactions as their counterparts in Cabo San Lucas simply because they're not as used to them.

The local American Express representative is **Turismo La Paz** (tel. 2-83-00 or 2-76-76, fax 5-52-72) at Calle Esquerro 1679, behind Hotel Perla and just around the corner from Hotel Plaza Real. Hours for AmEx service are Mon.-Fri. 0900-1400 and 1600-1800, Saturday 0900-1400.

Post and Telephone

The main post and telegraph office is at Revolución and Constitución, a block northeast of the cathedral; it's open Mon.-Fri. 0800-1300 and 1500-1900, Saturday 0800-1300.

The area code for La Paz is 112.

Immigration and Customs

If you're planning to cross the Sea of Cortez by ferry and haven't yet validated your tourist card, stop by the immigration office (tel. 2-04-29) on Paseo Obregón between Allende and Juárez. It's usually open Mon.-Fri. 0800-1500. The immigration office at the Pichilingue ferry terminal is open only an hour or so before each ferry departure.

The best place to obtain a temporary vehicle import permit (necessary for driving in mainland Mexico) is the **Aduana Maritima** office (tel. 2-07-30) at Paseo Obregón and Ignacio Bañuelos, opposite the Muelle Fiscal ("Public Pier") on the *malecón*. The permit can usually be processed on the spot—but leave a couple of days for processing just in case all the right bureaucrats aren't in.

GETTING THERE

Air

Marquéz de León International Airport (LAP) is 12 km south of the city; the airport access road leaves Mexico 1 at Km 9. Although it's a small airport, facilities include a couple of gift shops, two snack bars, rental car booths, LADATEL phones (cards available for purchase from the snack bar), and a fax/telegraph service.

La Paz's principal air carrier, **Aero California** (Paseo Obregón 550 at Bravo, tel. 5-10-23 or 2-83-92) flies daily nonstops to and from Culiacán, Guadalajara, Hermosillo, Loreto, Los Mochis, Los Angeles, Mazatlán, and Mexico City.

Aeroméxico (Paseo Obregón between Hidalgo and Morelos, tel. 2-00-91 or 2-16-36) offers daily nonstop flights to La Paz from Culiacán and Mexico City, as well as connecting flights to San Francisco, Tucson, and a number of Mexican cities.

Airport Transport: A company called **Transporte Terrestre** operates yellow-and-white vans between the city and the airport. The standard fare is US$9 *colectivo* (shared), US$18 private service for up to four persons. A regular taxi to the airport should cost around US$15. Some hotels operate airport vans that charge around US$3-4 per person.

Land

Intercity Bus: La Paz has two intercity bus terminals. From a terminal at calles Degollado and Gmo. Prieto, **Autotransportes La Paz** (tel. 2-21-57) runs buses to San José del Cabo (US$5.40, 10 times a day) and Cabo San Lucas (US$6.30, five times a day).

The **Central Camionera,** used mainly by Aguila and Autotransportes de Baja California (ABC), is located at Calle Jalisco and Av. Independencia. From here, northbound buses depart for Cd. Constitución (US$5.30, hourly 0700-2000), Loreto (US$9.25, four times daily), Santa Rosalía (US$15.25, three daily), Guerrero Negro (US$20, three daily), Ensenada (US$35.50, four daily), Tijuana (US$38.50, three daily), and Mexicali (US$44.40, one daily in the late afternoon).

Southbound, Aguila/ABC runs buses from this terminal eight times daily to the central Cape Region towns of El Triunfo (US$1.80), San Antonio (US$1.80), San Bartolo (US$2.40), Santiago (US$3.50), and Miraflores (US$3.50), continuing on to San José del Cabo (US$5.45) and Cabo San Lucas (US$6.35). More direct buses to Cabo San Lucas via Todos Santos operate six times daily between 0630 and 1900 for US$6.25. The fare as far as Todos Santos is US$4.80.

Driving: For now, Mexico 1 is the only federal highway leading to La Paz. A few years ago, a local consortium sponsored by CANACINTRA (National Chamber of Manufacturing Industries) announced plans to develop a new four-lane toll road that would run along the west coast from Ensenada to La Paz, instead of turning inland at El Rosario as does Mexico 11. So far the project is still in the discussion stages.

Sea

The ferry port at Pichilingue, 16 km (9.5 miles) northeast of downtown La Paz via Mexico 11, serves vehicle and passenger ferries between La Paz and the mainland destinations of Topolobampo (for Los Mochis) and Mazatlán. **SEMATUR** runs the ferries on those routes, and has tentative plans to begin a new route between La Paz and Puerto Vallarta, replacing the old Cabo San Lucas–Puerto Vallarta ferry discontinued several years ago.

You can book SEMATUR ferry tickets in advance at the ferry terminal (tel. 2-94-85), the city ticket office (tel. 5-38-33 or 5-46-66, fax 5-65-88) at calles 5 de Mayo and Gmo. Prieto, or Turismo La Paz (tel. 2-76-76 or 2-83-00) at the Hotel Perla.

For fares and schedules, see "By Sea" under "Getting There" in the On The Road chapter.

Vehicle Permits: Tourist cards must have a special endorsement (a temporary vehicle import permit) for vehicular travel on the Mexican mainland. These permits aren't needed for Baja California travel, but if you've driven down to La Paz and decide you'd like to take your wheels on a mainland-bound ferry, you'll need to get one before buying a ticket. The whole process operates more smoothly in Tijuana, so if you anticipate using the ferry service, doing the paperwork in advance will save time and hassle.

If for whatever reason you decide to take the ferry and haven't done the paperwork in advance, you can arrange the proper permit in La Paz. Simply apply at the customs office *(aduana)* near the downtown pier—*not* the Pichilingue ferry pier—a day or two in advance of departure. Bring your vehicle plus all immigration and registration papers, quadruple photocopies of your driver's license, proof of a U.S. insurance policy valid for six months from the date of application, and a credit card to post a "bond" of US$12. Without a temporary vehicle import permit, SEMATUR will not sell vehicle ferry tickets to non-Mexican citizens. For further information, see "Temporary Vehicle Import Permits" under "Getting There" in the On The Road chapter.

Private Boats: La Paz is an official Mexican port of entry, so the COTP office at the Muelle Fiscal has authority to clear yachts for movement throughout Mexican waters. The easiest way to arrange this is to check in at Marina de La Paz and let the marina staff process all port clearance papers. For Marina de La Paz clients, clear-in service is free, clear-out is US$10; for non-clients charges are US$5 in, US$15 out. Only one clearance in and out is required for entering and exiting the country; between Mexican ports the same papers can be presented. See "Boating" under "Sports and Recreation," above, for information on the five La Paz marinas.

BOB RACE

GETTING AROUND

You can reach most points of interest downtown on foot. For outlying areas, you can choose city buses or taxis, or rent a car.

City Bus

Regular city buses radiate in all directions from the *zona comercial* surrounding the Municipal Market on Calle Degollado. Each bears the name of either the principal street along its run or the district where the route begins and ends. Any bus marked "El Centro," for example, will end up near the Mercado Municipal at Revolución and Degollado. Bus fare anywhere in town is around US$.20.

From Terminal Malecón, Paseo Obregón 125, Transportes Aguila runs buses between La Paz and the Pichilingue ferry terminal (US$1.20, every two hours 0800-1200, hourly thereafter till 1800).

Taxi

Taxis can be found throughout El Centro, the downtown area between calles 5 de Mayo and Degollado (especially along the west end of Calle 16 de Septiembre in the shopping district), and in front of the tourist hotels. On the *malecón* (Paseo Obregón), the main taxi stands are in front of Hotel Los Arcos and Hotel Perla. The average taxi hire downtown costs around US$1.80-2.40. La Paz taxis don't have meters, so it's sometimes necessary to haggle to arrive at the correct fare.

Longer trips are more economical if you use a shared taxi van or *colectivo*. A *colectivo* from the *central camionera* to the center of town, for example, costs US$1.80 per person; by private taxi it's as much as US$5.40. Route taxis *(taxis de ruta)* operate along the main avenues

parallel to city buses for US$.25-.35 per person.

Car Rental

Several La Paz travel agencies can arrange auto rental, but rates are generally lower if you deal directly with a rental agency. **AMCA** (Calle Madero 1715, tel. 3-03-35); **Avis** (at Paseo Obregón between Piñeda and Marquéz de León, tel. 2-18-31 or 2-26-51); **Servitur Autorento** (Calle 5 de Febrero and Av. Abasolo, tel. 2-14-48); **Autorentos del Pacífico (Hertz)** (Paseo Obregón 2130, tel. 2-53-00); and **Thrifty** (Paseo Obregón and Lerdo de Tejada, also at Hotel Palmira and La Concha Beach Resort, tel. 5-96-96) all offer Volkswagen bugs and Golfs for US$25-40 per day, plus a per-kilometer charge. Nissan Tsuru IIs (Sentras), VW vans, and Jeeps are much more expensive, running US$65-83 per day plus kilometer charges, or US$106-159 per day including 200 free kilometers, tax, and insurance. All companies offer significant discounts for rentals of six days or more.

AMCA, Avis, Thrifty, and Hertz operate service counters at La Paz International Airport.

Fuel: La Paz is blessed with seven PEMEX stations, all offering Magna Sin (unleaded), Nova (leaded), and diesel.

SOUTHEAST OF LA PAZ

San Juan de los Planes–
Punta Arena de la Ventana

State highway BCS 286 begins south of La Paz off Mexico 1 (at Km 211) and leads southeast 43 km (26 miles) to the agricultural center of San Juan de los Planes. Along the way this paved road climbs over the northeastern escarpment of the Sierra de La Laguna (here sometimes given its own name, Sierra de las Cacachilas), then descends toward the coastal plains with a panoramic view of aquamarine Bahía de la Ventana and Isla Cerralvo in the distance.

At Km 38 a graded road branches northeast off BCS 286 eight km (five miles) to the fish camps of La Ventana and El Sargento on **Bahía de la Ventana.** Windsurfing is very good here due to the strong northeasterlies channeled through Canal de Cerralvo to the north. On-shore and inshore fishing is good all the way along the L-shaped bay; farther offshore in the Canal de Cerralvo, catches of marlin, skipjack, and dorado are common in the summer months. The gently sloped beach offers easy small-boat launching. If you don't fish, the bayshore still makes a worthwhile destination for blessedly secluded camping, swimming, and snorkeling, especially in the spring and fall (summers are hot). Isla Cerralvo lies about 16 km (10 miles) offshore.

Beach camping is available along the bay just north of the village of La Ventana; trash barrels, toilets, and running water are available at the camping area. Although you might expect someone to come along and collect a daily fee for camping here, we don't yet know anyone who's been charged. Basic supplies are available in La Ventana and San Juan de los Planes.

San Juan de los Planes, or Los Planes, as it's usually called, has several markets, a cafe, and around 1,500 inhabitants supported by farming (cotton, tomatoes, beans, and corn) or by fishing at nearby bays. From Los Planes, a graded road runs east 21 km (13 miles) to **Bahía de los Muertos,** a pretty, curved bay with primitive beach camping.

Historians don't know why a 1777 Spanish map named this shore "Bay of the Dead," but the name gained substance when a Chinese ship beached here in 1885 after being refused entry at La Paz harbor because the crew was suffering from yellow fever. After putting in at this bay, all 18 crewmen died; Mexican fishermen buried their bodies above the tideline and marked their graves with wooden crosses, a few of which still stand. In the early 1900s a community of American farmers tried unsuccessfully to cultivate the desert surrounding the bay; some died of thirst or hunger, adding to the bay's list of *muertos.* **Ensenada de los Muertos,** an abandoned port at the north end of the bay, was built in the 1920s for the shipping of ore from El Triunfo mines in the Sierra de La Laguna.

A lesser road branches northeast about three km before Los Muertos and leads eight km (five miles) to beautiful Punta Arena de la Ventana. The defunct **Hotel Las Arenas** was once a fishing and diving resort with its own 1,820-meter (6,000-foot) airstrip; it's up for sale now. The waters off Punta Arena de la Ventana reputedly offer Baja's best roosterfish angling; wahoo, amberjack, grouper, dorado, and billfish are also reportedly in abundant supply. Guided panga trips are available locally for US$50-75 per day. A bit south of the abandoned hotel, at **Punta Perico** ("Parakeet Point"), is a lively reef with varied depths of 3-25 meters (10-82 feet). You can pitch a tent or sleep under the stars anywhere along the north end of Bahía de los Muertos or around the bend at Punta Arena de la Ventana—no charge.

Bahía de los Muertos can also be reached from the south via a 47-km (29.5-mile) dirt road between Los Barriles and San Juan de los Planes. The road is fairly wide and flat from Los Barriles as far as Punta Pescadero and El Cardonal—13 km (8.5 miles) and 22 km (13.5 miles) respectively. North of El Cardonal, the road begins to rise along the Mesa Boca Alamo, eventually cutting inland and ascending steeply into the jagged, red Sierra El Carrizalito. Several miles of the road here wind around narrow, adrenalin-pumping curves with steep drop-offs. Contrary to popular belief, 4WD is not a necessity for this section of road, but careful driving and good road clearance are. Twenty-four km (15 miles) from El Cardonal, the road leaves the mountains and meets the paved end of BCS 286.

Isla Cerralvo

Across Bahía de la Ventana and Canal de Cerralvo lies **Isla Cerralvo,** one of the largest islands in the Sea of Cortez—about 30 km (18 miles) from north to south. At the time of early Spanish exploration, the island featured large pearl-oyster beds and was inhabited by a small group of Pericú Indians. Later the rugged island reportedly became a favored final resting place for the *vagabundos del mar,* Mexican-Indians who roamed the Sea of Cortez in dugout canoes until well into this century.

Today Cerralvo remains one of the least visited of Baja's large coastal islands, simply due to its location on the far side of the Península de Pichilingue. Coral-encrusted **Roca Montaña,** off the southeastern tip of the island, is an excellent diving and fishing location, as is **Piedras Gordas,** marked by a navigation light at the southwestern tip. Depths at these sites range 3-15 meters (10-50 feet). Other good dive sites include the rock reefs off the northern end (average depth 18-21 meters/60-70 feet), which feature a good variety of reef fishes, sea turtles, and shipwrecks. One of the reefs, **Arrecife de la Foca,** features an unidentified shipwreck with "Mazatlán" marked on the hull. **La Reina,** another reef at the north end of the island, is the site of a large steel-hulled freighter that sank half a century ago. Barely a hundred meters off the island's west shore are two adjacent rock reefs known as **La Reinita.**

Access to Isla Cerralvo is easiest from Bahía de la Ventana or Punta Arena, where beach launches are possible. From La Paz, it's a long haul around the Península de Pichilingue via Canal de San Lorenzo.

(top) Playa El Médano, Cabo San Lucas; (bottom, left) Westin Regina Resort Los Cabos, Corridor; (bottom, right) Hotel Finisterra, Cabo San Lucas

(top, left) *asadero,* Blvd. Marina, Cabo San Lucas; (top, right) Squid Roe, Cabo San Lucas; (bottom) El Triunfo, Central Cape

BOB RACE

CENTRAL AND EAST CAPE
SAN PEDRO TO MIRAFLORES

Along Mexico 1 between La Paz and San José del Cabo are a number of mining-turned-farming towns with cobblestone streets and 19th-century stone-and-stucco architecture. Nestled among well-watered arroyos in the Sierra de La Laguna, these neglected settlements now support themselves growing citrus, avocado, mangoes, corn, and sugarcane, and, to a lesser extent, serving the needs of passing travelers. Many of the families living in the central Cape Region are descended from Spanish settlers of the 18th and early 19th centuries. Others are newcomers—including a few *norteamericanos*—drawn by the area's solitude and simplicity.

San Pedro
This town appears—and quickly disappears—just before the junction of Mexico 1 and Mexico 19. *Carnitas* connoisseurs swear by **El Paraíso de San Pedro,** an unassuming roadside cafe on the highway's west side. The junction itself is reached at Km 185; if Cabo San Lucas is your destination, you must decide whether to take Mexico 19 via Todos Santos or the Transpeninsular Highway (Mexico 1) via El Triunfo, San Antonio, San Bartolo, Santiago, and Miraflores.

Unless you're in a hurry to reach Cabo San Lucas, Mexico 1 is the most scenic choice for drivers of autos and light trucks. South of San Pedro, Mexico 1 winds through the Sierra de La Laguna and features a succession of dizzying curves and steep grades. Hence for trailers, RVs, and other wide or lengthy vehicles, Mexico 19 is the better choice since it runs along relatively flat terrain.

El Triunfo and San Antonio
During the Jesuit missionary period, this section along the lower northern slopes of the sierra was earmarked for cattle ranching. Mining concessions moved in following the discovery of silver near San Antonio in 1748, and the settlement quickly grew into a town of 10,000 people, many of them Yaqui laborers.

When Loreto was heavily damaged by a hurricane in 1829, San Antonio briefly served as capital of the Californias before the capital was transferred to La Paz in 1830.

Gold and silver were discovered at El Triunfo ("Triumph"), seven km (4.5 miles) north of San Antonio, in 1862. By 1878 the large Progreso mining concern had established seven gold and silver mines that attracted a number of Mexican, French, English, Italian, German, and North American immigrants. The company paid for the first post office in the region, and also installed the first electrical and phone lines to La Paz.

Both towns bustled with frontier commerce through the end of the 19th century, when the ore began running out; then a hurricane in 1918 flooded the mines, and by 1925 both towns were virtually abandoned. Today El Triunfo has only around 500 residents, most of them involved in small-scale mining (extracting ore from leftover tailings) or the weaving of palm baskets. San Antonio, a farming community of around 1,000 set in a lushly planted valley that descends eastward all the way to the Sea of Cortez, boasts a PEMEX station with Magna Sin, a post office, and a few markets.

A number of historic adobe buildings in both towns have been restored, including El Triunfo's **Casa Municipal** and San Antonio's unusual 1825 church exhibiting train and paddlewheeler motifs.

Restaurant Las Glorias, on the east side of the highway through El Triunfo, is a good food stop. A fun time to visit San Antonio is 13 June, the feast day of St. Anthony, when the whole town (and El Triunfo) turns out for music and dancing.

San Bartolo

Beginning just past Km 128, San Bartolo is the greenest and lushest of the central Cape settings, thanks to a large spring gushing straight out of a mountainside into the arroyo. To complete the tropical picture, many homes sport thatched roofs. Mangoes, avocados, and other fresh fruits are available at roadside stands or in town. **Restaurant Los Burritos, Restaurant El Paso,** and two other unnamed eateries on the east side of the highway serve meals.

San Bartolo's patron saint day is 19 June, conveniently close to San Antonio's.

SANTIAGO

The largest of the central Cape Region towns (pop. 2,500), Santiago was founded as Misión de Santiago el Apóstol in 1723 by Italian padre Ignacio María Nápoli. The mission was abandoned in the latter half of the 18th century following a series of Pericú rebellions, and only in relatively recent times has agriculture revived the arroyo community.

Flanked by leafy fruit orchards, blue fan palms, and vegetable plots, a two-km road leads west from Mexico 1 (Km 85) across the wide, flat Arroyo de Santiago, dividing the town into Loma Norte and Loma Sur (North and South Slopes). Santiago and environs serves the region as an important source of palm leaves for making palapa roofs. *Palmeros* claim the fan-shaped fronds are best cut during a full moon, as rising sap makes the palm leaves last longer. Properly dried and stored, 250 palm leaves equals one *carga* or load, for which the *palmeros* receive US$30-50 depending on leaf quality.

A handful of *tiendas* line the town plaza; the town also offers a PEMEX station, hotel, supermarket stocked with local fruit and vegetables, post office, telegraph office, church, and the only zoo on the peninsula south of Mexicali. A small, rustic museum adjacent to the church at the corner of Calzada Misioneros and Calle Victoria contains colonial artifacts and local fossils; it's open Mon.-Fri. 0800-1300 and admission is free.

Among the residents of the small but nicely landscaped **Parque Zoológico** are a peccary, bear, coyote, fox, monkey, parrots, and ducks. Some of the animals are Cape Region natives. The park is open daily 0600-1800 and admission is free, though donations are gladly accepted. To bypass the town center and proceed directly to the zoo, take the left fork just after crossing the dry arroyo near the town entrance, then take the next left fork onto a levee road that curves along the south end of town to the zoo.

Santiago celebrates its patron saint day, the feast day of St. James, on 25 July.

Accommodations and Food

Casa de Huéspedes Palomar (tel. 112-2-06-04), south of the plaza on the east side of Calzada Misioneros, offers six tidy rooms around a courtyard for US$20 s/d a night. The highly regarded restaurant, decorated with local fossils, serves seafood, enchiladas, and burgers Mon.-Sat. noon-2030. Entrees start at US$6; *pescado mojo de ajo,* fish cooked in garlic butter, is a house specialty.

Vicinity of Santiago

The dirt road to the zoo continues southwest nine km (5.5 miles) to the village of **Agua Caliente** (also known as Los Manantiales),

TO CAÑON SAN DIONISIO AND LA LAGUNA

DIRT ROAD

TO EL TRIUNFO
AND LA PAZ

1

CERRO EL TEPETATE

DIRT ROAD

PALO VERDE

SANTIAGO

DIRT ROAD

SANTA
RITA
(HOT SPRINGS)
EL ENCINAL

SAN JORGE

SAN JORGE

DIRT ROAD

GRADED
ROAD

MESA CERRALVO

DIRT ROAD

DIRT ROAD

AGUA CALIENTE

LAS CABRAS

EL CHORRO
(HOT SPRINGS)

AGUA CALIENTE

LAS ESCOBAS DIRT ROAD

DIRT ROAD

LAS VINORAMAS

MESA LAS VINORAMAS

CERRO LA VENTANITA

DIRT ROAD

1

**SANTIAGO
TO MIRAFLORES**

TO CAÑON SAN BERNARDO

0   2 mi

0   2 km

BOCA DE LA SIERRA

MIRAFLORES

AIRSTRIP

EL RANCHITO

MESA
EL CAPULIN

SAN MARTIN

LA TINAJA

MESA LOS DIFUNTOS

DIRT ROAD

BOCA DE LA SIERRA

DIRT ROAD

CADUAÑO

CADUAÑO

GRADED
ROAD

TO CAÑON SAN PABLO

1

TO SAN JOSE DEL CABO

where a hot spring in a nearby canyon (about seven km/four miles west of the village) has been channeled into a concrete tub for recreational purposes. Camping is permitted in the canyon. Ask directions to two other hot springs in the area: **El Chorro** (west of Agua Caliente) and **Santa Rita** (north). The network of roads behind Santiago passes through dense thornforest in some spots and it's easy to get lost unless you keep a compass on hand or a good fix on the sun. If you can bring along a copy of the Mexican topographic map for this area (Santiago 12B34), all the better; each of these locales is clearly marked. Do not attempt these roads at night. If you continue south along the sandy road past Agua Caliente, you'll reach the town of Miraflores after 8.7 km (5.4 miles).

At the north end of Santiago, another dirt road leads northwest to **Rancho San Dionísio** (23.5 km/14.5 miles), where the Cañon San Dionísio approach to Picacho La Laguna begins. See "Sierra de La Laguna," below, for sierra hiking details.

At **Las Cuevas**, five km (3.1 miles) northeast of Santiago on Mexico 1 (around Km 93), is the turnoff to La Ribera and the East Cape.

Three km south of Santiago, a large cement sphere marks the **Tropic of Cancer** (latitude 23.5° N), south of which you are "in the tropics." As if to sanctify the crossing, an impressive Guadalupe shrine has been built next to the rather unattractive marker.

MIRAFLORES

A 2.5-km (1.5-mile) paved road to Miraflores branches west off Mexico 1 at Km 71 next to a PEMEX station. This ranching and farming community is known for leatherwork; **Curtiduría Miraflores** ("Miraflores Tannery"), just off the ac-

cess road between the highway and town, sells handmade leather saddles, bridles, whips, horsehair lariats, and other ranching gear as well as a few souvenir items such as leather hats, belts, and bags, and the occasional bleached cow skull. Custom orders are accepted. Look for a small sign on the right-hand side of the access road reading "Leather Shop."

Miraflores honors the Virgin of Guadalupe as its patron saint, so Fiesta Guadalupana (12 Dec.), venerated throughout Mexico, is celebrated especially fervently here.

Food

Restaurant Las Bugambilias, a small five-table palapa restaurant on the road into town, serves very tasty *burritos de machaca,* fish, *cocteles,* and ice-cold beer. The house *salsa picante* is *maravillosa* and the jukebox is well-stocked.

Taquería Niña, next to the market and plaza, makes good shrimp, fish, and *carne asada* tacos. Several *mercaditos* in town provide local produce and *machaca.*

Vicinity of Miraflores

A dirt road northwest of Miraflores leads to **Boca de la Sierra** ("Mouth of the Sierra"), a settlement at the mouth of Cañon San Bernardo—the second of the three canyons providing access deep into the Sierra de La Laguna (see the separate section on the sierra, below, for hiking information). *Ejido* farms in the Boca de la Sierra area cultivate vegetables and herbs—especially sweet basil—for Cape Region supermarkets and restaurants as well as for export to the United States.

Another dirt road southwest of town leads to the mouth of Cañon San Pablo, a third Laguna hiking route. Inquire at the tannery about guided trips into the sierra to view Indian rock-art sites.

SIERRA DE LA LAGUNA

The mountainous heart of the Cape Region extends southward from the Llano de La Paz (the plains just south of La Paz) to Cabo San Lucas, a distance of around 135 km (81 miles). Originally called Sierra de La Victoria by the Spanish, the interior mountains were renamed Sierra de La Laguna in the early Mexican era. These peaks are unique among sierras in the southern half of Baja California in that they're granitic rather than volcanic. And unlike the sierras to the north, the entire Laguna range is tilted eastward instead of westward, i.e., its steepest slopes are on the west side of the escarpment rather than the east.

Picacho de La Laguna (elevation 2,155 meters/7,090 feet), roughly in the sierra's center, is usually cited as the highest peak in the range,

although according to some sources **Cerro las Casitas**—approximately 6.5 km (four miles) southeast of Picacho de La Laguna and measuring 2,083 meters (6,835 feet) by most accounts—may be higher. Between these two peaks is a large, flat meadow called **La Laguna** (elevation 1,700 meters/5,600 feet). This depression held a mountain lake until around 1870 when Cañon San Dionísio became sufficiently eroded to drain away accumulated water.

Islands in the Sky

The meadow of La Laguna and other flats and high canyons in the sierra contain a number of "relict environments" preserving flora and fauna long ago lost on the arid plains below. The

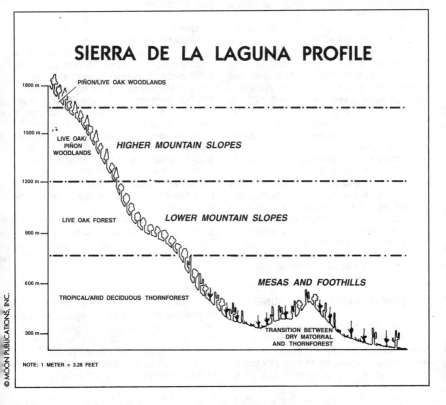

SIERRA DE LA LAGUNA PROFILE

1800 m — PIÑON/LIVE OAK WOODLANDS

1500 m —
LIVE OAK/
PIÑON
WOODLANDS
HIGHER MOUNTAIN SLOPES

1200 m —

LIVE OAK FOREST
LOWER MOUNTAIN SLOPES

900 m —

600 m —
MESAS AND FOOTHILLS

TROPICAL/ARID DECIDUOUS THORNFOREST

300 m —
TRANSITION BETWEEN
DRY MATORRAL
AND THORNFOREST

NOTE: 1 METER = 3.28 FEET

range's highlands, in fact, receive more annual precipitation—up to 89 cm (35 inches) per year in some microclimates—than any other place in Baja California.

These "islands in the sky" have gathered together a rare mix of desert, tropical, and subalpine species seen growing side by side nowhere else in North America. Among these are mosses and cacti, madrone and monkey flower, palm and willow, and other unlikely combinations. Of the 390 plant species known to grow in the sierra, at least 70 are reportedly indigenous. Undisturbed by human progress, deer, coyote, mountain lion, Pacific tree frog, and dozens of hummingbird species also thrive in the highland areas of the sierra.

The sierra flora has been little researched; the most recent detailed studies were undertaken in the 1890s by botanist T.S. Brandegee for the California Academy of Sciences. At elevations of 500-750 meters, tropical-subtropical deciduous forest and columnar cacti are the dominant flora (e.g., *mauto, palo blanco,* prickly pear, *cardón, palo adán*); from 750 to 1,200 meters, live-oak woodlands (encino, madrone) dominate; and above 1,200 meters a mix of live oak and piñon pine prevails. The foothills and mesas below are covered with dry *matorral*— low-growing cacti, succulents, thornscrub, and abundant herbs. Common species include barrel cactus, cholla, paloverde, ironwood, *damiana,* and oregano. Canyon walls may be draped with *zalate* (wild fig).

For many years, naturalists and outdoor enthusiasts clamored for the upper sierra to be declared a national park or preserve, and in June 1994 the Mexican government finally granted the Sierra de La Laguna official recognition as a "biosphere reserve." Such status prohibits any development within the reserve's core zone; as part of the plan, local ranchers are permitted to graze livestock in a buffer zone surrounding the reserve's protected core.

HIKING AND BACKPACKING

The Sierra de La Laguna is a popular hiking area for Cape residents, as it offers the opportunity to leave behind the fig trees and palms of the arid-tropical environment for a walk among cottonwoods and subalpine meadows. Three lengthy east-west canyons provide the principal access into the sierra: Cañón Dionísio, Cañón San Bernardo, and Cañón San Pablo. All three routes enable hikers to traverse the sierra's spine from east to west—or vice versa, although the western escarpment is considerably more precipitous. Primitive campsites are available along each of the three routes.

The northernmost and most popular route, via **Cañón San Dionísio,** leads directly to La Laguna—the range's largest and highest meadow. La Laguna lies at an altitude of just under 1,800 meters (6,000 feet), between Picacho de La Laguna and Cerro las Casitas, the sierra's tallest peaks. The scenery on this hike is impressive. A straight traverse of this route, starting from either side, is possible in three days, although this would allow little time for taking it easy. Add at least a day to these estimates to allow some time to enjoy La Laguna once you've reached it.

Seasons

The best backpacking season here is late fall, after the rainy season has passed and sierra streams and *tinajas* are full. Temperatures above 1,500 meters (5,000 feet) typically measure 12-22° C (54-72° F) during the day, 5-12° C (41-54° F) at night. In January and February, temperatures can dip below freezing at night, while daytime temps run around 10-20° C (50-68° F).

The warmest temperatures are usually encountered in May and June, when the mercury reaches around 25° C (77° F) during the day, 10-15° C (50-60° F) at night. Although the scenery isn't as spectacularly green this time of year, it's a fine time to beat the heat down on the coastal plains.

July-Oct. rains may wash out trails and flood the canyons. Rainfall peaks in August, averaging 7.5 cm (three inches) but sometimes reaching a drenching 20 cm (7.8 inches) for the month.

Supplies

A compass and good topo map are musts for any trip into the Sierra de La Laguna. To cover all three routes, you should possess copies of Mexico's relevant 1:50,000-scale topos: El Rosario F12B23, Las Cuevas F12B24, Todos Santos F12B33, and Santiago F12B34. (See "Hiking and Backpacking" in the On The Road chapter for recommended map sources.) Bring warm clothing and sleeping bags for the summit; morning frost isn't uncommon even in fall and spring. Long pants and sturdy hiking shoes—even at lower elevations—are recommended as a defense against the abundant cactus and nettles.

On the Cañon San Dionísio trail, bring all the water you'll need to reach La Laguna, as there are no dependable water sources on the way up, even in wet weather. An arroyo at La Laguna itself carries water year-round. On the Cañón San Bernardo trail, pools of water can be found along the way year-round. Water may be available from ranchos along the Cañón San Pablo trail, but bring your own to be safe. Be sure to use a water-purification system of some kind on all water sources in the mountains; although the water is generally uncontaminated, the presence of livestock precludes absolute safety.

Guides

For eastern ascents into the sierra, those unsure of their backpacking and orientation skills should consider hiring a local guide, since trails across the eastern escarpment are often obscured and junctions not always obvious. A guide can also prepare simple camp meals and point out items of natural interest—Indian rock art, flora and

© MOON PUBLICATIONS, INC.

fauna—that first-timers might otherwise miss. Guides are available in Santiago and Miraflores; simply ask around. For the Cañón San Dionísio route, you can sometimes arrange a guide at Rancho San Dionísio, just before the eastern trailhead.

The going rate for guides in Santiago is US$20-25 per day per person, plus an extra US$10 per day per pack animal. Rancho San Dionísio charges US$20 for a guide without mules, no matter how many people are hiking.

Many hikers make the western approach to Cañón San Dionísio from Todos Santos without a guide; the main difficulty is finding your way (or arranging a ride) to the trailhead. If you decide you want to hire a guide, inquire at the Sierra de La Laguna Water Co., just northeast of Todos Santos on the highway to La Paz. The water company should be able to arrange a trip with the very competent and personable Davíd Saisa, who lives near La Burrera at Rancho San Martín. Señor Saisa charges US$30 per day, more if you take along horses or burros as pack animals. It's also possible to arrange a guide through Hotel California in Todos Santos. Another guide in Todos Santos, Jesús Arballo, can be contacted through Vicki Arballo (tel. 5-01-80) at the corner of calles Pedrajo and Villarino.

Cañón San Dionísio:
Western (Todos Santos) Approach

Most hikers ascend to La Laguna from the western side, which is a steeper but more straightforward hike (and about two km shorter than from Rancho San Dionísio). Unlike the network of cattle trails on the east side—which are best negotiated with local guides—the western ascent can be easily accomplished without a guide. From the west side a roundtrip can be completed in two days.

Near Todos Santos, the sandy road to La Burrera leaves Mexico 19 about 100 meters south of the Punta Lobos turnoff. Past an old water tower, take the first left and continue straight through several intersections till the road ends at a gate and parking area. From the gate, follow the dirt road till you reach La Burrera (about 25 minutes away), where you'll see a sign in English advising hikers to follow marked trails (ironic since we've never seen any marked trails in the sierra). Also known as San Juan del Aserradero, this village on the sierra's western slopes lies around 17.5 km (11 miles) northeast of Todos Santos. Continue along this road another 20 minutes or so till you see a clearing on the right that has been used for camping; look for a sign reading "No tire basura" (Don't dump trash). Just past this sign, the road ascends to a small rise, at the top of which the main trail begins. After 30 meters or so of easy grade, the trail begins its long, steady climb straight up the mountain. Following this wide, established (rutted in places), 11-km (seven-mile) trail, you should reach La Laguna in 5-8 hours, depending on your pace. Along the way the vegetation changes quickly from desert and thornforest into lush piñon-oak woodlands; about 20 minutes before you reach La Laguna the forest canopy opens up to magnificent views of the sierra and Pacific Ocean.

Follow the arroyo that drains La Laguna at its southeast corner, near where the trail comes in from Rancho San Dionísio, to reach a 20-meter cascade with deep pools suitable for swimming.

The return descent along the same trail takes about four hours to reach La Burrera.

BOB RACE

If you need a ride to La Burrera from Todos Santos, your best bet is to inquire at Mini-Super La Siempre Viva (at the corner of calles Juárez and Marquéz de León) in the late morning, when ranchers from the western sierra sometimes turn up for supplies and gossip. Fees for such a ride are negotiable—some ranchers will give you a lift for gas money and a six pack of Tecate, others ask up to US$30.

Cañón San Dionísio:
Eastern (Santiago) Approach

From the east side of the sierra, count on three or four days to La Laguna and back with time to explore the area. The eastern mouth of the main canyon is reached via a dirt road to Rancho San Dionísio from Santiago (19 km/12 miles). From there it's a 13-km (eight-mile) hike west through the canyon mouth, then into a side arroyo and finally along the southern rim of the canyon to La Laguna. Piñon pine and Cape live oak began appearing about two-thirds of the way. This trail is relatively difficult to follow and is intersected by potentially confusing animal paths; a guide, available at Rancho San Dionísio or in Santiago, is highly recommended. If you decide to go it alone, be sure to carry a topo map and compass, and watch out for cattle trails branching off the main trail in every direction. Scout ahead at questionable junctions, even if it means going slower. Once you're up on the ridgeline you should be able to spot La Laguna in the distance and then confidently follow any trail heading that direction.

Those wishing to explore a bit can follow the canyon four km straight west of the ranch into a steep area of boulders; where the arroyo forks there's a 20-meter waterfall and deep pools suitable for swimming. Don't attempt to follow the canyon all the way to the meadow unless you're into some very serious bouldering and scrambling.

Near the northwest edge of the meadow itself are a couple of herder's shacks; just past these the trail cuts into the forest and divides; the southern branch descends to La Burrera, while the north branch ascends Picacho de La Laguna, a 1.5-hour hike away. (A lesser third trail leads to an arroyo with fresh water.) Easy to climb, the peak is bare of trees and provides splendid views of the surrounding terrain. Closer to the meadow, a hill surmounted by radio towers also makes a good vantage point.

Those wishing to traverse the sierra can descend westward from La Laguna another 11 km (seven miles) to La Burrera, see "Western (Todos Santos) Approach," above. About 20 minutes into the descent from the meadow, you'll come upon terrific views all the way to the Pacific Ocean. Roads from La Burrera meet Mexico 19 south and north of Todos Santos; the area east of these junctions is honeycombed with other dirt roads, but if you continue in a westerly direction you'll eventually come to the highway.

Cañón San Bernardo

The next route to the south, via **Cañón San Bernardo,** is a relatively easy (from east to west) hike that crests at around 900 meters (3,000 feet). The canyon trailhead is accessible via an eight-km (five-mile) dirt road from Miraflores to Boca de la Sierra, where the trail skirts a dam and follows the canyon to the crest, 16 km (10 miles) northwest. Several pools along the way provide fresh water year-round. From the 900-meter mark, the trail continues over the sierra to the village of Santo Domingo on the western side, for a total traverse of 22.5 km (14 miles). The Cañón San Bernardo crossing makes a good four- to five-day hike, although it's possible to make a quick overnight to the crest and back from the eastern approach.

Cañón San Pablo

Cañón San Pablo provides the southernmost route into the sierra, reaching an elevation of around 1,000 meters (3,250 feet). The canyon mouth is best approached by taking a 6.5-km (four-mile) dirt road west from Caduaño, a village four km (2.5 miles) south of Miraflores, to Rancho El Salto. From Rancho El Salto, it's approximately 10.5 km (6.5 miles) to the crest; the trail continues over the ridge and along a steeper 4.8-km (three-mile) westward descent to the village of El Guerigo on the other side, where a network of dirt roads leads west to Mexico 19. A leisurely El Salto–El Guerigo hike takes four to five days.

DRIVING ACROSS THE SIERRA

Visitors with sturdy, high-clearance vehicles can traverse the Sierra de La Laguna in dry weather via a road that leaves Mexico 1 about 16 km

(10 miles) south of Miraflores (about eight km/five miles north of Santa Anita). Among gringo road hogs this route is often called the "Naranjas road." From the Mexico 1 turnoff the road leads west-northwest 42 km (26 miles) to the village of **El Aguaje**, past the *ranchitos* of Cieneguita, San Pedro de la Soledad, and El Remudadero. The ungraded road passes a couple of 1,500- to 1,800-meter (4,900- to 6,000-foot) peaks before cresting at around 1,035 me-

ters (3,400 feet) and descending into a challenging set of sharp curves and grades approaching 30%. The track widens to a graded, gravel road near El Aguaje, then continues another 12.8 km (eight miles) before terminating at Mexico 19 near Playa Los Cerritos south of Todos Santos. Two INEGI topo maps, San José del Cabo F12B44 and La Candelaria F12B43, would make helpful—though not required—companions on this cross-sierra road trip.

EAST CAPE

The Cabo del Este ("East Cape") consists of a succession of scenic tropical coves and beaches extending from the northern end of Bahía de Palmas south to San José del Cabo, at the tip of the cape.

Beach camping is available along almost the entire length of the coast, although the area is developing gradually and some of the prettiest beaches now bear small-scale housing developments. Coastal development, in fact, is ongoing from Buena Vista all the way around the Cape to Cabo San Lucas, with land prices skyrocketing in recent years. Fortunately, there are still a few choice spots left where the fishing (some of the best in the world) and camping are free. The coastline north of Los Barriles as far as Bahía de los Muertos remains relatively untouched.

AROUND BAHÍA DE PALMAS

The gently curving shore of Bahía de Palmas, stretching 32 km (20 miles) from Punta Pescadero south to Punta Arena, began its commercial life in the 1960s as a fishing resort accessible only by yacht or private plane. Now that the Transpeninsular Highway swerves to within a couple of miles of the bay, it has become a full-fledged, drive-in fishing and windsurfing mecca.

In many places along the bay, anglers can reach the 100-fathom line less than a mile from shore, especially toward Punta Pescadero (Fisherman's Point) at the north end. Billfish frequent the area June-Dec., yellowtail Jan.-June, and roosterfish, wahoo, tuna, and dorado year-round (best in summer, however). Inshore catches include pargo, cabrilla, grouper, amberjack, wahoo, and pompano, plus the occasional yellowtail or rooster. The world-famous "Tuna Canyon," about 6.5 km (four miles) directly south of Punta Pescadero, reaches depths of 50 fathoms and has a year-round population of sizable yellowfin tuna; rocks along Tuna Canyon's submerged walls tend to cut the lines of all but the most skilled sportfishers. Guided fishing trips can be arranged at any of the hotels along

the bay—generally US$80-150 a day for a panga, US$200-325 a day aboard a fishing cruiser. You can launch trailered or cartopped boats off sandy beaches or at the boat ramp just north of the Hotel Buenavista Beach Resort (see "Buena Vista," below).

Sailboarders flock to Los Barriles Nov.-April when sideshore winds—collectively called El Norte and aided by thermals from the Sierra de La Laguna—blow 18-30 knots for weeks at a time. The rest of the year, you'll have to settle for around 12-14 knots—not too shabby. During the high-wind season, inshore water temperatures average around 22-24° C (72-75° F), with air temperatures in the 25-29° C (78-85° F) range. The same basic conditions can be found all the way north to El Cardonal. Several hotels on the bay rent windsurfing equipment and provide basic instruction.

With such favorable recreational conditions, it's little wonder legions of gringo anglers, boaters, and sailboarders are buying up property along the bay to build vacation and retirement homes. The Barriles–Buena Vista area is starting to look like a San Diego suburb. Several roads branch east off Mexico 1 between Kilometers 110 and 105 to hotels and trailer parks—most owned by gringos—scattered along the central section of Bahía de Palmas. Because there are no real zoning regulations, construction varies from flimsy palapa extensions to impressive beach homes. Construction trash is unfortunately a common sight; in some spots an unmistakable stench indicates improper installation of cesspools. Those seeking more solitude and less development can head north of Los Barriles to Punta Pescadero at the northern end of Bahía de Palmas, or farther north to El Cardonal.

Punta Pescadero and El Cardonal
The sandy, washboard road to Punta Pescadero and El Cardonal heads north from Los Barriles—look for a turnoff from Mexico 1 signed El Cardonal. The road crosses a couple of arroyos that could be problematic in heavy rains.

At the extreme north end of Bahía de Palmas (13.6 km/8.5 miles north of Los Barriles) is the **Hotel Punta Pescadero** (24831 Alicia

Los Barriles
windsurfing

HOWARD MOREHEAD, COURTESY OF VELA HIGHWIND CENTERS

Pkwy., Box C-320, Laguna Hills, CA 92653-4696, tel. 800-426-2252), a small fishing resort on 125 palm-studded acres overlooking a sandy beach. A room costs US$90 s/d and comes with sea views, a private veranda, a/c, satellite TV, and refrigerator; some also have fireplaces. The resort features a restaurant and bar, dive shop with compressor, pool, lighted tennis court, nine-hole golf course, landing strip (1,065 meters/3,500 feet, Unicom 122.8), and rental equipment for scuba and free diving, boating, and fishing. Petroglyphs are visible in nearby rock caves that once served as Indian burial sites. The unpaved side road out to the actual point is not recommended for RVs or trailers.

Farther north along this same road, the little-known **Restaurant Marimar,** a mile north of Punta Pescadero, serves simple but well-prepared seafood.

Past Punta Pescadero and technically at the south end of Bahía de los Muertos, you'll come to **El Cardonal** (23 km/14 miles from Los Barriles). Inshore coral heads here provide worthwhile underwater scenery, while nearby prehistoric cave paintings reportedly depict marlin, turtles, and human figures. The Canadian-owned **El Cardonal Resort** (tel./fax 112-1-00-40, VHF channel 25; in the U.S./Canada tel. 514-767-6036, fax 767-7180) offers tidy apartments as well as spaces for RV and tent camping. Each of the large studios comes with kitchenette and ceiling fan, and costs US$49 a night, US$225 per week, US$385 for two weeks, or US$599 per month.

Tent camping costs US$7 per day, two-way hookups are US$8, and full hookups cost US$10. A dump station is available, as are fishing boats (pangas and a 32-foot cruiser), ice, and equipment for fishing, windsurfing, and snorkeling.

Beyond El Cardonal, the road continues northward along the coast, then west across the Sierra El Carrizalito to San Juan de los Planes (see "San Juan de los Planes–Punta Arena de la Ventana" under "Southeast of La Paz," above, for further details on this route).

Los Barriles

In the center of the bay at Los Barriles are the **Hotel Playa del Sol** (Baja Reservations, P.O. Box 9016, Calabasas, CA 91372, tel. 818-591-9463, 800-368-4334 in California) and **Hotel Palmas de Cortez** (same contact information). Hotel Playa del Sol has 26 air-conditioned rooms, an oceanfront pool, tennis and volleyball courts, an outdoor terrace restaurant, bar with satellite TV, rental gear (for fishing, kayaking, mountain biking, and windsurfing), and charter boats for sportfishing (US$110-250 per day, not including fishing permits). Rooms cost US$55 s, US$80 d, US$105 t, and US$130 q. The hotel is closed in September.

About 300 meters south of Hotel Playa del Sol—and just a half-mile off the highway—the Hotel Palmas de Cortez offers 28 air-conditioned rooms for US$55 s, US$85 d; 10 deluxe suites for US$85 s, US$120 d; and 10 two-bedroom condos that sleep up to six for US$150. Facilities include a restaurant and bar, pool, tennis and racquetball courts, a 990-meter (3,250-foot) landing strip (Unicom 122.8), windsurfing gear, charter boats (US$115-250, not including fishing permits), and equipment for both fishing and hunting. Dove and quail hunting in the nearby Sierra de La Laguna is reportedly good.

Camping and RV Parks: North of Hotel Playa del Sol are **Martin Verdugo's Trailer Park** (A.P. 17, Los Barriles, BCS 23501, tel. 114-1-00-54) and **Playa de Oro RV Resort** (3106 Capa Drive, Hacienda Heights, CA 91745, tel. 818-336-7494 in the U.S.). Both have beach frontage, dump stations, flush toilets, showers, laundry, boat ramps, and full hookups for US$10 for two people, plus US$2 for each additional person; tentsites cost US$5 a night at Verdugo's, US$7 at Playa de Oro. Verdugo's operates a restaurant; Playa de Oro features an ocean view and bonded boat storage, plus a few cabins for rent. Both parks can arrange fishing trips. On the west side of the dirt road north, the smaller **Juanito's Garden** (tel. 114-1-00-24, fax 1-01-63) has trailer spaces without hookups for US$6-8 a night.

Free primitive camping is available in the area north of these three parks, usually referred to by gringos as the "North Shore."

Food: Los Barriles has but one restaurant, **Tío Pablo's,** a large, smartly designed palapa-style structure with ceiling fans, a well-stocked bar, sports TV, and a menu of salads, sandwiches, and burgers; it's open daily 1130-2200.

Windsurfing: During the high-wind season, two windsurfing centers in Los Barriles can arrange package deals that include the use of state-of-the-art equipment, lessons geared to your level, air transportation, and accommodations. **Baja Surf Club** (tel. 800-551-8844 in the U.S.) is based at the Hotel Palmas de Cortez, while **Vela Windsurf Resort** (351-C Foster City Blvd., Foster City, CA 94404, tel. 415-525-2070 or 800-223-5443 in the U.S./Canada) uses both Hotel Playa del Sol (formerly Playa Hermosa) and Hotel Palmas de Cortez. The Playa del Sol has the best beach launch overall. Seven-night packages cost US$665-902 at Hotel Playa del Sol or US$735-840 at Hotel Palmas de Cortez; rates include all windsurfing equipment, instruction at every level, accommodation, meals, tax, and service.

During the second week of January, Vela Windsurf Resort and sailboard manufacturer Neil Pryde co-host the annual Baja Champi-onships sailboard race at Los Barriles. The week before the competition, the center offers a race clinic staffed by world-class instructors. Non-windsurfing spectators are welcome to watch the event from shore, and to join in on the beach barbecues and partying. For more information, contact Vela Windsurf Resort.

Buena Vista
About 6.5 km (four miles) south of Los Barriles at Buena Vista is old-timer **Rancho Buena Vista** (P.O. Box 673, Monrovia, CA 91016, tel. 114-1-01-77; tel. 818-303-1517 in the U.S./Canada, or 800-258-8200 outside CA). The resort has a nice restaurant and bar facing the sea, a pool, tennis and volleyball courts, fishing tackle (including fly-fishing equipment), cruisers, windsurfing gear, a boat ramp, and air-conditioned cottages for US$60-130 per night for two, plus US$45 for each additional guest.

Hotel Buenavista Beach Resort (16211 E. Whittier Blvd., Whittier, CA 90603, tel. 310-943-0869, 800-752-3555 in CA only), about a kilometer farther south, offers rooms in a converted hacienda as well as condo-style units for US$85 s, US$135 d, or US$185 t, including three meals. Additional guests pay US$25 each. Rooms without meals are available for US$65 s and US$84 d, plus US$15 for each additional person. Facilities include pool, tennis court, mineral spa, and equipment for fishing and hunting. The Buenavista Beach Resort also offers special package deals that include accommodations, all meals, and several days of guided fishing.

Casa de Rafa (tel. 112-5-36-36, ext. 163) is a relatively new bed and breakfast with six rooms; it's just off the highway near Km 109.

Food: The modest but popular **Restaurant La Gaviota,** out on the highway, offers a standard list of fresh seafood (including fish tacos), *antojitos, carne a la tampiqueña,* and breakfasts. It's open daily 0800-2100. The Gaviota also sports a jukebox stocked with *norteña* tunes. **Restaurant Calafia,** on Mexico 1 near the Buena Vista police station, offers good shrimp tacos and tables with views of Bahía de Palmas. Usually open for lunch and early dinner only.

Diving: Although there's little to interest the underwater tourist in Bahía de Palmas, **Vista Sea Sport** (tel./fax 114-1-00-31, VHF channel 71) in Buena Vista offers dive trips south to Cabo Pulmo and Los Frailes, and north to El

Cardonal, as well as air fills, diving-gear rentals, and PADI scuba certification courses.

South to Punta Colorada

About two km south of Hotel Buenavista Beach Resort is the modest **La Capilla Trailer Park,** with flush toilets, showers, and full hookups for US$7-8 a day. Farther south, just north of Punta Colorada, lies the palapa-style **Rancho Leonero** (8691 El Rancho, Fountain Valley, CA 92708, tel. 714-375-3720 or 800-696-2164) with 18 spacious rooms and bungalows, restaurant and bar, pool, jacuzzi, fully equipped dive center, and rental fishing gear. Rates run US$125 d per night for rooms, $150-175 d for suites or bungalows (the more expensive ones front the beach), plus $32.50 a night for each additional guest. All rooms have sea views. Rancho Leonero's restaurant is considered one of the best on the East Cape. Fishing charters start at US$120 a day for smaller pangas.

Punta Colorada, at the south end of the bay (16 km/10 miles east of Mexico 1 via the La Ribera road), features the **Hotel Punta Colorada** (P.O. Box 9016, Calabasas, CA 91372, tel. 112-1-00-50 or 1-00-46; tel. 818-222-5066 or 800-368-4334 in the U.S./Canada). Roosterfish fanatics often choose to stay here since the roosterfishing off nearby Punta Arena is usually the best in Baja. Large rooms cost US$50 s, US$80 d. Like the competition to the north, Hotel Punta Colorada has its own airstrip (1,000 meters/3,300 feet, Unicom 122.8). Guided hunting and fishing trips are available. The hotel is closed September and the first week of October.

Surfing: One of Baja's least-known surfing spots—simply because no one expects surf this far up the Sea of Cortez—can be found at **Punta Arena,** just below Punta Colorada. A left point break can crop up here anytime during the March-Nov. southwest swell, but the peak surf usually comes in late summer or early fall—*chubasco* season.

LA RIBERA TO SAN JOSE DEL CABO

El Camino Rural Costero ("The Rural Coastal Road")

About halfway down the infamous Coastal Road between La Ribera and Pueblo La Playa stands a brass plaque commemorating the road's May 1984 grading. For first-time drivers who have braved washouts and sandpits to read it, the sign never fails to elicit a few chuckles. Big plans claim the road will soon be paved—such claims have been around for several years now. In spite of the rough access, certain areas along the Coastal Road—e.g., Cabo Pulmo and Los Frailes—are filling up with small-scale housing/resort developments. Yet plenty of open space for beach camping is still available.

Contrasting strongly with the budding resort developments are several ranchos along the road that raise cattle, goats, pigs, and sheep—mostly without fencing. If you substitute fiberglass pangas for dugout canoes, the ranchos today appear much as they must have in 1941, when John Steinbeck described Cabo Pulmo:

On the shore behind the white beach was one of those lonely little rancherías we came to know later. Usually a palm or two are planted nearby, and by these trees sticking up out of the brush one can locate the houses. There is usually a small corral, a burro or two, a few pigs, and some scrawny chickens. The cattle range wide for food. A dugout canoe lies on the beach, for a good part of the food comes from the sea. Rarely do you see a light from the sea, for the people go to sleep at dusk and awaken with the first light.

In general, driving conditions along the Coastal Road are suitable for passenger cars of average road clearance; even smaller RVs sometimes manage to make it all the way. Sand can be a problem in places, and shoulders are invariably soft. Weather plays an important role in day-to-day conditions; following late-summer or early-fall storms, parts of the Coastal Road can be impassable. Make inquiries before embarking on the trip and be prepared to turn back if necessary. The unpaved 77-km (48-mile) stretch between El Rincón and San José del Cabo can take up to four hours.

La Ribera

To reach the Coastal Road from the north, take the paved road signed La Ribera east at Km 93 off Mexico 1 (at Las Cuevas). This 20-km (12-

mile) road passes through La Ribera (La Rivera), a small town of around 2,000 with a PEMEX station, church, *tortillería,* cemetery, banana and mango trees, trailer shelters, and simple homes lining up along a network of sandy roads overlooking a sand beach. Worn palapa shelters at the south end of the beach can be used for camping when not occupied by fishermen. Several *mercaditos* in the village offer local produce and other supplies for long-term visitors.

Just north of La Ribera, in a large mango orchard near the beach, the tidy and well-run **Correcamino Trailer Park** (no phone, CB channel 66) offers shady tent/camper/RV spaces with full hookups for US$8 per day. Facilities include hot showers and flush toilets.

A sandy road just south of Correcamino Trailer Park leads .6 km (.4 miles) to a casuarina-shaded beach where you can camp for free. A point at the north end of the small bay (also accessible from Correcamino) creates a surf break during heavy southwest swells.

CABO PULMO

Another paved road section branches south from La Ribera, meeting both the unpaved road east to Punta Colorada and the Coastal Road. The section of the Coastal Road from here to Cabo Pulmo, 26.5 km (16.5 miles) south of La Ribera, is usually in fair condition. The paving is slowly moving south along an interior track parallel to the current Coastal Road; rumor says it

will hit the coast again at Bahía de Los Frailes. Eventually the road is supposed to be paved all the way to San José del Cabo, but completion is probably at least five years distant.

Bahía Pulmo
Noted for its reef-building corals, this tidy bay is bounded by Cabo Pulmo to the north and Corral de Los Frailes to the south. The bay is ringed by coarse white-sand beaches, most of them readily accessible from the parallel Coastal Road. Baja California pearling once reached it's southernmost point here.

A pristine, fine-sand beach known as **Playa La Sirenita** ("Mermaid Beach," named for a rock formation whose silhouette resembles the head and bust of a female figure), lies against the north escarpment of Corral de Los Frailes at the bay's southeastern tip. Best reached by small boat or kayak from the village of Cabo Pulmo, the beach's crystal waters are protected from southerly winds in the summer and early fall; rock reefs close by offer snorkeling opportunities. There's just enough room above the tideline for undisturbed overnight camping.

Farther south around the wide headland of **Corral de Los Frailes** (named for a rock formation with a resemblance to hooded friars), a colony of sea lions lives among geometric boulder piles.

Take the first sand road that isn't barbwired north of Corral de Los Frailes to reach **Playa Corral de Los Frailes,** a one-man fish camp with a beach sheltered from most onshore winds.

Playa Sirenita

Pulmo Reef System

The bay's reef system, the northernmost of only three coastal reefs in North America, is rich with tropical marinelife and hence a favorite snorkeling and scuba-diving destination. Adding to its attraction is the fact that it's easily accessible from shore.

The reef consists of eight hard coral fingers scattered throughout the bay, from Cabo Pulmo at the north end to Corral de Los Frailes at the southern end. Four finger reefs extend from the center of bayshore: two solid lengths called **Las Navajas**; an unnamed broken length used by (harmless) nurse sharks as a breeding zone; and a solid, kilometer-long finger known as **El Cantil.** Water depths along these four reefs range 4.5-10.5 meters (15-35 feet).

Farther offshore (up to 3.2 km/two miles), running more or less parallel to the bayshore, are the reef fingers of **La Esperanza** (around 18 meters/60 feet), **El Bajo de los Meros** (15 meters/50 feet), and **Outer Pulmo** (30 meters/100 feet).

Soft coral heads can be found at **El Islote**—a rock island near La Esperanza—and at **Las Casitas,** rock caves just off Corral de Los Frailes at a depth of 13 meters (45 feet).

The reef system here is very delicate; reef corals can't tolerate temperatures lower than 21° C (70° F) and must have clear water since debris settling on their disks and tentacles will kill them. All of these corals are important breeding grounds for several marine species, so if the corals die it will negatively impact all manner of fish in the area.

The University of La Paz is currently surveying the bay for possible national-park status. Meanwhile the Mexican government has declared Pulmo Reef an underwater nature preserve—no fishing or anchoring at the reef (or anywhere in Bahía Pulmo) is permitted. Shore development remains the reef's biggest ecological challenge, since the corals rely on unpolluted and unimpeded runoff. If resorts or housing developments further expand along Bahía Pulmo, the reef will probably perish.

Diving and Boating

Optimum visibility in the waters around Pulmo Reef occurs March-October. Aside from the natural reefs cited above, directly off Cabo Pulmo (the cape itself) lies the wreck of *El Vencedor,* a tuna boat that sank in 1981 and which now forms an excellent artificial reef. Pilot whales are commonly seen in the vicinity in April, large jack crevalles Aug.-September.

Ask for personable José Luis Murrieta in Cabo Pulmo if you're interested in a guided dive or boat service. His **Pepe's Dive Center** (A.P. 532, Cabo San Lucas, BCS, tel. 114-5-39-00, ext. 193; in the U.S./Canada tel. 619-489-7001 or 208-726-9233) offers a complete diving service (including equipment rentals and air fills) to 14 dive sites in the area. **Juan Castro** also operates a small dive center out of Cabo Pulmo. Rates from either run an economic

*Pepe's Dive Center,
Cabo Pulmo*

US$35 per person for a one-tank dive tour, US$55 for a two-tank tour, US$25 for snorkeling tours, and US$40 for night dives. English-speaking Pepe offers a PADI-approved scuba resort course for US$75 or full scuba certification for US$350.

Pepe is also happy to arrange boat trips for non-divers interested in touring the bay, Playa La Sirenita, and the Corral de Los Frailes seal colony. Although a local resident recently constructed an illegal concrete boat ramp at the north end of bay, by law boats are supposed to be launched from the beach.

Fishing

Neither sport nor commercial fishing is permitted in Bahía Pulmo, but inshore north of Cabo Pulmo anglers can find giant seabass, snapper, pargo, ladyfish, and roosterfish. Offshore are grouper, sierra, skipjack, dorado, marlin, and tuna. The latter gamefish are found closer in at Bahía Los Frailes farther south, but anywhere along this coastal stretch the heavyweights can come within three km (two miles) of the shoreline, according to *The Baja Catch*. Peak months for most varieties are May-June and Oct.-November.

Practicalities

In the midst of Cabo Pulmo village, **Cabo Pulmo Beach Resort** (P.O. Box 774, Ketchum, ID 83340, tel. 208-726-9233, fax 726-5545) offers palapa-roofed, solar-powered *cabañas* by the day, week, or month. The bay is just a short walk from each. Rates run US$45-75 per night for two persons, varying according to the size and style of each *cabaña*. Additional guests pay US$12.50 per day each. All accommodations come with kitchenettes or full kitchens, plus all bed and bath linens; some feature patios, decks, or barbecue grills. Weekly rates of US$240-400 and monthly rates of US$950-1575 are also available.

You can camp for free on the beach at the south end of Bahía Pulmo.

Cafe Cascade, a rustic collection of tables beneath a palapa shelter next to a small trailer (adjacent to the resort and near the road), provides a changing menu of fish (the cafe's own or bring your catch), pizza, tacos, vegetable enchiladas, soups, homemade breads, cinnamon rolls and other delights prepared by an American cook. Popular with divers during the dive season, the simple restaurant has an especially cozy ambience at night when illuminated by hurricane lamps. Nancy appreciates two hours notice for a full-course dinner (US$11); drop in anytime for breakfast or lunch.

Tito's, a casual palapa restaurant on the opposite side of the road, provides simple fish meals, beer, and drinking water—when you can find the proprietors.

Getting There: Most visitors drive themselves to Cabo Pulmo via the Coastal Road. With advance notice, the Cabo Pulmo Beach Resort can arrange roundtrip transportation from Los Cabos airport for up to four people for US$100.

BAHIA DE LOS FRAILES

About eight km (five miles) south of Cabo Pulmo village is a sandy spur road east to gently curving, white-sand Bahía de Los Frailes. With Bahía Pulmo just to the north serving as a protected nursery, onshore and inshore fishing is unusually good here. Surfcasters can land roosterfish and, within a couple miles of shore, boating anglers can hook yellowfin tuna, leopard grouper, skipjack, dorado, and marlin.

Windsurfers will find a steady cross-shore breeze at the bay's south end. The bay plummets here as deep as 210 meters (688 feet).

According to the owner of Hotel Bahía Los Frailes, Indian rock art can be found inland nearby.

Accommodations and Food

Hotel Bahía Los Frailes (220 Montgomery St., Suite 1019, San Francisco, CA 94104, tel. 415-956-3499 or 800-762-2252; tel. 114-2-22-46 in Mexico) consists of a set of well-constructed, nicely furnished cottages with high palapa roofs facing the south side of the bay. Rates run US$90 per adult (children under 15 US$50, under five free) for a room and three meals. One-bedroom suites cost US$110 per adult (same rates for children as regular rooms), while two-bedroom suites with four queen-size beds and two baths go for US$400 for four guests including meals. Pangas (but no tackle) are available for rent from US$80 per day.

Beach camping is permitted along the north end of the bay—a nominal fee may be collected.

LOS FRAILES TO
SAN JOSE DEL CABO

South of Los Frailes, the Coastal Road deteriorates rapidly, but those with sturdy vehicles and steady nerves will be rewarded by secluded arroyo campsites and vignettes of disappearing ranch life. About 12.5 km (7.5 miles) south of Los Frailes is **Rancho Tule,** followed after 5.5 km (3.5 miles) by **Rancho Boca de La Vinorama.** A late summer beach break sometimes hits at Boca del Tule, sending a few clued-in surfers scurrying across the landscape in this direction.

Just south of Vinorama, a graded dirt road heads west across the lower Sierra La Trinidad, via the ranching settlement of **Palo Escopeta,** to meet Mexico 1 near San José Viejo, a distance of 34 km (21.7 miles). Although roughly the same distance as the remainder of the Coastal Road to San José, the Palo Escopeta road often rides more smoothly and quickly. Hence, unless you're heading for a specific spot along the coast between Pueblo La Playa and La Vinorama, it's normally faster to cut across the hills here to Mexico 1 rather than follow the coast.

From La Vinorama along the coast, it's another five km (three miles) and 1.5 km (one mile) southwest respectively to **Rancho San Luis** and **Rancho Santa Elena.** Following another 5.5-km (3.5-mile) section is the small dairy farm of **La Fortuna,** after which the road improves a bit for 24 km (15 miles) before terminating at **Pueblo La Playa,** a fishing village on the eastern outskirts of San José del Cabo.

Jutting from the coast about 10.3 km (6.4 miles) before Pueblo La Playa is **Punta Gorda,** known for good onshore/inshore fishing and, in a southwest swell, surfing. Surfers know the break as "Santa Cruz," the name of a small ranchería nearby. Just north of Punta Gorda, **Rancho Rocas del Mar** (tel. 114-2-37-76) offers a furnished cottage with kitchenette near a sandy cove for US$65 per night or US$390 per week. The gringo owners can arrange fishing trips and rental equipment for kayaking, snorkeling, or diving.

Around 10 km (six miles) offshore lie the world-famous **Gorda Banks,** a pair of seamounts that are a hot-spot for marlin and wahoo fishing. *Pangeros* are sometimes available for guide fishing trips out to the Banks, but it's easiest to hire someone at La Playita, the beach behind Pueblo La Playa farther on. If you have your own boat, beach launching is generally easier at La Playita. Guided scuba trips to the Gorda Banks can be arranged through dive outfitters in Cabo San Lucas.

The last couple of kilometers between Pueblo La Playa and San José del Cabo is more tropical than the entire East Cape, with mango trees, huge banyan trees, and wild sugarcane.

BOB RACE

SAN JOSE DEL CABO AND THE CORRIDOR

SAN JOSE DEL CABO

Although closer to Los Cabos International Airport, San José del Cabo represents the quieter, more traditional resort of the twin Cabos—San José and San Lucas. A somewhat older tourist crowd frequents San José (pop. 25,000), leaving Cabo San Lucas to partying singles and young couples.

The Jesuit padres who founded a mission community here in the 18th century wisely situated San José on a mesa that slopes down toward the beach a couple of kilometers south. Century-old brick and adobe buildings, many of them proudly restored, line the main streets radiating from the plaza and church. These are interspersed with Indian laurel trees and other greenery, making San José one of the most pleasant pedestrian towns in the Cape Region.

The architecture thins out and becomes more modern as you descend toward the beach, culminating in a golf course, condos, resort homes, and the Zona Hotelera. Because of the town's mesa geography, the beachfront hotels thankfully don't obscure the view from town. Areas to the north and east of town are dotted with irrigated orchards producing mangoes, avocados, bananas, and citrus.

As the *cabecera* (roughly equivalent to "county seat") of the Municipio de San José del Cabo, the town enjoys well-maintained streets and city services. Employment in the public as well as private sector has lured a variety of talented Bajacalifornios to establish residence here. A number of *norteamericanos* also have retirement or vacation homes in the area, although the overall gringo presence, whether resident or visiting, is much smaller than in Cabo San Lucas.

CLIMATE

San José del Cabo's climate, influenced by its tropical latitude, estuarine environment, and proximity to both sea and desert, belongs in the classic tropical-arid category. Average maximum temperatures run 30° C (86° F) in January, up to 40° C (104° F) in June, the warmest month. Average minimum temperatures in the winter are around 18° C (64.4° F), though rare recordings as low as 3° C (37.4° F) have been taken.

Average annual rainfall amounts to just 32 cm (12 inches), low enough to be called semi-

Map labels:

TO AIRPORT AND LA PAZ

GALERIA LOS CABOS
CALLE ZARAGOZA
CALLE IGNACIO
CALLE COMONFORT
CALLE OBREGON

ASADERO LOS CANDILES
CALLE MUÑOZ
SAN JOSE INN
PIETRO RISTORANTE ITALIANO
PLAZA MIJARES

HOTEL DIANA
HOTEL POSADA TERRANOVA
BANCOMER
CALLE DEGOLLADO
HOTEL CECI
HOTEL COLLI
CONSEJO MUNICIPAL (CITY HALL)

IMSS HOSPITAL
CALLE DOBLADO
CALLE CASTRO
IGUANA BAR
CALLE GUERRERO
TROPICANA INN

TAQUERIA EL INDIO
SUPERMERCADO GRUPO CASTRO
MERCADO MUNICIPAL
CALLE CORONADO
CLUB ECLIPSE

PANADERIA SAN JOSE (BAKERY)
CALLE M.M. DE JUAREZ
CALLE JUAREZ
CALLE HIDALGO
POST OFFICE

TO PUEBLO LA PLAYA AND EAST CAPE

SEE "SAN JOSE DOWNTOWN" MAP

SAN JOSE DEL CABO

CALLE MORELOS

BUS TERMINAL
CALLE CANSECO
EL SUPER BURRO

THRIFTY CAR RENTAL

BLVD. MIJARES

PASEO DEL ESTERO

ESTERO SAN JOSE

0   0.2mi
0   0.2km

CERRO DE LA VIGIA

HOWARD JOHNSON PLAZA SUITES RESORT

CAMPO DE GOLF

PRESIDENTE FORUM RESORT

MOON

TO BRISAS DEL MAR TRAILER PARK, PLAYA COSTA AZUL, AND CABO SAN LUCAS

FONATUR (GOVERNMENT OFFICES)
LAS MISIONES DE SAN JOSE

PASEO SAN JOSE

HOTEL BEST WESTERN POSADA REAL
HOTEL AGUAMARINA

PLAZA LOS CABOS

PLAYA CALIFORNIA

FIESTA INN

PACIFIC OCEAN

desert. September is typically the wettest month, while virtually no rainfall is usually recorded Feb.-July. Even "wet" September usually has just three or four rainy days, with total rainfall for the month under 10 cm (four inches). Like much of the Cape Region, San José is subject to occasional tropical storms called *chubascos* Aug.-October. On rare occasions a storm may bring torrential downpours, as in 1993 when a late-arriving November *chubasco* caused serious damage—via flooding—to beachside condos and hotels.

HISTORY

The Pericús who frequented the San José area before the Spanish *entrada* called the area "Añuiti," a name whose meaning has been lost. Spanish galleons first visited Estero San José—the mouth of the Río San José—to obtain fresh water near the end of their lengthy voyages from the Philippines to Acapulco in the late 17th and early 18th centuries. During this period the estuary was known among sea-

LEGEND OF THE FLAME

San José's colorful history is footnoted by a little-known episode featuring a shipwrecked Irishman. Fleeing political strife in 18th-century Ireland, John O'Brien and several of his countrymen sailed to the New World—along the same route followed by Sir Francis Drake and earlier English explorers—only to become stranded at Estero San José in 1795. After marrying a local Pericú woman, O'Brien refused rescue when his father and the rest of the Irish crew were later picked up by a ship on its way back to the British Isles.

From this point in the story onward, facts merge with fable as O'Brien gained legendary status among the Bajacalifornios as "La Flama" (The Flame) for his red hair and fiery disposition. Also known as Juan Colorado ("Red John"), or more prosaically as Juan Obregón, the Irishman set out on a lifetime adventure throughout the Californias as far north as San Francisco, working as a cowboy and singing the nostalgia-tinted praises of San José del Cabo everywhere he went. For O'Brien, San José replaced the Emerald Isle as his homeland, and one imagines him crying in a shot of tequila instead of ale as he expresses his longing for "San José del Arroyo," as imagined in Walter Nordhoff's book *The Journey of The Flame:*

On seeing our dear Valley of San José del Arroyo for the last time, with the cattle grazing everywhere, on both sides of the fertile land, on the hillsides, I remembered the violent stampedes of the wild bulls and the delicious sips of warm milk I stole, and I thought: If heaven is like this valley, I can only repeat after the Indians, 'Father, lead us there!'

How many times, in subsequent years, someone galloping by my side in the desert has asked me, 'Where are you from, countryman?' And when I answered him 'From San José!', something crept into his voice that no other place is capable of evoking when he asked: 'Would that be San José del Arroyo?' Then the horses could scatter, the cattle begin a stampede, the water be a thousand burning leagues away, or death lie close by in ambush for us, and nevertheless we had to stop. Because when two who love this Arroyo Valley meet and know each other, everything else loses importance.

men as Aguada Segura ("Sure Waters") and, less commonly, San Bernabe, a name left behind by Sebastián Vizcaíno during his coastal navigations. As pirate raids along the coast between Cabo San Lucas and La Paz became a problem, the need for a permanent Spanish settlement at the tip of the cape became increasingly urgent. The growing unrest among Guaicura and Pericú Indians south of Loreto also threatened to engulf mission communities to the north; the Spanish had to send armed troops to the Cape Region to quell Indian uprisings in 1723, 1725, and 1729.

In 1730 Jesuit Padre Nicolás Tamaral traveled south from Misión La Purísima and founded Misión Estero de las Palmas de San José del Cabo Añuiti (or Misión San José del Cabo, for short) on a mesa overlooking the Río San José, some five km north of the current town site. Due to the overwhelming presence of mosquitoes at this site, Tamaral soon moved the mission to the mouth of the estuary, on a rise flanked by Cerro de la Vigía and Cerro de la Cruz. During the mission's first year, Jesuit records show the padre baptized 1,036 *salvajes* ("savages"), while at the same time establishing fruit orchards and irrigated farmlands.

Tamaral and the Pericús got along fine until he pronounced an injunction against polygamy, long a tradition in Pericú society. Wrote Tamaral about Pericú men:

It is highly difficult to induce them to leave the great number of women they have, because women are very numerous among them. Suffice it to say that the most ordinary men have at least two or three . . . because the larger the number of their women, the better served they are and better provided with everything necessary, as they lie in perpetual idle-

ness in the shade of the trees, and their women work looking in the woods for wild roots and fruits to feed them with, and each one tries to bring her husband the best to be found in order to win his affection in preference to the others.

After Tamaral punished a Pericú shaman for violating the anti-polygamy decree, the Indians rebelled and burned both the San José and Santiago missions in October 1734. Tamaral was killed in the attack. Shortly thereafter, the Spanish established a presidio, which served the dual purpose of protecting the community from insurgent Indians and the estuary from English pirates.

By 1767, virtually all the Indians in the area had died either of European-borne diseases or in skirmishes with the Spanish. Surviving mission Indians were moved to missions farther north, but San José del Cabo remained an important Spanish military outpost until the mid-19th century when the presidio was turned over to Mexican nationals.

During the Mexican-American War (1846-48), marines from the U.S. frigate *Portsmouth* briefly occupied the city. A bloody siege ensued, but the Mexicans prevailed under the leadership of Mexican naval officer José Antonio Mijares. Plaza Mijares, San José's town plaza, is named for him. As mining in the Cape Region gave out during the late 19th and early 20th centuries, San José lost population along with the rest of the region. A few sugarcane farmers, cattle ranchers, and fishermen began trickling into the San José area in the '30s, and in 1940 the church was rebuilt.

San José remained largely an agricultural backwater known for its avocados, mangoes, citrus, and other fruits until the Cape began attracting sportfishers and later the sun-and-sand set in the '60s and '70s. Since the late '70s, FONATUR (Fondo Nacional de Fomento del Turismo, or National Foundation for Tourism Development) has sponsored several tourist and residential development projects along San José's shoreline. Fortunately, the development has done little to change San José's Spanish colonial character, and local residents take pride in restoring the town's 18th-century architecture and preserving its quiet, laid-back ambience.

SIGHTS

Plaza Mijares

The shady town plaza at the intersection of Blvd. Mijares and Zaragoza—San José's two main streets—is a well-tended expanse of brick with a number of benches and a gazebo. At the west end of the plaza is the twin-towered **Iglesia San José,** built in 1940 on the site of the original 1730 Misión San José del Cabo. A mosaic over the main entrance depicts a scene from the infamous 1734 Pericú uprising, with Indians shown dragging Padre Tamaral toward a fire, presumably to be burned alive.

During the Dec.-March tourist season, the town holds a fiesta every Saturday evening in Plaza Mijares.

Estero San José

The freshwater Río San José meets the Pacific Ocean at this 125-acre estuary, just east of the Presidente Forum Resort. A sandbar at the

Estero San José

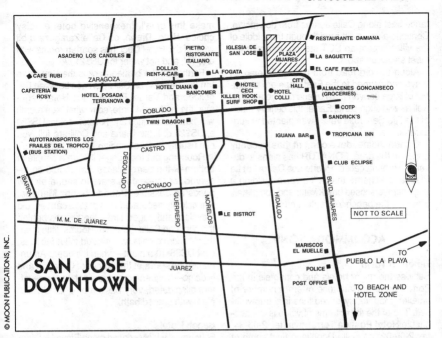

© MOON PUBLICATIONS, INC.

SAN JOSE DOWNTOWN

NOT TO SCALE

TO PUEBLO LA PLAYA

TO BEACH AND HOTEL ZONE

mouth of the river forms a scenic lagoon surrounded by tall palms and marshgrasses, a habitat for over 200 species of birds including brown pelicans, ring-necked ducks, common egrets, and herons. Canoes can be rented at the Presidente for paddling around the lagoon.

A public footpath, **Paseo del Estero,** follows the estuary and river through scenic fan palms, river cane, and tule, a perfect habitat for birdwatching. The path begins at the Presidente and comes out on Blvd. Mijares near a modern water-treatment plant.

**Museo Regional/
El Centro Cultural Los Cabos**
Next to the Presidente and alongside the estuary stands a small building containing modest exhibits of fossils, ceramics, and historical photos of turn-of-the-century San José. Museum supporters plan to add a small aquarium and art exhibits sometime in the near future.

Posted hours for the center are Tues.-Sun. 1000-1300 and 1600-1800, but in practice hours are erratic. Admission costs US$1.80 for adults, US$.60 for children.

Zona Hotelera
FONATUR has developed 4,000 shoreline acres adjacent to San José into a hotel-recreation zone. Thus far, the zone contains six resort hotels, an 18-hole Campo de Golf, a shopping center, and several condo and housing developments. Some of the nicest homes are found along the north side of the golf course.

The wide, sandy beach here, known either as Playa Hotelera or Playa California, is perfect for sunbathing, but the undertow is very strong. FONATUR is discussing a proposal to develop a small marina on the shore between the Presidente Forum Resort and Posada Real hotels.

La Playita and Pueblo La Playa
Just east of San José via Calle Juárez is a beach area called La Playita ("Little Beach"), adjacent to the village of Pueblo La Playa. An ocean beach away from the hotel zone, La Playita offers pangas for rent and free camping. This area can be reached by walking along the beach northeast of Presidente Forum Resort about a kilometer, or by walking a similar dis-

tance east along Calle Juárez from downtown. Continue along a dirt road through the middle of the village, past an SCT station, to reach the most secluded spots.

Along the dirt road from here to Pueblo La Playa and beyond to the East Cape are a number of large banyan *(zalate)* and mango trees as well as wild sugarcane. Earlier this century much of the Río San José valley was planted in sugarcane.

Gringo home development has recently begun in the area. FONATUR has plans to develop a marina called "Puerto Los Cabos" at La Playita, a scheme that will involve building a huge semi-enclosed breakwater and completely dredging the beach to create a harbor.

ACCOMMODATIONS

Hotels in Town

Besides the major hotels and condotels in the Zona Hotelera, San José offers a number of smaller, moderately priced inns in the town itself. Top of the list in terms of value is the hospitable **Hotel Posada Terranova** (tel. 2-05-34, fax 2-09-02) on Calle Degollado (just south of Zaragoza), a converted home with 18 clean, air-conditioned rooms with TV for US$35 s, US$40 d. The inn also features an intimate dining room with an outdoor eating section and a bar.

The **Tropicana Inn** (tel. 2-09-07 or 2-25-80, fax 2-15-90; tel. 415-652-6051 in the U.S.) features attractively decorated rooms around a tile-and-cobblestone fountain courtyard behind the Tropicana Bar and Grill on Blvd. Mijares. Room rates are US$75 s/d Nov.-March, US$44-65 s/d the rest of the year. All rooms come with air-conditioning and direct-dial telephones; other hotel facilities include a swimming pool and complimentary transport to La Playita and Playa Palmilla.

Budget: Friendly and economical **Hotel Colli** (tel. 2-07-25), on Calle Hidalgo between Zaragoza and Doblado, offers 12 simple but comfortable rooms for US$25 s, US$30 d, US$35 t with fan and private bath, or US$33 s, US$38 d with a/c and private bath.

Around the corner the very basic **Hotel Ceci,** at Calle Zaragoza 22 opposite the church, rents 14 rooms with fan for only US$15 s, US$17 d, US$19 t. At night, busy Calle Zaragoza might

make this small, inexpensive hotel a noisy choice. **Hotel Diana,** on Calle Zaragoza a bit west of the Hotel Ceci, has spartan rooms with a/c, TV, and hot water for US$21 s/d.

Farther off the beaten track is the **San José Inn** (tel. 2-09-24) on Calle Obregón between Degollado and Verde. Formerly the Hotel Pagamar, the inn has 14 large, somewhat bare rooms with basic furnishings and hot showers for US$20 s, US$25 d. If the Diana and Colli are full, you can usually count on finding a room here.

Rounding out the budget list are a couple of bottom-of-the-barrel places that should be reserved for those desperate to spend as few pesos as possible. **Posada Señor Mañana,** whimsically decorated with plants, canoes, old tricycles, and caged birds, languishes behind the plaza on Calle Obregón. Rooms, little more than concrete cells with shared toilet facilities, cost US$8-10 a night—when it's open. An unnamed **hostería** at the corner of Obregón and Hidalgo—frequented by transient workers—offers dilapidated, very basic rooms for US$3 a night with shared bath.

Beach Hotels

Four hotels widely spaced along Playa Hotelera are seldom full except in the peak months of December through mid-April. Friendly negotiation can often net a savings of as much as 40% off the usual rack rate. Rates given below do not include 20% tax and service.

Best of the bunch is the 250-room **Presidente Forum Resort Los Cabos** (tel. 2-02-11, fax 2-01-32; tel. 800-327-0200 in the U.S./Canada), a well-designed resort next to the Estero San José with large pool, tennis courts, jacuzzis, fitness center, beach palapas, poolside restaurant, coffee shop, video disco, and auto/ATV rental. The Presidente was recently transformed from a one-only hotel into an all-inclusive resort in which one daily rate covers accommodation, three meals a day (including buffets and a la carte dinners), open bar, service charges, all entertainment and recreational activities, and two nighttime theme parties weekly. The resort also maintains a playground and offers special children's activities. Spacious rooms come with air conditioning, satellite TV, minibar, and telephone. Rates run US$160 during low season, US$170 in the shoulder season (15 July-2 Sept. and 1 Nov.-22 Dec.), and US$200 during peak season (23 Dec.-14 April). Children 6-12 are accommodated at US$20 per day; under six free.

Next west along the beach is the well-maintained **Hotel Best Western Posada Real** (tel. 2-01-55 or 800-528-1234 in the U.S./Canada), where 150 rooms and suites with a/c, telephone, and satellite TV run US$55-60 s/d in the low season, US$85-90 s/d in the high season. Hotel facilities include pool, tennis court, jacuzzi, and restaurant. Most rooms offer ocean views.

A bit farther west, the three-story, 99-room **Hotel Aguamarina** (tel. 2-02-39, fax 2-02-87; tel. 800-342-AMIGO in the U.S./Canada) features clean, standard rooms for US$50-70; even lower rates may be available when occupancy is low.

The last place within the beach hotel zone is the **Fiesta Inn** (tel. 2-07-93 or 800-343-7821 in the U.S./Canada), where rooms with a/c, TV, and phones cost US$70 s/d in the off-season, US$100 s/d at the peak. The Fiesta Inn provides a restaurant and pool.

On the Campo de Golf, a 10- to 15-minute walk from the beach, **Howard Johnson Plaza Suites Resort** (tel. 2-09-99 or 800-654-2000 in the U.S./Canada) offers one-, two-, and three-bedroom apartments with kitchens for US$90-129 in the low season, US$90-140 in the high season.

Condos

Several condominium complexes in the golf course and beach area and on the hill west of Mexico 1 rent vacant units to visitors for anywhere from US$65 a night for a studio or one-bedroom unit to US$300 for a deluxe two- or three-bedroom unit. Discounted weekly and monthly rates are usually available. Local companies that help arrange condo rentals include **Baja Properties** (Doblado and Morelos, tel. 2-09-88, fax 2-09-87) and **Laguna Vista Real Estate** (A.P. 66, San José del Cabo, BCS, tel./fax 2-05-23).

A few complexes will take reservations directly. Along the south edge of the Campo de Golf, **Las Misiones de San José** (tel. 2-14-01, fax 2-14-01) offers 60 two-bedroom condos—with choice of ocean, pool, or golf course views—for US$110 a night. All condos come with a/c, full kitchens, and private terraces.

Southwest of San José del Cabo proper, next to Playa Costa Azul at Km 29, **La Jolla de Los Cabos** (tel. 2-30-00, fax 2-05-46; tel. 8v 5104 in the U.S./Canada) features 196 one- and two-bedroom suites and condos for US$98-155. Facilities include four pools and a gym. **Mira Vista Beachfront Condos** (tel. 2-05-23), in the same area, rents one-bedroom condos by the week (only) for US$700.

Camping and RV Parks

Brisas del Mar Trailer Park (mailing address A.P. 45, San José del Cabo, BCS, tel. 2-28-28), 3.2 km (two miles) southwest of San José off Mexico 1 at Km 28, is so far the only beachfront RV park in the Cabos area. As such, it's often full in the high snowbird season, mid-November through mid-February. For two people/one vehicle, full-hookup RV slots run US$13 and tent spaces US$6, plus US$1.50 per additional guest. Facilities include flush toilets, showers, a laundry, pool, restaurant, and bar. Some full-timers have built studio apartments on the grounds, and these may occasionally become available as rentals. Brisas del Mar is easy to miss; watch carefully for the small sign.

You can camp free on the beach at La Playita between San José and Pueblo La Playa and between Brisas del Mar Trailer Park and the water. Back from the beach in Pueblo La Playa itself, **El Delfín Blanco RV Park** (A.P. 147 San José del Cabo, BCS 23400, tel./fax 2-11-99) rents spaces with full hookups for US$12 a night. Palapa bungalows are also available for rent.

FOOD

Most of San José's fashionable restaurants are found along Blvd. Mijares and Calle Zaragoza in the vicinity of the plaza. These eateries are, for the most part, geared to Mexican diners as well as foreigners—so far the town harbors no equivalents to Cabo San Lucas's Giggling Marlin or Squid Roe.

As a general rule, the closer a restaurant to the plaza, the more expensive the menu. To save money and/or experience local flavor, seek out the spots where San José residents eat—most are in the western part of town toward Mexico 1. At the west end of Calle Doblado are several inexpensive taco stands and *fruterías*. The Mercado Municipal features a section of side-by-side *loncherías* open 0700 till around 1600 or 1700.

Boulevard Mijares

$$ El Café Fiesta (tel. 2-28-08): Right on the plaza on the premises of the former Café Europa, this friendly, cozy cafe-bistro offers espresso coffees, omelettes, salads, burgers, pastries, desserts, and daily specials of "light Mexican food." Open daily 0700-2200.

$$-$$$ Damiana (tel. 2-04-99): Named for the Cape Region's legendary herbal aphrodisiac, and housed in a restored 18th-century townhouse, this is one of the most romantic settings in either San José or San Lucas. The front room is a tastefully decorated bar, followed by an indoor dining area in the middle room, and a patio dining area—candlelit in the evening—in the lushly foliated rear courtyard. House specialties include shrimp, lobster, abalone, and steak. A complimentary taste of *damiana* liqueur is served to guests upon request. Open daily 1030-midnight, serving *almuerzo,* lunch, and dinner.

$$ Iguana Bar (tel. 2-02-66): Although more of a bar than a restaurant, the Iguana serves a variety of well-prepared seafood, ribs, chicken, and Mexican dishes. In the evenings, the restaurant transforms into a nightclub with live music. Open daily 1100-0100.

$$ Mariscos El Muelle: This outdoor grill and collection of palapa-shaded tables features good seafood at reasonable prices. Just north of the road to Pueblo Playa. Open daily 1100-2300.

$-$$ Sandrick's (tel. 2-12-70): Informal late-lunch, après-beach kind of place, specializing in fajitas, burgers, and chimichangas. Open daily except Tuesday 1400-2100.

$$ Tropicana Bar & Grill (tel. 2-09-07): Large, touristy restaurant-bar with outdoor patio, big-screen sports TV, and music and dancing at night. The menu is basic Tourist Mex/Fake Caribbean, but the drinks are strong. Open daily for lunch and dinner.

Calle Zaragoza

$-$$ Asadero Los Candiles (no phone), on Calle Degollado just north of Calle Zaragoza: A recently established outdoor grill with excellent mesquite-grilled *arrachera* (skirt steak, often called fajitas in the U.S. and in some parts of northeastern Mexico). Also serves quesadillas, vegetarian *brochetas, tacos machos* (mild chile pepper stuffed with chopped *arrachera* and cheese inside a folded tortilla), barbecued ribs, *frijoles charros, cebollas asadas* (grilled onions), fresh guacamole, potatoes baked with cheese and sour cream, and other delights. Not to be missed. Open daily from around 1900 till around 2300.

$ Cafetería Rosy: Inexpensive *antojitos* and *licuados.* On Calle Zaragoza near Café Rubi; open 0700-2200.

$-$$ La Cenaduría (no phone): This new eatery opposite the plaza on the south side of Zaragoza is a very welcome addition to the San José restaurant scene. The simple menu covers a range of standard mainland-style *antojitos,* including tostadas, *gorditas, pozole, flautas,* enchiladas, quesadillas, tamales, tacos, *carne asada,* and *pollo en mole.* Open daily 1100-2100.

Calle Zaragoza,
San José del Cabo

$-$$ Jazmín: A casual local eatery with fresh juices and *licuados,* Mexican breakfasts, French toast and pancakes, *chilaquiles,* burgers, tortilla soup, *tortas,* tacos, tostadas, fajitas, *carne asada,* and seafood. Just off Zaragoza on Morelos, opposite the *nevería.* Open daily for breakfast, lunch, and dinner.

$$-$$$ La Fogata: This restaurant specializes in steaks and seafood, along with a few Mexican dishes. Popular for its huge, gringo-style portions. Opposite Bancomer; open daily for breakfast, lunch, and dinner.

$$ Posada Terranova (tel. 2-05-34), on Calle Degollado just south of Zaragoza: This family-run inn features a small dining room and bar, and outdoor seating. The menu offers a good variety of high-quality Mexican and American breakfasts. Open daily 0700-2200.

$$-$$$ Pietro Ristorante Italiano (tel. 2-05-58): This tastefully decorated restaurant-bar near La Fogata serves Italian food for lunch (1145-1545) and dinner (1745-2315).

$ El Recreo: Good fish and shrimp tacos are available at this small stand with tables out front just north of the church on the plaza.

$ Cafetería Arco Iris: Next door to Hotel Diana, this diner-style place serves inexpensive *licuados, tortas,* and burritos.

Other Locations

$$ Amigos Pizza (tel. 2-05-70): Oriented toward a younger crowd, with decent pizzas and recorded music and videos. Open daily 0830-2300.

$-$$ Asadero Las Hornillas: Specializes in mesquite-grilled chicken, steaks, and burgers, for a mostly local clientele. Toward the west end of Calle Doblado; open daily 1200-2100.

$ Baja Natural (no phone): Delicious fresh juices, malts, green salads, fruit salads, and other fruit and vegetable concoctions. On the south side of Calle Doblado between Hidalgo and Morelos; open Mon.-Sat. 0900-2000.

$$-$$$ El Caribeño, Presidente Forum Resort, Zona Hotelera: This palapa-roofed restaurant on the beach wins the grand prize for most atmospheric breakfast spot. It's open daily 0700-1130, serving Mexican and international fare.

$$-$$$ Le Bistrot (tel. 2-11-74): A very nicely decorated, slightly formal restaurant with good French and European cuisine, omelettes, salads, sandwiches. On Calle Morelos between Coronado and Juárez, near the telecommunications tower; open Tues.-Sun. 1300-2200.

$ Huatabampo: Local spot with inexpensive seafood cocktails, tacos, and burritos; west end of Calle Doblado.

$$ Los Dos Ricardos (tel. 2-30-68): A typical but out-of-the-way, palapa-roofed seafood place. On the road through Pueblo La Playa; open daily 1100-2200.

$ Restaurant El Descanso: Housed in an old adobe building, this 24-hour eatery serves *menudo, pozole, birria, barbacoa,* tamales, and other Mexican soul food. On Calle Castro, diagonally opposite the Mercado Municipal.

$-$$ Restaurant El Sinaloense: This sparkling little Mexican restaurant, popular with the business-lunch crowd, serves well-prepared seafood, fish tacos, and burritos. In the Plaza Los Cabos shopping center, between the golf course and hotel zone in the FONATUR district; open Mon.-Sat. 1100-2100.

$ Restaurant El Super Burro: Small, family-run palapa restaurant with seafood, *carnes rojas* (Mexican steaks), tacos, and burritos. On the south side of Calle Canseco, east of the main bus station; open daily for lunch and dinner.

$-$$ Taquería Indio, off the west side of Mexico 1 on Calle Malvarrosa (one street north of Calle Canseco) in the Colina de los Maestros neighborhood: Similar to Asadero Los Candiles; very good corn on the cob *(elotes), tacos de carne asada,* quesadillas, *frijoles charros, cebollas asadas,* and potatoes *(papas),* with choice of shrimp, mushrooms, steak, or corn. Lots of fresh condiments. Generally open 1800-midnight.

$ Twin Dragon: The better of San José's two Chinese restaurants for inexpensive Cantonese dishes. On the south side of Calle Doblado between Guerrero and Morelos; open Mon.-Sat. for lunch and dinner.

Groceries

The **Mercado Municipal,** between calles Castro and Coronado in the west part of town, provides fresh fruits and vegetables, fish, meats, a *licuado* stand, and a cluster of *loncherías;* it's open daily from dawn to dusk.

More expensive canned and imported foods, plus beer and liquor, are available at decades-old **Almacenes Goncanseco,** Blvd. Mijares 14-18 (opposite city hall); this supermarket accepts credit cards. A couple of smaller grocery stores are located along the west end of Calle Zaragoza.

Facing the east side of Mexico 1, just north of the west end of Calle Doblado, **Supermercado Grupo Castro** is larger and more well-stocked than Almacenes Goncanseco. Better yet is the large and modern **Supermercado Plaza,** located a half kilometer north of town on the east side of Mexico 1. Both of these supermarkets can supply just about any food/liquor/ice needs.

Toward the west end of Calle Zaragoza is **Pastelería y Panadería La Princesa,** with a good selection of Mexican cakes, pastries, and bread. Pricier European-style baked items are available at **La Baguette,** Blvd. Mijares 10, on the east side of the plaza, near Café Europa.

Tortillería Perla, diagonally opposite the hospital on Calle Doblado, sells corn tortillas by the kilo Mon.-Sat. 0500-1500, Sunday 0500-1200. On the west side of Mexico 1, almost opposite the west end of Calle Doblado, **Tortillería de Harina** supplies flour tortillas during roughly the same hours. Along the same side of the highway, just south of Calle Doblado, **Panadería San José** has the usual tongs-and-tray baked goods.

Coffee—ground, whole bean, or fresh-brewed—can be purchased at **Café Rubi,** toward the west end of Calle Zaragoza near where the street bends north.

ENTERTAINMENT AND EVENTS

Bars and Discos
While San José doesn't offer as much of a night-time party scene as Cabo San Lucas, neither does the town close down at sunset—although in low season it may seem that way. The most relaxed spot is the **Iguana Bar** (tel. 2-02-66) on Blvd. Mijares, where live bands play a mix of Latino and international pop. Popular **Tropicana Bar & Grill** (tel. 2-09-07) across the street features lounge-lizard folk music in the front room and canned music in the back. Both bars host a two-drinks-for-the-price-of-one happy hour in the late afternoon.

The **Club Eclipse,** near the Iguana on Blvd. Mijares, is a sizable video disco pushing "Daks" (daiquiris) and "Margs" (margaritas). The Presidente Forum Resort has its own **Bones Video Disco** for folks who don't want to leave the Zona Hotelera. Both are open 1800-0300 daily.

Events
On most Saturday evenings during the Dec.-March high tourist season San José hosts a fiesta in Plaza Mijares. Although mostly held for the benefit of tourists, lots of locals attend as well. Typical events include folk dances, mariachi performances, cockfight demonstrations, and piñata breaking, with food vendors and arts-and-crafts sales. Profits from food and beverage sales go to local charities and service clubs.

San José's biggest annual festival is held 19 March, the feast day of its patron saint: In addition to music, dancing, and food, celebratory activities include horse races and parades.

SHOPPING

Near the intersection of Blvd. Mijares and the road to Pueblo La Playa, about halfway between the Zona Hotelera and the plaza, is a large open-air market selling inexpensive Mexican handicrafts; it's generally open 1100-2100. Higher-quality and higher-priced arts and crafts are offered in shops along the east end of Calle Zaragoza and the north end of Blvd. Mijares, including **Copal** (handmade furniture, antiques, rugs, folk art, and ceramics), **Bye-Bye** (T-shirts and souvenirs), **La Casa Vieja** (folk art, jewelry, beachwear), **Galería El Dorado** (modern sculpture), and **La Mina** (silver jewelry).

Galería Los Cabos, on Calle Hidalgo north of Obregón, sells a unique assortment of antique and rattan furniture, stoneware, crafts, decorator items, and locally made barrel-back chairs.

Arte Diseño Decoración (ADD) (tel. 2-27-77), on Calle Zaragoza near Hidalgo, sells high-quality, original home accessories and furniture—perfect for anyone looking to furnish a vacation home.

Killer Hook Surf Shop, on Calle Hidalgo between Zaragoza and Doblado, stocks a variety of surfing, snorkeling, and other water-sports equipment, as well as T-shirts and stickers. Killer Hook also has a branch opposite Playa Costa Azul, southwest of town, where you can rent surf gear. Next door to Killer Hook's town shop is **Clio,** a small boutique featuring fashions for young women.

Publicaciones May, on the north side of Calle Doblado near the street's west end, carries a large collection of books, magazines, and newspapers—though mostly in Spanish.

Organización Sierra Madre (tel. 24151), on Blvd. Mijares near Sandrick's, sells T-shirts emblazoned with endangered species, books on natural Mexico, and other ecologically conscious souvenirs. Proceeds from the sale of these items support a variety of conservation efforts in Baja California and northwestern Mexico, including cleanups of Estero San José.

SPORTS AND RECREATION

Fishing

All hotels in the Zona Hotelera can arrange guided fishing trips. Since San José has no harbor or marina, all trips are in pangas. One of the more reputable outfits is **Victor's Sportfishing** (tel. 2-10-92), headquartered at Hotel Posada Real. You can also hire pangas directly from the *pangeros* at the beach next to Pueblo La Playa. Whether using a guide arranged through one of the hotels or at La Playita, it's best to bring your own rods and tackle as the quality of local guide-supplied gear is rather low.

Onshore and inshore catches include cabrilla, grouper, roosterfish, sierra, snapper, jack crevalle, pompano, and occasional yellowtail. Farther offshore you might catch tuna, dorado, and sailfish. One of Baja's best marlin and wahoo grounds is Bancos Gorda (Gorda Banks), two seamounts about 16 km (10 miles) southeast of San José. Striped marlin are seen year-round in Cape Region waters; angling for dorado, roosterfish, and sailfish is best in the late summer and early fall.

If you're going out on your own, or just want to try a little surfcasting from the beach, you can rent rod-and-tackle sets for US$6 a day at **Killer Hook Surf Shop** on Calle Hidalgo downtown.

BOB RACE

roosterfish

Golf and Tennis

Surrounded by FONATUR condotel projects, the **Campo de los Cabos** ("Los Cabos Country Club," also known simply as "Campo de Golf") features a well-groomed, 18-hole golf course with a sea view. Another nine holes are planned for the future. This is a challenging course; the third hole extends 540 yards, with a lake in the middle of the fairway. The greens fee is US$18; carts (US$14) and clubs (US$12) are available for rent. Tee-offs can be scheduled daily 0700-1600.

The club also features tennis courts, a pool, clubhouse, pro shop, restaurants, and a bar.

Race and Sports Book

A branch of Tijuana's **LF Caliente,** attached to the Fiesta Inn, offers off-track and sports betting using Vegas odds in a bar-restaurant setting. You don't have to gamble to enjoy a drink or a meal while watching the club's bank of closed-circuit TVs. Hours are 0900-2200 Sun.-Thurs., 0900-midnight Fri.-Saturday.

SERVICES

Changing Money

Two banks in town offer foreign-currency exchange services, open Mon.-Fri. 0830-1130. The lines at **Bancomer,** one block west of the plaza at calles Zaragoza and Morelos, are generally the longest; during high tourist season if you're not in line by 1100, you might not make it to the foreign-exchange window before it closes. On the other hand, Bancomer offers an automatic teller machine, so if you've brought along a Visa debit card (or an ATM card on the Cirrus system) you can avoid the lines altogether.

Banca Serfin, two blocks west of Bancomer on Calle Zaragoza, usually has shorter lines. Banca Serfin has an ATM next to the Supermercado Grupo Castro, just north of Calle Doblado on the east side of Mexico 1.

There don't appear to be any *casas de cambio* in San José, although the major hotels will gladly take your dollars at a low exchange rate.

Post and Telephone

San José's post and telegraph office, on Blvd. Mijares, is open Mon.-Fri. 0800-1700. The public telephone office on Calle Doblado, opposite the hospital, offers direct-dial long-distance phone service. LADATEL booths, the most convenient public phones for making international calls, can be found at calles Doblado and Muñoz and on Calle Hidalgo between Obregón and Comonfort. There are also several private long-distance services in town.

San José's area code is 114.

COTP

Although it's unlikely any international boaters will be needing a Captain of the Port since there are as yet no marinas or harbors in San José del Cabo, the town does have its own **Capitania de Puerto**. The office sits at the east end of Calle Doblado after it crosses Blvd. Mijares.

SEDESOL

A *subdelegación* office of the Secretaría de Desarollo Social (SEDESOL), the government organ responsible for ecological protection, can be found at the southwest corner of Calle Obregón at Morelos.

Laundry

Laundry Vera offers assisted or do-it-yourself laundry services Mon.-Sat. 0800-2000. It's just east of Restaurant El Super Burro and the main bus station on Calle Canseco.

Storage

Los Cabos Mini & RV Storage (tel. 2-09-76 or 310-924-5853 in the U.S.) offers locked, garage-style storage units within a fenced and lighted complex with 24-hour security. One of the few services of its kind anywhere in northwestern Mexico, the storage facility can be found at Km 37 on Mexico 1 (about five km south of Los Cabos International Airport).

TRANSPORTATION

Air

Los Cabos International Airport (SJD), 12.8 km (eight miles) north of San José del Cabo via Mexico 1, services both San José and Cabo San Lucas. The airport includes several snack bars, souvenir shops, and a money-exchange service. There are no seats in the waiting area for arriving flights, a minor inconvenience for those meeting incoming passengers. An offi-

---

USEFUL SAN JOSE DEL CABO TELEPHONE NUMBERS
(San José del Cabo area code: 114)

Police: 2-00-57
Red Cross: 2-03-16
General Hospital: 2-01-80
Tourism Office: 2-00-13

---

cial port of entry, Los Cabos' paved, 2,195-meter (7,200-foot) runway is tower-controlled (Unicom 118.9), offers fuel, and can receive DC-10s and 747s. Auto rental agencies with airport booths include AMCA, National, Avis, Hertz, Dollar, and Thrifty.

Four airlines—Aero California, Alaska, Continental, and Mexicana—fly into Los Cabos. **Aero California** (tel. 3-08-27 or 3-08-48) has daily nonstop flights to Los Cabos from Los Angeles and Phoenix. **Alaska** (tel. 2-10-15) schedules nonstop flights to Los Cabos from Los Angeles and San Diego, with connecting flights from Anchorage, Palm Springs, Phoenix, Portland, San Francisco, and Seattle/Tacoma. **Mexicana** (tel. 2-06-06 or 2-02-30) offers nonstop flights to Los Cabos from Los Angeles, Guadalajara, and Mazatlán, with connecting flights from Chicago, Los Angeles, Sacramento, San Diego, Mexico City, Monterrey, Puerto Vallarta, and Tokyo. Continental (tel. 2-38-80) recently began offering nonstops between Houston and Los Cabos.

Mexicana maintains a ticket office at Plaza Los Cabos on Paseo San José in the Zona Hotelera; Aero California's office is in the Centro Comercial Plaza in Cabo San Lucas. Mexicana and Aero California also have ticket counters at Los Cabos airport; Alaska and Continental handle ticket sales only at the airport.

For San Francisco and Los Angeles residents, one of the best air deals around is offered by SunTrips (tel. 800-786-8747), a charter company with roundtrip air fares from SFO and LAX to Los Cabos as low as US$119-149 for a seven-night stay during low season, up to US$300 Dec.-March. SunTrips can also arrange charter connections through California from Boston and New York for another US$100-150.

Airport Transport: A taxi from the airport to any destination in San José del Cabo costs US$4 per person or US$11 for an entire taxi.

Departure Tax: Los Cabos International Airport collects a US$12 departure tax from every passenger, payable in cash only.

Bus

From San José's main bus station (tel. 2-11-00) on Calle V.G. Canseco, Aguila/ABC runs 10 buses per day to La Paz (US$5.40) and 10 buses to Cabo San Lucas (US$.90). The last bus to Cabo San Lucas leaves around 2000. Each day at 1600 a first-class bus also leaves for the 24-hour trip all the way to Tijuana (US$44.40). The bus station features a small cafeteria and a *licuado* stand.

Autotransportes Los Frailes del Trópico (tel. 2-21-57) on Calle Ibarra between Castro and Doblado runs vans and small buses to Cabo San Lucas for US$1.50.

Vehicle Rental

Several auto rental agencies—AMCA (tel. 2-13-14, or 800-832-9529 in the U.S./Canada), Dollar (tel. 2-06-71, or 800-800-4000 in the U.S./Canada), Hertz (tel. 2-09-30, or 800-654-3131 in the U.S./Canada), National (tel. 2-04-04, or 800-328-4567 in the U.S./Canada), Thrifty (tel. 2-09-62, or 800-367-2277 in the U.S./Canada), Avis (tel. 2-11-80, or 800-331-1212 in the U.S./Canada)—maintain desks at Los Cabos International Airport as well as offices in or near town. Rates average US$29 a day (or US$174 per week) for a non-a/c VW bug, US$46 (US$276 per week) for a non-a/c VW Golf or Ford Topaz, US$49 (US$294 per week) for a Golf or Topaz with a/c, US$54 (US$324 per week) for an a/c Nissan Tsuru II, US$64 (US$384 per week) for a Jeep Wrangler, and US$63 (US$378 per week) for a VW Combi van. Some companies also offer a "topless" or open-air VW bug for US$25 a day (US$150 per week). These prices usually include unlimited free kilometers; if the companies decide to add per-kilometer charges, which sometimes happens during a strong high season, you can usually negotiate for a free-kilometers rate.

In town, Dollar runs an office at the corner of Guerrero and Zaragoza; Thrifty and AMCA have offices on the highway near the town entrance, next to a Nissan dealer, while Hertz has a lot a little north of town on the east side of highway, with National practically next door.

Vagabundos (no phone), next to the Presidente Forum Resort, rents motor scooters and ATVs for US$8-10 an hour or US$22-30 per day.

Taxi

Visitors staying in town or at the beach are able to see most of what San José has to offer on foot. If you tire of walking, typical taxi fares are US$1.80 from the Zona Hotelera to the plaza downtown, US$2.40 from downtown to Pueblo La Playa, US$6.60 from town to Los Cabos airport. Taxis congregate in front of the beach hotels and along Blvd. Mijares toward the plaza.

THE CORRIDOR

The Transpeninsular Highway's 29-km (18-mile), four-lane stretch between San José del Cabo and Cabo San Lucas provides access to numerous beaches, coves, points, and tidal pools along the Pacific Ocean/Sea of Cortez. Known officially as the Corredor Naútico ("Nautical Corridor"), or more commonly in English simply as "the Corridor," the whole strip is sometimes called Costa Azul or "Blue Coast," although this is also the name of a single beach near San José.

Private companies are starting to string utility poles along the Corridor. Already the highway is well-lit along its northeast end between San José del Cabo and the Westin Regina Los Cabos. Most of the roads branching south of the highway are unpaved. Almost all can be negotiated by ordinary passenger vehicles, though the overall number of public access roads is declining fast due to private development. In some cases it's necessary to park along the highway or in a nearby hotel parking lot and walk down to the beach.

Near Km 17 Mexico's ruling party constructed a monolith inscribed "Construido en Solidaridad" to mark the highway's 1993 completion. In November of the same year, a rainstorm heavily damaged the just-completed highway, destroying the three bridges spanning major arroyos along the route. Repairs and/or alternate routes were completed within weeks, and today this roadway represents one of Mexico's finest non-toll routes.

BEACHES AND ACTIVITIES

One after another, beautiful beaches and coves hug the coastline between San José and Cabo San Lucas. Some are hidden from highway view by bluffs, others are marked by resort development.

To find these beaches, follow the SEDESOL signs (older signs may read "SEDUE") along Mexico 1 labeled "Acceso a Playa." Sometimes these signs include the name of the beach, sometimes not. The accompanying key lists all those beaches accessible from the highway.

Swimming

Not all the Corridor beaches are suitable for year-round swimming. Starting from the San José end, one of the best is **Playa Costa Azul,** where a long strip of sand next to the Mykonos and La Jolla condo developments is gently washed by low breakers (except during the *chubasco* season—see "Surfing," below). At

BEACHES BETWEEN SAN JOSE DEL CABO AND CABO SAN LUCAS

BEACH	NEAREST KM MARKER	DISTANCE WEST OF KM MARKER, IN METERS
Costa Azul	29	500
Acapulquito	27	600
Arroyo Seco/Punta Palmilla	26	400
Punta Bella	24	400
Buenos Aires	22	400
El Mirador	20	—
San Carlos	19	—
El Zalate	17	500
Costa Brava	17	100
Cantamar	16	700
Del Tule	15	400
Punta Chileno	14	—
Santa María	12	200
Twin Dolphin (Las Viudas)	11	500
Barco Varado ("Shipwreck")	9-10	—
Cabo Bello	6	200
Cemeterio	4	—

(previous page) islets near Isla Espíritu Santo; (this page, top) Cabo San Lucas;
(this page, bottom) Bahía Santa María (Joe Cummings)

Playa Chileno

Zipper's, a palapa restaurant at the south end of the beach, surfers, surfer wannabes, and tourists fill up on tasty mesquite-grilled hamburgers, fish burgers, chili, chiles rellenos, and quesadillas; it's open Mon.-Sat. 1100-2300, Sunday 0830-2300. A palapa extension under construction will eventually feature live music.

Farther southwest, a new breakwater has tamed the waters along a lengthy stretch of beach north of the Hotel Meliá Cabo Real, part of **Bahía El Bledito.** Look for an access road just north of Km 20. As the huge Cabo Real development expands, public access may change though hopefully access won't be (illegally) denied.

A little more than halfway to Cabo San Lucas, the wide crescents of sand rimming Bahía Chileno and Bahía Santa María constitute two of the Corridor's most popular and accessible swimming beaches. **Playa Chileno** is larger and more well-endowed with public facilities. Visitors walk through a gate in the chain-link fence protecting the beach from vehicles and follow a path through a grove of fan palms to reach the beach itself. The palms provide natural shade, a component lacking at most other Corridor beaches. Free public restrooms and showers are available, while Cabo Acuadeportes rents water-sports equipment from a booth at the south end of the beach. Beneath the houses perched on headlands at either end of the bay are rocky areas with good snorkeling. Though very picturesque and suitable for swimming, **Playa Santa María** offers a much smaller beach and is short on facilities and shade; it's a beach best enjoyed by snorkelers and divers rather than swimmers.

Playa Las Viudas ("Widows Beach"), more commonly known as Twin Dolphins Beach, is reached via a rough sand turnoff at Km 12 next to the private entrance to the Hotel Twin Dolphins. Vehicles with high road clearance will fare better than ordinary sedans. The tan-colored beach—actually several scalloped beaches separated by small rocky points—tends to be on the pebbly side, though the swimming is usually good.

Northeast of Cabo San Lucas at Km 4, little-known **Playa Cemeterio** offers calm swimming and white sands. Conditions are similar to those at Cabo's Playa El Médano but with fewer people.

Surfing

Although Los Cabos is less famous than Baja's northern and central Pacific coast for surf, the summer southwest swell brings decent wave action to the tip of the peninsula, when most of the west coast points are flat. The surf reaches peak height during the *chubasco* season, late summer to early fall. Probably the most dependable surfing area between San José and Cabo San Lucas is **Playa Costa Azul,** at Km 29-28, where a grinding shore-breaker called "Zippers" is sometimes backed by Hawaii-style outside breaks in heavy swell. **Punta Palmilla,** below the Hotel Palmilla at Km 28-27, whips out a decent point break, while the bay to the point's immediate north, **Playa Acapulquito,** offers a good reef break in heavy swell.

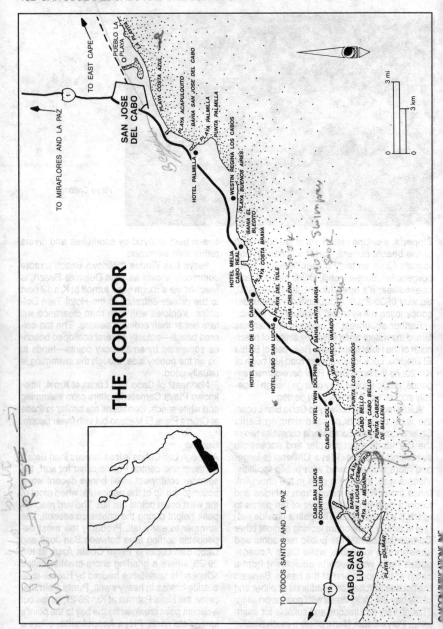

THE CORRIDOR

TO MIRAFLORES AND LA PAZ

TO EAST CAPE

PUEBLO LA O PLAYA LA PALMILLA

SAN JOSE DEL CABO

Playa Costa Azul
Playa Acapulquito
Bahia San Jose del Cabo
Playa Palmilla
Punta Palmilla

HOTEL PALMILLA

WESTIN REGINA LOS CABOS

Playa Buenos Aires

Bahia El
Bledito

HOTEL MELIA CABO REAL

Playa Costa Brava

Playa del Tule

Bahia Chileno

Playa Chileno

HOTEL PALACIO DE LOS CABOS

Bahia Santa Maria

HOTEL CABO SAN LUCAS

Playa Barco Varado

Punta Los Anegados

HOTEL TWIN DOLPHIN

Playa Cabo Bello

Cabo Bello

CABO DEL SOL

Punta Cabeza de Ballena

Playa Cabo Bello

Playa San Lucas (Cemeterio)

Playa El Medano

Bahia San Lucas

CABO SAN LUCAS COUNTRY CLUB

CABO SAN LUCAS

TO TODOS SANTOS AND LA PAZ

Playa Solmar

3 mi

3 km

0   0

Reef breaks sometimes occur at **Playa Buenos Aires,** at Km 22 (but beware strong rips), and **Playa Cabo Real,** Km 20; then there's a gap until **Playa Cantamar** at Km 16 and **Punta Chileno** at Km 14, both offering workable point breaks. **Playa Cabo Bello,** between Kilometers 6 and 5 (near the Hotel Cabo San Lucas), is known for a consistent reef break nicknamed "Monuments" for the H-shaped concrete monument that used to stand next to the highway near here. This break is fueled by northwest swell refracted off Cabo San Lucas, and is the easternmost break for winter surfing.

Most of these beaches now feature some sort of condo or resort development in progress but there's always a way to drive through or around them: it's illegal to restrict public beach access.

Diving
Several beaches along the Corridor feature rock reefs suitable for snorkeling and scuba diving, particularly **Playa Santa María** (Km 12), **Playa Chileno** (Km 14), and **Playa Barco Varado** (Shipwreck Beach, Km 9-10). Santa María offers rocky reefs at either end of a protected cove at depths of 13 meters (40 feet) or less. The north point displays sea fans and gorgonians, along with the usual assortment of tropical fish. The south end has sea caves, coral outcroppings, and large rocky areas inhabited by reef fish and lobster.

The remains of the Japanese tuna boat *Inari Maru No. 10,* stranded on rocky shoals in 1966, is the main diving destination at Shipwreck Beach. A local story says that when Cabo *pescadores* noticed the Japanese vessel fishing illegally, they extinguished the nearest lighthouse beacon and rigged a light of their own that lured the boat onto the shoals after nightfall. The hull and other wreckage lie within 2-26 meters (6.5-85 feet) of the bay surface; there are also scenic rock reefs in the vicinity. Tidal pools containing starfish and sea urchins are located along the beach.

HOTELS AND GOLF RESORTS

Five of Los Cabos's priciest and best-situated hotels grace the coast along the Corridor. Designed to appeal to the well-heeled hedonist seeking a degree of privacy and seclusion not

found in Mexican beach resorts like Puerto Vallarta, Cancún, Mazatlán, or Acapulco (and avoiding the hot, rainy summers elsewhere in coastal Mexico), these resorts take full advantage of their desert remoteness. Don't forget to pack your irons and woods; golf is quickly becoming almost as big an attraction as beachgoing and fishing now that the area boasts several world-class golf courses.

Even if you have no plans to stay in the area, the hotel bars are worth a visit for a drink and the ocean view.

Hotel Palmilla Resort
Covering 384 hectares (950 acres) of Punta Palmilla near Km 27 is the Cape's first major resort, built in 1956 by "Rod" Rodríguez, son of former Mexican President Abelardo Luis Rodríguez. Coconut palms, clouds of hibiscus, and sweeping sea views dominate the grounds. Facilities include a pool; tennis, croquet, paddleball, and volleyball courts; a giant outdoor chessboard; stables; a restaurant and bar; a chapel used for weddings; and a 1,370-meter (4,500-foot) illuminated airstrip (Unicom 122.8). The Hotel Palmilla maintains its own sportfishing fleet, offering panga trips (one to three anglers) for US$250 per day or long-range cruises (one to four anglers) for US$395 per day. Scuba-diving programs cost US$45-65 for guided beach dives, US$55-75 for boat dives.

A Jack Nicklaus–designed, 27-hole golf course recently opened its first 18 holes at the Palmilla and by all accounts it's a splendid course. Nicklaus himself, though admitting his bias as the designer (this is his first course in Latin America), claims the 17th and 18th holes are the best finishing holes in the world. The course's signature hole is the 440-yard, par 4 "Mountain Five," which necessitates a long drive across two desert arroyos. Gray water is used to irrigate the fairways and greens, easing the strain on the Los Cabos water supply. Guests may play for a greens fee of US$75 per 18 holes Nov.-May, US$50 June-Oct.; nonguests are charged US$100 Nov.-May, US$75 June-October. Fees include golf cart, practice balls, and use of the driving range. The golf course serves as the centerpiece of a new 384-hectare (950-acre) development surrounding the original hotel with fairway homes, a network of paved roads, clubhouse, and tennis complex.

The Palmilla's room rates vary from US$135 s/d/t/q (US$145 on weekends) in summer in the Garden section to US$275 (US$315 weekends) for a Vista Suite in winter. Two-bedroom Primera Suites sleeping up to four are also available for US$410-450 (summer) or US$550-625 (winter); five-bedroom Casas cost from US$800 (summer weekday) to US$1000 (winter weekend). These rates don't include the 10% tax and 15% service. For information contact Hotel Palmilla Reservations (4343 Von Karman Ave., Newport Beach, CA 92660-2083; tel. 714-833-3033 or 800-637-2226). In Baja, dial (114) 2-05-83 for the hotel, (114) 2-05-02 for the golf course.

If even the Hotel Palmilla's La Cantina bar seems beyond your budget, you might at least enjoy the beach below by stopping in at **Restaurant-Bar Pepe's** on Playa Palmilla, where the first drink is on Pepe; if he's not in attendance, the first *two* drinks are on the house.

Westin Regina Resort Los Cabos

Hidden from the highway by brick-hued Cerro Colorado, just past Km 22 on the Transpeninsular Hwy. (only 10 minutes drive from San José del Cabo), the new *gran turismo*-class Westin Regina Los Cabos opened in 1994 at a cost of US$200 million, making it the most expensive hotel ever built in Mexico. Renowned Mexican architect Javier Sordo Madaleno endowed the bold curvilinear design with a bright palette of colors abstracted from the surrounding geological, floral, and marine environment. A Zen-like rock-and-cactus garden on a hillside overlooks a dramatic seaside pool fed by a sophisticated water recycling system. On the opposite hillside to the immediate north of the hotel stand numerous pastel-colored time-share and residential units managed by the hotel.

All 243 rooms and suites come with sea views, large marble bathrooms, ceiling fans, a/c, in-room safes, refreshment bars, satellite TV, and IDD phone for US$158-279 s/d per night; palatial suites start at US$410. These rates do not include 10% tax and 10% service charge.

Restaurant Arrecifes commands a view of the wave-battered beach below; the eclectic menu emphasizes Mediterranean, sushi, and seafood. A restaurant on the ground floor, **La Cascada,** specializes in Mexican and seafood;

Westin Regina Resort

there is also a poolside snack bar. Guests have golf privileges at the new Cabo Real golf course, about 2.5 km southwest. For information or reservations, call the Westin Regina Resort at (114) 2-90-00, fax 2-90-11; tel. 800-228-3000 in the U.S./Canada, or 91-800-90-223 in Mexico.

Hotel Meliá Cabo Real

A bit farther down the highway at Km 19.5 the new Hotel Meliá Cabo Real presides over scenic Bahía El Bledito. Rated a *gran turismo* resort, the Meliá Cabo Real's 292 rooms and suites—almost all with ocean view—are laid out like a squared-off horseshoe around a huge pyramid-topped lobby. Guests can swim at the beach (tamed by the addition of a rock jetty) or in the hotel's large pool.

A sprawling 1,012 hectares (2,500 acres) of adjacent land is currently being developed as a resort that will eventually include a 27-hole Robert Trent Jones, Jr. golf course with two lakes, as well as another 2,000 hotel rooms, 1,500 condo units, 450 family home lots, and five beach clubs. The golf course is open to hotel guests staying at the Westin Regina Los Cabos and the Meliá Cabo Real, as well as to the general public for a green fee of US$50 per nine holes; call (114) 3-03-61 in Mexico for course information.

Well-appointed rooms with all the amenities, including a safe box, cost US$80-180 per night, plus tax and service. For information or reservations, contact the Meliá Cabo Real at (114) 3-09-67, fax 3-10-03; tel. (800) 336-3542 in the U.S./Canada.

Hotel Palacio de Los Cabos

Formerly called Hotel María Gaviota, the Palacio de Los Cabos (P.O. Box 2-57, La Paz, BCS 23040, tel. 114-3-33-77, fax 5-86-55) overlooks Playa Cantamar near Km 17. Though not in the same class as the Corridor's *gran turismo* resorts, the hotel's 40 one- and two-bedroom suites come with full kitchen, sitting room, satellite TV, and a/c, and start at a bargain (in this neighborhood) US$90 per night, not including tax and service. The nicely landscaped premises feature a pool, restaurant, bar, and health center.

Hotel Cabo San Lucas

Farther southwest between Km 15 and 14, the **Hotel Cabo San Lucas** (tel. 213-205-0055 or 800-733-2226 in the U.S.) perches on Punta Chileno facing Playa del Tule. Another heavy hitter in the colonial-luxury league, the Cabo San Lucas came along early in the game in 1958 and features its own hunting ranch, as well as sportfishing excursions, horseback riding, a three-level swimming pool, a dive cen-

ter, a 1,200-meter (3,950-foot) airstrip, and an Asian art gallery. The reef below the hotel, on the Playa Chileno side of the point, is suitable for snorkeling and surfing. Almost more Hawaiian than Mexican in overall style, the hotel charges US$80-100 in summer, US$120-180 in winter. One- and two-bedroom apartments that sleep up to four guests are available for US$260 a night, three- to seven-room villas cost US$920-1410 (plus 20% tax and service).

Hotel Twin Dolphin

One of the Corridor's original 1950s triumvirate is the Twin Dolphin Hotel (tel. 3-04-96 in Los Cabos; tel. 213-386-3940 or 800-421-8925 in the U.S.) at Km 11. Like the Palmilla, the Twin Dolphin offers splendid ocean views. Playa Santa María, to the immediate north, is one of Los Cabos' best snorkeling/diving beaches. The hotel has its own fishing fleet, an 18-hole putting green, dive center, pool, tennis courts, horseback riding, restaurant, and bar. The 50 oceanfront rooms, each with private terrace, cost US$225 s, US$310 d, and US$20 for each additional guest (plus 20% tax and service).

Cabo del Sol

Jack Nicklaus has designed his second set of Mexican fairways on 730 hectares (1,800 acres) of land between Playa Barco Varado and Cabo Bello (near Km 7). Seven of the course's holes feature dramatic oceanfront play along the shore of Bahía de Ballenas. On the drawing board are the usual housing sites, a tennis center, and a small exclusive hotel—most likely a Grand Hyatt. For information on the golf course, call (114) 3-31-49.

CABO SAN LUCAS

Cabo San Lucas and San José del Cabo enjoy equal access to the great beaches along the Corridor between the two towns, but because the San Lucas harbor provides shelter for a sizable sportfishing and recreational fleet, the preponderance of the 300,000-plus yearly Los Cabos visitors station themselves here rather than in San José or along the Corridor. Several cruise lines also feature Cabo San Lucas on their itineraries. With a permanent population of only 25,000, many of them retirees, the tourist-resident ratio runs higher than elsewhere in the Cape Region, especially during the peak Nov.-March tourist season.

Yet in spite of all the tourists—most of whom confine themselves to the waterfront—Cabo manages to retain something of a funky, small-town feel. Away from Blvd. Marina, many of the unpaved, sand streets are lined with the *tortillerías,* hardware shops, and markets typically found in any small coastal Mexican town.

Named for the slender cape extending eastward from Baja California's southernmost tip, Cabo San Lucas is the only city in Mexico with a marine preserve within its city limits. Created in 1973, the protected 36-square-km (14-square-mile) patch of sea and shore designates special boat lanes, boating speed limits, and restricted fishing and recreation craft areas, all under the watchful eye of Grupo Ecológico de Cabo San Lucas. Nowhere else among Mexi-

co's top-drawing seaside resorts will you find such pristine beaches within so short a distance (5-10 minutes by boat taxi) of the town center.

Outside this area, however, hotel and condo development marches ahead. Pedregal—a fashionable hillside district to the west—the marina, and Playa El Médano to the east are all chockablock with condos and villas. Next to undergo development will probably be the large section of unused harborfront property near the inner harbor entrance, where an old cannery and ferry pier sit abandoned.

While yachting and sportfishing bring an older, early-to-bed crowd to Cabo, the town's nightlife attracts an energetic youth market, creating a more vibrant ambience than is found at relatively staid San José del Cabo, 29 km (18 miles) northeast. As the last stop on the 1,700-km (thousand-mile) transpeninsular Baja road trip, Cabo also acts as a receptacle for old Baja hands looking for a few days or weeks of R&R before beginning the long return drive across relatively unpopulated desert landscapes.

Thus, as residents and repeat visitors will point out, you never know who you'll run into in Cabo; yachties on their way to and from exotic South Pacific ports, cops on a fishing vacation, Baja road warriors, honeymoon couples, Mexico City denizens cleaning out their lead-filled lungs, rockers resting up after a continental tour, or Montana cowboys escaping the snow—

they've all set themselves temporarily adrift in the Pacific, like the Cape itself as it inches westward from mainland Mexico.

CLIMATE

At a latitude (22° 55' 44") below the Tropic of Cancer, Cabo San Lucas is sunny and mild year-round. The town's location at the confluence of the Pacific Ocean and the Sea of Cortez means ocean currents and airstreams from both sides of the peninsula tend to moderate the general climatic influences of each; neither the cool Pacific nor the warm Cortez completely dominates in any given season. Hence summers aren't as hot as in La Paz (220 km north on the Cortez side), and winters aren't as cool as in Todos Santos (72 km north on the Pacific).

The average temperature in August is 27° C (81° F), in January 18° C (64° F). Maximum temperatures rarely exceed 33° C (92° F) and minimum readings seldom fall below 13° C (56° F).

Cabo San Lucas boasts an average of 360 days of sunshine a year. Annual rainfall averages a scant 19 cm (7.5 inches), most falling Aug.-October. Brief showers are sometimes encountered as late as November or early December.

HISTORY

The Pericús and the English

In pre-Cortesian times the only humans enjoying Cabo San Lucas were the Pericús, one of the nomadic Guaycura Indian groups that inhabited the Cape Region for hundreds if not thousands of years. Standard anthropology says that, like other Amerindians in North and South America, the Pericús were descendants of Asian groups who traversed the prehistoric land bridge between the Eurasian and American continents. One fringe theory, however, suggests the Pericús may originally have come from Tahiti. The tip of the Cape dangles just north of latitude 22°, with the star Arcturus overhead; Tahitian navigators traditionally followed Arcturus on their course to Hawaii, and it's possible that during bad weather a fleet of Tahitian boats were blown off course until east of the Hawaiian islands. Picking up on the Arcturus route, their next logical landfall would have been the Cape. Seventeenth- and early 18th-century English descriptions of the Pericús lend at least partial credence to the theory by pointing out how much the Pericús' physical and social characteristics differed from that of other Amerindians of the same era.

Spaniard Juan Rodríguez Cabrillo made first contact with the Pericús here in 1542 while exploring the coastline. Sir Francis Drake stopped off here in 1578, followed by privateer Thomas Cavendish in 1587. English pirating exploits inspired the Spanish to gain a stronger foothold on the Cape and in 1596 explorer Sebastián Vizcaíno spent a week, then returned in 1602 to map the region with cartographer Gerónimo Martín Palacios. Vizcaíno strongly recommended the establishment of a colony at Cabo San Lucas; Loreto, farther north on the Sea of Cortez, was selected instead, leaving Cabo to the English for another hundred years.

English pirates continued to use the harbor as a hiding place for attacks on Manila galleons until the mid-18th century. Woodes Rogers anchored here in 1709, when he and his crew captured the Spanish galleon *Encarnación*. Another English corsair, George Shelcocke, landed in 1721 and carried out a regional survey that included extensive drawings of the Pericú. In his descriptions, Shelcocke wrote:

The men are tall, straight, and well formed; they have very large arms and black, thick, poorly cared for hair, which does not reach the thighs, as a previous sailor reported on his voyage [apparently a rebuke to Woodes Rogers's earlier descriptions], nor even barely to the shoulders. The women are smaller; their hair is longer than the men's and sometimes almost covers their faces, Some of both sexes have a good appearance, although of a darker color than other Indians I have seen in these seas, as they have a dark copper color. The reader may reasonably conclude that they cannot be more savage, but there is much difference between what one would think on first sight of them, and what they truly are: because from everything I could observe of their behavior with each other and us, they are endowed with all imaginable humanity, and might shame some other nations . . . because during our entire stay there, constantly among so many hundreds of them, we observed only perfect harmony; when one of us gave something edible to one of them in particular, he always divided it into as many parts as there were people around, and normally reserved the smallest part for himself.

The First Settlers

During the remainder of the Spanish colonial era, Cabo's natural harbor was periodically used by passing galleons, but since it offered no source of fresh water and scant protection during the late-summer storm season when *chubascos* rolled in from the southeast, it was largely ignored in favor of San José del Cabo, where fresh water was abundant.

The Mexican independence movement largely bypassed San Lucas, although the Chilean ship *Independence,* sent by Lord Thomas Cochrane (admiral of Chile's newly independent navy) under the command of Capt. William Wilkinson, visited Cabo in 1822 in support of the Mexican struggle. The visit accomplished little as a military exercise since Spain had already granted Mexican independence the previous year, but it may have sparked renewed

interest in San Lucas as a convenient harbor in this part of the world. By the turn of the century, an enterprising group of Bajacalifornios began the processing and shipment of bark from the local *palo blanco (Lysiloma candida)* tree, a key ingredient in leather tanning. The principal route for the bark trade ran between Cabo San Lucas and San Francisco; shipping traffic gradually increased, and the lighthouse now known as Faro Viejo was built at nearby Cabo Falso in 1890.

In 1917 an American company floated a tuna cannery from San Diego to San Lucas to take advantage of the abundance of tuna in the area. As San Lucas gathered a small population, a roadbed to San José del Cabo, the nearest federal government seat, was laid in the 1920s. By the 1930s, a cannery and a small fishing village inhabited by around 400 hardy souls occupied the north end of the Cabo San Lucas harbor. Fish-canning remained the backbone of the local economy until the cannery was heavily damaged by a hurricane in 1941. During WW II the area was all but abandoned as Japanese submarines cruised the Pacific coast; Cabo seemed destined for obscurity.

Marlin Alley and
La Carretera Transpeninsular

Fortunately for San Lucans, post–WW II leisure travel brought fly-in anglers, who spread the word that Cabo was a gamefish paradise. The Cape sportfishing craze of the '50s and '60s—

harbor, Cabo San Lucas

when the waters off the peninsula's southern tip earned the nickname "Marlin Alley"—expanded the population to around 1,500 by the time the Transpeninsular Highway was completed in 1973. Following the establishment of the highway link between the U.S. and Cabo San Lucas, the town was transformed from a fly-in/sail-in resort into an auto-and-RV destination.

When Baja California Sur received statehood in 1974, a ferry route from Puerto Vallarta on the mainland was established, thus opening the area to increased Mexican migration. The construction of Los Cabos International Airport near San José del Cabo in the '80s brought Cabo within reach of vacationers who didn't have the time for a six-day drive from border to Cape and back. The establishment of a water pipeline between San José and San Lucas further loosened the limits on development.

Today the local economy rests on the provision of tourism services—hotels, restaurants, fishing, diving, and other water sports—and on the construction industry, which supplies the growing need for leisure, residential, and business structures throughout the lower Cape Region. At the moment Cabo San Lucas's population is roughly equal to that of San José del Cabo, the *cabecera* or *municipio* seat—but it is possible the San Lucas population may soon exceed its older twin's. A vocal group of San Lucans are campaigning for the Cabo area to separate from San José's jurisdiction and become the state's sixth *municipio*.

LAND'S END

A large cluster of granitic batholiths, carved by wind and sea into fantastic shapes, tumbles into the sea at the Cape's southernmost point. Forming the coccyx of a rocky spine that reaches northward all the way to Alaska's Aleutian Islands, the formations are collectively known as **Finisterra,** or Land's End.

El Arco, a rock outcropping at the tip of Land's End, has become Cabo San Lucas's most immediately recognizable symbol. During low tide you can walk along Playa del Amor to the 62-meter (200-foot) rock formation, which features an eroded passage through the middle. El Arco is also known as the "Arch of Posei-

rock formations, Land's End

don" since it marks the "entrance" to a precipitous submarine canyon—the perfect throne room for the King of the Seas—just offshore. Running northwest from El Arco and Playa del Amor are several more unnamed rock formations, including two large granite clusters as tall or taller than El Arco. These should be of interest to rock climbers.

Just offshore stand **Los Frailes** ("The Friars"), two rock islets frequented by sea lions. A smaller, bird-limed rock pinnacle off the northeast side of the cape, **Roca Pelicanos** ("Pelican Rock"), serves as a crowded pelican roost. The base of the pinnacle, about six meters (20 feet) down, is richly endowed with marinelife, including coral, sea fans, gorgonians, sea urchins, and numerous tropical fish. Recent reports from divers say visibility at the rock is declining, however, due to discharge from boats moored in the outer harbor.

Cerro La Vigía, rising 150 meters (500 feet) above the harbor, once served as lookout point for English pirates awaiting Manila galleons to

CABO SAN LUCAS

CALLE MIJARES

TP EL FARO VIEJO

ORTEGA

SUPER POLLO

TO TODOS SANTOS

TO CANDELARIA AND TODOS SANTOS

CALLE JUVENTUD

FRUTERIA LIZARRAGA

ALIKAN

12 DE OCTUBRE

OBREGON

CARRANZA

CABO SAN LUCAS

HIDALGO

MATAMOROS

ABASOLO

OCAMPO

ZARAGOZA

MORELOS

LEONA VICARIO

MENDOZA

GOMEZ FARIAS

16 DE SEPTIEMBRE

TO SAN JOSE DEL CABO, LOS CABOS AIRPORT

LAZARO CARDENAS

BANAMEX

IMMIGRATION OFFICE

REVOLUCION

20 DE NOVIEMBRE

HOTEL CASABLANCA

TELMEX

LIBERTAD

COTP

BUS TERMINAL

DOLLAR RENT-A-CAR

POST OFFICE

16 DE SEPTIEMBRE

PESCADERIA EL DORADO

CARLOS

EL PESCADOR

LATITUDE 22+

NIÑOS HEROES

LA DORADITA

ATUN'S

PLAZA ARAMBURO

SQUID ROE

STUDIO 94

LA PERLA

HOTEL MAR DE CORTEZ

CARLOS 'N CHARLIE'S

PLAZA BONITA

PIZZA OCEANA

PLAZA MI CASA

TACOS CHIDOS

SIESTA SUITES

HOTEL DOS MARES

GIGGLING MARLIN

BOAT RAMP

CABO ISLE MARINA OFFICE

PAVO REAL

BAHIA CONDO HOTEL

CASA RAFAEL

EDITH'S JAZZ CAFE

TO CLUB CABO

MADERO

GUERRERO

ZAPATA

HOTEL MARINA

PLAZA NAUTICA

HOTEL MARINA FIESTA

PIRATE'S COVE INN

PUEBLO BONITO RESORT

CLUB CASCADA

EL CORAL RESTAURANT

MARINA BLVD.

PLAZA LAS GLORIAS

MARINA CABO PLAZA

RESTAURANT BAR LAS PALMAS

HOTEL MELIA SAN LUCAS

U.S. CONSULATE

QUESARIA DEL PACIFICO

ROMEO Y JULIETA

SIGHTSEEING BOATS

MARINA

PLAYA EL MEDANO

HACIENDA BEACH RESORT

CAMINO PESCADORES

OLD FERRY OFFICE

SPORTFISHING

PLAYA ESCONDIDA

HOTEL FINISTERRA

GALEON RESTAURANT

OLD CANNERY

OLD CANNERY PIER

PLAYA BALCONCITO

BAHIA SAN LUCAS

0   0.25mi

0   0.25km

CERRO LA VIGIA

ASTON TERRASOL CABO

HOTEL SOLMAR

PLAYA SOLMAR

PACIFIC OCEAN

PLAYA DEL AMOR

LAND'S END

LOS FRAILES

© MOON PUBLICATIONS, INC.

plunder. Today it's still an excellent vantage point for viewing Land's End, the town, the marina, Playa Solmar (the beach next to the Hotel Solmar), and Cabo Falso. A steep trail begins just behind the old cannery on the harbor and leads to La Vigía's summit, which is marked by a crucifix.

BEACHES

Beachgoers can choose among five beaches close to the downtown area and a string of beaches and coves along the San José del Cabo to Cabo San Lucas Corridor.

Playa El Médano

The most popular and easily accessible local beach, Playa El Médano ("Dune Beach") extends several kilometers along Bahía San Lucas northeast from the inner harbor's entrance channel. This is Baja's most heavily used beach—it's packed with swimmers and sunbathers during peak vacation periods—and is one of the few local beaches where swimming is safe year-round. Besides swimming and lying on the sand, a variety of other activities here entertain beachgoers. Beach vendors rent pangas, Jet Skis, inflatable rafts, sailboards, snorkeling equipment, volleyball equipment, palapas, and beach furniture. Several palapa bars and restaurants scattered along the beach—Playa Brujita Beach Club, The Office, El Delfín, and Las Palmas—offer cold beverages and seafood.

Minor annoyances at Playa El Médano include the jewelry and rug vendors who plod up and down the beach (they won't persist if you show no interest) and the condo developments in the background that mar the view of the Sierra de La Laguna foothills.

Playa del Amor

Cabo's next most popular beach can only be reached by boat or by a difficult climb over two rock headlands along the ocean. Named one of Mexico's 10 best beaches by *Condé Nast Traveler* magazine, Playa del Amor ("Love Beach," also known as Playa del Amante, "Lover's Beach") lies near the tip of Cabo San Lucas—the cape itself, not the town—just northwest of the famous arch-shaped rock formation featured in virtually every Los Cabos advertisement. The wide, sandy, pristine beach actually extends across the cape behind the arch to the other side, forming two beachfronts—one on the Bahía San Lucas and one on the Pacific. The latter is sometimes whimsically called "Divorce Beach."

Only the beachfront facing the bay is generally safe for swimming. Bring along a cooler full of beverages, as the entire area is free of vendors and commercial enterprises. Unless you have a portable beach umbrella, go early in the day to command one of the shady rock overhangs. The southeast end of the bay features a series of coral-encrusted rocks suitable for snorkeling; a deep submarine canyon lying only 50 meters (164 feet) offshore is a popular scuba-diving site.

You can reach Playa del Amor by water taxi from the marina for US$5, or take a glass-bottom boat tour (US$7) and arrange a drop-off at the beach. Any tour boat in the vicinity will give you a ride back to the marina upon presentation of your ticket stub; the last tour boat leaves the marina at 1500. In calm seas, you can also rent a kayak on Playa El Médano and paddle across the inner harbor entrance to the beach.

Those skilled at bouldering can reach the south side of the beach by climbing from the east end of Playa Solmar (in front of the Hotel Solmar) over two rocky points that separate the two beaches. The climb is best attempted during low tide, when the cove between the rock formations reveals a sandy beach useful as a midway rest-stop. The second set of rocks, to the east, is more difficult than those to the west; turn back after the first set if you've reached the limit of your climbing skills.

Playa Solmar

This very wide, very long beach running along the southwestern edge of the cape is accessible via the road to Hotel Solmar. The strong undertow and heavy surf makes it a sunbathing-and-wading-only beach. Solmar's biggest advantage is its lack of people, even during peak tourist seasons.

Cannery Beaches

Next to the abandoned Planta Empacadora, the old tuna cannery on the south side of the inner harbor entrance, are two small public beaches virtually ignored by most Cabo visitors. The first, **Playa Escondida** ("Hidden Beach"), lies next to the cannery pier and is easily reached by walking along the west bank of the marina and alongside the main cannery building. The sand extends only around 50 meters (164 feet), less in high tide, but it's popular with local Mexican families because Dad can fish from the pier while the kids play in the calm water. During a recent visit I watched a local resident haul in a 4.5-kilo (10-pound) tuna with a handline here.

Playa Balconcito ("Little Balcony Beach"), a bit larger than Playa Escondida, lies beyond the pier on the other side of the cannery toward the sea. You must walk along a stone ledge—part of the cannery foundation—to get there.

Corridor Beaches

Northeast of Cabo San Lucas—on the way to San José del Cabo—are a number of uncrowded, relatively pristine beaches suitable for swimming, fishing, camping, snorkeling, and scuba diving. See "The Corridor," above, for names and locations.

ACCOMMODATIONS

Cabo San Lucas offers a greater number and variety of hotels than neighboring San José. Most are in the US$50-110 range although four hotels charge under US$35 a night and several cost well over US$100 in winter and early spring.

Unless otherwise noted, rates quoted below are for peak season, usually Nov.-May. Some hotels may offer a 15-20% discount March through October. Add 10% hotel tax to all rates; some hotels may charge an additional 10-15% service charge. All area codes are 114.

Downtown Hotels

Although Cabo's beaches are the average visitor's preferred address, you can save considerably by staying downtown and walking or driving to the beach. One of the best values downtown is the friendly and efficient **Siesta Suites Hotel** (Calle Zapata between Guerrero and Hidalgo, tel./fax 3-27-73, tel./fax in U.S. 909-945-5940), near the better downtown restaurants and one block from the marina. Each of the 15 immaculate rooms is quiet and has a full kitchen. Four of

the rooms have ceiling fans but no a/c; these rent for US$41 s/d per night or US$275 per week. The rest of the rooms have a/c, and go for US$50 s/d daily or US$330 weekly. Because of price and location, Siesta Suites is a popular spot; advance reservations are recommended, even in summer (when fishing's high season lures droves of North American anglers).

On the same street is the very economical and friendly **Hotel Dos Mares** (Calle Zapata s/n, tel. 3-03-30), which rents adequate, non-a/c rooms for US$20 s, US$26 d, or rooms with stove, fridge, and dishes for US$34.

Another economical choice is the two-story **Hotel Marina** (tel. 3-24-84), nearby at Blvd. Marina at Guerrero, where 16 clean and tidy a/c rooms fill up fast for US$27 a night, and seven large a/c suites with refrigerators cost US$45 a night. On the premises are a modest pool and jacuzzi. One drawback is that it can get a bit noisy during peak season (Dec.-March), when the hotel is jam-packed and there's lots of pedestrian traffic on Blvd. Marina.

Three blocks back from the marina, old gringo standby **Best Western Hotel Mar de Cortez** (Blvd. Lázaro Cárdenas and Guerrero, tel. 3-00-32, or 800-347-8821 or 408-663-5803 in the U.S.) trades on its American franchise name to stay full virtually all season. Rooms surrounding a pleasant pool and patio cost US$27-29 s, US$31-52 d. Room rates drop a bit in summer. Service is generally poor to indifferent.

A bit further off the beaten track, on Calle Revolución a half block east of Morelos (and close to the bus terminal), the refurbished **Hotel Casablanca** (tel. 3-02-60) offers 15 basic rooms with ceiling fans for US$22 s, US$30 d. Although lacking in atmosphere, the Casablanca has the advantage of being relatively quiet.

Playa El Médano Hotels

The preponderance of Cabo's beach hotels are found along this long strip of sand southeast of the town center. Surrounded by coconut palms, the stately mission-style **Hacienda Beach Resort** has presided over the south end of the beach since 1960. Spacious a/c rooms (114 in all), some with ocean views, cost US$92-175 s/d; the more expensive two-story units feature sleeping lofts and full kitchens. On the grounds are a pool, tennis court, aquatic center, small-boat anchorage, restaurant, and bar. For infor-

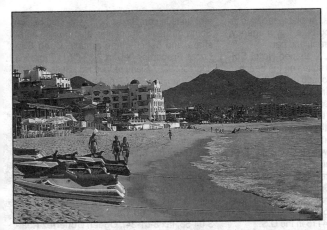

Playa El Médano

mation or reservations, contact the Hacienda Beach Resort (tel. 3-01-22, fax 3-06-66; tel. 213-655-2323 or 800-733-2226 in the U.S./Canada).

Moving northeast along the beach, next up is the **Hotel Meliá San Lucas** (tel. 3-44-44, fax 3-04-20; tel. 310-410-1024 in the U.S.), a multistory resort built in a horseshoe shape around a large pool and patio area. The Meliá's 190 rooms and suites, all with ocean view, start at US$165 s/d. Facilities include IDD telephones, in-room safes, a pool, tennis court, restaurants, and bars.

A couple of hundred meters northeast along the beach is the striking **Pueblo Bonito Resort**, a white, five-story building topped by blue-tiled domes and arrayed in a horseshoe around pool and patio, similar in conception to its immediate neighbor. The 149 junior and luxury suites come with IDD telephones, satellite TV, kitchenettes, and ocean views for US$175-210 a night (summer rates US$50 less). In addition to its large pool, the hotel offers a health club. For further information contact the Pueblo Bonito Resort at 3-29-00, fax 3-19-95, (800) 252-8008 or (800) 442-5300, fax (619) 456-8005 in the U.S.

Behind the aforementioned El Médano hotels, not on the beach but with beach access, are several good choices. Twelve-room **Casa Rafael** (formerly Villa Alfonso's, tel. 3-07-39, or 408-459-9494 or 800-524-5104 in the U.S.), tastefully decorated in Mexican-colonial style, offers standard doubles for US$90, suites for US$100, or deluxe doubles with jacuzzi for US$150, all with good ocean views. Rooms with

handicapped access are available; also on the premises are a pool, jacuzzi, and fitness room.

Pirate's Cove Inn (tel. 3-02-68), at the end of Camino de los Pescadores just a few meters from the beach, is a funky four-room place run by an old and established Cabo San Lucas family. They usually rent rooms by the month only, but if a room becomes available for a few nights, the cost is US$40 per night.

Farther east along Playa El Médano, between San Vicente and Vagabundos RV parks, **Club Cabo** (tel./fax 3-33-48) rents seven suites with full kitchens for US$45-60 a night. Club Cabo is primarily an RV park; accommodations are separated from the beach by a road.

Playa Solmar Hotels

Two of Cabo's most distinguished hotels are secluded from the rest of town by the rocky ridge leading to Land's End. Impressively constructed high on the ridge itself, overlooking the beach and Pacific Ocean, is the 1968-vintage **Hotel Finisterra** (tel. 3-01-00, fax 3-05-90; tel. 714-476-5555 or 800-347-2252 in the U.S.). A new tower wing extends from the beach below all the way to the original hotel and lobby area, to which it is connected by a bridge. Also new is a 1,040-square-meter (11,200-square-ft.) swimming pool with jacuzzis and swim-up bar, right on the beach. Rooms in the old wing cost US$75-120 d, US$100-145 t, while one-bedroom suites in either wing go for US$135-155, two-bedroom suites US$250-270. Some of the rooms and suites in the old wing feature marina rather than ocean views. Available facilities include lighted tennis courts, a travel agency, wedding chapel, restaurant, and bar.

The modern-looking, V-shaped **Hotel Solmar Suites** features 90 suites on the beach itself, plus 32 time-share/condo units overlooking the beach, at rates ranging US$130-225 in season. All suites have ocean views; some of the condos do not. Down at the original beach wing are two heated pools with swim-up palapa bars and jacuzzis, tennis courts, and an aquatic center. The Solmar is renowned for its fishing fleet; special all-inclusive fishing packages are popular during the late-summer fishing season. The hotel's dive boat, the *Solmar V,* is one of the finest in Baja. For information contact the Hotel Solmar Suites at 3-35-35, fax 3-04-10; tel. (213) 459-9861 or (800) 878-4115 in the U.S.

Marina Hotels

Three hotels flank the innermost marina area. The largest, a sprawling, 287-room, pseudo-Pueblo-style pink structure nicknamed "Cabo Jail" because it takes so long to walk from one end to another, is **Plazas Las Glorias** (tel. 3-12-20, fax 3-12-38; tel. 713-448-2829 or 800-342-2644 in the U.S.). All rooms come with a/c, telephones, refrigerators, and in-room safety box for US$110-145. Facilities include a pool, restaurants, bars, shopping center, travel agency, and a beach club at Playa El Médano.

Along the northeast side of the marina, near the Cabo Isle Marina office, stands **Marina Fiesta Resort & Hotel** (tel. 3-26-89, fax 3-26-88; tel. 800-332-2252 in the U.S.). The hotel's 144 suites come with kitchenettes and cost US$120-340 depending on size and time of year. Next door, overlooking the east side of the marina, the **Marina Cabo Plaza** (tel. 3-18-33, in the U.S. tel. 800-524-5104 or 510-652-6051, fax 510-652-9039) charges a reasonable US$70-80 s/d, US$80-90 with kitchenette. Both the Marina Fiesta and Marina Cabo Plaza have swimming pools; Playa El Médano is a 10-minute walk away.

Condominiums, Time Shares, and Beach Homes

Some of the best deals for families or small groups are rental condos, which usually sleep up to four for US$40-165 per night. Many real-estate and property-management companies rent units in complexes not mentioned below. Some of these companies also handle time-share and beach-home rentals. **Cabo San Lucas Properties** (tel./fax 3-32-62; U.S. mailing address: 9297 Siempre Viva Rd., Suite 40-497, San Diego, CA 92173) can arrange rental condos with full kitchens, satellite TV, and laundry service starting at US$40 a night (US$250/week, US$475 per month); in Cabo the office is opposite the Giggling Marlin Restaurant on Calle Matamoros and Blvd. Marina. **Earth, Sea, and Sky Tours** (tel. 800-745-2226 in the U.S./Canada) books everything from studio condos to multiroom beachfront villas.

Other companies with a broad variety of rental units in the Los Cabos area include **Pinal y Asociados** (A.P. 68, Cabo San Lucas, BCS, tel. 3-04-58, fax 3-01-34), **Ogden Gutiérrez Realty** (A.P. 427, Cabo San Lucas, BCS, tel. 3-25-58), and **Los Cabos Property Management** (A.P. Cabo San Lucas, BCS 23410, tel. 3-11-64, fax 3-11-62).

The following condo sites take reservations directly (rates do not include tax and service). **Bahía Condo Hotel** (tel. 3-18-88, or 800-982-5599 in the U.S./Canada), just off Camino de los Pescadores above Playa El Médano, rents units with ocean views and kitchenettes for US$95-110 a night. **Club Cascadas** (tel. 3-07-38), at the east end of El Médano next to Pueblo Bonito Resort, is a nicely designed time-share complex with one- to three-bedroom interconnected villas that rent for US$105-515 in season; on the premises are two pools and tennis courts.

The **Hotel Solmar Suites** (see "Playa Solmar Hotels," above) rents a number of time-share/condo units on the hill overlooking Playa Solmar. Next door, the **Terrasol Cabo** (tel. 3-03-83; in the U.S. 408-459-9494 or 800-524-5104) rents studios for US$140, one-bedroom units for US$190, and two-bedroom units for US$300 (up to four people); all come with full kitchens and ocean views. On the premises are two pools, a sauna, health club, restaurant, and bar. You can walk to the beach from both the Solmar and Terrasol.

Camping and RV Parks

Shady and well-kept **El Faro Viejo Trailer Park** (A.P. 64, Cabo San Lucas, BCS), at Matamoros and Mijares in the northwestern section of town on the way to Todos Santos, offers 30 spaces for

US$12 for two with full hookups, flush toilets, showers, a laundromat, and a reputable restaurant-bar. This park tends to fill up Nov.-May.

Three km northeast of Cabo San Lucas off Mexico 1, the **Vagabundos del Mar RV Park** (tel. 3-02-90; tel. 707-374-5511 or 800-474-2252 in the U.S.), has 81 slots with full hookups for US$15 for two plus US$3 per additional guest; discounts are available for members of the Vagabundos del Mar travel club. Facilities include restaurant, bar, flush toilets, showers, a pool, and laundry. The nearby **San Vicente Trailer Park** (tel. 3-07-12) has full hookups for US$10-12, plus showers, a rec room, bar, and restaurant.

Between San Vicente and Vagabundos RV parks and Playa El Médano is **Club Cabo** (tel./fax 3-33-48), best accessed by following the road to Club Cascada from Mexico 1 and turning left before the beach. This small campground offers 10 tentsites and 10 RV slots with full hookups for US$10-13 a night; toilets and hot showers are available. Club Cabo also rents seven suites with full kitchens for US$45-60 a night.

Also northeast of town, at Km 4 on the south side of Mexico 1, is the 24-site **Cabo Cielo RV Park,** with full hookups for US$10, flush toilets, potable tap water, and showers. Tent campers are welcome. On a rise at Km 5.5 on the highway, **El Arco Trailer Park** (tel. 3-06-13) commands a view of the town and Bahía San Lucas even though it's on the north side of the highway. El Arco has many permanent shelters and few vacancies; when available, full hookups cost US$12, tentsites US$6. The park features flush toilets, a pool, and a large palapa restaurant with distant bay views.

Just a bit farther east along the highway near Km 7, the **Villa Serena RV Park** (tel. 3-05-09) sits on a scenic bluff overlooking the ocean and a rocky beach. Many semipermanent, nicely constructed RV shelters and bungalows are cropping up so that fewer of the 85 slots are available on a drive-in basis, but you have a better shot here than at El Arco. Full hookups cost US$14 per vehicle with two persons, US$2 for each additional guest. Facilities include showers, flush toilets, pool, fitness center, jacuzzi, restaurant, and bar.

You can camp on the beaches farther northeast along Mexico 1 (see "The Corridor") or northwest along Mexico 19 (see "North of Cabo San Lucas").

FOOD

Downtown Cabo San Lucas is riddled with restaurants and bars, most of open-air design, with menus that attempt to cover all the bases—seafood, Mexican, and steak. Because Cabo is Baja's number-one resort town, prices are above what you'd find in La Paz, Ensenada, Tijuana, or other tourist areas. Quality is also generally high since Cabo attracts chefs from all over Mexico and beyond. One complaint: Cabo restaurants sometimes hold back on the chiles in Mexican dishes and table salsas, hence picante-lovers may be forced to request extra chiles or fresh *salsa cruda* to bring things up to the proper level of heat.

Mexican

$$ **Carlos'n Charlie's** (tel. 3-21-80), opposite The Place at Cabo on Blvd. Marina: Despite its main function as a place for tourists to drink themselves silly, Cabo's latest Grupo Anderson restaurant serves good Mexican food. Volleyball court on the premises. Open daily 1130-midnight.

$$ **Cilantro's Bar & Grill** (tel. 3-29-00), Pueblo Bonito Resort, Playa El Médano: One of the better hotel-oriented Mexican restaurants, featuring mesquite-grilled seafood and homemade tortillas. Open daily 1100-2300.

$ **La Perla,** Blvd. Lázaro Cárdenas at Guerrero: Supported by a mainly local clientele, this simple Mexican eatery features inexpensive *desayuno, comida corrida, tortas,* tacos, burritos, quesadillas, and *licuados.* Open daily 0730-1630 only.

$$-$$$ **Mi Casa** (tel. 3-19-33), Calle Cabo San Lucas opposite the plaza: Often cited as the most authentic Mexican restaurant in Cabo, Mi Casa is tastefully designed with a half-palapa, half-open-air dining room encircled by pastel murals intended to look like a small central Mexican village. The menu lists dishes from all over Mexico, including fajitas, *mole verde, mole poblano, pipián, carne asada a la tampiqueña, pollo borracho,* and *cochinita pibil.* The food is good but doesn't always match menu descriptions. Open daily noon-2200.

$$ Pancho's (tel. 3-09-73), Calle Hidalgo off Blvd. Marina: Specializes in huge Mexican platters at reasonable prices, good Mexican breakfasts, plus over 85 brands of tequila. Mexican beer costs US$1 a bottle, house tequila shots US$.30. Open daily 0600-2300.

$$ Salsitas (tel. 3-17-40), Plaza Bonita, Blvd. Marina: This mall restaurant is mostly a tourist scene, serving Mexican food adapted for gringo palates, but is one of the only restaurants outside Plaza Las Glorias with marina views. Nice terrace tables. Open daily 0630-2300.

Seafood

$$$ Casa Rafael (tel. 3-07-39), Plaza Bonita: Formerly Villa Alfonso's, the elegant dining room at this small hotel specializes in *nacional novelle,* or Nouvelle Mexican cuisine, served a la carte or as a seven-course, fixed-price meal. The changing menu also features several international dishes. Open Mon.-Sat. 1800-2230; reservations suggested.

$-$$ El Coral, opposite Plaza Las Glorias on Blvd. Marina: This rambling outdoor restaurant serves inexpensively priced Mexican and seafood meals; nowhere else in town can you consume a lobster dinner for US$10. Open daily 1100-2300.

$-$$ El Pescador, Zaragoza and Niños Héroes: A humble palapa restaurant with very good Baja-style seafood—oysters, shrimp, and red snapper are specialties—at low prices. A piece of the old Cabo, and still patronized by locals. Open daily 0800-2100.

$$ The Fish Company (tel. 3-14-05), Guerrero and Zapata next to the Río Grill: Small eatery with a simple but very well-prepared

menu of fresh fish *empanizada* (breaded) or *al mojo de ajo* (in garlic butter), plus grilled shrimp, *carne a la tampiqueña,* fajitas, chiles rellenos, and enchiladas. Ice-cold beers cost US$1 apiece; good, inexpensive breakfasts are also available. Open daily 0800-2200.

$$ Giggling Marlin (tel. 3-11-82), Calle Matamoros near Blvd. Marina: Better for appetizers and booze than entrees. Most tourists come here to snap photos of themselves hanging upside down—like landed marlins—from the restaurant's block-and-tackle rig. Others come for the big-screen satellite TV. Open daily 0700-0100.

$$ La Placita (tel. 3-14-99), in front of the Hotel Marina on Blvd. Marina: Casual palapa restaurant with good service and moderately-priced steak, lobster, and shrimp. Open daily 0900-2100.

$$ Las Palmas (tel. 3-04-47), Playa El Médano: This was the first palapa restaurant on Médano, and most residents agree it's still the best, in spite of the ugly concrete addition. The grilled seafood is always a good choice. Open daily 1100-2300.

$$ Mariscos Mocambo, west side of Calle Morelos just south of Almacenes Grupo Castro (between calles 16 de Septiembre and Niños Héroes): A very casual, local-style place with a huge seafood menu and good prices. Open daily 1100-2200.

$$-$$$ Río Grill (tel. 3-13-35), Blvd. Marina, near Calle Zapata: One of the nicer outdoor restaurant-bar combinations in the central marina area, with live music nightly and well-prepared steak, lobster, shishkebab, and Mexican combos. Open daily noon-midnight.

$$-$$$ Señor Sushi (tel. 3-13-23), Blvd. Marina and Guerrero: Don't be fooled, no sushi here. Instead the energetic staff serves seafood platters, ribs, fajitas, and huge drinks from the Tai Won On Bar. Open daily 1030-0100.

$-$$ The Shrimp Factory (tel. 3-11-47), Blvd. Marina: This no-frills, open-air place serves shrimp only by the half kilo or kilo; each order comes with salad, bread, and crackers. Open daily noon-2200.

$$ Squid Roe (tel. 3-06-55), Blvd. Lázaro Cárdenas at Zaragoza: One of the many Grupo Anderson restaurant-bars in Mexico that combine zany, tourist-on-the-loose fun with tried-and-tested menus based on regional cuisine. House

specialties at this one include seafood, barbecue ribs, and Mexican combos; the kitchen will cook fish you bring in. Open daily noon-0300.

American, European, and Japanese

$$$ Da Giorgio: (tel. 3-29-88), Km 5.5 on the Corridor, adjacent to the Misiones del Cabo complex: This well-designed palapa restaurant with long-distance views of Land's End has upstaged all other local Italian venues with high-quality pasta and seafood entrees. Open daily 0800-2300.

$-$$ Latitude 22+, Blvd. Lázaro Cárdenas between Morelos and Vicario, opposite the boat ramp: More of a bar than a restaurant, with American fare available throughout the day. Daily specials include roast chicken, pork chops, chicken-fried steak, meat loaf, and roast beef. Open 0700-midnight daily.

$$ MerMed (Mer Mediterranée) Restaurant (tel. 3-41-00), second floor of Plaza de los Mariachis near Carlos'n Charlie's on Blvd. Marina: A new, airy, aqua-walled, casual-but-sharp restaurant serving seafood, French, and Californian cuisines. Open daily 1100-1500 and 1800-2200.

$$$ Pavo Real (tel. 3-18-58), Camino de los Pescadores, near Playa El Médano: Highly regarded continental kitchen presided over by a German chef. The changing menu features creative delights such as blackened tuna with tomato-almond chutney, dorado in pecan crust, and other original recipes. Open daily 1800-2200 only.

$$$ Ristorante Italiano Galeón (tel. 3-04-43), Blvd. Marina, just south of the Hotel Finisterra entrance: Elegant restaurant with harbor views, specializing in Neapolitan cuisine and pizzas baked in wood-fired ovens. Live piano music nightly; open 1600-2300.

$$-$$$ Romeo y Julieta (tel. 3-02-25), Blvd. Marina near Hotel Finisterra: An Italian menu featuring fresh pasta and wood-fired pizzas. Open daily 1600-midnight.

$$-$$$ La Terraza Restaurant Bar (tel. 3-17-99), inside Plaza Bonita, second floor: Good sushi and Japanese grill (teppanyaki) amidst tasteful decor. Open Wed.-Mon. 1600-2300 only.

Tacos and Fast Food

The local food scene is concentrated along Calle Morelos, where a string of stands offers tacos, carne asada, and mariscos at the lowest prices in town. The *taquerías* seem to change owners and names every other year or so, but rarely close down completely. You'll also find a cluster of inexpensive restaurants serving seafood cocktails, chicken, and *tortas* at the south end of Calle Ocampo where it meets Blvd. Lázaro Cárdenas.

From December to March a trolley cart at the corner of Blvd. Lázaro Cárdenas and Guerrero assembles delicious custom fruit salads for US$1.30 a cup, including your choice of sliced papaya, watermelon, cucumber, mango, orange, cantaloupe, and jicama, with a squeeze of lime. Salt and chile powder optional.

Two American chain restaurants recently crept into Cabo: a **KFC** opposite Señor Sushi on Blvd. Marina and a **Domino's Pizza** at Plaza Naútica (complete with a fleet of delivery motorcycles). Still not a single McDonald's in sight, but for how much longer?

$-$$ Ali's Burger, Calle Morelos and 16 de Septiembre: An old but still exotic standby for quick American breakfasts, burgers, and North African couscous. French spoken; open daily 0700-2300.

$-$$ Broken Surfboard (Restaurant San Lucas), Calle Hidalgo, opposite the east extension of Calle Zapata: A local institution for over 20 years, this casual, open-air spot serves reasonably priced breakfasts, sandwiches (try the marlin *torta*), seafood, and *licuados*. Surfers are invited to scribble something on the wave mural. Open daily 0700-2100.

$ El Pollo de Oro, Blvd. Lázaro Cárdenas at Morelos: A longtime favorite for Sinaloa-style barbecued chicken, as well as grilled shrimp, lobster, and ribs. Good breakfasts. Open daily 0700-2300.

$ El Pollo Sinaloense, Calle Zaragoza and 20 de Noviembre: Similar to El Pollo de Oro, fewer tourists. Open 1100-2200.

$ La Doradita, corner of Matamoros and Niños Héroes: This street vendor specializes in tasty seafood tacos stuffed with fish, oysters, shrimp, scallops, or octopus; the *ceviche* is also good. Usually open midday till mid-evening.

$$ Pizza Los Cabos (tel. 3-18-20, VHF 68), Calle Guerrero just south of Madero: Decent pizza, starting at US$8, centrally located. Open daily noon-2300.

$$ Pizza Océana (tel. 3-23-48), Blvd. Lázaro Cárdenas just west of the plaza (look for the surfboard over the door): Run by a Spaniard and his Mexican wife, friendly Océana serves very tasty, good-quality pizza at reasonable prices. Open Tues.-Sun. 1230-2230.

$ **Super Pollo** (tel. 3-07-88), Calle Morelos and Ortega: Part of the Sinaloa-style chicken chain found throughout Baja. Very reliable. Open daily 1100-2200.

$ **Tacos El Chilorio,** Blvd. Lázaro Cárdenas at Ocampo, opposite La Perla: No-frills place with good, quick, inexpensive *tacos de carne asada.* Open Mon.-Sat. 1000-2200.

$ **Tacos Chidos,** Calle Zapata: A tiny diner with excellent fish tacos, *torta milanesa, sopes,* and chicken tamales at low prices. Open Tues.-Sat. 0800-1900, Sunday 0800-1700.

$ **Taquería Maury,** west side of Calle Morelos just south of 20 de Noviembre: Delicious *tacos de carne asada,* quesadillas, and baked potatoes *(papas)* served plain or with cheese and/or *carne asada.* Open daily 1100-2200.

$$ **Wabo Grill,** Calle Guerrero: This Van Halen–owned nightclub serves excellent taco platters, tortas, tortilla soup, burgers, and breakfasts on its outdoor patio. Open daily 0700-2300.

Ice Cream

$$ **The Creamery,** Blvd. Marina opposite Plaza Las Glorias: Serves a delicious nonfat ice cream as well as coffee, donuts, and pastries. Open daily 0800-2100.

$ **Helados Bing,** next door to Squid Roe on Blvd. Marina. The Cabo branch of Mexico's best ice cream parlor chain. Assorted flavors. Open daily 1000-2200.

Trailer Park Restaurants

$$ **El Arco,** Km 5.5, Mexico 1: A large, airy restaurant with a distant view of Bahía San Lucas. The menu includes a variety of seafood, Mexican, and American dishes. Open Wed.-Mon. for breakfast, lunch, and dinner.

$$ **El Faro Viejo** (tel. 3-19-27), Calle Matamoros and Mijares: Renowned for steak, seafood, and ribs. Open daily 1700-2200.

$$-$$$ **The Trailer Park at La Golondrina** (tel. 3-05-42), Camino de los Pescadores: Same owners as El Faro Viejo, focusing on lobster, seafood, and Mexican. Open Tues.-Sun. 0700-2200.

Groceries

Cabo's several supermarkets stock a variety of Mexican and U.S. foodstuffs—from fresh Mexican cheeses to Sara Lee frozen cheesecake—plus cooking and cleaning supplies, and even motor oil. Ranging from small to huge, they include **Almacenes Grupo Castro** (southwest corner of Calle Morelos and Revolución), **Supermercado Sánliz** (three locations: Blvd. Marina and Madero; calles Ocampo and Matamoros; calles León Vicario and López Mateos), and **Supermercado Plaza** (at Plaza Aramburo, calles Lázaro Cárdenas and Zaragoza). Supermercado Plaza stocks the largest selection of both domestic and imported foods.

Pescadería El Dorado at calles Niños Héroes and Matamoros stocks a large selection of fresh finfish and shellfish. Inside the old entrance to Pedregal, off Blvd. Marina near the U.S. consulate, **Quesaría del Pacífico** (tel. 3-36-60) carries fresh eggs, butter, cheese, meats, bacon, and sausages; it's open Mon.-Sat. 0800-1300 and 1500-1800. A smaller but fancier delicatessen, **Cabo Gourmet,** is on Blvd. Lázaro Cárdenas near Restaurant La Perla, between Ocampo and Abasolo.

The most conveniently located place to buy fresh tortillas is **Tortillería Perla** (tel. 3-01-21) on the west side of Calle Abasolo just south of Calle 16 de Septiembre.

La Baguette (on Blvd. Lázaro Cárdenas east of the plaza) carries European and American-style baked goods including pastries, bagels, and breads; it's open Mon.-Sat. 0830-1930.

Frutería Lizarraga (tel. 3-12-15), at Calle Matamoros and Av. de la Juventud, stocks a very good selection of fruits and vegetables; several local hotel and restaurant chefs shop here.

The best shopping area for beer and liquor is the string of *subagencias* and *licores* along Calle Matamoros.

ENTERTAINMENT AND EVENTS

Bars and Discos

Nightlife in Cabo starts in the bars downtown near the marina and after midnight moves to the discos, which stay open till 0300 or 0400. Tourists bent on getting well-primed for the

THE LA BAMBA SYNDROME

In Mexico, all it takes is the right combination of circumstances—a hotel lounge or tourist bar, plenty of tequila or Tecate, and a table full of sunburned gringos—and sooner or later someone will be stricken by what might be called the La Bamba Syndrome. Initial symptoms are a desperate urge to hear or sing the song "La Bamba." If a live Mexican band (it doesn't matter whether they're mariachis or *norteños*) or even a lone guitarist is present, those afflicted by the syndrome will begin shouting at the musician(s) "La Bamba! La Bamba! Play La Bamba!" Victims are convinced they must hear La Bamba or else they'll die.

The desperation appears very convincing, as the victim's face becomes increasingly flushed if the strains of La Bamba don't ring out immediately. Finally, the *músicos* give in—perhaps hesitating just a bit longer than necessary in order to relish the victim's suffering—and begin banging out those three chords that would bring relief to the sufferer. But in order to prolong recovery, the LBS victim usually begins singing along with the music, shouting out an unintelligible mixture of mispronounced Spanish, pseudo-Spanish, and improvised English lyrics to the song. The syndrome is sometimes contagious, but if others in the room don't join in on their own, the original victim will often cajole other gringos to follow his (it's almost always a guy) example.

When the song's over, some LBS sufferers are temporarily cured, but in others the condition only becomes aggravated and they may demand other gringo chestnuts like "Guadalajara" or, in the worst cases, even "La Cucaracha." When it goes this far, even the musicians begin to suffer, along with all the gringos (and locals, if they haven't already made hasty exits) who were hoping to hear something a little more authentic or up-to-date, or who hoped that they might at least be able to enjoy themselves without the distractions of a raging La Bamba maniac.

If you're ever in a bar or restaurant that has musical entertainment and an organized tour from the States arrives, consider calling in the tab and leaving, as conditions are ripe for a mass LBS outbreak. And should you become afflicted yourself, at least try to get the lyrics halfway right. (Certain variations are acceptable.) "La Bamba," incidentally, is a Veracruz-style song; if you want to hear something local, ask for *la música norteña*.

---

evening pack the **Río Grill** (Blvd. Marina at Zapata), **Giggling Marlin** (Calle Matamoros and Blvd. Marina), or the two-story **Squid Roe** (Blvd. Lázaro Cárdenas at Zaragoza). Squid Roe's dance floor, with bleachers, distinguishes it from the surrounding bar scene.

The **Whale Watcher Bar** at the Hotel Finisterra has a somewhat more sedate but well-attended 1530-1730 happy hour that features two drinks for the price of one. The bar features an excellent mariachi group Thurs.-Sun., and great Pacific views every day of the week.

One of the oldest and funkiest bars in town is **Latitude 22+** ("Lat 22"), on Blvd. Lázaro Cárdenas between Morelos and Vicario opposite the boat ramp. This is a yachtie's hangout with authentic marine decor assembled from salvaged boats. There's a pool table in back. Prices for drinks (very good Bloody Marys) and food are very reasonable; the bar is open Wed.-Mon. 0700-2300 and offers a happy hour 1600-1800.

The **Hacienda Beach Resort** has a lively bar that doubles as a weekend social center for resident gringos. For something more sedate, show up for the nightly live piano music (1600-2300) at the **Ristorante Italiano Galeón.** Live and recorded jazz (mostly '40s and '50s repertoire) is presented nightly 1800-0100 at **Edith's Jazz Cafe** near Playa El Médano, on the west side of the Camino de los Pescadores; enjoy views of Bahía Cabo San Lucas and Land's End as long as the sun's up.

Cabo's discos begin filling up around 2300 but the crowd doesn't really break a sweat till around midnight or later. The town's first dance club, **Opera** (formerly Luka's), on the northeast edge of town near the PEMEX station on Blvd. Lázaro Cárdenas, is still in vogue as is the newer **Studio 94** at Plaza Bonita. The latter features a state-of-the-art laser show and sound system.

Californians tend to prefer **Cabo Wabo** on Calle Guerrero, a dance club owned by the rock group Van Halen; the music here alternates between a recorded mix (with video) and live bands. Cabo Wabo was built in 1989 and named for a Van Halen song describing the "wobble" exhibited by tourists walking around town after a night of club-hopping. Members of Van Halen put in the occasional—make that rare—appearance, as do Los Tres Gusanos, a locally organized trio headed by Van Halen vocalist Sammy Hagar. The atmosphere is loose, though not beachy.

To take a step further on the wild side, sign up for one of the "Tour of the Edge" pub crawls arranged by **Baja Travel** (tel. 3-19-34) to backstreet bars and strip clubs of questionable reputation.

Al Anon meets daily at 6 p.m. above the pool at the Hacienda Beach Resort.

Events

Cabo San Lucas hosts several sportfishing tournaments throughout the year. The largest is the **Bisbee's Black and Blue Marlin Jackpot Tournament,** held for three days each October. The purse for the contest has exceeded US$850,000, making it the world's richest marlin tournament. Proceeds go to local charities. For information call **Bisbee's** (tel. 3-16-22) or the Hotel Finisterra in Cabo San Lucas.

Another notable yearly event falls around the Festival of San Lucas on 18 October, part of a week of music, dancing, and feasting in the Mexican tradition.

SHOPPING

The streets of Cabo are filled with souvenir shops, street vendors, clothing boutiques, and galleries—probably more shops of this type per capita than anywhere else in Baja. For inexpensive handicrafts—rugs, blankets, baskets, leatherwork—from all over Mexico, check the outdoor **Mercado Mexicano** on Calle Hidalgo at Obregón; for the best prices you'll have to bargain. Another place where bargaining is useful is the **Tianguis Marina,** an outdoor souvenir market on the southwest side of the inner harbor toward the old ferry pier. Typical items here include black-coral sculptures, T-shirts, and costume jewelry.

Among the better shops in town are **Casas Mexicanas** in front of Restaurant Mi Casa on Calle Cabo San Lucas, with Talavera ceramics,

religious art, pewter, wood and wrought-iron furniture; **Gaby's Huaraches** on Lázaro Cárdenas just east of Matamoros, offering all types and sizes of Mexican-made leather sandals as well as cloned sport sandals; **Faces of Mexico** next door to Pancho's Restaurant, selling Mexican masks and other ethnic art; **Taxco Silver,** on Calle Hidalgo opposite Capitan Lucas Restaurant, with the best selection of silver jewelry; and **Joyería Albert,** a branch of the reputable Puerto Vallarta jeweler located on Calle Matamoros.

The newer shopping centers are all found along the marina side of Blvd. Marina. Modern **Plaza Bonita** faces the marina and contains a number of shops offering tourist-oriented sportswear, jewelry, and souvenirs. Two of the more interesting shops here are **Dos Lunas** (handpainted clothing), and **Cartes** (rustic colonial furniture, arts and crafts, and classy home-decor accessories). **Books/Libros** (tel. 3-31-71) in Plaza Bonita stocks an excellent selection of English-language paperbacks, magazines, maps, books on Baja, children's books, and U.S. newspapers. The bookshop is open daily 0900-2100.

A newer shopping center near the marina, **Plaza Naútica,** contains a branch of **Bye-Bye,** a Mexican chain selling souvenirs and T-shirts at reasonable prices. Also in Plaza Naútica, the useful **Cabo Sports Center** sells beach supplies (coolers, umbrellas, etc.), sports sandals, and varied equipment for golf, swimming, surfing, boogie-boarding, and mountain-biking.

Plaza Marina, attached to the Hotel Plaza Las Glorias on the marina, also contains a few shops; good buys in leather are available at **Navarro's** (tel. 3-41-01). Still under construction is a complex next to Plaza Bonita called **The Place at Cabo,** which reportedly will encompass a hotel and villas, plus shopping and dining outlets.

Because Blvd. Marina is such a popular shopping and strolling area, several time-share vendors (the kind that provoke local T-shirts reading "What part of 'No' don't you understand?") have set up booths along the street. So far every booth sits on the north side of Blvd. Marina; walk along the south side of this road (the side with the shopping malls) to avoid the worst of the come-ons.

SPORTS AND RECREATION

Fishing

After swimming and lying on the beach, sportfishing is Cabo's number-one outdoor activity. An average of 50,000 billfish—marlin, sailfish, and swordfish—a year are hooked off the cape, more than anywhere else in the world. The biggest trophy of all, the *marlín azul* (blue marlin), can reach five meters (16 feet) in length and weigh close to a ton; in the Cape area, it's not unusual to hook 200- to 400-kilogram (440- to 880-pound) blues. A smaller species, the *marlín rayado* (striped marlin), grows to over 270 kilograms (600 pounds), while the *marlín negro* (black marlin) is almost as big as the blue.

To catch a glimpse of these huge gamefish, stop by the sportfishing dock on the marina's west side around 1500-1600, when sportfishing boats return with their catches. Note the flags flown over the boats; a triangular blue flag means a billfish has been bagged while a red flag with a T means one has been tagged and released. All Cabo sportfishing outfits request that anglers release billfish to fight another day; some even require it. Instead of skinning and mounting these beautiful fish, they recommend bringing a video camera along to record the catch from start to finish. Even where customers demand to keep a billfish, the Sportfishing Association of Los Cabos stipulates that only one billfish per boat may be killed (you can catch and release as many as you like).

Good marlin-fishing spots include **Banco San Jaime,** 29 km (18 miles) southwest of Cabo Falso, and **Banco Golden Gate,** 31 km (19 miles) west of Cabo Falso. Dorado and wahoo are also common in the same areas. Sportfishing cruisers—powerboats equipped with electronic fish-finders, sophisticated tackle, fighting chairs and harnesses, and wells for keeping live bait—are the angler's best chance for landing large gamefish.

Almost unbelievably, marlin are also somewhat common just beyond the steep dropoffs

WORLD FISHING RECORDS SET IN BAJA

The nonprofit International Game Fish Association (IGFA) tracks world records set for each species of gamefish according to weight, weight/test ratio (fish weight to line test), place where the catch was made, and other significant record details. World-record catches achieved by Baja anglers for specific line classes include those for the following fish: Pacific blue marlin, striped marlin, Pacific sailfish, swordfish, roosterfish, dolphinfish (dorado), gulf grouper, California yellowtail, Pacific bonito, bigeye trevally, spotted cabrilla, spearfish, giant sea bass, white seabass, California halibut, Pacific jack crevalle, black skipjack, yellowfin tuna, Pacific bigeye tuna, and chub mackerel.

Baja anglers hold all-tackle records—highest weight of any fish species regardless of line test—for gulf grouper, roosterfish, Pacific amberjack, white seabass, spotted cabrilla, rainbow runner, black skipjack, yellowfin tuna, Pacific jack crevalle, chub mackerel, and California yellowtail.

For information on IGFA membership and record entries, write to IGFA, 3000 East Las Olas Blvd., Fort Lauderdale, FL 33316. Membership includes a copy of the IGFA's annual *World Record Game Fishes Book*—which contains a list of all current fishing records—and the bimonthly *International Angler* newsletter. IGFA members are also eligible for discounts on fishing charters offered by several sportfishing outfitters in Cabo San Lucas.

blue marlin

BOB RACE

between Los Frailes and Cabo Falso, an area easily reached by panga or skiff. Without the technology of a fishing cruiser, panga marlin-fishing becomes the most macho hook-and-line challenge of all—the resulting fish stories reach *Old Man and the Sea* proportions. For anglers with more humble ambitions, black seabass, cabrilla, sierra, and grouper are available in inshore waters; surfcasters can take corvina, ladyfish, sierra, and pargo.

Guided cruiser trips are easy to arrange through any major Cabo hotel. Solmar, Finisterra, and Meliá Cabo Real each have their own fleets. **Pisces Fleet** (tel. 3-12-88, fax 3-05-88), opposite Supermercado Sánliz at Blvd. Marina and Madero, is one of the more reliable independent outfitters; others can be found along the west side of the harbor. Rates average US$450 a day for a six-person, 36-foot fishing cruiser, US$335 on a 28-foot cruiser, US$250 a day on a 26-footer (around US$100 per half-day), or US$175 per couple on a 31-foot party boat. Charter boats generally hold up to six anglers; rates include tax, license, gear, and ice.

Pangas are available in Cabo San Lucas, but most panga-fishing trips operate out of San José del Cabo. Either place, the typical panga trip costs US$125 in a three-person, 22-foot boat. Panga rates usually don't include rental gear and sometimes don't include licenses. When inquiring about rates—panga or cruiser—ask whether the quote includes filleting of edible gamefish. The better outfits include fish preparation and packing among their services at no extra charge. You can also arrange to have fish processed and vacuum-packed through **Cabo Smokehouse** (tel. 3-33-96).

The best surfcasting in the immediate area is at **Playa Solmar.** You can also fish from the old pier extending from the abandoned tuna cannery at the entrance to the harbor.

Minerva's Baja Tackle (tel. 3-12-82), next door to Pisces Fleet, is well stocked with lures and other tackle designed specifically for Cabo sportfishing. Minerva's is also the official IGFA representative in the area.

Boating

Cabo San Lucas is a major Baja California boating center (1,227 yacht arrivals in 1993) although harbor size and facilities don't match those of La Paz. The outer harbor anchorages are mostly occupied by sportfishing cruisers; recreational boaters can moor off Playa El Médano to the northeast.

Within the inner harbor, first dredged in the early '70s, is the **Cabo Isle Marina** (tel. 3-12-51 or 3-12-52, fax 3-12-53; tel. 310-541-3830 in the U.S.), with showers, pool, snack bar, dry-storage facilities, chandlery, and 338 slips, complete with electricity and satellite TV. The marina can accommodate boats up to 45 meters (148 feet) long. Permanent and monthly renters at Cabo Isle Marina have priority over short-term visiting boaters; daily rentals are available on a first-come, first-served basis for US$12 per day for the first 25 feet of boat length, plus US$.50 for each additional foot, not including tax. Visiting boaters should call the marina 15 days before arrival to check on the availability of slips. The Cabo Isle Marina office is open Mon.-Sat. 0900-1700, Sunday 1000-1500. The marina's condos are occasionally available as rentals and the adjacent Marina Fiesta Resort and Hotel usually has vacant rooms.

Also in the inner harbor are two boat ramps, one near the old ferry pier and one at the northeast end of the harbor near Plaza Las Glorias. A fuel dock is located between the old ferry pier and the abandoned cannery, just inside the entrance to the inner harbor. Cabo San Lucas is an official Mexican port of entry; the COTP office is on Calle Matamoros at 16 de Septiembre.

Boat Cruises: Dos Mares operates a fleet of glass-bottom tour boats that depart frequently from the marina and from Playa El Médano between 0800 and 1500 each day. The standard 45-minute tour costs US$7 pp and covers Pelican Rock, the famous Land's End arch, and the sea lion colony. For no extra charge, the crew will let passengers off at Playa del Amor near the arch; you can flag down any passing Dos Mares boat and catch a ride back to the marina later in the day. Simpler launches without glass bottoms will do the same trip, including beach dropoff and pickup, for US$5.

Sunset Cruises: Bay trips with all the beer and margaritas you can drink are also popular and usually last around two hours and 15 minutes. You can make reservations at the marina or at most hotels; tickets cost US$20-40 pp depending on whether dinner is included. The *Pez Gato* (tel. 3-37-97, VHF channel 18), a 42-foot catamaran, offers a US$30 sunset all-the-margaritas-you-can-drink cruise that leaves from the Hacienda Beach Resort dock (the cruise can be booked through any hotel).

Nautilus VII: Using a mixture of photos, videos, and live viewing, this air-conditioned, partially submerged "submarine" offers passengers the opportunity to experience underwater life in the bay without donning snorkel and fins. The *Nautilus VII* departs from the Plaza Las Glorias dock at 1000, 1100, noon, and 1500 daily. Tickets cost US$23 pp, children 5-16 half price, under five free.

Paddling, Sailing, and Windsurfing

The onshore surf is mild enough at Playa El Médano for launching wind- and paddle-powered craft easily. You can rent kayaks, canoes, Hobie catamarans, sailboards, and Sunfish sailboats from **Cabo Acuadeportes** (tel. 3-01-17, VHF radio 82) at the Hacienda Beach Resort on Playa El Médano, for paddling or sailing along the beach or across the harbor to Land's End.

In stormy conditions it's not a good idea to try paddling or sailing across the harbor entrance. Be sure to inform the vendors where you plan to take the craft; they'll know the conditions and advise accordingly. Watch out for powerboats, yachts, and cruise ships; larger craft have the de facto right of way. Novices should stick to Playa El Médano no matter what the conditions.

Diving and Snorkeling

Cabo is a unique diving destination since it's in the middle of a transition zone between tropical and temperate waters. Strikingly large fish like amberjack, hammerheads, and manta rays—which are partial to temperate waters—mix with the smaller, more colorful species typical of tropical waters.

It's also unique in that several snorkeling and scuba sites are only a 15- to 25-minute boat ride from the marina. Snorkelers find the base of the cliffs on each side of **Playa del Amor,** about three meters (10 feet) deep, worth exploring for coral and tropical fish. Nearby **Pelican Rock,** some six meters (20 feet) deep, is a bit more challenging. Strong divers, on calm days, can swim south around the arch to the seal colony at Los Frailes to frolic with the creatures.

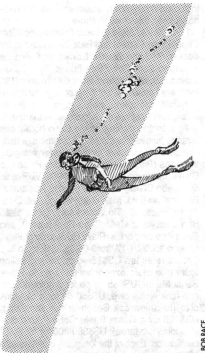

BOB RACE

Divers with experience below 30 meters (100 feet) can visit a vast **submarine canyon** that begins just 50 meters (164 feet) off Playa del Amor. Part of a national marine preserve, the canyon is famous for its "sandfalls,"—streams of sand tumbling over the canyon rim at a depth of around 30 meters and forming sand rivers between rock outcroppings. At a depth of around 40 meters (130 feet), the outcroppings give way to sheer granite walls, where the sand rivers drop vertically for over two kilometers (to a depth of around 2,750 meters/9,000 feet). The size of the sandfalls and sand rivers depends to a large extent on climatic conditions; during long spells of very calm weather they may even come to a halt.

The phenomenon was first documented by a Scripps Institute of Oceanography expedition in 1960 and later made famous in one of Jacques Cousteau's television documentaries. The edges of the canyon walls are also layered with colorful coral, sea fans, and other marinelife. These in turn attract schools of tropical fish, including many open-ocean species not ordinarily seen this close to shore.

Dives further afield to **Cabo Pulmo** (see "East Cape" in the Central and East Cape chapter for details) and the **Gorda Banks** can also be arranged from Cabo San Lucas. The Gorda seamounts, at a depth of around 41 meters (135 feet), are famous for sightings of huge tuna, amberjacks, groupers, manta rays, and whale sharks (the latter are the largest fish in the world).

As with sportfishing, many Cabo hotels can arrange guided dive trips and equipment rentals. Independent outfitters include **Underwater Diversions** (Plaza Marina, attached to Plaza Las Glorias facing the marina, tel. 3-04-04, VHF radio 65), **Cabo Diving Services** (next to Restaurant El Coral on Blvd. Marina at Hidalgo, tel. 3-16-58, VHF radio 10), **Tío Watersports** (at the Meliá San Lucas and Meliá Cabo Real hotels), and **Cabo Acuadeportes** (Playa El Médano or Playa Chileno, tel. 3-01-17, fax 3-06-66, VHF radio 82). Typical rates are US$25-45 pp for snorkeling tours (the more expensive tours go to Playa Santa María), US$35-40 pp for a guided local, one-tank scuba dive, US$50-60 for a two-tank dive (to Shipwreck Beach or the sandfalls), US$110 for a Gorda Banks/Cabo Pulmo dive (including two tanks), US$350-400 for full PADI certification. Each of the foregoing outfitters also offers dive equipment sales and rental.

Operated by the Hotel Solmar Suites, the 34-meter (112-foot) *Solmar V* (tel. 310-546-2464, fax 545-1672; tel. 800-344-3349 in the U.S./Canada) offers luxury live-aboard dive trips to the Gorda Banks, Los Frailes, El Bajo, Cabo Pulmo, and other more remote sites. The wood-and-brass-fitted boat features two onboard air compressors and a dive platform for easy exits. Prices are US$995 for four-day trips, and US$1495-2375 for six- and seven-day trips, including all land transfers, food and beverages (including wine and beer), accommodations in a/c staterooms (each with TV and VCR), and up to three guided dives per day.

The *Pez Gato,* a large catamaran moored at Playa El Médano, offers a six-hour tour to scenic Bahía Santa María (see "Beaches and Activities—Diving" under "The Corridor" in the San Jose del Cabo and The Corridor chapter). The tour costs US$50 per adult (US$25 children) and includes a Mexican breakfast served on the way out, two hours of swimming and snor-

keling at Santa María, and *ceviche*, tuna salad, and beer on the way back. The boat departs at 1000 and returns around 1400.

Divers seeking equipment rentals only can expect the following daily rates in Cabo: wetsuit US$3.60-6; mask and snorkel US$2.40-3; fins US$2.40-3; wetsuit, fins, and mask US$9; weight belt and weights US$2.40-3; regulator US$7.20; tanks US$6 each; BCD vest US$3.60-5.40; Hawaiian-sling spearguns US$4.20; underwater camera and film US$12; air fills US$3.

Vigilantes Marinos (A.P. 13, Cabo San Lucas, BCS 23410), a local divers group, has taken up the cause of protecting Cabo's marine environment from illegal fishing, head dumping, and other ecologically harmful practices. In addition to supporting the enforcement of existing laws, the group's Mexican, English, and American members educate local diving guides in safe dive tactics and undertake periodic beach- and bottom-cleaning sessions.

Golf

Three world-class golf resorts are located along the highway between Cabo San Lucas and San José del Cabo: **Cabo del Sol** (tel. 3-31-49), **Palmilla Resort** (tel. 2-05-02), and **Cabo Real** (tel. 3-03-61). For details on these courses, see "Hotels and Golf Resorts" under "The Corridor" in the San Jose del Cabo and The Corridor chapter.

About one km north of the Cabo city limits, the 300-hectare (746-acre) **Cabo San Lucas Country Club** (tel. 3-19-22), is currently under construction. The course will have views of Land's End and Bahía San Lucas from each fairway, and five tee-offs for each hole (back, championship, member, forward, and front). At 600 yards (par 5), the seventh hole is said to be the longest in Mexico. To avoid drawing excessively from the Cape's precious aquifer, gray water from the resort spends a month cycling through a series of duckweed ponds until the fast-growing plant renders the water safe for irrigation. Along with fairway homes, the resort will feature tennis, swimming, and fitness clubs.

Bungee Jumping

Baja Bungy and Beach Bar (tel. 3-27-73), near the Villa de Palmar time-share complex off Mexico 1 just northeast of town, features a crane rig for bungee-jumping. They claim they haven't lost a jumper yet, but don't drink too many margaritas first. The cost is US$35 per jump; T-shirts and videos are available.

Horseback Riding

Rancho Collins (tel. 3-36-52) at the Hotel Meliá San Lucas offers horseback riding by the hour or on trail rides. The hourly rate is a relatively high US$20; better value is the 3.5-hour trail ride to dune-encircled El Faro Viejo ("The Old Lighthouse," built in 1890) for US$45. Take this ride in the morning or at sunset for maximum scenic effect. A 1.5-hour, US$35 beach ride is also available.

ATV Trail Rides

The sandy beaches and dunes in the Cabo San Lucas area are open to ATVs (all-terrain vehicles) as long as they're kept away from swimming areas (Playa El Médano) or turtle-nesting areas (Cabo Falso). Any of the hotels in town can arrange ATV tours for US$40-45 pp per half-day (four hours), US$70 pp all day (six hours). The basic route visits sand dunes, the ruins of El Faro Viejo, and a 1912 shipwreck; the six-hour tour adds La Candelaria, an inland village known for its mango trees and *curanderos* (traditional healers). Vendors along Blvd. Marina also book these trips.

Whalewatching

Whales pass within a few hundred meters of Cabo San Lucas throughout the year, but the most activity occurs during gray whale migration season, Jan.-March. The Dos Mares tour-boat fleet operates whalewatching trips from the marina during the migration season for US$30 pp. With binoculars you can also see passing whales from the Hotel Finisterra's Whale Watcher's Bar.

Race and Sports Book

LF Caliente in Plaza Naútica near the marina features a full-service bar and restaurant, a bank of closed-circuit television screens tuned to various sporting events, and the opportunity to place bets based on Las Vegas odds on thoroughbred and greyhound races, as well as on American football, basketball, baseball, and other games. You don't have to gamble to watch the TVs or use the facilities. Hours are Mon.-Fri. 0900-midnight, Sat.-Sun. 0800-midnight.

INFORMATION AND SERVICES

Tourist Information

Cabo San Lucas has no government tourism offices or information booths, although FONATUR maintains an office on the marina. Its representatives are always interested in speaking with potential investors but they don't distribute general tourist information. Information on Los Cabos—maps and hotel lists—can be obtained from the state tourism office in La Paz (between Kilometers 6 and 5 on Mexico 1, tel. 2-11-99, fax 2-77-22).

Magazines and Newspapers

The annual magazine *Los Cabos Guide* contains a number of features, ads, annotated lists, and announcements concerning hotels, restaurants, clubs, and recreational events as well as local social and business news. It's offered for sale at some local newsstands, but free copies can be collected at real estate offices. The local Spanish-language newspaper is *El Heraldo de Los Cabos*.

USA Today and *The News* (from Mexico City) are usually available at the **Supermercado Sánliz** at Blvd. Marina and Madero, as well as at other larger grocery stores catering to gringos. **Books/Libros** in Plaza Bonita carries *The News*, *USA Today*, and the *Los Angeles Times*.

Post and Telephone

Cabo's post office, on Calle Matamoros just north of 16 de Septiembre, is open Mon.-Fri. 0800-1100, 1500-1800. Public telephone booths are found at various locations throughout town, including the main plaza.

The area code for Cabo San Lucas is 114.

USEFUL CABO SAN LUCAS TELEPHONE NUMBERS

(Cabo San Lucas area code: 114)

Police: 3-39-77
Red Cross: 3-33-00
IMSS Hospital: 3-04-80
Port Captain: 3-01-71
Immigration: 3-01-35
U.S. Consulate: 3-35-66

Immigration

Cabo's *migración* office is on Blvd. Lázaro Cárdenas between Gómez Farías and 16 de Septiembre.

Changing Money

U.S. dollars are readily accepted throughout Cabo, although in smaller shops and restaurants you'll save money if you pay in pesos. Three banks offer foreign exchange services (0830-1200): **Bancomer** (Calle Hidalgo and Guerrero), **Banamex** (Calle Hidalgo and Blvd. Lázaro Cárdenas), and **Banca Serfin** (Plaza Aramburo). Hotel cashiers will also gladly change dollars for pesos, albeit at a lower rate than the banks'.

Except in emergencies, stay away from Cabo's moneychangers, which charge high commissions or sell currency at low exchange rates. **Baja Money Exchange** (at Plaza Náutica and three other locations around town), for example, lists an exchange rate N$.19 lower per U.S. dollar than the going bank rate; on top of this the office charges 5% commission on personal checks, and 5% plus bank fees for wire transfer or cash advances. Although this is expensive, many visiting foreigners—too timid to try a Mexican bank—line up for such services.

U.S. Consulate

The U.S. State Department has terminated the consular position in Mulegé and moved it to Cabo San Lucas. The small office (tel. 3-35-36) is on Blvd. Marina near the west side of the bay and is open Mon.-Fri. 1000-1300. The consular staff can assist U.S. citizens with lost or stolen passports and other emergency situations.

Laundry

Lavamatica Cristy (tel. 3-29-59) and **Lavandería Evelyn,** both opposite Restaurant El Faro Viejo on Calle Matamoros, offer banks of washing machines for self-service laundry; ask the attendants to start the machines for you. Or you can pay (by weight) to have the washing, drying, and ironing done by the staff—one-day service is the norm. Both are open Mon.-Sat. 0700-2000. Several other *lavanderías* are scattered around town.

Tintorería Supernova, in the Plaza Aramburo shopping center off Blvd. Marina, does dry cleaning.

Travel Agencies

Cabo's major hotels—Solmar, Finisterra, Hacienda, Plaza Las Glorias—have their own travel agencies for making air reservations and flight changes or arranging local tours. In town, the most reliable and long-running independent is **Los Delfines** (tel. 3-13-96 or 3-13-97) on Calle Morelos; it's open Mon.-Fri. 0830-1800, Saturday 0830-1500.

TRANSPORTATION

Air

See "Transportation" under "San José del Cabo" in the San Jose del Cabo and The Corridor chapter for details on domestic and international service to **Los Cabos International Airport.** The airport is 12.8 km (eight miles) north of San José del Cabo. **Mexicana** (tel. 3-04-11) has a Cabo San Lucas office at calles Niños Héroes and Zaragoza; **Aero California** (tel. 3-37-00) is in Plaza Náutica, Blvd. Marina.

Sea

The SCT Cabo San Lucas–Puerto Vallarta ferry service was suspended five years ago; SEMATUR, the private corporation that took control of the formerly government-owned ferry line between Baja and the mainland, has no plans to reinstate service. The nearest ferry service to the mainland operates from La Paz to Mazatlán (see "Getting There" in the La Paz chapter).

Cabo Isle Marina is the main docking facility for transient recreational boats; bow-stern anchorages are also permitted in the outer bay.

Land

Buses to/from La Paz: Autotransportes Aguila and Autotransportes de Baja California (ABC) operate 14 buses a day (0600-1830) to La Paz from Cabo's main intercity bus depot at Calle 16 de Septiembre at Zaragoza. Fare is US$6. Eight of the departures go via Todos Santos, which is the quickest route (about 3.5 hours total), while the other six go via San José del Cabo (4-4.5 hours) for the same fare.

Buses to/from San José: Aguila/ABC runs around 11 buses a day (0645-2000) to San José del Cabo; the trip takes 30-45 minutes and costs US$1.50 per person.

Buses to/from Todos Santos: Eight buses a day run to Todos Santos (about two hours from Cabo San Lucas) for US$6 per person; the last bus to Todos Santos leaves Cabo at 1800.

Driving: If you've driven down from the U.S. border, congratulations—you've reached "Land's End." If you've arrived via the La Paz ferry terminal and plan to drive north to the U.S., count on three eight-hour days (Mulegé first night, Cataviña second night) or 2.5 dawn-to-dusk days (Santa Rosalía first night, San Quintín second night). If you stretch your itinerary to include a week's driving time, you'll have a safer trip and more of an opportunity to enjoy the sights along the way.

Local Transportation
Shuttles and Taxi: Shuttle vans from Los Cabos International Airport to Cabo San Lucas cost US$10 per person. A private taxi costs US$50 for the whole cab. In Cabo itself, you can easily get around on foot, bicycle, or scooter, though taxis are available for US$1.80-2.40 a trip.

Water Taxi: You can hire harbor skiffs from the marina in front of Plaza Las Glorias to Playa El Médano (US$2.50 per person one way) and Playa del Amor (US$5 roundtrip only). In the reverse direction, skiffs are plentiful at El Médano, but for del Amor, advance arrangements for a pickup are necessary.

Vehicle Rental: You can rent VW sedans or vans at Los Cabos International Airport (see "Transportation—Vehicle Rental" under "San José del Cabo" in the San Jose del Cabo and The Corridor chapter). In Cabo, they can also be rented—albeit more expensively than at the airport—at **AMCA Rent-A-Car** (at the old entrance to Pedregal off Blvd. Marina, tel. 3-25-15), **Dollar** (Blvd. Lázaro Cárdenas and Mendoza, tel. 2-01-00), and **Thrifty** (next to Lat 22+, Blvd. Lázaro Cárdenas s/n, tel. 3-16-66). Rates vary from around US$27 a day plus US$.22 per km for a no-frills VW bug to US$55/day and US$.28/km for a Nissan Tsuru II (Sentra).

Vendors along Blvd. Marina rent mopeds, ATVs, and motorcycles for US$6 an hour or US$24 per day.

Tours
Several local travel agencies and hotels offer land tours of the area, typically US$45 for the city and El Faro Viejo, US$85 for La Candelaria and Todos Santos.

If you'd like a bird's-eye view of the Cape, **Helitours Aventura** (Plaza Bonita, tel. 3-35-11) arranges helicopter tours. A 10-minute flight around the bay costs US$38.50 per person and takes in all the local landmarks. Also available are more expensive 20-minute flights out to Cabo Real and back, or 30 minutes to San Jose and back along the Corridor.

For information on bay tours, see "Boating" under "Sports and Recreation," above.

palo blanco

BOB RACE

BOB RACE

WEST CAPE

NORTH OF CABO SAN LUCAS

Although a paved, two-lane highway—Mexico 19—extends the full 76 km (47 miles) between Cabo San Lucas and Todos Santos (and beyond all the way to La Paz), this is still the least developed coastal stretch on the lower Cape. Wags say it's only a matter of time before this area is dotted with resorts; housing developments are already slowly appearing along the southern end of the highway outside Cabo San Lucas. Local resistance to development—especially in the Todos Santos area—is growing, so perhaps the area farther north will remain preserved and relatively pristine.

Cabo Falso–Playa Migriño

About three km west of the Cabo San Lucas city limits is **Cabo Falso,** once incorrectly thought to be Baja California's southernmost point. The wide beach along Cabo Falso is protected as a nesting ground for sea turtles; visitors aren't permitted within 50 meters (165 feet) of the surf line. The dunes behind the beach, however, are a popular destination for rented ATVs from Cabo San Lucas. The abandoned lighthouse, **El Faro Viejo,** signaled ships from 1895 to 1961; the original lens is now installed in a newer lighthouse higher on the beach. Surrounded by loose sand for at least a half mile,

the old lighthouse can only be approached on foot, ATV, or horse.

Past Cabo Falso the highway begins climbing over the southwestern foothills and coastal plateaus of the Sierra de La Laguna to reach the small ranching settlement of Migriño after about 21 km (13 miles). **Playa Migriño,** accessed at Km 94 or 97, is a long section of beach next to Estero Migriño, a small estuary linked with Río Candelaria. In winter, surfers can catch a point break at the north end of the beach. Different sections of Playa Migriño are accessible via a network of sandy roads; several spots are suitable for camping.

La Candelaria

From Mexico 19 an 11-km (6.8-mile), ungraded dirt road runs inland along the north side of the arroyo formed by Río Candelaria to this small, picturesque village in the foothills of the lower Sierra de La Laguna. Palapa-roofed adobe and block homes, a small church, a school, split-rail and *carrizal* fences, and saddled burros tethered to palo verde and mesquite trees set the scene. Irrigated gardens grow mango, citrus, guava, avocados, and papayas.

La Candelaria is known throughout the Cape Region for its *curanderos* (healers). Tourism flacks in Los Cabos call the curandero culture "white magic," but in reality the local villagers simply have a way with medicinal herbs, which grow in the sierra in some abundance. A palm oasis lies in a shallow canyon on the northwest edge of the quiet village, where an underground stream is dammed to irrigate mangoes, corn, and bamboo. Pigs wander in and out of the canyon, seeking cool mud around the pumphouse.

Several local artisans produce rustic pots and cane baskets—look for a sign reading "Pottery" in the village if you're interesting in purchasing these crafts.

Hikers may enjoy the hilly, tropical-arid thorn-forest in the area. Bring plenty of water, even in the winter, as the sun bakes everything unprotected by shade. At the edge of town near an old cane mill is a hill surmounted by a cemetery that can be reached on foot. Look for the headstone of Rafael Salvatierra, whose engraved dates of birth and death indicate he lived to the age of 130; opinions are divided as to whether the dates are accurate, although several generations ago residents in this area often passed the century mark.

Getting There: The quickest way to La Candelaria is via the sandy arroyo road from Mexico 19 near Playa Migriño, while the road from Cabo San Lucas via the Mexico 1 bypass is longer and more scenic. If you enter one way and leave the other you can form a loop without backtracking.

To find the road from downtown Cabo San Lucas, begin driving toward San José along Blvd. Lázaro Cárdenas, then turn left at a sign marked "La Paz Via Corta" directly opposite the entrance to Club Cascada. You are now heading northwest toward Todos Santos and La Paz. After passing a soccer field on the left, look for a power plant on your right and turn onto the wide dirt road next to the plant (1.7 km/1.1 miles from the Via Corta intersection); this turnoff lies opposite the entrance to Minisuper El Langostine and a *llantera* at calles Morelos and Reforma.

From this intersection, La Candelaria is 27.7 km (17.2 miles) away according to my odometer (the highway sign says 23 km). Make another right 4.3 km (2.7 miles) from the highway at a road signed "La Candelaria" and "Los Pozos" through a fence and cattle guard. As you ascend the foothills of the sierra into relatively dense thornforest (very green in early fall) and stands of *cardón* and *pitahaya,* it's not unusual to see cattle or burros in the road, so drive slowly. The road forks at Los Pozos, about 12 km

(7.5 miles) from the highway; the ranching settlement of Los Pozos consists of charming ranchitos and adobe ruins. Take the right fork, pass a small chapel at 14 km (8.9 miles), and follow signs for La Candelaria and La Trinidad.

The road begins climbing at this point, and 18.5 km (11.5 miles) from the highway you should be able to see the Pacific Ocean to the west. Around 21 km (13 miles) from the highway comes a signed turnoff for Rancho San Ramón, followed at 26.4 km (16.4 miles) by a turnoff for La Trinidad. Less than a mile later you'll arrive at La Candelaria.

Note: Almost any type of vehicle can safely navigate the Cabo San Lucas–Candelaria road in dry weather. Low-lying Los Pozos—almost halfway to La Candelaria—may flood in heavy rains, so if it begins raining during the first half of the drive, turn back. Once you're past Los Pozos, keep going! Becoming stranded in La Candelaria would beat getting mired in Los Pozos.

La Candelaria–Playa Migriño: If you continue along the same road past La Candelaria, it curves westward and parallels the deep, wide Río Candelaria arroyo on its way to the Pacific coast. The road drops to the bottom of the arroyo and passes a couple of ranchitos, then reaches Mexico 19 near Migriño about 5.6 miles from La Candelaria. This section of road is sandy and narrow in spots, so drivers must take care not to stray off the track into sand traps; since the road runs across the bottom of an arroyo, it could be very risky during or after a hard rain.

If you plan to do this loop starting at the top—from Mexico 19—the unsigned arroyo turnoff lies three km (1.9 miles) south of the Km 94 marker, or about a half km (.3 miles) north of the main Playa Migriño turnoff.

Playa Migriño–Todos Santos

Of the many deserted beaches strung out along this stretch of the Pacific parallel to Mexico 19, one of the easiest to reach is **Playa Las Cabrillas** (turnoff at Km 81). Flat and sandy, this beach was named for the plentiful seabass that can be caught from shore. Grass-tufted dunes provide partial windscreens for beach camping, which is free.

El Pescadero (pop. 1,500), at Km 62, is little more than a plaza lined with *tiendas* and a cafe, surrounded by farms and fishing shacks. East of El Pescadero, a network of dirt roads leads southeast approximately 56 km (35 miles) across the Sierra de La Laguna to Mexico 1 between Santa Anita and Caduaño; parts of the road are graded but the middle section is passable only by sturdy, 4WD vehicles.

Rancho Nueva Villa, just before Km 60, is a well-known farm producing fruits and vegetables without chemical pesticides or fertilizers. You can sometimes purchase organic produce from the farm's roadside stand.

TODOS SANTOS

One of the more lushly vegetated arroyo settlements in the Cape Region, Todos Santos (pop. 4,000) makes a good midpoint stopover for Cabo San Lucas– or La Paz–bound travelers on Mexico 19, offering several seafood restaurants, cafes, and fruit stands; a few modest hotels, bed and breakfasts, and RV parks; and a PEMEX station. Long-term visitors can explore the nearby as-yet-undeveloped Pacific beaches and the steep western escarpment of the Sierra de La Laguna, or simply hang out and soak up the small-town ambience.

The town itself sits on a *meseta* (low plateau) buttressing the sierra foothills. Looming over Todos Santos to the east, the sierra provides an underground stream that irrigates dozens of orchards laden with mango, avocado, guava, papaya, citrus, coconut, and other fruits. Most of these are cultivated along wide Arroyo de la Reforma to the town's immediate north in an area commonly known as **Las Huertas** or "The Orchards." At the west end toward the beach is **La Poza,** a small freshwater lagoon favored by resident and migrating waterfowl. North of town, amidst a dense palm grove, is another natural pool where local children go swimming.

Beneath the town's sleepy surface, behind the century-old brick-and-adobe facades, lives a small, year-round colony of artists, surfers, and organic farmers who have found Todos Santos the ideal place to follow their independent pursuits. A number of La Paz residents maintain homes here as temporary escapes from the Cortez coast's intense summer heat; these are complemented by a seasonal community of California refugees from the high-stress film and media worlds who make the town their winter retreat. Several small farms in the area specialize in organic produce for the North American market.

A rave writeup in the May 1993 issue of *Travel And Leisure* ("... a new Mexican Oz in the making, destined to become the Carmel of Baja") briefly stimulated outside interest, much of it focusing on real estate—the town's streets are now tacked with For Sale signs. With each passing year the town seems to move a little closer toward becoming, if not the next Carmel, then perhaps the next San José del Cabo.

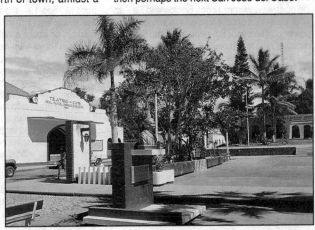

plaza,
Todos Santos

CLIMATE

Straddling the Tropic of Cancer, Todos Santos has perhaps the coastal Cape Region's most comfortable climate. December through February nights are cool, days warm. In March and April the air begins warming up but the ocean reaches its coldest annual temps (still comfortable for swimming).

Increasing air temperatures in June interact with the cooler seas to bring a marine fog in the evenings; visitors are often surprised how cool the nights are during this month. July through September are peak rainfall months, although the Sierra de La Laguna partially blocks the heavier storms coming from the Mexican mainland that affect Los Cabos. The November 1993 storm that inundated San José and Cabo San Lucas, for example, barely touched Todos Santos. At the same time, because of its location on a *meseta* facing the Pacific, it receives the ocean's overall cooling effect and hence temperatures are almost always lower than in Cabo San Lucas, San José, or La Paz, all of which are heated to greater or lesser degrees by the warmer Sea of Cortez. When it's 38° C (100° F) in La Paz, for example, Todos Santos will register just 32° C (90° F).

The rain tapers off in October as temperatures descend a bit. November usually brings beautiful, sunny weather with an abundance of greenery.

HISTORY

The earliest traces of human habitation in the Todos Santos area date back 3,000 years to "Matancita Man," the defleshed and painted remains (thus indicating a second burial) of a tall male who lived to at least 75 years on a vegetable and animal-protein diet. The first Spaniard to sight the oasis, Jesuit Padre Jaime Bravo, found nomadic Guaicuras availing themselves of the inland water source and collecting shellfish along the coast.

Padre Bravo established a farm community and "visiting mission" *(misión de visita)* called Todos Santos here in 1724 to supply the water-poor mission community at La Paz with fruits, vegetables, wine, and sugarcane. By 1731

Todos Santos was producing 200 burro-loads of *panocha*—raw brown sugar—annually, along with figs, pomegranates, citrus, and grapes. Two years later, deeming the local Guaicuras amenable to missionization, Padre Sigismundo Taraval founded Misión Santa Rosa de las Palmas at the upper end of the arroyo about two km inland from the Pacific. Taraval fled to Isla Espíritu Santo near La Paz following a 1734 native rebellion, and the mission returned to visiting-chapel status the following year.

The Guaicura population in the vicinity was soon wiped out by smallpox and Pericús were brought in to work fields irrigated by springs connected to Arroyo de la Reforma. Reinstated as a *misión de vista* in 1735, Todos Santos outgrew La Paz by the mid-1700s; Padre Bernardo Zumziel in fact spent more time in Todos Santos than at the mission in La Paz from 1737 until 1748. Renamed Nuestra Señora del Pilar de Todos Santos in 1749, the town served as Spanish military headquarters for La Escuadra del Sur, the southern detachment of the Loreto presidio. This enabled the community to weather the Pericú rebellions to the southwest in Santiago and San Jose del Cabo. Polish Jesuit padre Carlos Neumayer presided over the mission from 1752 until his death in Todos Santos in 1764. Todos Santos remained an important mission settlement until secularization in 1840.

When Governor Luis del Castillo Negrete ordered the distribution of church lands to the local community in 1841, he was contested by Padre Gabriel González, a local priest and former president of the mission who had used mission property for his own farming and ranching, becoming a powerful local trader in the process. González's armed rebellion was put down in 1842; the priest and his followers fled to Mazatlán.

Anglo whalers visiting Todos Santos in 1849 praised the town as "an oasis" with "friendly and intelligent people." In the post-mission era, Todos Santos thrived as Baja's sugarcane capital, supporting eight sugar mills by the late 1800s. While carrying out a survey of Cape Region flora for the California Academy of Sciences in 1890, botanist T.S. Brandegee commented on the area's beauty and bounty. During this period handsome hotels, theaters, municipal offices, and homes for painters and sculptors were built.

Sugar prices dropped precipitously following WW II, and all but one mill closed when the most abundant freshwater spring dried up in 1950. The remaining mill closed in 1965 though smaller household operations continued into the early '70s. The town faded into near obscurity.

Around 1981 the spring came back to life, and the arroyo once again began producing a large variety and quantity of fruits and vegetables. Three years later, Mexico 19 was paved between San Pedro and Cabo San Lucas, opening Todos Santos to tourists and expatriates for the first time.

BEACHES

North

Miles of virgin sand stretch north and south from Todos Santos along the Pacific. A sandy road at the southwest edge of town off Calle Juárez parallels a wide, planted arroyo past a palm-hidden freshwater lagoon (La Poza) to the nearest beach, **Las Pocitas** (also known as La Poza de Lobos). The undertow and shore break here are usually too heavy for swimming, but it's a great spot for watching the sunset.

Follow Calle Topete across the arroyo through Las Huertas, in the neighborhood sometimes known as El Otro Lado ("The Other Side"), to find a sand road leading west to **Playa La Cachora**, another good sunset-watching and strolling beach with roiling waters too strong for most swimmers.

A wider network of sand roads crosses the arroyo and runs north parallel to the beach for some 26 km (16 miles) past small coconut and papaya orchards to larger farms at Las Playitas and El Carrizal, then heads inland to join Mexico 19. Several sandy tracks branch west off this road to a lengthy succession of dune-lined beaches. For much of the year the surf isn't suitable for swimming, though you can surf the beach break at **La Pastora** (named for a meadow some distance from the break of the same name). Look for a large, lone palapa standing over the beach well north of town. The beaches offer secluded sunbathing and beachcombing. El Carrizal itself has changed back and forth from farm to campground to the latest scheme, a "desert theme park" that promises tent camping, rooms, a restaurant, and pool (call 112-4-02-61 for the latest).

Beyond El Carrizal a rough dirt road snakes north along and away from the coast 57 km (36 miles) to a cluster of Ranchos—Los Inocentes, El Rosario, El Tepetate, and El Tomate—where another dirt road leads northeast 29 km (18 miles) to meet Mexico 1. Sand beach lines the entire coastline here all the way north to **Punta Márques** (about 24 km/15 miles north of Rancho El Tomate) and **Punta Conejo** (11 miles north of **Punta Márques**). Both points offer excellent surfing and windsurfing in the winter and early spring. Self-contained beach camping is permitted anywhere along the shore.

While walking along any of the northern beaches close to the surf line, watch out for "sneaker" waves that rise up seemingly out of nowhere to engulf the beach; though rare, accidental drownings have occurred on these beaches. During the late *chubasco* season, especially September, small blue jellyfish called *aguas malas* are commonly encountered in inshore waters.

Punta Lobos

About two km (1.2 miles) south of the town limits via Mexico 19, a signed, unpaved access road suitable for most vehicles leads 2.4 km (1.5 miles) to Punta Lobos, a rocky point at the south end of a sandy cove. The cove is named for a resident colony of sea lions. The surf here is usually okay for swimming but take a good look at the currents before leaping in. This cove is used as a launching point for the local fishermen, so there's usually a small fleet of pangas toward the point. The pangas usually bring the catch in after 1500; sometimes fresh fish can be bought directly from the *pangeros*. The ruins of an old cannery lie at the side of the access road toward the beach; north along the beach stands a lighthouse. Swimming in the lighthouse area is not recommended.

A small spring-fed lagoon lies behind the south end of the beach, marked by a large Virgin shrine. A narrow trail leads up and over the 215-meter (700-foot) headland to a panoramic view of the beach and sea below. On the other side of the headland you can see sandy **Puerto Campechano** and, farther south, **Puerto Algodones.** The latter can also be reached via a very rough dirt road that runs southwest off the Punta Lobos access road. According to local history, Algodones was used for the ship-

*abandoned cannery,
Punta Lobos*

ping of tomatoes and sugarcane from the 1930s through the '50s; snorkeling is good at the rocky headlands at each end. You will also find a colony of sea lions here.

Punta Lobos can be reached on foot from town by following Calle Pedrajo southwest past Hotel Miramar one long block till you meet a wide dirt road. Turn left here and follow the road until you can see the lighthouse on the right; take the next wide dirt road heading in that direction till you reach Punta Lobos. This walk takes 30-40 minutes.

Playa San Pedrito

Just north of El Pescadero between Km 56 and 57 is an unsigned, 2.5-km (1.5-mile) dirt road west to **Playa San Pedrito**, known as "Palm Beach" to the local gringos. Stretched between two rocky points and backed by Mexican palms and a saltmarsh, this scenic beach offers good camping, fishing, and a steady beach break for surfing. For swimming, the middle 100 meters or so in the center of the cove is usually the safest; toward the north and south ends, the water looks deceptively shallow and inviting but riptides have been known to carry swimmers out of the cove into open ocean or onto the rocks.

At the southern end of the cove, toward Punta San Pedro, is a small, semipermanent encampment of surfers and world travelers seeking *la grande vida* for as few pesos as possible. Trails lead across the headlands at either end of the cove to beach vistas. In back of Punta San

Pedro, the slopes of **Cerro Los Viejos** offer a rough but scenic hike.

This beach is sometimes incorrectly called "Playa San Pedro"; Mexican topographic surveys will confirm its original name as Playa San Pedrito—"Little San Pedro Beach"—since it's smaller than Playa San Pedro, immediately south of Punta San Pedro.

Getting There: In 1993 the most direct road to San Pedrito was marked with a sign reading "Road Closed"; all the local residents and surfers used it anyway. The road intersects several other sandy tracks; when you see a ruined mansion off to your right, make sure you take the left fork that curves around to the south end of the palm orchard. If you head straight toward the middle or north end of the orchard you'll run into the saltmarsh and have to hike a couple of hundred yards through tall saltgrass and mud to reach the beach. The more commonly used road between Km 56 and 57 leaves the highway almost opposite the Campo Experimental on the left.

Playa San Pedro

Just south of Punta San Pedro begins the long **Playa San Pedro** (7.4 km/4.6 miles south of the Todos Santos town limits), which is stony at the north end but sandy for a long stretch south. Surfing here is sometimes as good as or better than that at San Pedrito, and it's a lot easier to find: the 3.1-km (1.9-mile) access road is clearly marked. San Pedro has an RV/tent campground called "San Pedrito," which leads many

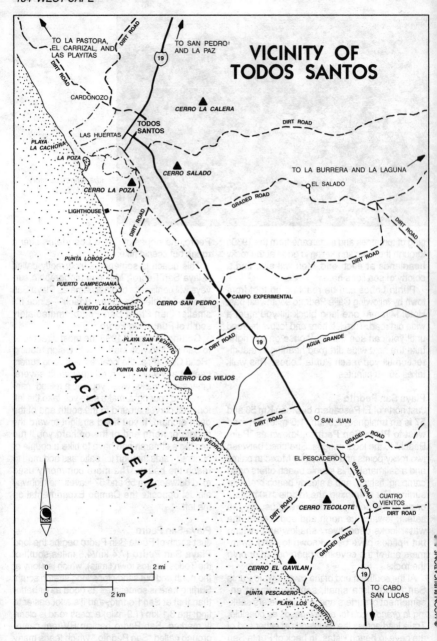

people to call this beach "Playa San Pedrito," further confusing this beach with the less frequented cove to the north. During the winter surfing season, the local ejido sometimes collects a US$1.80 parking fee for vehicles parked in the small area at the end of the road near Punta San Pedro.

The beach's south end, toward Punta Pescadero, is sometimes called Playa Pescadero.

Playa Los Cerritos and South

South of El Pescadero at Km 64 (12.8 km/eight miles south of Todos Santos) a good dirt road branches 2.7 km (1.7 miles) southwest to **Playa Los Cerritos,** another fine beach for camping and fishing. Because the beach is sheltered by Punta Pescadero at its north end, swimming is usually safe. During the winter the northwest swell tips a surfable point break. A tidy, cactus-landscaped campground offers space for tent or trailer camping.

Near Playa Los Cerritos a 55-km (34-mile) unpaved, graded road east off the highway to El Aguaje crosses the Sierra de La Laguna to meet Mexico 1 about 16 km (10 miles) south of Miraflores; see "Sierra de La Laguna" in the Central and East Cape chapter, for details.

Access to free beach campsites is available via several dirt roads branching off Mexico 19 at Km 70-71, Km 75, Km 86, and between Km 89 and 90. **Punta Gaspareño,** near Km 73, catches a right point break.

For destinations south of Punta Gaspareño, see "North of Cabo San Lucas," above.

ACCOMMODATIONS

Hotels and Motels

The two-story, colonial-style **Hotel California** (tel. 5-00-02, fax 5-23-33), on Calle Juárez between Morelos and Marquéz de León, has 16 clean, renovated rooms for US$35 s, US$42 d, US$48 t plus a small pool, bar, and restaurant. Some of the wooden floors contain planks taken from a Norwegian shipwreck half a century ago. The management can arrange pack excursions into the Sierra de La Laguna as well as nearby scuba, fishing, and hunting trips. Since it's right on one of the town's main streets, road noise creeps into the rooms, but it's still the most popular spot in town for first-time visitors.

Opposite the Hotel California on Calle Juárez, the basic but adequate **Motel Guluarte** (tel. 5-00-06) has clean rooms with hot water showers for US$18 s, US$20 d.

Villas del Trópico (tel. 5-00-19), Calle Colegio Militar at Ocampo, offers six simple, well-furnished apartments inside a shady, walled complex for US$100-125 a week, US$300-500 per month. Nightly stays can probably be arranged in the off season, May to October, for US$35-40 a night. Outdoor washing machines may be used at no charge. Three RV slots with palapas and three-way hookups are available for US$12 per night.

Near the south entrance to town, in a dusty but quiet neighborhood, the modern **Santa Rosa Hotel and Apartments** (tel. 5-03-94) on Calle Olachea offers eight large, well-maintained studio units with kitchenettes for a bargain US$30 a night, less for long-term stays. In fact, for long-term stays this is your best choice in town. Facilities include a good pool and an enclosed parking area. The signed turnoff for the Santa Rosa is three blocks south of the PEMEX station, after which it's another two blocks west to the hotel.

In the same neighborhood as the Santa Rosa, but a step down in amenities, is the often-empty **Hotel Miramar** (tel. 5-03-41) at calles Mutualismo and Pedrajo. The two-story, L-shaped motel contains 10 rooms—clean, small, with two twin beds in each room—for US$14 s, US$17 d. On the premises are a pool, small restaurant, and laundry.

Bed and Breakfasts

The newly opened **Hostería Las Casitas** (A.P. 73, Todos Santos, BCS 23300, tel. 5-02-88), on Calle Rangel between Obregón and Hidalgo, offers a cluster of charming, renovated *carrizo* cottages amid tropical landscaping. One suite with private bath and queen and double beds runs US$45 a night, while two rooms with shared shower facilities and private half baths cost US$35 each. Another room looking out on the adjacent plant nursery costs just US$25 a night with shared bathroom facilities. All rates include a full breakfast of Mexican and international dishes, fresh juices, and coffee or herb tea served on an outdoor shaded terrace. From May to October all rates are lowered by US$5.

Hostería Las Casitas

Another new bed and breakfast, **Todos Santos Inn** (tel./fax 5-00-40), occupies a newly restored turn-of-the-century building on Calle Topete. Rates for the beautifully appointed rooms include breakfast and run US$85 a night during the high season and US$65 during the low season.

Camping and RV Parks

North of town a maze of sandy roads leads to a string of undeveloped beaches suitable for camping. During peak season *ejidatarios* occasionally ask campers for US$2-3 per person.

El Molino Trailer Park (tel. 5-01-40), at the southeast edge of town off Mexico 19, has become a permanent RV community that doesn't rent spaces by the day anymore. RVers interested in long-term leases can try their luck. Facilities include flush toilets, showers, a laundry, and cafe.

Primitive beach camping is possible on Playa San Pedrito (sometimes called "Palm Beach"), 2.5 km (1.6 miles) west of Km 57; during high season someone may be around to collect a fee of US$3 a night for up to three campers at one site; additional campers are charged US$1. Some people prefer to sleep in the ruins of the old mansion set back from the beach behind the palms and marsh—the site supposedly has fewer insects than in the palms and, on the mansion's second floor, there's often a good breeze. Water is available from a spring at the south end of the beach; treat before drinking. A reminder: This beach is often mistakenly called Playa San Pedro.

San Pedrito RV Park (tel. 5-01-70 or 5-01-47), about 6.5 km (four miles) south of town off Mexico 19 (3.2 km west of Km 59) on Playa San Pedro, has full hookups for US$12.50 (negotiable to US$10 in the off season), and tentsites with simple palapa shelters for US$3 a night. The park has flush toilets, hot showers, laundry facilities, a pool, bar, and restaurant.

Ejido-operated **Los Cerritos Trailer Park** at Playa Los Cerritos (see "Beaches," above) offers RV/camper/tentsites with sewer hookups and nearby toilet facilities for US$4 a day or US$24 a week; the daily rate drops to US$3 per day May-October. A few palapa sites on the beach are available for US$4.50 a night. Outside the park you may camp anywhere on the beach for US$1.80 a night, free in the off season.

The same people who run The Message Center in Todos Santos have recently established **The Trees** at Km 62 on Mexico 19 (El Pescadero), offering hot showers, laundry, shade, and travel information to campers and travelers. Campsites and motel rooms may be added in the coming year.

Farther south toward Cabo San Lucas (especially between Km 80 and 95) are several more unsigned beaches where camping is free.

Hostería Las Casitas (see "Bed and Breakfasts," above) has some space for tent campers at US$5 per tent and one camper, plus US$2.50 for each additional person.

FOOD

For a small, relatively undiscovered town, Todos Santos has a surprising number of places to eat, though some seem to flourish and die with each successive tourist season.

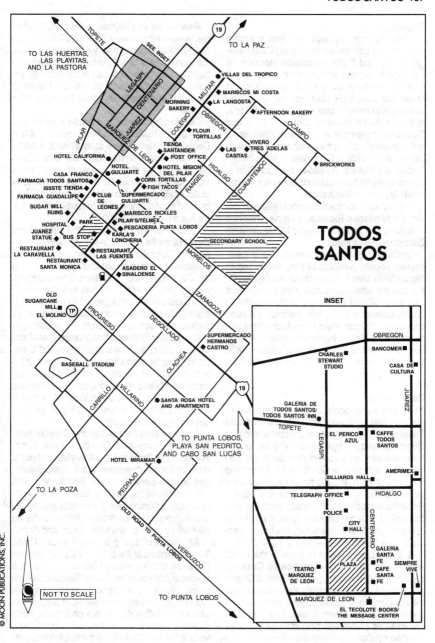

TO LAS HUERTAS,
LAS PLAYITAS,
AND LA PASTORA

TOPETE

SEE INSET

19

TO LA PAZ

LEGASPI

CENTENARIO

JUAREZ

MARQUEZ DE LEON

PILAR

MILITAR

VILLAS DEL TROPICO

MARISCOS MI COSTA

LA LANGOSTA

MORNING
BAKERY

OBREGON

COLEGIO

AFTERNOON BAKERY

OCAMPO

FLOUR
TORTILLAS

HIDALGO

VIVERO
TRES ADELAS

TIENDA
SANTANDER
POST OFFICE

LAS
CASITAS

HOTEL CALIFORNIA

HOTEL
GULUARTE

CUAUHTEMOC

HOTEL MISION
DEL PILAR

BRICKWORKS

CASA FRANCO

CORN TORTILLAS

RANGEL

FARMACIA TODOS SANTOS

ISSSTE TIENDA

FISH TACOS

FARMACIA GUADALUPE

SUPERMERCADO
GULUARTE

CLUB
DE
LEONES

SUGAR MILL
RUINS

MARISCOS RICKLES

HOSPITAL

PARK

PILAR'S/TELMEX

JUAREZ
STATUE

BUS STOP

PESCADERIA PUNTA LOBOS

SECONDARY SCHOOL

KARLA'S
LONCHERIA

RESTAURANT
LA CARAVELLA

RESTAURANT,
LAS FUENTES

MORELOS

RESTAURANT
SANTA MONICA

**TODOS
SANTOS**

ASADERO EL
SINALOENSE

ZARAGOZA

OLD
SUGARCANE
MILL
EL MOLINO

TP

PROGRESO

DEGOLLADO

INSET

BANCOMER

OBREGON

SUPERMERCADO
HERMANOS
CASTRO

OLACHEA

19

CHARLES
STEWART
STUDIO

CASA DE
CULTURA

BASEBALL STADIUM

VILLARINO

CARRILLO

SANTA ROSA HOTEL
AND APARTMENTS

GALERIA DE
TODOS SANTOS/
TODOS SANTOS INN

JUAREZ

TOPETE

LEGASPI

EL PERICO
AZUL

CAFFE
TODOS
SANTOS

TO PUNTA LOBOS,
PLAYA SAN PEDRITO,
AND CABO SAN LUCAS

BILLIARDS HALL

AMERIMEX

HOTEL MIRAMAR

PEDRAJO

TELEGRAPH OFFICE

HIDALGO

TO LA POZA

POLICE

CENTENARIO

OLD ROAD TO PUNTA LOBOS

VERDUZCO

CITY
HALL

GALERIA
SANTA
FE

TEATRO
MARQUEZ
DE LEON

PLAZA

CAFE
SANTA
FE

SIEMPRE
VIVE

NOT TO SCALE

© MOON PUBLICATIONS, INC.

MARQUEZ DE LEON

EL TECOLOTE BOOKS/
THE MESSAGE CENTER

TO PUNTA LOBOS

Taquerías

Several humble roadside vendors maintain more-or-less permanent sites along Calle Colegio Militar and Calle Degollado (Mexico 19 South); others come and go with the seasons. A string of vendors along the south end of Colegio Militar offer inexpensive but tasty fish, usually either shark or dorado, and shrimp tacos. **Pilar's,** at the northeast corner of Colegio Militar and Zaragoza, is the most well known for fish tacos, but a smaller unsigned vendor on the opposite corner, same side of the street, is even better. **Tacos de Pollos Asados,** next to Pilar's, serves fantastic barbecued chicken—by the half or whole, or in chicken tacos.

A good spot for seafood cocktails and *ceviche* is **Mariscos Rickles,** a simple unsigned vendor station on Calle Colegio Militar between Zaragoza and Morelos.

On Calle Degollado at the south end of town, the very popular **Asadero El Sinaloense** serves dependable *carne asada,* tacos, and quesadillas at a few sheltered outdoor tables next to a van. Also offered during the cooler months is *champurrado,* a thick, hot, delicately spiced chocolate and cornmeal drink found throughout mainland Mexico but less commonly seen in Baja. El Sinaloense starts serving between 1830 and 1900 and stays open till around midnight, Thurs.-Tuesday.

Restaurants

Popular among locals as well as gringos for seafood and Mexican dishes, **Restaurant Las Fuentes** (tel. 5-02-57) sits at the corner of calles Degollado and Colegio Militar. The seafood is fresh and beer is served with frosted mugs. You can enjoy it in either a well-lighted indoor dining area or outdoors around three fountains on a patio planted with bougainvillea and palms. Prices are moderate. *Pescado empapelado,* fish baked in paper with tomatoes, mild chiles, and various other condiments, is a house specialty. Las Fuentes is open daily 0700-2100.

A notch or two lower in price is the much more rustic, sand-floor **Mariscos Mi Costa** at the north end of Calle Colegio Militar at Ocampo. *Pescado frito* (fried fish), *camarones al mojo de ajo* (shrimp in garlic butter), and seafood *cocteles* are house specialties. The similar **El Pariente de Ensenada** next to Hotel Misiones del Pilar on Colegio Militar is also good.

Restaurant Las Tejitas, in the Hotel California, is open for breakfast 0700-1030 and dinner 1800-2100. In spite of a very competent kitchen, the restaurant is usually empty except when a backpacking or cycling tour is booked into the hotel. During high season the hotel hosts a Tuesday seafood buffet that receives high marks.

Old standby **Restaurant Santa Monica,** just north of the PEMEX station on Mexico 19 (Calle Degollado), serves very tasty shrimp, lobster, and *carne asada* dinners at reasonable prices. Service can be slow but everything is made from scratch. One of the house specialties is *pollo estilo Santa Monica,* a quarter chicken braised in something akin to barbecue sauce. It's open daily 0700-2200.

Call it chic, call it trendy, but the atmospheric **Café Santa Fé** (tel. 5-03-40), on Calle Centenario off Marquéz de León facing the plaza, has become *the* place to eat and be seen during the Dec.-March tourist season. The changing, mostly Italian menu emphasizes the use of fresh, local ingredients (including organic vegetables) to produce wood-fired pizza, ravioli (a shrimp and lobster version is the house specialty), *pasta primavera,* lasagna, fresh seafood, octopus salad, and the occasional rabbit. Complementing the menu are espresso drinks, a full wine list, *tiramisu,* and fresh fruits. The service is crisp, and prices match the cafe's aristocratic flair. The Santa Fé is open Wed.-Mon. noon-2100; the restaurant closes each year in October during the town fiesta.

A new venture financed by the Coppola family of Los Arcos and Finisterra hotel fame, **Restaurante Italiano La Caravella,** is about to open at the southwestern end of Calle Juárez, just beyond Benito's statue. Borrowing a little from the Santa Fé, La Caravella will feature indoor-outdoor dining, wood-fired grills and ovens, and a modern Italian menu. Unlike the Santa Fé it will be open for breakfast, lunch, and dinner.

Another well-run gringo operation, **Caffé Todos Santos,** at the corner of Centenario and Obregón a block west of the Bancomer, is a welcome addition to the Todos Santos breakfast scene. Housed in a historic corner building with lots of light, the cafe offers excellent cappuccino and other coffee drinks, hot chocolate, fresh pastries, waffles, omelettes, deli sandwiches, vegetarian sandwiches, ice cream, bagels, granola, fruit shakes (made with produce from the owner's farm), and other snacks. It's open Tues.-Sun. 0700-2000 most of the year, till 2100 during high tourist season.

Hostería Las Casitas (see "Bed and Breakfasts" preceding) serves very good Mexican and international breakfasts to the public daily 0900-noon. The "Don Juan"—fluffy scrambled eggs folded in a flour tortilla seasoned with *chipotle* mayonnaise, fried potatoes on the side—is highly recommended.

Groceries

The usual assortment of staples can be bought at any of several markets in town, which include: **Supermercado Guluarte** (next to Motel Guluarte), **ISSSTE Tienda** (Calle Juárez between Zaragoza and Morelos), and **Supermercado Hermanos Castro** (Calle Degollado). Castro is the only market open on Sunday and the only one open late (till 2200). Seventy-year-old **Siempre Viva**, at calles Juárez and Marquéz de León, opens around 0700, which is an hour or two earlier than the others. Siempre Viva stocks household wares and a few ranch supplies as well as groceries; meats, cheeses, produce, and honey sold here come from local farms and ranches.

Two unsigned bakeries, one open in the morning and one in the afternoon, sell *bolillos, pan dulce,* and other Mexican-style baked goods. The **morning bakery** (open 0700-noon, closed Sunday) is at the end of an alley off Calle Colegio Militar between Hidalgo and Obregón, while the **afternoon bakery** (1300 till around 1800 or until they sell out, closed Sunday) operates from a house at the north end of Calle Rangel near Ocampo. Per order, the morning bakery will also roast small pigs or lambs for around US$12 apiece in its clay *horno.*

You can buy tortillas by the kilo at the **Tortillería Todos Santos** on Calle Colegio Militar between Morelos and Marquéz de León. **Pescadería Punta Lobos,** a seafood market on Calle Zaragoza just south of Calle Colegio Militar, sells fresh fish and shellfish; hours are daily 0830-1600. Even fresher seafood can often be purchased from the *pangeros* at Punta Lobos, south of town.

Fresh tropical fruits—mango, guava, figs—are most abundantly available toward the middle and end of the rainy season, i.e., Aug.-Sept.,

although certain fruits, such as papaya, are available year-round. Fresh vegetables peak in January and February.

Just north of town on the way to La Paz, along the east side of Mexico 19, a string of vendors sell candies and pastries made from local produce, including tasty *empanadas* (turnovers) made from mango, guava, and *cajete* (goat milk caramel); *panocha* (brown sugar cakes); lemon peel and coconut candies; and refreshing sugarcane juice.

ENTERTAINMENT AND EVENTS

Museums and Theater

The new **Casa de Cultura** on Calle Juárez at Obregón displays a modest collection of artifacts evoking the anthropology, ethnography, history, and natural history of the region, along with small displays of modern art and handicrafts. Hours hadn't been set at press time but expect something along the lines of Mon.-Fri. 0830-1700, Saturday 0830-1300.

Nicely restored **Teatro Marquéz de León,** at calles Legaspi and Marquéz de León, hosts musical and folkloric dance performances from time to time, especially during the annual October fiesta. Before the Teatro de la Ciudad in La Paz was built, this was the only proper theater in the state of Baja California Sur.

Simple outdoor cinemas—featuring grade-C Mexican films with the usual *ranchero/narcotraficante* themes—are sometimes set up next to the soccer field near Las Huertas.

Dancing

La Langosta, at calles Colegio Militar and Obregón, doubles as the town's bar and disco. Live *norteña* bands often play on weekends; usually there's no cover, but the place doesn't start to fill till around 2300.

The local **Lions Club** (Cueva de los Léones) holds Saturday evening dances at their hall opposite the Hotel California. A small cover charge is collected at the door; there's an additional fee to sit at a table.

Events

During the last weekend in January the **Todos Santos Arts and Crafts Show** is held at the Casa de la Cultura. Sponsored by Artosan—a

local nonprofit group devoted to the enhance-
ment of local cultural and educational opportunities—the show features sculptures, paintings,
ceramics, and other visual works by local artists
as well as a few out-of-towners. The show is
young, but will probably become an important
Cape event over the next few years.

In late February Artosan also sponsors a
Home and Garden Tour that allows visitors to
tour some of the town's more historic or visual-
ly notable homes, some restored by resident
gringos. For further information on either of the
above events, contact Artosan (A.P. 16, Todos
Santos, BCS 23300, tel. 5-00-50, fax 5-02-92).

March is the month for **artist-led workshops.**
Potter Barbara Campbell-Moffitt offers five-day
pottery workshops, while artist and jewelry designer Randall Gunther leads courses of similar
length focusing on nature drawing. Exact dates
and venues are yet to be announced; for further
information, contact Ginny Hoyt, P.O. Box 131,
Tomé, New Mexico 87060 (tel. 505-866-0582).

Fiesta Todos Santos is held around the feast
day of the town's patron saint, Virgen del Pilar,
on 12 October. For four days beginning the second Saturday of the month, residents enjoy
dances, cockfights, theater performances, and
other merriment centered around the church
and town plaza.

For 12 days beginning **Día de Guadalupe**
(12 Dec.), Todos Santos Catholics participate in
nightly candlelight processions to the plaza
church. The celebrations culminate in a midnight mass on **Christmas Eve.**

SPORTS AND RECREATION

Much of the outdoor recreation enjoyed in the
Todos Santos area—e.g., fishing, swimming,
and surfing—focuses on the coast; see "Beaches," above, for beach descriptions.

Fishing
Pangas and fishing guides may be hired at
Punta Lobos for US$20 per hour with a three-
hour minimum. Many of the same gamefish
commonly found from Cabo San Lucas to La
Paz can be caught offshore here. English-
speaking *pangero* Marco Torres is an experienced guide; he can be contacted in advance
through Hotel California.

Surfcasting, though possible at any of the
Todos Santos area beaches, is safest and eas-
iest at Playa San Pedrito (Palm Beach), Playa
San Pedro, and Playa Los Cerritos.

Whether fishing onshore or inshore, you'll
need to bring your own rods, tackle, and lures.
Live bait can be purchased from the local fishermen at Punta Lobos.

Whalewatching
Although you won't see as many whales close
to shore as farther north in Bahía Magdalena (an important calving bay for the Pacific
gray whale), newborn calves and their mothers
do swim by on their "trial run" to the Sea of
Cortez before beginning the long migration back
to the Arctic Circle. The best months for spotting
grays are Dec.-April.

With a pair of binoculars and some luck, you
can stand on any beach in the vicinity and spot
grays (and other whales) spouting offshore.
For a much better view from shore, climb Punta
Lobos (see "Beaches," above). *Pangeros* at
Punta Lobos will take up to five passengers
out to see the whales for US$30 an hour; in-
quire at the beach or at any of the hotels in
town.

Surfing
Most of the Pacific breaks near Todos Santos
(Playa San Pedro, Playa Los Cerritos, La Pastora) hit their peak during the northwest swell,
Dec.-March. See "Beaches," above, for beach
locations. The nearest place to rent boards or
buy wax is Cabo San Lucas.

Experienced surfers who paddle around the
larger points at Punta Lobos and Punta San
Pedro during the late summer southern swell
will sometimes turn up a nice break, although
the usual summer custom is to head for the
Corridor between Cabo San Lucas and San
José del Cabo, or to lesser known spots around
the east side of the Cape (see "Los Frailes to
San José del Cabo," under "East Cape" in the
Central and East Cape chapter).

Baseball and Billiards
Todos Santos fields its own baseball team at
the **stadium** on calles Rangel and Villarino.

A **billiards hall** on Centenario and Hidalgo offers the usual Mexican forms of billiards and
pool.

Yoga

Satchidananda Expeditions (tel./fax 5-01-51; P.O. Box 180176, Coronado, CA 92178, tel. 619-645-8012) custom-designs health programs for individuals or couples in Todos Santos. Typical activities include instruction in yoga, meditation, and tai chi, plus vegetarian meals, daily massage, hiking, cycling, and kayaking. Regular yoga classes are held several times weekly at a bungalow on the north side of the arroyo.

Baja Herbal Intensive

Occasional three-day workshops at Hostería Las Casitas educate participants in the identification, uses, and preparation of indigenous medicinal plants. The cost is US$85 per person; contact Pam Hyde-Nakai at (602) 743-3980 in the U.S., or Lee Moore at (114) 5-02-18 in Todos Santos.

SHOPPING

Although Todos Santos hardly compares with Cabo San Lucas or San José del Cabo when it comes to variety and quantity, a few interesting, high-quality shops have opened during the last year or two.

The tiny **Casa Franco,** on Calle Juárez just south of Morelos, carries a selection of rustic, handmade furniture, as well as regional arts and crafts (including pottery from La Candelaria). Casa Franco may soon be moving two blocks southwest near the pharmacies.

Nearby at the corner of Juárez and M. de León, in the new Plaza de los Cardones commercial center, **El Tecolote Books/Libros** (tel. 5-02-88) carries a good selection of foreign and Mexican magazines (including surf magazines), new and used paperbacks (trades welcome), and local arts and crafts. The shop is open Mon.-Sat. 1000-1700. Owner Jane Perkins is a good source of local tourist information. **Muebles Martín,** in the same plaza, sells graceful *palo de arco* furniture and cane-bottomed chairs.

On Calle Topete at Centenario, opposite Caffé Todos Santos, recently opened **El Perico Azul** stocks local crafts and women's clothing, along with hard-to-find deli items. If you're looking for tropical plants—bougainvillea, hibiscus, jasmine, oleander, and more—to decorate your local villa, sooner or later you'll end up at **Vivero Las Tres Adelas,** a plant nursery at calles Rangel and Obregón.

Agua Sierra de La Laguna (about one km north of town on Mexico 19), and **La Cristalina** (on Calle Juárez opposite the Hotel California) are the primary sources of purified water for the town. You can purchase water or ice here in just about any quantity. Beer is available from any market in town, or from the *depositos* on Calle Colegio Militar (adjacent to the post office) and on Calle Degollado near the gas station; the former is slightly less expensive.

Tienda Santander, on Calle Colegio Militar between calles Marquéz de León and Hidalgo, sells handcrafted ranching accoutrements collectively known as *talabartería*—saddles, lariats, bridles, chaparreras, and boots—as well as *huaraches* (leather sandals), engraved machetes, and other farm/ranch hardware.

Artist Studios

Several North American artists live in Todos Santos, some year-round, others only part-time. One of the year-rounders is **Charles Stewart,** who has a home gallery—usually referred to as "Stewart House" (officially known

BOB RACE

as Estudio Caballo del Mar)—at the corner of Centenario and Obregón. You can't miss this little 1810-vintage house smothered in foliage and singing birds. Formerly of Taos, New Mexico, Stewart works mostly in watercolors and pastels; among his more recently conceived media are small *retablo*-style pieces that feature colorful Bajacalifornio pictograph motifs on salvaged wood.

Stewart's work can also be found at the new **Galería de Todos Santos** at the corner of Topete and Legaspi in the same building as the Todos Santos Inn. Owned by American artist Michael Cope, the gallery focuses on the work of artists who reside in Baja California. The works displayed are of high quality; something new graces the gallery walls every six weeks or so.

Next door to the Café Santa Fe, the **Galería Santa Fe** displays the work of Italian artist Ezio Colombo and other local artists. The owner of the **Hostería Las Casitas** (see "Bed and Breakfasts" under Accommodations) shows some of her work in glass media in a small gallery on the *hostería* grounds.

INFORMATION AND SERVICES

Tourist Information
Although Todos Santos has no tourist office as such, you can usually find someone to answer your questions at any of the gringo-run establishments in town (e.g., Caffé Todos Santos, El Tecolote Libros, Todos Santos Message Center). If you speak Spanish and seek information on the sierra backcountry, try Siempre Viva at the corner of calles Juárez and Marquéz de León; this is where sierra ranchers traditionally come to supplement foods they produce at home.

The Todos Santos Book, written by local resident Lee Moore and available at El Tecolote Libros (see "Shopping," above), contains lots of useful information on things to see and do in the area.

Changing Money
Bancomer, at the corner of calles Juárez and Obregón, is open Mon.-Fri. 0830-1300. To change travelers checks, be sure to arrive before 1100.

Post and Telephone
Todos Santos' **post office** is on Colegio Militar (Mexico 19) between Hidalgo and Marquéz de León. It's open Mon.-Fri. 0800-1300 and 1500-1700.

Long-distance phone calls can be made from the rustic **public telephone office** at Pilar's at Calle Colegio Militar and Calle Zaragoza; it's open daily 0700-1900. Be wary of the new private phone services that charge outrageous rates for long-distance calls; the phone office at Pilar's and the front desk phone at the Hotel California are hooked into the latest ripoff system from the United States. Ask to use TelMex or, if you have an access number for your long-distance carrier at home, use that; of course there will be a surcharge, but that's usually cheaper than using the fly-by-night long-distance services that charge as much as US$14 a minute.

The Message Center (Centro de Mensaje Todos Santos) (A.P. 48, Todos Santos, BCS 23300, tel./fax 5-02-88) can give you a quick long-distance-rate comparison between TelMex, AT&T, and other telephone companies. The office charges a reasonable surcharge over whichever long-distance service you choose. In addition to long-distance calling, this office offers fax, courier, mail forwarding, and answering services. The Message Center is open mid Oct.-May, Mon.-Sat. 0800-1700, Mon.-Fri. 0800-1300 and 1500-1700 the rest of the year.

The area code for Todos Santos is 114.

Real Estate
Of the several real estate companies that handle local property transactions as well as general inquiries on rentals, leases, and sales, **AmeriMex** (Juárez and Hidalgo, A.P. 16, Todos Santos, BCS 23300, tel. 5-00-50, fax 5-02-92) is the only one that maintains an office year-round and is the only company with local roots.

Pharmacies
Farmacia Todos Santos (tel. 5-00-30) and **Farmacia Guadalupe** (tel. 5-03-00), both on Calle Juárez, can fill prescriptions any time of day or night.

Laundry
The *lavandería* attached to the Hotel Miramar is open Mon.-Sat. 0800-1600, Sunday 0800-noon.

Transportation

Seven Aguila buses a day run between Todos Santos and La Paz to the north and Cabo San Lucas to the south. Either bus trip takes about two hours and costs US$3 per person; a bus through to San José del Cabo (four daily departures) costs US$4.80. Buses arrive at and depart from the corner of Calle Colegio Militar and Calle Zaragoza, opposite Pilar's fish taco/phone office.

BOOKLIST

DESCRIPTION AND TRAVEL

Burleson, Bob, and David H. Riskind. *Backcountry Mexico: A Traveler's Guide and Phrase Book*. University of Texas Press, 1986. Part guidebook, part anthropological study covering northern Mexico with some relevance to Baja California backcountry travel.

Cudahy, John. *Mañanaland: Adventuring with Camera and Rifle Through California in Mexico*. Duffie and Co., 1928. Provides an interesting glimpse of pre-WW II Baja, but no outstanding revelations.

Cummings, Joe. *Baja Handbook*. Moon Publications, 1994. If you like the Cape Region, you'll probably love the rest of Baja California Sur and Baja California to the north. Now in its second edition, this guide covers the entire peninsula from Tijuana to Cabo San Lucas.

Cummings, Joe. *Northern Mexico Handbook*. Moon Publications, 1994. A new guidebook—and the first ever published in English—to a largely undiscovered region that shares many geographical and cultural characteristics with Baja California. The book covers mainland Mexico's nine northernmost states—Sonora, Sinaloa, Chihuahua, Durango, Coahuila, Nuevo León, Tamaulipas, Zacatecas, and San Luis Potosí.

Mackintosh, Graham. *Into A Desert Place*. Graham Mackintosh Publications, P.O. Box 1196, Idyllwild, CA 92549. A thoroughly engaging report of Mackintosh's walk around the entire coastline of Baja California over the course of two years. Destined to become a classic of gringo-in-Baja travel literature for its refreshingly honest style and insights into Baja fish-camp and village life.

Miller, Max. *Land Where Time Stands Still*. Dodd, Mead, and Co., 1943. A classic travelogue that chronicles Baja life during WW II, when Mexicans alternately fell prey to German and American propaganda.

Steinbeck, John. *The Log from the Sea of Cortez*. Viking Press, 1941. This chronicle of the author's Baja research voyage with marine biologist Ed Ricketts (the inspiration for *Cannery Row* protagonist "Doc") reveals Steinbeck as a bit of a scientist himself. Annotated with Latin, the book is full of insights into Pacific and Sea of Cortez marinelife as well as coastal Bajacalifornio society. Sprinkled throughout are expositions of Steinbeck's personal philosophy, implicit in his novels but fully articulated here. Also reveals the source for his novella *The Pearl*.

HISTORY AND CULTURE

Paz, Octavio. *The Labyrinth of Solitude: Life and Thought in Mexico*. Grove Press, 1961. Paz has no peer when it comes to expositions of the Mexican psyche, and this is his best work.

Robertson, Tomás. *Baja California and its Missions*. La Siesta Press, 1978. Robertson was the patriarch of an old Baja California–Sinaloa family of northern European extraction as well as a patron of Baja mission restoration. His useful amateur work synthesizes Baja mission history from several sources; like its sources, the book contains a few minor contradictions and muddy areas.

NATURAL HISTORY

Krutch, Joseph Wood. *The Forgotten Peninsula: A Naturalist in Baja California*. University of Arizona Press, 1986 (reprint from 1961). Combines natural history and a curmudgeonly travelogue style to paint a romantic portrait of pre-Transpeninsular-Highway Baja.

Nickerson, Roy. *The Friendly Whales: A Whalewatcher's Guide to the Gray Whales of Baja California*. Chronicle Books, 1987. A light study, with photographs, of the friendly-whale phenomenon in Laguna San Ignacio, where gray whales often initiate contact with humans.

Roberts, Norman C. *Baja California Plant Field Guide*. Natural History Publishing Co., 1989. Contains concise descriptions of over 550 species of Baja flora, more than half illustrated by color photos.

Scammon, Charles Melville. *The Marine Mammals of the Northwestern Coast of America*. Dover Publications reprint, 1968. Originally published in the 19th century by the whaler who almost brought about the gray whale's complete demise, this is *the* classic, pioneering work on Pacific cetaceans, including the gray whale.

Wiggins, Ira L. *Flora of Baja California*. Stanford University Press, 1980. This weighty work, with listings of over 2,700 species, is a must for the serious botanist. But for the average layperson with an interest in Baja vegetation, Norman Roberts's *Baja California Plant Field Guide* (see above) will more than suffice.

Zwinger, Ann Raymond. *A Desert Country near the Sea*. Truman Talley Books, 1983. A poetic collection of essays centered around Baja natural history (including a rare passage on the Sierra de La Laguna), with sketches by the author and an appendix with Latin names for flora and fauna.

SPORTS AND RECREATION

Fons, Valerie. *Keep It Moving: Baja by Canoe*. The Mountaineers, 1986. Well-written account of a canoe trip along the Baja California coastline; recommended reading for sea kayakers as well as canoeists.

Kelly, Niel, and Gene Kira. *The Baja Catch*. Apples and Oranges, 1993. The latest version of this fishing guide pushes it firmly to the top of the heap. Contains extensive discussions of tackle and expert fishing techniques, detailed directions to productive fisheries, and numerous maps.

Lehman, Charles. *Desert Survival Handbook*. Primer Publishers, 1990. A no-nonsense guide to desert survival skills; should be included in every pilot's or coastal navigator's kit.

Romano-Lax, Andromeda. *Sea Kayaking in Baja*. Wilderness Press, 1993. This inspiring 153-page guide to Baja kayaking contains 15 one- to five-day paddling routes along the Baja coastline, plus many helpful hints on kayak camping. Each route is accompanied by a map; although these maps are too sketchy to be used for navigational purposes, a list of Mexican topographic map numbers is provided so that readers can go out and obtain more accurate material.

Williams, Jack. *Baja Boater's Guide, Vols. I and II*. H.J. Williams Publications, 1988. These ambitious guides, one each on the Pacific Ocean and the Sea of Cortez, contain useful aerial photos and sketch maps of Baja's continental islands and coastline.

Wong, Bonnie. *Bicycling Baja*. Sunbelt Publications, 1988. Written by an experienced leader of Baja cycling tours, this book includes helpful suggestions on trip preparation, equipment, and riding techniques as well as road logs for 17 different cycling routes throughout the peninsula.

Wyatt, Mike. *The Basic Essentials of Sea Kayaking*. ICS Books, 1990. A good introduction to sea kayaking, with tips on buying gear, paddling techniques, safety, and kayak loading.

REAL ESTATE

Combs-Ramirez, Ginger. *The Gringo's Investment Guide*. Monmex Publishing, 1994. Succinct but complete advice on buying and selling real estate in Mexico.

Peyton, Dennis John. *How to Buy Real Estate in Mexico*. Law Mexico Publishing, 1994. The most thorough and in-depth reference available in English on buying Mexican property. Anyone considering real estate investments in Mexico should read this book before making any decisions.

SPANISH PHRASEBOOK

PRONUNCIATION GUIDE

Consonants

c—like 'c' in "cat" before 'a', 'o', or 'u'; like 's' before 'e' or 'i'

d—as 'd' in 'dog', except between vowels, then like 'th' in "that"

g—before 'e' or 'i', like the 'ch' in Scottish "loch" elsewhere like 'g' in "get"

h—always silent

j—like the English 'h' in "hotel" except stronger

ll—like the 'y' in "yellow"

ñ—like the 'ni' in "onion"

r—always pronounced as strong 'r'

rr—trilled 'r'

v—similar to the 'b' in "boy" (not as English 'v')

z—like 's' in "same"

b, f, k, l, m, n, p, q, t—as in English

Vowels

a—as in "father" except shorter

e—as in "hen"

i—as in "machine"

o—as in "phone"

u—usually as in "rule;" when it follows a 'q' the 'u' is silent; when it follows an 'h' or 'g' it is pronounced like 'w' except when it comes between 'g' and 'e' or 'i', when it is also silent

USEFUL WORDS AND PHRASES

Greetings and Civilities

Hello!—*¡Hola!*

Good morning—*Buenos días*

Good afternoon—*Buenas tardes*

Good evening, good night—*Buenas noches*

(*Buenas* can be used when you're not sure of the time of day.)

How are you?—*¿Cómo está?*

Fine—*Muy bien*

So-so—*Así así*

Thank you very much—*Muchas gracias*

You're welcome—*de nada* (literally, "it's nothing")

Yes—*Sí*

No—*No*

I don't know—*Yo no sé*

It's fine; okay—*Está bien*

Good; okay—*Bueno*

Please—*Por Favor*

(To your) health!—*¡Salud!* (used in toasting or after someone sneezes)

Excuse me—*Dispénseme*

Pardon me—*Perdóneme*

I'm sorry—*Lo siento*

Goodbye—*Adiós* (can also be used as a passing hello)

What?—*¿Mande?* (as in "Could you repeat that?")

Terms of Address

I—*yo*

you (formal)—*usted*

you (familiar)—*tú*

he/him—*él*

she/her—*ella*

we/us—*nosotros*

you (plural)—*ustedes*

they/them (all male or mixed gender)—*ellos*

they/them (all female)—*ellas*

Mr., sir—*señor*

Mrs., madam—*señora*

miss, young lady—*señorita*

Communication Problems

I don't speak Spanish well.—*No hablo bien español.*

I don't understand.—*No entiendo.*

Speak more slowly, please.—*Hable más despacio, por favor.*

Repeat, please.—*Repita, por favor.*

How do you say . . . in Spanish?—*¿Cómo se dice . . . en español?*

Do you understand English?—*¿Entiende el inglés?*

Is English spoken here? (Does anyone here speak English?)—*¿Se habla inglés aquí?*

Getting Directions

Where is . . . ?—*¿Dónde está . . . ?*
How far is it to . . . ?—*¿Qué tan lejos está a . . . ?*
from . . . to . . . —*de . . . a . . .*
Does this road lead to . . . ?—*¿Conduce a . . . este camino?*
highway—*la carretera*
road—*el camino*
street—*la calle*
block—*la cuadra*
kilometer—*kilómetro*
mile—*milla* (commonly used near the U.S. border)
north—*el norte*
south—*el sur*
west—*el oeste*
east—*el este*
straight ahead—*al derecho* or *adelante*
to the right—*a la derecha*
to the left—*a la izquierda*

At a Hotel

Is there a hotel near here?—*¿Hay un hotel cerca de aquí?*
inn—*posada*
guesthouse—*casa de huéspedes*
Can I (we) see a room?—*¿Puedo (podemos) ver un cuarto?*
What is the rate?—*¿Cuál es el precio?*
Does that include taxes?—*¿Están incluídos los impuestos?*
Do you accept credit cards?—*¿Acepta tarjetas de crédito?*
cash only—*solo efectivo*
a single room—*un cuarto sencillo*
a double room—*un cuarto doble*
with twin beds—*con camas gemelas*
with a double bed—*con una cama de matrimonio*
with bath—*con baño*
without bath—*sin baño*
shared bath—*baño colectivo*
hot water—*agua caliente*
cold water—*agua fría*
heater—*calentador*
air conditioning—*aire acondicionado*
towel—*toalla*
soap—*jabón*
key—*llave*
blanket—*cubierta* or *manta*
toilet paper—*papel higiénico*
ice—*hielo*

Post Office

post office—*la oficina de correos* (or *el correo*)
I'd like some stamps.—*Quiero unas estampillas.*
I'd like to send this . . . —*Quiero mandar esto . . .*
by air mail—*por correo aéreo*
certified mail—*certificado*
I'd like to send this parcel.—*Quiero mandar este paquete.*
Is there any mail for me? My name is . . . —*¿Hay correo para mí? Me llamo . . .*

Telephone

telephone office—*caseta de teléfono*
I want to make a call to . . . —*Quiero llamar a . . .*
collect call—*por cobrar*
person-to-person—*persona a persona*
a long-distance call—*una llamada de larga distancia*
I want to speak with . . . —*Quiero hablar con . . .*
Is . . . there?—*¿Está . . . ?*
S/he's not here.—*No está.*
The line is engaged.—*La línea está ocupada.*

Changing Money

I want to change money.—*Quiero cambiar dinero.*
traveler's checks—*cheques de viajero*
What's the exchange rate?—*¿Cuál es el tipo de cambio?*
Is there a commission?—*¿Hay comisión?*
bank—*banco*
currency exchange office—*casa de cambio*

Making Purchases

I need . . . —*Necesito . . .*
I want . . . —*Deseo . . .* or *Quiero . . .*
I would like . . . (more polite)—*Quisiera . . .*
Is/are there any . . . here? (Do you have . . . ?)—*¿Hay . . . aquí?*
How much does it cost?—*¿Cuánto cuesta?*
Can I see . . . ?—*¿Puedo ver . . . ?*
this one—*ésta/éste*
that one—*ésa/ése*
I'll take this one.—*Me llevo éste.*
expensive—*caro*
cheap—*barato*
cheaper—*más barato*

Driving

Full, please (at a gasoline station).—*Lleno, por favor.*

My car has broken down.—*Se me ha descompuesto el carro.*

I need a tow.—*Necesito un remolque.*

Is there a garage nearby?—*¿Hay un garaje cerca?*

Is the road passable with this car (truck)?—*¿Puedo pasar con este carro (troca)?*

With four-wheel drive?—*¿Con doble tracción?*

It's not passable.—*No hay paso.*

traffic light—*semáforo*

traffic sign—*señal*

gasoline (petrol)—*gasolina*

gasoline station—*gasolinera*

oil—*aceite*

water—*agua*

flat tire—*llanta desinflada*

tire repair shop—*llantera*

Auto Parts

fan belt—*banda de ventilador*

battery—*batería*

fuel pump—*bomba de gasolina*

water pump—*bomba de agua*

spark plug—*bujía*

carburetor—*carburador*

distributor—*distribuidor*

axle—*eje*

clutch—*embrague*

gasket—*empaque, junta*

filter—*filtro*

brakes—*frenos*

tire—*llanta*

hose—*manguera*

starter—*marcha, arranque*

radiator—*radiador*

voltage regulator—*regulado de voltaje*

Public Transport

bus stop—*parada del autobús*

main bus terminal—*central camionera*

airport—*aeropuerto*

ferry terminal—*terminal del transbordador*

I want a ticket to . . . —*Quiero un boleto a . . .*

I want to get off at . . . —*Quiero bajar en . . .*

Here, please.—*¡Aquí, por favor.*

How much do I owe you?—*¿Cuánto le debo?*

Hiking and Camping

Where does the trail (path) start?—*¿Dónde empieza la vereda (el sendero)?*

Is camping permitted here (there)?—*¿Se puede acampar aquí (allá)?*

Is there drinking water?—*¿Hay agua potable?*

Is there water there?—*¿Hay agua allá?*

water hole—*tinaja*

spring—*ojo de agua*

well—*pozo*

backpack—*mochila*

sleeping bag—*bolsa de dormir*

tent—*carpa*

firewood—*leña*

charcoal—*carbón*

fire—*fuego*

matches—*cerrillos* or *fósforos*

crossing—*cruce*

on foot—*a pie*

by horse, mule, or burro—*a bestia*

I want to rent (buy) . . . —*Quiero rentar (comprar) . . .*

. . . a burro—*un burro*

. . . a horse—*un caballo*

. . . a mule—*una mula*

Geography

island—*isla*

hill—*cerro* or *colina*

mountain—*montaña*

mountain range—*sierra*

forest—*bosque*

large canyon—*barranca*

medium-size canyon—*cañón*

streambed, wash, small canyon—*arroyo*

valley—*valle*

waterfall—*catarata*

river—*río*

lagoon or lake—*laguna*

bay—*bahía*

sea—*mar*

beach—*playa*

point, headland—*punta*

Fishing

(also see the chart "Fish Translator" in the On the Road chapter)

Where's the best fishing around here?—*¿Dónde está la mejor pesca por aquí?*

What kind of fish is that?—*¿Qué clase de pescado es?*

I'd like to fish for . . . —*Quiero pescar . . .*
I'd like to rent a *panga.*—*Quiero rentar una panga.*
How much does it cost?—*¿Cuánto cuesta?*
What time do we meet?—*¿A qué hora nos encontramos?*
I'd like to buy some bait.—*Quiero comprar unas carnadas.*
Let's fish here.—*Vamos a pescar aquí.*
Slower.—*Más despacio.*
Faster.—*Más rápido.*
Let's go back.—*Vamos a regresar.*
Gaff it.—*Engánchalo.*
Release it.—*Déjelo.*
Can we take it?—*¿Podemos llevarlo?*

Numbers

0—*cero*
1—*uno* (masculine) *una* (feminine)
2—*dos*
3—*tres*
4—*cuatro*
5—*cinco*
6—*seis*
7—*siete*
8—*ocho*
9—*nueve*
10—*diez*
11—*once*
12—*doce*
13—*trece*
14—*catorce*
15—*quince*
16—*diez y seis*
17—*diez y siete*
18—*diez y ocho*
19—*diez y nueve*
20—*veinte*
21—*veinte y uno*
30—*treinta*
40—*cuarenta*
50—*cincuenta*
60—*sesenta*
70—*setenta*
80—*ochenta*
90—*noventa*
100—*cien*
101—*ciento y uno*
200—*doscientos*
500—*quinientos*

1000—*mil*
2000—*dos mil*
20,000—*veinte mil*
million—*millón*

Days of the Week

Sunday—*domingo*
Monday—*lunes*
Tuesday—*martes*
Wednesday—*miércoles*
Thursday—*jueves*
Friday—*viernes*
Saturday—*sábado*

Time

What time is it?—*¿Qué hora es?*
one o'clock—*la una*
two o'clock—*las dos*
at two o'clock—*a las dos*
ten past three—*las tres y diez*
six a.m.—*las seis en la mañana*
six p.m.—*las seis en la tarde*
noon—*el mediodía*
midnight—*la medianoche*
today—*hoy*
tomorrow—*mañana*
yesterday—*ayer*
tonight—*esta noche*
last night—*anoche*
this week—*esta semana*
last week—*la semana pasada*
next year—*el próximo año*
last month—*el mes pasado*
two years ago—*hace dos años*

Miscellaneous

more—*más*
less—*menos*
better—*mejor*
a little—*un poco*
a very little—*un poquito*
large—*grande*
small—*pequeño*
hot (temperature)—*caliente*
hot (spicy)—*picante*
cold—*frío*
quick—*rápido*
bad—*malo*
difficult—*difícil*
easy—*fácil*

GLOSSARY

abarrotes—groceries

aduana—customs service

arroyo—canyon, dry wash, or stream

bahía—bay

basura—trash or rubbish; the sign No Tire Basura means "Don't throw trash"

boca—literally "mouth," a geographic term describing a break in a barrier island or peninsula where sea meets lagoon

calle—street

callejón—alley or lane

cañón—canyon

cardón—*Cereus pringelei,* the world's tallest cactus

carrizo—cane reed

casa de huéspedes—guesthouse

cerro—mountain peak

cerveza—beer

colectivo—van or taxi that picks up several passengers at a time for a standard per-person fare, much like a bus

CONASUPO—Compañía Nacional de Subsistencias Populares ("National Company for Popular Subsistence")

correo—post office

COTP—Captain of the Port

curandero—traditional healer

desertland—biotic community with an average annual precipitation of 25 cm (10 inches) or less

efectivo—cash payment

ejido—collectively owned agricultural lands

ensenada—cove or small bay

FONATUR—Fondo Nacional de Fomento del Turismo ("National Foundation for Tourism Development")

gringo—Mexican slang for Caucasian foreigner

hostería—hostelry, inn

IMSS—Instituto Mexicano del Seguro Social ("Mexican Social Security Institute")

ISSSTE—Instituto de Seguridad y Servicios Sociales para Trabajadores del Estado ("Security and Social Services Institute for Government Workers")

laguna—lagoon, lake, or bay

llano—plains

malecón—waterfront promenade

mariscos—literally "shellfish," but often used as a generic term for seafood

mercado—market

municipio—the next administrative unit below the state, Mexico's equivalent to a county

palacio municipal—literally "municipal palace," equivalent to city or county hall in the U.S.

palapa—umbrella-like shade shelter or roof made from thatched palm leaves

panadería—bakery

panga—fiberglass fishing boat

parada—bus stop

PEMEX—Petróleos Mexicanos ("Mexican Petroleum")

pensión—boardinghouse

playa—beach

pre-Cortesian—a reference to Mexican history before the arrival of the Spanish conquistador Hernán Cortés, i.e., before 1518; other terms with the same meaning include "precolumbian" and "prehispanic"

presidio—military garrison

punta—point

ramal—branch road

refresca—soda or soft drink

SECTUR—Secretaría de Turismo ("Secretariat of Tourism")

SEDESOL—Secretaría de Desarollo Social ("Secretariat of Social Development")

tienda—store

tinaja—pool or spring

topes—speed bumps

ultramarinos—delicatessen-liquor store

INDEX

Italicized page numbers indicate information in captions, charts, illustrations, maps, or special topics.

ABOUT THE AUTHOR

MARK DOWNEY

Joe Cummings has written about travel and culture for 15 years. Attracted to geographical extremes, his first in-depth journeys were in the river deltas and rainforests of Southeast Asia, where he worked as a Peace Corps volunteer (Thailand) and university lecturer (Malaysia), and later contributed to popular guidebooks on Thailand, Laos, Malaysia, Singapore, Burma, Indonesia, and China.

Joe became infatuated with desert terrains while exploring the Sierra del Carmen and Chihuahuan Desert reaches of Texas's Big Bend Country for Moon's Texas Handbook. His love of South Texas border culture, including norteña music and food, eventually spilled over into Northern Mexico and Baja California, where he has undertaken intensive Spanish language courses and lived with a Mexican family. After covering over 30,000 miles of Mexican roads by car and four-wheel-drive, he has decided to build a home in Mexico.

MOON TRAVEL HANDBOOKS

THE IDEAL TRAVELING COMPANIONS

Moon Travel Handbooks provide focused, comprehensive coverage of distinct destinations all over the world. Our goal is to give travelers all the background and practical information they'll need for an extraordinary, unexpected travel experience.

Every Handbook begins with an in-depth essay about the land, the people, their history, art, politics, and social concerns—an entire bookcase of cultural insight and introductory information in one portable volume. We also provide accurate, up-to-date coverage of all the practicalities: language, currency, transportation, accommodations, food, and entertainment. And Moon's maps are legendary, covering not only cities and highways, but parks and trails that are often difficult to find in other sources.

Below are highlights of Moon's Mexico Travel Handbook series. Our complete list of Handbooks covering North America and Hawaii, Mexico, Central America and the Caribbean, and Asia and the Pacific, are listed on the order form on the accompanying pages. To purchase Moon Travel Handbooks, please check your local bookstore or order by phone: (800) 345-5473 Monday-Friday 8 a.m.-5 p.m. PST.

MOON OVER MEXICO
MEXICO TRAVEL HANDBOOK SERIES

"The finest are written with such care and insight they deserve listing as literature."

—*American Geographical Society*

BAJA HANDBOOK   by Joe Cummings, 360 pages, **$15.95**
"Very thorough. Particularly useful are the additions of sidetrips for travelers eager to trek off the beaten path" —*Arizona Daily Star*

CABO HANDBOOK   by Joe Cummings, 205 pages, **$14.95**
The southern tip of Mexico's Baja peninsula features two of the country's most popular tourist destinations–Cabo San Lucas and La Paz. Author Joe Cummings chronicles the rich history and culture of this region in *Cabo Handbook*. Discover 19th-century stone-and-stucco architecture in La Paz, hike in the Sierra de La Laguna, or wander through the aisles of Mercado Mexicano. A master navigator of the road less traveled, Cummings guides visitors to rustic fruitstands and remote adobe villages, as well as the resorts of Los Cabos.

CANCUN HANDBOOK   by Chicki Mallan, 260 pages, **$13.95**
"Finally, there is a thorough, well-organized and clearly presented guidebook for the independent traveler venturing to Mexico's eastern shores to soak up more than sun and sand."
—*Small Press Magazine*

CENTRAL MEXICO HANDBOOK
by Chicki Mallan, 350 pages, **$15.95**
"A most enjoyable read, even for the armchair traveler . . . Of particular interest are the discussions and descriptions of the lesser-known sites." —*Frankfurter Allegemaine Zeitung*

MEXICO HANDBOOK
by Joe Cummings and Chicki Mallan, 1000 pages, **$21.95**
This is the definitive guide on Mexican travel from the preeminent publisher of regional Handbooks on Mexico. Veteran authors Joe Cummings and Chicki Mallan have teamed up to create a single-volume reference that combines practical travel information with the cultural insight that is standard in the Moon Handbook series. Organized by region, *Mexico Handbook* is more user-friendly and comprehensive than competing all-Mexico guidebooks. Suggestions for outdoor recreation are voluminous, and excursion travelers will appreciate the driving information, including tips on renting cars and hundreds of up-to-date maps.

NORTHERN MEXICO HANDBOOK
by Joe Cummings, 528 pages, **$16.95**
"Fill in an important gap in Mexican travel information—and does it with great style." —*Adventures in Mexico*

PACIFIC MEXICO HANDBOOK   by Bruce Whipperman, 428 pages, **$16.95**
"An excellent overview of life along the Pacific coast." —*Small Press Magazine*

PUERTO VALLARTA HANDBOOK
by Bruce Whipperman, 300 pages, **$14.95**
Puerto Vallarta Handbook brings the insight of an award-winning travel writer to one of Mexico's most popular destinations. Join author Bruce Whipperman on a tour through the lush hundred-mile stretch between San Blas and Puerto Vallarta, the villages and quiet beaches areound the Bay of Banderas, and the historic city of Guadalajara. Discover the charm of Old Puerto Vallarta or the excitement of Fiesta de Mayo. With regional history and special features on Mexico's diverse population, this guidebook provides visitors with a cultural perspective to an increasingly popular destination.

YUCATAN PENINSULA HANDBOOK
by Chicki Mallan, 400 pages, **$15.95**

"Amazing in its comprehensiveness, this guide will encourage even the armchair traveler to get up and go to experience the many facets of this unusual part of the world." –*Fort Lauderdale Tribune*

STAYING HEALTHY IN ASIA, AFRICA, AND LATIN AMERICA
by Dirk G. Schroeder, ScD, MPH, 200 pages, **$11.95**

"Your family doctor will not be able to supply you with this valuable information because he doesn't have it."
—*Whole Earth Catalog*

"Read this book if you want to stay healthy on any journeys or stays in Asia, Africa, and Latin America."
—*American Journal of Health Promotion*

TRAVEL MATTERS

Travel Matters is Moon Publications' free quarterly newsletter, loaded with specially commissioned travel articles and essays that tell it like it is. Recent issues have been devoted to Asia, Mexico, and North America, and every issue includes:

Feature Stories: Travel writing unlike what you'll find in your local newspaper. Andrew Coe on Mexican professional wrestling, Michael Buckley on the craze for wartime souvenirs in Vietnam, Kim Weir on the Nixon Museum in Yorba Linda.

Transportation: Tips on how to get around. Rick Steves on a new type of Eurail pass, Victor Chan on hiking in Tibet, Joe Cummings on how to be a Baja road warrior.

Health Matters: Articles on the most recent findings by Dr. Dirk Schroeder, author of *Staying Healthy in Asia, Africa, and Latin America*. Japanese encephalitis, malaria, the southwest U.S. "mystery disease" . . . forewarned is forearmed.

Book Reviews: Informed assessments of the latest travel titles and series. The Rough Guide to *World Music,* Let's Go vs. Berkeley, Dorling Kindersley vs. Knopf.

The Internet: News from the cutting edge. The Great Burma Debate in rec.travel.asia, hotlists of the best WWW sites, updates on Moon's massive "Road Trip USA" exhibit.

There are also booklists, Letters to the Editor, and anything else we can find to interest our readers, as well as Moon's latest titles and ordering information for other travel products, including Periplus Travel Maps to Southeast Asia.

To receive a free subscription to *Travel Matters*, call (800) 345-5473, write to Moon Publications, P.O. Box 3040, Chico, CA 95927-3040, or e-mail travel@moon.com.

Please note: subscribers who live outside the United States will be charged $7.00 per year for shipping and handling.

MOON TRAVEL HANDBOOKS

MEXICO
Baja Handbook (0528). $15.95
Cabo Handbook (0285) $14.95
Cancún Handbook (0501). $13.95
Central Mexico Handbook (0234) $15.95
*Mexico Handbook (0315) $21.95
Northern Mexico Handbook (0226) $16.95
Pacific Mexico Handbook (0323) $16.95
Puerto Vallarta Handbook (0250) $14.95
Yucatán Peninsula Handbook (0242). $15.95

CENTRAL AMERICA AND THE CARIBBEAN
Belize Handbook (0307). $14.95
Caribbean Handbook (0277) $16.95
Costa Rica Handbook (0358). $18.95
Jamaica Handbook (0129) $14.95

NORTH AMERICA AND HAWAII
Alaska-Yukon Handbook (0161). $14.95
Alberta and the Northwest Territories Handbook (0676) . . . $17.95
Arizona Traveler's Handbook (0536) $16.95
Atlantic Canada Handbook (0072) $17.95
Big Island of Hawaii Handbook (0064) $13.95
British Columbia Handbook (0145) $15.95
Catalina Island Handbook (3751) $10.95
Colorado Handbook (0137). $17.95
Georgia Handbook (0609) $16.95
Hawaii Handbook (0005) $19.95
Honolulu-Waikiki Handbook (0587). $14.95
Idaho Handbook (0617) $14.95
Kauai Handbook (0013). $13.95
Maui Handbook (0579) $14.95
Montana Handbook (0544) $15.95
Nevada Handbook (0641). $16.95
New Mexico Handbook (0153) $14.95
Northern California Handbook (3840) $19.95
Oregon Handbook (0102). $16.95
Texas Handbook (0633). $16.95

Utah Handbook (0684) $16.95
Washington Handbook (0552). $15.95
Wyoming Handbook (3980) $14.95

ASIA AND THE PACIFIC
Bali Handbook (3379) $12.95
Bangkok Handbook (0595). $13.95
Fiji Islands Handbook (0382). $13.95
Hong Kong Handbook (0560) $15.95
Indonesia Handbook (0625) $25.00
Japan Handbook (3700). $22.50
Micronesia Handbook (3808) $11.95
Nepal Handbook (3646). $12.95
New Zealand Handbook (3883) $18.95
Outback Australia Handbook (3794) $15.95
Philippines Handbook (0048) $17.95
Southeast Asia Handbook (0021) $21.95
South Korea Handbook (3204). $14.95
South Pacific Handbook (3999) $19.95
Tahiti-Polynesia Handbook (0374) $13.95
Thailand Handbook (3824) $16.95
Tibet Handbook (3905) $30.00
*Vietnam, Cambodia & Laos Handbook (0293) $18.95

INTERNATIONAL
Egypt Handbook (3891). $18.95
Moon Handbook (0668) $10.00
Moscow-St. Petersburg Handbook (3913). $13.95
Staying Healthy in Asia, Africa, and Latin America (0269) . . $11.95

* New title, please call for availability

PERIPLUS TRAVEL MAPS
All maps $7.95 each

Bali	Hong Kong	Penang
Bandung/W. Java	Jakarta	Phuket/S. Thailand
Bangkok/C. Thailand	Java	Sarawak
Batam/Bintan	Ko Samui/S. Thailand	Singapore
Cambodia	Kuala Lumpur	Vietnam
Chiangmai/N. Thailand	Lombok	Yogyakarta/C. Java

WHERE TO BUY MOON TRAVEL HANDBOOKS

BOOKSTORES AND LIBRARIES: Moon Travel Handbooks are sold worldwide. Please write to our sales manager for a list of wholesalers and distributors in your area.

TRAVELERS: We would like to have Moon Travel Handbooks available throughout the world. Please ask your bookstore to write or call us for ordering information. If your bookstore will not order our guides for you, please contact us for a free title listing.

> **Moon Publications, Inc.**
> **P.O. Box 3040**
> **Chico, CA 95927-3040 U.S.A.**
> **Tel: (800) 345-5473**
> **Fax: (916) 345-6751**
> **E-mail: travel@moon.com**

IMPORTANT ORDERING INFORMATION

PRICES: All prices are subject to change. We always ship the most current edition. We will let you know if there is a price increase on the book you order.

SHIPPING AND HANDLING OPTIONS: Domestic UPS or USPS first class (allow 10 working days for delivery): $3.50 for the first item, 50 cents for each additional item.

EXCEPTIONS:

Tibet Handbook and *Indonesia Handbook* shipping $4.50; $1.00 for each additional *Tibet Handbook* or *Indonesia Handbook.*

Moonbelt shipping is $1.50 for one, 50 cents for each additional belt.

Add $2.00 for same-day handling.

UPS 2nd Day Air or Printed Airmail requires a special quote.

International Surface Bookrate 8-12 weeks delivery: $3.00 for the first item, $1.00 for each additional item. Note: Moon Publications cannot guarantee international surface bookrate shipping. Moon recommends sending international orders via air mail, which requires a special quote.

FOREIGN ORDERS: Orders that originate outside the U.S.A. must be paid for with either an international money order or a check in U.S. currency drawn on a major U.S. bank based in the U.S.A.

TELEPHONE ORDERS: We accept Visa or MasterCard payments. Minimum order is US$15.00. Call in your order: (800) 345-5473, 8 a.m.-5 p.m. Pacific Standard Time.

ORDER FORM

Be sure to call (800) 345-5473 for current prices and editions or for the name of the bookstore
nearest you that carries Moon Travel Handbooks • 8 a.m.–5 p.m. PST.
(See important ordering information on preceding page.)

Name: _____ Date: _____

Street: _____

City: _____ Daytime Phone: _____

State or Country: _____ Zip Code: _____

QUANTITY	TITLE	PRICE

	Taxable Total	_____
	Sales Tax (7.25%) for California Residents	_____
	Shipping & Handling	_____
	TOTAL	_____

Ship: ☐ UPS (no P.O. Boxes) ☐ 1st class ☐ International surface mail

Ship to: ☐ address above ☐ other _____

Make checks payable to: **MOON PUBLICATIONS, INC.** P.O. Box 3040, Chico, CA 95927-3040
U.S.A. We accept Visa and MasterCard. **To Order:** Call in your Visa or MasterCard number, or send
a written order with your Visa or MasterCard number and expiration date clearly written.

Card Number: ☐ **Visa**   ☐ **MasterCard**

☐☐☐☐ ☐☐☐☐ ☐☐☐☐ ☐☐☐☐

Exact Name on Card: _____

Expiration date: _____

Signature: _____

F/95–M

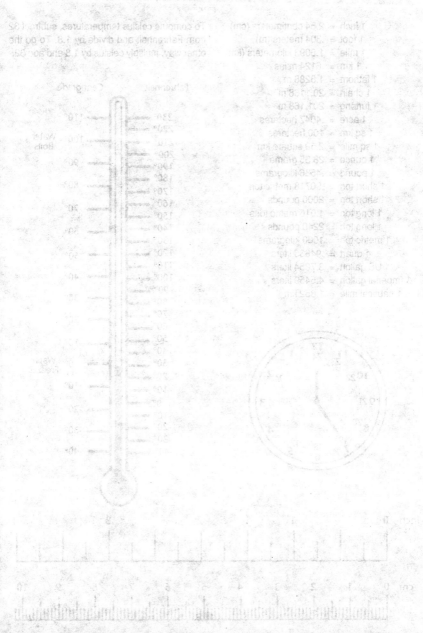

THE METRIC SYSTEM

1 inch = 2.54 centimeters (cm)
1 foot = .304 meters (m)
1 mile = 1.6093 kilometers (km)
1 km = .6124 miles
1 fathom = 1.8288 m
1 chain = 20.1168 m
1 furlong = 201.168 m
1 acre = .4047 hectares
1 sq km = 100 hectares
1 sq mile = 2.59 square km
1 ounce = 28.35 grams
1 pound = .4536 kilograms
1 short ton = .90718 metric ton
1 short ton = 2000 pounds
1 long ton = 1.016 metric tons
1 long ton = 2240 pounds
1 metric ton = 1000 kilograms
1 quart = .94635 liters
1 US gallon = 3.7854 liters
1 Imperial gallon = 4.5459 liters
1 nautical mile = 1.852 km

To compute celsius temperatures, subtract 32 from Fahrenheit and divide by 1.8. To go the other way, multiply celsius by 1.8 and add 32.

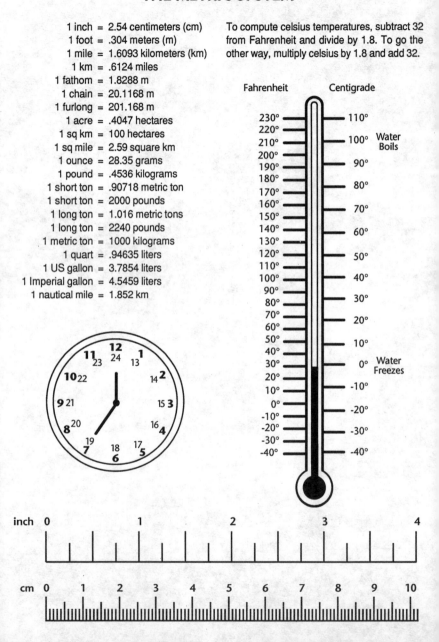